The Political Economy of Post-Soviet Russia

Vladimir Tikhomirov
Deputy Director
Contemporary Europe Research Centre
University of Melbourne
Australia

D1480848

First published in Great Britain 2000 by
MACMILLAN PRESS LTD
Houndmills, Basingstoke, Hampshire RG21 6XS and London
Companies and representatives throughout the world

A catalogue record for this book is available from the British Library.

ISBN: 0–333–77888–X

First published in the United States of America 2000 by
ST. MARTIN'S PRESS, INC.,
Scholarly and Reference Division,
175 Fifth Avenue, New York, N.Y. 10010

ISBN 0–312–23086–9

Library of Congress Cataloging-in-Publication Data
Tikhomirov, V. I. (Vladimir Igorevich)
The Political economy of post-Soviet Russia / Vladimir Tikhomirov.
p. cm.
Includes bibliographical references and index.
ISBN 0–312–23086–9 (cloth)
1. Russia (Federation)—Economic conditions—1991– 2. Russia (Federation)–
–Economic policy—1991– I. Title
HC340.12 .T545   2000
338.947'009'049—dc21

99–053112

This book is printed on paper suitable for recycling and made from fully managed and sustained forest sources.

10 9   8   7   6   5   4   3   2   1
09 08 07 06 05 04 03 02 01 00

Printed and bound in Great Britain by
Antony Rowe Ltd, Chippenham, Wiltshire

The Political Economy of Post-Soviet Russia

Also by Vladimir Tikhomirov

ANATOMY OF THE 1998 RUSSIAN CRISIS (*editor*)

CHURCH AND POLITICAL STRUGGLE IN SOUTH AFRICA: The Role of Religion in Development of South African Society (*in Russian*)

DEVELOPMENT OF POLITICAL THOUGHT IN SOUTH AFRICA, 1948–1988 (*in Russian*)

IN SEARCH OF IDENTITY: Five Years since the Fall of the Soviet Union (*editor*)

STATES IN TRANSITION: Russia and South Africa

THE PARTY OF APARTHEID: Socio-Political Evolution of the National Party of South Africa

Contents

List of Tables

List of Graphs

List of Maps

Introduction

Starting from the late 1980s, when the then Soviet leadership began to make first timid attempts to reform the ill-functioning and over-bureaucratised command economy, issues related to the strategy, tactics and limitations of reforms continued to remain the forefront of public debates in Russia. Any moves to restructure Soviet systems of social and economic management, and, in the later years, to change property rights in the country, were met with a fierce political opposition. Politics and economics in post-Soviet Russia became so closely interrelated, that it became simply impossible to measure any successes or failures of what seemed like a purely economic policy without taking into consideration political circumstances that surrounded adoption and implementation of that or other decisions. In a sense, Russian economic reform was caught in the crossfire between opposing national political trends (reformists against "old-thinkers", communists), growing centre-region and region-region political and social divisions, emerging problems and contradictions in Russia's relations with its former allies, both within the former Soviet Union and within the Eastern Bloc.

The constant and severe intervention of political factors in the course of implementation of Russian economic reforms, no matter how predictable, is now viewed by many reformists as the major reason behind the ultimate failure of the Russian reform experiment, at least in its initial form. However, it was very naïve of Russian leaders to expect that the political effect of radical social and economic changes, which have a direct and large impact on the lives of people, will be small and easily manageable. Within 4–6 months from the start of radical reforms in early 1992 inability or failure of the Gaidar government to contain growing political pressures had drastically limited its reform capability and finally forced this government to resign. Consecutive Russian governments have also tried to find a balance between opposing and often contradictory pressures, which in the end did not bring the desired economic change but also did not halt the unreformed economy from a continuing collapse.

Despite much talk about reforms that was heard from Russia since the late 1980s, there was amazingly little done in practice. Yes, indeed, Russia has a moved far away from the centralised Soviet economic model it had just a decade ago. While in the late 1980s about 90% of Russian GDP was produced at state owned or controlled enterprises, in the late 1990s a similar share was produced by the private sector. During the same decade new market structures were created and new institutions have emerged – banks, stock exchanges, export–import companies, etc. But all much of these developments were no more than a façade for a largely diminished but still functioning command economy. In general terms privatisation in the economy had no effect on the national production dynamics and by the end of the 1990s the private sector in Russia was even less profitable than the state-owned sector. Moreover, the majority of these privatised firms were technically insolvent, but continued to operate with financial blessing from the authorities. Much of the most visible and, until recently, most cited achievements of the reform years – emergence of non-state banking and a relative stability of Russia's financial system – were wiped away in one day, following the official announcement of Russia's default on state debt repayments on 17 August 1998.

With the mirage of promised economic prosperity moving further and further away, in the past few years the Russian ruling elite mainly concentrated on its achievements in restructuring of the Soviet authoritarian political system as a major justification of its reform effort. But, ironically, it was the way that the political reform was carried out that largely prevented Russia from achieving much more impressive reform results. It is my view that in the course of Yeltsin's reform a communist system based on an authoritarian and repressive rule was replaced by a political structure that resembles Western-type democracies but which, nevertheless, is also highly authoritarian in character. In the latter system the principle of centralisation of political power in the hands of the Communist Politburo was substituted by the unlimited powers of closest associates of the Russian President in the centre and in the regions. And like its predecessor, this system relied heavily on bureaucratic support. Therefore, it is no surprise that in reform years the number of public servants in Russia grew rapidly: by the end of 1998 Russia had more bureaucrats than it had under communists.

As in the Soviet times, the majority of the electorate could only observe political struggles in the Kremlin, unable to significantly influence their outcome. Results of all post-Soviet parliamentary elections in Russia were a clear indication of the growing electoral discontent with policies of the Russian leadership. This was a dramatic change from the last pre-reform years when Russian reformists enjoyed an almost unhindered public support. Growing support for opposition parties was symptomatic of a deep political and psychological change that took place within the Russian society. It clearly pointed towards a widening gap between "the people" and "the authorities" which was very similar to the one that existed in the Soviet political system. "Democratic idealism" – a common political stance shared by many Russians in the first years of reform – which led many of them to believe that free elections could bring to power leaders capable of improving the lives of ordinary people, was consistently giving way to feelings of cynicism and anger. In socio-psychological terms, this resulted in reappearance of the division between "them" and "us" or between, on the one hand, the new political and economic elite (popularly named "the new nomenklatura") and, on the other, the masses of outsiders (or "the common people").

Modern Russia gives a wealth of factual, anecdotal and empirical evidence, which indicates that the political stability in the country rests on a critical balance. In the late 1990s, despite years of reform and almost a decade of political freedoms, Russia, as ever before, was still under the shadow of an impending political confrontation. How could it happen, that, after almost ten years of reforms, Russia found itself even farther away from reaching its initial reform objectives than it was in the early 1990s? In this study I will attempt to give some answers to this important question.

It is hard to understand modern Russian developments solely by using economic, sociological or political methods. Politics and economics in contemporary Russia became almost inseparable. In the same way as the economy of the former Soviet Union was largely a product of the grand political experiment of the communist party, the post-Soviet Russian economic model also represented a rather artificial creation, closely linked to its Soviet heritage.

The main goal of the book is to analyse successes reached and mistakes made in the course of implementation of reforms in the post-Soviet Russia during the period between 1992 and 1998. My major argument is that, despite few successes, the economic mismanagement on part of the Russian reformists caused the development of a deep socio-economic crisis in the country. In its turn, this crisis had major political implications for the future of Russia, such as a dramatic decline of the popular support for the cause of reform, the gradual transformation of the early "nomenklatura capitalism" into a distinctive Russian model of "oligarchic capitalism", and a rapid increase in influence of various extremist and nationalist movements in the Russian Federation.

Until mid-1998 some success achieved by Russian reformists in the financial sphere and in mass privatisation gave at least some credibility to the Yeltsin regime. In their public statements reformists often stressed the importance of these achievements for the future of the market economy in Russia and predicted grave consequences in case these achievements were to be reversed. However, they often tended to evade explanations of how these achievements were made and what strategic consequences their reform has had for the Russian economy. Thus, a typical line of argument often heard from reformists like Yegor Gaidar or Anatoly Chubais is that it is *the result* and not *the means* of achieving that are of the overall importance to the future of reform.

I strongly disagree with this type of argumentation. I would argue that very often, certainly in the Russian case, the means of achieving a certain goal have greatly undermined the efficiency and validity of the results that were reached and might well have an effect which will be diametrically opposite to what was hoped to be achieved initially. I believe that an unjustified rush in the destruction of the Soviet system of economic management in the early 1990s resulted in an almost total reliance of the consecutive Russian reformist governments on borrowing as a major source of revenues for the shrinking state budget. Sooner or later this policy would have led to the collapse of Russia's fragile financial system and would have had a devastating effect on the country's state finances. Thus, the August 1998 crisis was a natural continuation of and a logical conclusion to the type of "reform" that Russian reformists chose to implement from early 1992.

Most of Russian recent reforms have had dire effects on the national economy. Throughout the post-Soviet years all Russian major production indicators were constantly and rapidly going south. It is the Gaidar-Chernomyrdin governments that hold the responsibility for implementation of most of these so-called reforms. The majority of Russian post-Soviet governments was made up from an amazing combination of the worst kind of Soviet-type bureaucrats, lacking vision and knowledge, and self-trained free-market apologists with very little concern for the needs of the real economy. These initiators of a new grand social experiment in Russia were never short of Western consultants and support. The result of their combined efforts was the creation of yet another "Potemkin village" in (parts of) Russia, this time in an attempt to model Western-type capitalism. Oases of prosperity, like Moscow, were neighbouring vast areas of economic and social depression, while many Russian regions that were located far away from the nation's capital were on the verge of breaking away from the federation, often finding themselves in a situation of low to high-level civil war.

The August 1998 crisis has clearly demonstrated that haste and rigidity in the initial implementation of reforms greatly undermined chances of Russia's successful transformation and its eventual transition to a working market economy. By 1998 ideas of free market and economic liberalism in Russia became largely discredited by the failure of the earlier reform efforts, while those politicians that were still advocating them were enjoying an extremely limited and declining support among the Russian electorate. This was an almost total reverse of the situation that existed in Russia seven years earlier, at the time when reforms commenced. It is my belief that it was not the traditional conservatism of Russian voters or their lack of democratic experience that were to blame for that. Russian post-communist reformists themselves will have to carry a great deal of responsibility if, in the end, Russia chooses not to support them or their ideas.

The declining power base of the Russian leadership, both within the bureaucracy and within the society, and the reform commitments, it made earlier, have greatly limited the ability of political manoeuvring of the Yeltsin regime. The result was a growing split in the interests of Russia's federal and local leaders, as well as between reformists and the masses. The high level of fragmentation of political life in post-Soviet Russia had effectively blocked the development of a working system of democratic political management and led to a steady growth of anti-democratic and even authoritarian political tendencies. The existence of fragmented politics, however, during the larger part of the 1990s allowed Russian leaders to successfully manipulate the electorate.

By the end of 1998 the development of an acute financial and economic crisis in Russia had put strict limitations on the political flexibility of the Yeltsin regime. These critical developments in Russia had their own internal roots, but their effects were significantly intensified first by the Asian financial crisis and then by the collapse of the Russian financial market in August 1998. The fragile economic stability, which was maintained in Russia during 1995–96 almost exclusively as a result of increased state borrowing on internal and external markets, in the course of 1997 and early 1998 was put under severe pressure when, following international efforts to stabilise Asian economies, foreign financial resources became scarce and significantly more expensive.

This global "shock therapy" forced the Russian leadership in 1998 to start a grand revision of its reform strategy. The Russian reform began in January 1992 when the reformist Gaidar government announced its ambitious plans of restructuring of the Soviet economy. The main aim of that policy was decentralisation of the over-centralised state system of management of the national economy, privatisation of state-owned enterprises, and the formation of legal, financial and other structures facilitating the development of market economic mechanisms. In early 1992 the reform started with the introduction of price, currency and trade liberalisation followed at the end of the year by the privatisation campaign. Lifting of state control over prices almost immediately sparked off a huge inflation wave, which very soon became one of the major obstacles to the continuation of the reform. Although the Russian government has been successful in controlling and lowering the inflation rate since 1995, this has not stopped the economy from sliding further and further into recession.

The dramatic falls in production indicators and standards of living experienced by Russia and the majority of ex-Soviet states in the post-1991 period could be attributed to a number of factors, the most important of which are: (a) the high level of mutual dependency, general backwardness and inflexibility of the socio-economic systems these newly independent states inherited from the over-centralised Soviet system which made independent management of their economies extremely difficult and greatly intensified the already existing socio-economic crisis in these states; (b) the lack of experience in management and legal affairs in a market environment on the part of political and economic elites in these countries, which caused serious legal confusion and created too many legal loopholes, even a certain "power vacuum", resulting in an unprecedented growth in corruption as well as in economic and other crimes; (c) the economic difficulties and social costs caused by transition to the market economy in ex-Soviet states, which proved to be much higher than anticipated by reformists at the start of the reforms, forcing the majority of the leaders of these republics to make significant alterations to the initially proclaimed strategies which brought the whole reform process to a standstill and exacerbated the crises.

These factors affect developments in all of the former Soviet republics, although their strength and effects vary greatly. In some regions of the ex-USSR, like Transcaucasia and parts of Central Asia, post-Soviet political instability has led to a situation of ongoing civil war which has had an even more devastating effect on economic and social transformations in these areas. At the end of 1994 political instability spread to the Russian Federation with the outbreak of the bloody Chechen War.

Despite the differences in their economic, social, political and ethnic background, not one of the former Soviet states has yet shown any signs indicating a genuine recovery. The key to successful change seems to lie in the ability of post-Soviet leaders to co-ordinate their transition policies, in such a way as to facilitate, rather than destroy, the existing benefits of their mutual co-operation. This raises the more general issue of the inter-relation between political independence (the nationalism factor) which frames the ideologies of the majority of ruling elites in these states, and the *de facto* economic dependency (moves towards integration) which these states was inherited from the Soviet Union. The clearest illustration of the struggle between these two tendencies is the history of the Commonwealth of Independent States (CIS). During years of its existence the CIS has failed to fulfil its proclaimed objectives of facilitating closer co-operation between its members, mainly because of strong internal pro-independence (i.e. anti-integration) political pressures in most of its member-states.

The future of social and economic transformations in the former Soviet Union (FSU) is largely dependent on the success of the transition to democracy and a market economy in the biggest of its former republics, the Russian Federation. Russia accounts for 70–80% of the total industrial output of the FSU and, through energy supply chains, holds in its hands a very effective lever of control over developments in all of the other ex-Soviet states. Russia is also the indisputable military leader in the area and, in the event of a major crisis, still has the potential to bring all the other ex-Soviet states into its political and strategic domain. Since the collapse of the USSR Russia has also proved to be a clever and sometimes ruthless political manipulator in the area, on many occasions strongly and consistently safeguarding its own interests.

However, continuing attempts by the Russian leaders to reinstall Russia as the dominant force on the ex-Soviet territory are being blocked by the growing weakness of its economy. Even the Russian military might has become questionable following the humiliating defeat of

Table 1   Russia's General Economic Performance in the Three Critical Periods of 20th Century

End of the period as % to the start of the period (=100)

	Russia in WWI and Civil War, 1913–22	USSR in WWII, 1940–45	Post-Soviet Russia, 1990–96
National income	55.6	83.1	54.7[c]
Gross industrial output	31.0[a]	91.8	47.5
Gross agricultural production	66.3	57.0	62.5
Volumes of capital investment	40.3[b]	89.0	24.3

NOTES:
[a] 1913–21.
[b] 1918–20.
[c] 1990 to mid-1996.

Sourced and calculated from:
Narodnoe khozyaistvo SSSR v 1960 godu, Moscow: TsSU, 1961, pp.152, 219, 368; *Narodnoe khozyaistvo RSFSR. Statisticheskii sbornik*, Moscow: StatUpravlenie RSFSR, 1957, p.67; *Narodnoe khozyaistvo SSSR za 60 let*, Moscow: TsSU, 1977, p.277; *Narodnoe khozyaistvo SSSR, 1922–1982*, Moscow: TsSU SSSR, 1982, pp.52, 227; *Rossiiskii statisticheskii ezhegodnik. 1994*, Moscow: Goskomstat, 1994, pp.262, 371; *Rossiiskii statisticheskii ezhegodnik. 1995*, Moscow: Goskomstat, 1995, p.267; *Rossiya v tsifrakh. 1996*, Moscow: Goskomstat, 1996, pp.164–81.

Russian federal troops in the civil war in Chechnya. In Table 1 I compare four main indicators of economic development in the first six years of the post-Soviet Russian reform (1990–96) with the economic performance of Russia and the USSR during the two major crises, which the Russian nation has gone through during the 20th century. These were World War I, the 1917 Russian Revolution and the Civil War (1913–22), and World War II (1940–45). In all of these cases I took as a base year the last pre-crisis year (respectively, 1913, 1940 and 1990).

Data in Table 1 clearly indicates that already by 1996 the scale of crisis in post-Soviet Russia was similar to or even larger than the scope of the two other major crises that the country experienced during the 20th century. There was, however, one significant difference. While in the two earlier cases crises have begun as a result of external military intervention (war), the crisis of the 1990s was not caused by any warfare but essentially by internal developments. Despite that, the destructive effect of this latter crisis, both in economic and social areas, was comparable to a wartime situation.

Although the breakout of the modern Russian crisis coincided with the start of the Russian reform, it would be major mistake to blame solely post-Soviet reforms for its eruption. The roots of this crisis lie in the economic and political system that existed in the Soviet Union. The transformation and modernisation of this system proved to be an extremely difficult task, both for the last Soviet communist leader, Mikhail Gorbachev, and for the first Russian president, Boris Yeltsin.

While many of the difficulties and problems in the Russian transition to a market economy and a democratic political system evolved from Russia's Soviet heritage, still many other came as a result of wrong decisions taken by the Russian leadership in the recent years. By the late 1990s, however, it became increasingly difficult to blame only the Soviet past for all Russia's problems. It is the current political leadership that will have to carry a large part of responsibility for the way Russia developed, at least in the second half of the 1990s.

As the title suggests, this book is not only about economics, nor it is solely about politics. The main interest that I had when I started working on this study was the nature and combination of those political and economic factors that played and continue to play a major role in framing of Russian developments in the post-Soviet period. From the start of the Russian reform the Soviet political legacy with its centralised political and economic system ensured that political factors have played a crucial role in drafting and implementation of the national economic strategy. The dependency of economy on politics in modern Russia is probably at one of the highest levels in the world. The deepening of the crisis during the 1990s made the Russian economy even more weak and that, in turn, increased the influence of politics in the economy even further.

In recent years much has already been written on the problems of Russian economic and political transition. But, with the exception of a number of case studies, very few studies have centred on social and economic developments in Russian regions. This book also attempts to analyse what effect Russian post-Soviet reforms have had on Russia's 12 economic and 89 administrative regions, particularly from the point of view of the interrelation between national and regional socio-economic and political trends. The book covers mainly the period between 1990 and 1998.

In my analysis I concentrate on both the national dynamics and the dynamics of developments in main groups of regions. For the purpose of comparison I selected nine administrative regions of Russia and divided them into mining, agricultural and manufacturing groups, in accordance with their major economic profile. The regions I selected for the "mining group" are Kemerovskaya oblast', Tyumenskaya oblast' and the Sakha Republic; for the "manufacturing group" – St. Petersburg, Samarskaya oblast' and Khabarovskii krai; and for the "agricultural group" – Belgorodskaya oblast', Krasnodarskii krai and Stavropolskii krai.

The combined output of some major industrial and agricultural commodities by these groups of regions is presented in Table 2. While mining regions had the dominant share in the Russia's national production of some main primary commodities (oil, gas and coal), the manufacturing group of regions played an important role in the national production of some manufactured goods (cars). Agricultural production, and especially industrial processing of some major agricultural products, was in 1997 developed in all three groups of regions, but the agricultural group clearly had a significantly larger share in the national totals than the other two groups. Ratios of agricultural output to GDP were also significantly higher in agricultural group of regions than in the other two groups.

Table 2   Groups of Regions by Economic Profile, 1996–97

a) Shares in Russian national development indicators, 1996 (%)

	Industrial output	Agricultural output	GDP
Mining regions	11.7	8.8	12.0
Manufacturing regions	7.2	5.9	6.8
Agricultural regions	3.0	18.6	3.7

b) Regional industrial and agricultural output in relation to regional GDP, 1996 (%)

	Industrial output	Agricultural output
Mining regions	62.6	4.7
Manufacturing regions	68.2	5.5
Agricultural regions	52.5	32.0

c) Shares in Russian gross production of selected products and commodities, 1997 (%)

	Crude oil	Natural gas	Coal	Vehicles	Grains	Meat	Milk
Mining regions	65.4	91.9	42.7	0.0	2.6	4.0	3.6
Manufacturing regions	2.8	0.0	0.7	75.2	3.1	2.2	2.1
Agricultural regions	0.8	0.4	0.0	0.0	12.7	9.1	6.7

NOTES:
Mining: Kemerovo, Tyumen' and Sakha only.
Manufacturing: St. Petersburg, Samara and Khabarovsk only.
Agriculture: Belgorod, Krasnodar and Stavropol only.

Source: *Regiony Rossii*. 1998, Vols.1 and 2, Moscow: Goskomstat, 1998.

The division of selected regions into these three groups made it possible to analyse variations in the dynamics of industrial, agricultural, social and political developments that exist between Russia's regions. Some of the most important economic and political indicators are also presented in the book in the form of chloropleth maps covering all 89 of Russia's administrative units.

In addition to analysis of Russia's recent economic and social performance, the book also attempts to give an overview of some recent important political developments, like the evolution of the Russian reform strategy, the formation of post-Soviet business and political elite, and changes in political preferences of the Russian electorate.

The study is based on a variety of sources. However, the larger part of the social and economic analysis is based on the official Russian statistical series. The reliability of Russian statistical materials remains a major concern, both among academics as well as policy-makers. The scandal that broke out in June 1998 when the chairman of the Russian State Statistical Committee (*Goskomstat*), Yuri Yurkov, was arrested on charges of falsification of statistical data in order to help large companies to evade taxes,[1] did not help in raising the credibility of these official economic data.

The radical restructuring of the Russian national economy, ongoing changes to the ownership of companies, the growth in market services, many of which were non-existent in the Soviet times, changes in accounting systems – all these factors have made the work of Russian statisticians in the post-Soviet period more difficult than ever before. Since 1994 *Goskomstat* and its regional branches have gradually been moving towards international statistical standards.[2] By the mid-1996 the old Soviet system of formal accounting of production was replaced by a system of national accounting. This brought the Russian statistical series in line with international standards. However, some major problems remained, including ways data were collected from the so-called "unorganised" sectors of the economy or the "shadow economy". In order to incorporate these developments Russian statisticians developed special coefficients. That sparked off an ongoing debate on the issue of whether these coefficients were truly representative of reality. Amazingly, in contrast to the Soviet times, a large number of analysts and observers were now accusing Russian statistical offices of underestimating, and not overestimating like earlier, real dynamics of production and change in GDP indicators.[3] At the same time other group of economists argued that these dynamics continued to be grossly overestimated.[4]

Some major problems of the current Russian statistics are caused by the following factors: (a) existing difficulties in collection of reliable data from the "shadow economy" and small business operations, most of which for taxation evasion purposes are unreported; (b) conflicting incentives that force some Russian producers to under-report their output while others to overstate it (in order to raise their credit status); and (c) problems in calculation of gross indicators (particularly price deflators due to a rapid and dramatic change in the system of prices in a situation of high inflation).[5] These problems, although they are new to Russian statisticians, are generally considered to be quite common shortcomings of statistical reporting in practically all Western countries. At the same time, economic and social dynamics as presented in the Russian statistical data are often confirmed from other sources, e.g., numerous media reports from the ground that also point to the fact that during the 1990s Russia was experiencing a major and deepening social and economic crisis. The author supports the view of the group of Western and Russian analysts who suggest that although Russian statistical series do have some faults, nevertheless they managed to accurately reflect main trends in Russian post-Soviet developments.[6]

Notes

1. *The Economist*, 13 June 1998.
2. See: "Rossiiskaya statistika ukhodit ot totalnogo utchyota", *Finansovye Izvestiya*. Cit. from *Biznes-TASS*, 31 August 1994.
3. World Bank economists Misha Belkindas and Olga Ivanova quoted in *Monitor*, Vol.3, No.221, 25 November 1997.
4. Grigory Khanin and Igor Birman, cited in *Moskovskie novosti*, 29 September–5 October 1997. In March 1997 *Goskomstat* was accused of manipulating Russian GDP figures through increasing its allowance for the shadow economy from 20% to 23% (*The Financial Times*, 25 March 1997, *Open Media Research Institute (OMRI) Daily Digest*, No.59, 25 March 1997; "Russia shadow economy shown in statistics", *Reuters*, 4 April 1997).
5. For more information and discussion on the subject see *Voprosy ekonomiki*, No.5, May 1993, pp.4–21; James H. Noren, "Statistical reporting in the states of the former USSR", *Post–Soviet Geography*, Vol.35, No.1, January 1994, pp.13–37; Szyrmer, Janusz M., "Eastern European Monitor", *EAST: Economies and Societies in Transition*, Vol.2, Issue 1, Spring 1995 (www.ssc.upenn.edu/east/spring95/janusz.html).
6. See James H. Noren, op.cit.; Stephen G. Wheatcroft, "Re-Visiting the Crisis Zones of Euro–Asia", *Russian and Euro-Asian Bulletin*, Melbourne, March 1997, Vol.6, No.3, p.6; Robert McIntyre, "Data Fraud", *Johnson's Russia List (JRL)*, 20 May 1998.

1
Dynamics of Development in the Real Sector of Economy

1.1   Russian industry in the post-Soviet era

Negative economic tendencies that started to develop in the Soviet economy in the late 1970s and evolved into a major crisis in the early 1990s had a direct and adverse effect on Russian industry. The large, poorly managed and grossly ineffective enterprises that formed the majority of Russian industrial enterprises, turned out to be extremely sensitive to any significant changes to the way in which they operated and were managed. Gorbachev's attempts to reform the ailing Soviet economy in the late 1980s were met with growing resistance from the industrial lobby; the latter, however, resisted the changes because in most cases reforms were accompanied by sharp falls in production levels.[1]

The inability of these enterprises to restructure, together with the reluctance of industrial mangers to reform[2] greatly hampered Gorbachev's reform actions and, in the end, brought the industrial reform to a standstill. In early 1992 the post-Soviet government of reformers re-activated the process of industrial transformation. But the situation in 1992 differed greatly from the earlier reform attempts: in the post-Soviet period the liberalisation of prices and the beginnings of privatisation meant that most industries found themselves overnight in a completely changed economic environment. Their influence on the general economic developments was minimal and, for that matter, most industries were pressed to adjust to the changed circumstances rather than to resist the changes.[3]

In the first few months of Gaidar's reforms many industrial managers with a certain amount of enthusiasm greeted new developments, mainly because they saw price liberalisation as a way of maximising profits without the need to reform or restructure.[4] However, very soon more and more industrial enterprises started to fall victim to the post-Soviet race of prices when their customers were unable to pay high prices for their produce, while the workers demanded higher and higher wages to cope with the inflation wave.[5]

These developments were also accompanied by either the complete withdrawal of or sharp cuts to state credits to industry, and the Gaidar government's attempts to keep inflation under control by reducing the money supply to the economy. The idea was that these measures would eventually force enterprises to reduce prices and to enter into competition with other local or foreign producers for Russian markets. But as early as mid-1992 the government had to retreat from the implementation of its reform strategy when accumulation of non-payments within industry and of delays in salary payments reached a critical level. Because of the monopolistic position that many industrial producers occupied in the Russian economy, any attempts to force them to compete for internal markets were doomed. Industrial enterprises remained inflexible, outdated and huge; their managers were very sceptical of the reforms, which many of them did not understand. In this situation the industrial producers preferred to keep on raising prices for their produce, hoping that at some later stage the situation would settle down or that the state would come to the rescue, as it had always done before throughout the Soviet period. As a result, by mid-1992 sales of industrial products fell sharply; many enterprises had no money in their bank accounts and stopped making payments to suppliers and employees.

The levels of industrial production in Russia reflected these negative changes. Table 1.1 shows that between 1990 and 1992 Russian industrial production fell by 25%; a further 30% fall was recorded in the following four years of post-Soviet reforms. While all of the main branches of industry recorded significant falls in their production indices in the post-Soviet period, the rates of decline varied greatly between the branches of industry. In 1990–98 production of electricity and fuel (oil, coal and gas) fell the least, by 24% and 34% respectively. On the other hand, developments in Russian light industry (textile, clothing, footwear, etc.) were tantamount to a national disaster: in 1998 the volume of production in that branch of industry in constant prices was less than 18% of the 1990 level. The high-tech industries grouped in Table 1.1 in the "machine-building" branch also experienced a dramatic decline of 63% between 1990 and 1998. On the whole, the figures in Table 1.1 indicate that the industries that experienced falls of less that 50% during 1990–98 were those that were

Table 1.1 Volumes of Production by Branch of Industry (constant prices, 1990 = 100)

	1990	1991	1992	1993	1994	1995	1996	1997	1998[a]
All industry	100.0	92.0	75.0	65.0	51.0	49.5	47.5	48.5	45.9
Electricity	100.0	100.3	96.0	91.0	83.0	80.5	78.9	77.3	75.4
Fuel	100.0	94.0	87.0	77.0	69.0	67.6	66.9	67.1	65.4
Ferrous metallurgy	100.0	93.0	77.0	65.0	54.0	58.9	57.7	58.3	53.6
Non-ferrous metallurgy	100.0	91.0	68.0	59.0	54.0	55.1	52.9	55.5	52.8
Chemical and oil-refinery	100.0	94.0	73.0	58.0	44.0	47.5	44.2	45.5	42.1
Machine building	100.0	90.0	77.0	65.0	45.0	40.5	38.5	40.0	37.0
Forestry and wood-processing	100.0	91.0	78.0	63.0	60.5	58.1	48.2	48.7	48.5
Construction materials	100.0	98.0	78.0	65.0	61.8	58.7	48.7	46.8	44.0
Light industry	100.0	91.0	64.0	49.0	34.8	24.7	19.3	18.9	16.7
Food-processing	100.0	91.0	76.0	69.0	63.5	58.4	56.1	55.7	54.6

NOTES:

[a] Preliminary data.

Sources:

Rossiiskii statisticheskii ezhegodnik. 1995, Moscow: Goskomstat, 1995, p.311;
Sotsial'no-ekonomicheskoe polozhenie Rossii. 1995 g., Moscow: Goskomstat, 1996, p.19; *Sotsial'no-ekonomicheskoe polozhenie Rossii, janvar'-iyun' 1996 g.*,
Moscow: Goskomstat, 1996, p.12; *Rossiya v tsifrakh. 1996*, Moscow: Goskomstat, 1996, p.281; *Sotsial'no-ekonomicheskoe polozhenie Rossii. 1996 g.*,
Moscow: Goskomstat, 1997, pp.14–6; *Rossiiskii statisticheskii ezhegodnik. 1997*, Moscow: Goskomstat, 1997, p.330; *Sotsial'no-ekonomicheskoe
polozhenie Rossii. 1997 g.*, Moscow: Goskomstat, 1998, pp.26–7; *Rossiiskii statisticheskii ezhegodnik. 1998*, Moscow: Goskomstat, 1998, p.379;
Sotsial'no-ekonomicheskoe polozhenie Rossii. 1998 g., Moscow: Goskomstat, 1999, p.16.

Table 1.2 The Structure of Production of Major Industries in Russia (% to the total, constant prices)

	1990	1991	1992	1993	1994	1995	1996	1997	1998[a]
Electricity	5.4	5.8	6.7	7.4	8.6	8.8	9.4	17.1	15.8
Fuel	17.1	19.1	19.3	20.0	22.7	23.1	24.5	17.4	15.6
Ferrous metallurgy	8.5	8.3	8.5	8.3	8.7	9.8	10.3	7.9	7.8
Non-ferrous metallurgy	10.2	9.8	9.0	9.0	10.4	10.9	11.3	5.5	7.3
Chemical and oil-refinery	9.1	9.1	8.6	8.0	7.6	8.4	8.2	7.2	6.6
Machine building	21.5	20.6	21.4	21.1	18.4	17.2	16.7	18.8	20.2
Forestry and wood-processing	4.9	4.7	5.0	4.7	4.2	4.3	3.6	3.7	3.9
Construction materials	3.4	3.5	3.4	3.4	3.0	2.9	2.4	4.1	3.6
Light industry	9.0	8.7	7.4	6.7	4.5	3.2	2.5	2.2	1.8
Food-processing	10.9	10.5	10.7	11.4	11.9	11.3	11.2	14.5	15.0
Other	0.0	0.0	0.0	0.0	0.0	0.0	0.0	1.6	2.4
Total	100.0	100.0	100.0	100.0	100.0	100.0	100.0	100.0	100.0

NOTES:
[a] Preliminary data.

Calculated and sourced from:
Promyshlennost' Rossii. 1996, Moscow: Goskomstat, 1996, p.8; *Sotsial'no-ekonomicheskoe polozhenie Rossii. 1996 g.*, Moscow: Goskomstat, 1997, pp.15–6; *Rossiiskii statisticheskii ezhegodnik. 1996*, Moscow: Goskomstat, 1996, p.493; *Sotsial'no-ekonomicheskoe polozhenie Rossii. 1994 g.*, Moscow: Goskomstat, 1995, pp.12–3; *Rossiiskii statisticheskii ezhegodnik. 1998*, Moscow: Goskomstat, 1998, p.382; *Sotsial'no-ekonomicheskoe polozhenie Rossii. 1998 g.*, Moscow: Goskomstat, 1999, p.17.

directly linked to Russia's major exports, i.e. minerals and energy-carriers (oil and gas). On the other hand, all manufacturing industries were more deeply affected by the changes than the minerals sector was. In short, it might be argued that in the course of the post-Soviet reforms Russian industry was gradually reorienting itself towards low-tech production (Table 1.2).

The shares of the major branches of industry in the gross production of these branches are presented in the Table 1.2. Between 1990 and 1996 five industries have significantly increased their shares in overall production: electricity, fuel, ferrous and non-ferrous metallurgy, and food-processing. The significant increases in the shares of electrical and fuel production can be explained by a relatively low decline in these sectors compared to other industries (see Table 1.1). During the same period the shares of light industry and machine building fell dramatically: their combined share in overall production in 1990 was 30% but it dropped to 22% in 1998.

An analysis of industrial production dynamics using the physical volumes of production of the main industrial commodities in Russia gives approximately the same picture (Table 1.3). While in 1990–98 production of electricity and gas decreased by 12–24%, manufacturing industries experienced slides in production for some commodities between 50% and 93% over the same period.

The larger part of high-tech products was traditionally produced in Russia (and in the former Soviet Union) by enterprises within the military-industrial complex.[7] The sharp decline in manufacturing that took place after the collapse of the USSR[8] (which is demonstrated by the data series presented in the tables above) also had a serious effect on production dynamics in the Russian military-industrial complex. Moreover, the production slump in the military industry was significantly larger than in the civilian industries. While in 1997 the production volume in the Russian industry was 53% of the 1991 level, the gross output in the military-industrial complex fell to just 27% (Table 1.4a). Military output in that sector generally fell more sharply than civilian output. The crisis in the military-industrial complex was also accompanied by a sharp reduction in the number of people employed in that sector which in 1996 was 51% of what it was in 1991.

Between 1991 and 1996, with the sole exception of ship-building, all main branches of the military-industrial complex recorded falls of more than 50% in production of military output (Tables 1.4b, 1.4c and 1.4d). The largest decline was in the production of the most sophisticated high-tech military products: electronic and communications

Table 1.3   Annual Production of Major Industrial Commodities in Russia

a) In physical volumes

	1990	1991	1992	1993	1994	1995	1996	1997	1998[a]
Electricity, bn kWh	1 082	1 068	1 008	957	876	860	847	834	826
Crude oil, mln t	516	462	399	354	318	307	301	306	294
Natural gas, bn cubic m	641	643	641	618	607	595	601	571	564
Coal, mln t	395	353	337	306	272	263	257	245	232
Cast iron, mln t	59.4	48.9	46.1	40.9	36.5	39.8	37.1	37.3	34.1
Steel, mln t	89.6	77.1	67.0	58.3	48.8	51.5	49.3	48.5	43.8
Trucks, th	665	616	583	467	183	143	134	146	142
Plastics, th t	3 258	2 963	2 544	2 246	1 669	1 804	1 411	1 578	1 591
Chemical fibre, th t	674	529	474	349	198	216	134	129	130
Paper, th t	5 240	4 765	3 608	2 884	2 216	2 773	2 302	2 226	2 441
Cement, mln t	83.0	77.5	61.7	49.9	37.2	36.5	27.8	26.7	26.0
All fabrics, mln square m	8 449	7 619	5 090	3 739	2 197	1 774	1 431	1 565	1 395
TV sets, th	4 717	4 439	3 672	3 987	2 240	1 005	313	327	324
Processed meat, th t	6 629	5 815	4 784	4 099	3 282	2 416	1 937	1 535	1 307
Whole milk products, mln t	20.8	18.6	9.8	8.4	7.2	5.6	5.3	5.2	5.3

Table 1.3 *continued*

b) Indices, 1990 = 100

	1990	1991	1992	1993	1994	1995	1996	1997	1998[a]
Electricity	100.0	98.7	93.2	88.4	81.0	79.5	78.3	77.1	76.3
Crude oil	100.0	89.5	77.3	68.6	61.6	59.5	58.3	59.3	57.0
Natural gas	100.0	100.3	100.0	96.4	94.7	92.8	93.8	89.1	88.0
Coal	100.0	89.4	85.3	77.5	68.9	66.6	65.1	62.0	58.7
Cast iron	100.0	82.3	77.6	68.9	61.4	67.0	62.5	62.8	57.4
Steel	100.0	86.0	74.8	65.1	54.5	57.5	55.0	54.1	48.9
Trucks	100.0	92.6	87.7	70.2	27.5	21.5	20.2	22.0	21.4
Plastics	100.0	90.9	78.1	68.9	51.2	55.4	43.3	48.4	48.8
Chemical fibre	100.0	78.5	70.4	51.8	29.4	32.1	19.9	19.2	19.3
Paper	100.0	90.9	68.9	55.0	42.3	52.9	43.9	42.5	46.6
Cement	100.0	93.4	74.3	60.1	44.8	44.0	33.5	32.2	31.3
All fabrics	100.0	90.2	60.2	44.3	26.0	21.0	16.9	18.5	16.5
TV sets	100.0	94.1	77.8	84.5	47.5	21.3	6.6	6.9	6.9
Processed meat	100.0	87.7	72.2	61.8	49.5	36.4	29.2	23.2	19.7
Whole milk products	100.0	89.4	47.1	40.4	34.6	26.9	25.5	25.0	25.6

NOTES:
[a] Preliminary data.

Sources:
Rossiiskii statisticheskii ezhegodnik. 1995, Moscow: Goskomstat, 1995, pp.325–43; *Sotsial'no-ekonomicheskoe polozhenie Rossii. 1995 g.*, Moscow: Goskomstat, 1996, pp.299–309; *Sotsial'no-ekonomicheskoe polozhenie Rossii. 1996 g.*, Moscow: Goskomstat, 1997, pp.17–39; *Rossiya v tsifrakh. 1996*, Moscow: Goskomstat, 1996, pp.296–309;*Sotsial'no-ekonomicheskoe polozhenie Rossii. 1997 g.*, Moscow: Goskomstat, 1998, pp.40–71; *Rossiiskii statisticheskii ezhegodnik. 1997*, Moscow: Goskomstat, 1997, pp.325–43; *Rossiiskii statisticheskii ezhegodnik. 1998*, Moscow: Goskomstat, 1998, pp.397–423; *Sotsial'no-ekonomicheskoe polozhenie Rossii. 1998 g.*, Moscow: Goskomstat, 1999, pp.30–63.

equipment, armaments and military chemical products, aircraft and other aviation products (Table 1.4c). Among the civilian products manufactured by enterprises in the military-industrial complex in 1991–96, components for nuclear power stations, ship-building and aviation experienced much lower decline than other branches (Table 1.4d).

Table 1.5 lists the indices of production of some major civilian products of the Russian military-industrial complex. Between 1991 and 1996 production of sophisticated electronic equipment (videocassette

Table 1.4   Production Dynamics in the Russian Military-Industrial Complex (constant prices, 1991 = 100)

a) General dynamics[a]

	1991	1992	1993	1994	1995	1996	1997
Gross output including:	100.0	82.0	68.9	44.8	38.1	31.2	27.3
Military output	100.0	62.0	43.4	26.5	21.2	16.9	13.6
Civilian output	100.0	93.0	82.8	55.5	48.2	40.0	...
Employment	100.0	91.0	80.1	67.3	57.8	50.9	...

b) Total output by branch

	1991	1992	1993	1994	1995	1996
Aviation	100.0	84.0	68.0	36.1	31.0	22.3
Ship-building	100.0	89.0	78.3	58.0	55.1	41.3
Radio equipment	100.0	84.0	78.1	49.2	34.0	26.5
Communications	100.0	74.0	57.7	32.3	21.3	15.4
Electronics	100.0	72.0	47.5	26.1	21.7	14.8
Weaponry	100.0	84.0	68.9	42.7	32.0	26.3
Armaments and chemical	100.0	70.0	57.4	36.7	29.0	20.9
Missile and space	100.0	94.0	89.3	63.4	58.3	39.7
Nuclear	100.0	100.0	103.0	82.4	81.6	84.8

c) Military output by branch

	1991	1992	1993	1994	1995
Aviation	100.0	61.0	39.0	18.3	17.1
Ship-building	100.0	81.0	61.6	53.6	57.3
Radio equipment	100.0	59.0	46.6	33.1	22.5
Communications	100.0	56.0	39.8	23.5	13.6
Electronics	100.0	42.0	15.1	8.6	8.6
Weaponry	100.0	66.0	51.5	34.5	27.2
Armaments and chemical	100.0	23.0	23.7	19.7	16.1
Missile and space	100.0	64.0	59.5	41.7	36.2
Nuclear	100.0	97.0	74.7	49.3	36.0

Table 1.4 *continued*

d) Civilian output by branch

	1991	1992	1993	1994	1995
Aviation	100.0	113.0	102.8	59.6	49.5
Ship-building	100.0	95.0	87.4	64.7	64.0
Radio equipment	100.0	102.0	103.0	57.7	39.8
Communications	100.0	91.0	74.6	40.3	29.0
Electronics	100.0	84.0	61.3	33.7	27.3
Weaponry	100.0	92.0	76.4	45.8	33.9
Armaments and chemical	100.0	86.0	69.7	41.8	32.6
Missile and space ·	100.0	105.0	100.8	75.6	71.1
Nuclear	100.0	103.0	112.3	93.2	96.0

NOTES:
[a] Estimates by the Russian Academy of Sciences show even more dramatic falls: in 1996 the total output stood at 22.2% of the 1991 level, military production – at 12.2% and civilian production – at 29% of the 1991 level.[6]

Sourced and calculated from:
Rossiya-1996. Ekonomicheskaya konyuktura. 1–2. Moscow: Tsentr ekonomicheskoi konyuktury, June 1996, p.94; *Rossiya-1997. Ekonomicheskaya konyuktura. 1*. Moscow: Tsentr ekonomicheskoi konyuktury, March 1997, p.109; *Promyshlennost' Rossii. 1996*, Moscow: Goskomstat, 1996, pp.11–12; *Promyshlennost' Rossii. 1998*, Moscow: Goskomstat, 1998,

Table 1.5 **Indices of Production of Some Major Civilian Commodities in the Military-Industrial Complex, 1991 = 100**

	1991	1992	1993	1994	1995	1996
Metal-cutting equipment	100.0	93.0	87.4	37.6	35.7	24.3
Diesel engines and generators	100.0	89.0	72.1	25.2	23.5	20.6
Cargo train cars	100.0	73.0	47.5	22.8	15.5	14.2
Personal computers	100.0	43.0	38.7	22.8	12.3	34.2
Refrigerators	100.0	85.0	91.0	59.1	27.8	5.8
Washing machines	100.0	74.0	65.9	34.2	20.2	11.3
VCRs	100.0	143.0	84.4	21.9	6.8	1.8
Colour TV sets	100.0	80.0	83.2	40.8	11.8	3.4
Motorcycles	100.0	81.0	68.9	22.0	9.7	6.4

Sourced and calculated from:
Rossiya-1996. Ekonomicheskaya konyuktura. 1–2. Moscow: Tsentr ekonomicheskoi konyuktury, June 1996, p.96; *Rossiya-1997. Ekonomicheskaya konyuktura. 1*. Moscow: Tsentr ekonomicheskoi konyuktury, March 1997, p.110.

recorders and TV sets) stopped almost completely. Despite greatly increased use of personal computers in Russia during those years, the production of personal computers in 1991–96 fell by two-thirds. According to the figures presented in Tables 1.4 and 1.5, the situation in the military-industrial complex could generally be characterised as disastrous. Like the rest of the Russian manufacturing sector, in the post-Soviet period the military industry in Russia was experiencing a sharp and uninterrupted decline. By the mid-1990s the production of sophisticated, high technology products had almost totally halted. The falling output in Russian industry also had an adverse effect on many consumers of Russian-made industrial goods, including the armed forces.

Another aspect of the post-Soviet reform that had an extremely negative impact on Russia's industrial performance was the problem of enterprise non-payments.[9] This problem emerged at the very start of the reform in early 1992. As mentioned above, the removal of state control over the pricing system was immediately interpreted by many industrial managers of the then state-run enterprises as the freedom to increase prices as a way of maximising profits. Price hikes unbalanced the whole system of prices, both for intermediate goods and final products. At the same time the government's attempts to keep money supply under control created a situation in which the majority of consumers had no money to pay for the goods. Lack of funds put many Russian enterprises on the brink of bankruptcy; however, rather than declaring their companies insolvent, Russian industrial managers preferred to delay outstanding payments (for supplies of intermediate goods and salary payments) while lobbying the state for new credits or seeking credits from commercial banks.

By the time privatisation of state property began in late 1992, the majority of state industrial enterprises were in dire financial straits. For this reason one would hardly expect that the stakes at privatisation auctions would be high; and indeed, in the majority of cases, in 1992–94 state property was sold for nominal sums which were far below cost. At the same time, financial havoc caused by the increasing price race, and accumulating industrial non-payments and delayed wages, could not be stopped by simple transfers of property rights for enterprises. Like their state-owned counterparts, the newly privatised companies were operating in an economic environment where most industrial players were constantly experiencing large delays in payments and enormous difficulties in finding customers for their produce.

Table 1.6 demonstrates the scale of the problem of non-payments in post-Soviet Russia. During the first year of reform non-payments had grown from zero to 15.7% of GDP, or US$7.2 billion (Table 1.6a). Of the total amount of delayed payments in the beginning of 1993, 57%

Table 1.6 Non-Payments and Loss-Making Enterprises in the Russian Economy

a) Crisis of payments by enterprises

	01-Jan-93	01-Jan-94	01-Jan-95	01-Jan-96	01-Jul-96	01-Jan-97	01-Jan-98	01-Jan-99
Billions current roubles								
Total overdue credit payments including:	2 985	58 300	95 975	238 900	382 345	514 421	756 135	1 230 613
Non-payments to suppliers	1 254	29 034	56 780	122 300	186 341	245 937	344 688	585 993
Delayed salary payments	29	766	4 200	13 380	21 654	34 705	39 678	170 147
Other (incl. budget & state funds)	1 702	28 500	34 995	103 220	174 350	233 779	371 769	474 473
Millions current US dollars								
Total overdue credit payments including:	7 193	46 752	27 035	51 487	74 691	92 207	126 868	59 594
Non-payments to suppliers	3 021	23 283	15 994	26 358	36 402	44 083	57 834	28 377
Delayed salary payments	69	614	1 183	2 884	4 230	6 221	6 657	8 240
Other (incl. budget & state funds)	4 102	22 855	9 858	22 246	34 059	41 903	62 377	22 977
Overdue payments as % to GDP	*15.7*	*34*	*15.7*	*14.4*	*35.9*	*22.8*	*28.3*	*45.8*

b) Loss-making enterprises, industry only

	01-Jan-93	01-Jan-94	01-Jan-95	01-Jan-96	01-Jul-96	01-Jan-97	01-Jan-98	01-Jan-99
Numbers as % of all enterprises	15.3	14.0	32.5	36.0	39.0	43.0	47.3	49.2
Volume of losses as % to the volume of gross revenues of all enterprises	1.5	2.6	18.3	14.8	31.2	56.4	55.8	103.5

Sourced and calculated from:
Sotsial'no-ekonomicheskoe polozhenie Rossii (monthly statistical bulletins from Goskomstat), 1993–99.

were caused by delays in state funding. Five years later the state share in the gross amount of non-payments fell to 49%, but the total volume had increased to the astronomical sum of US$126.9 billion. Attempts by the Primakov government to solve the non-payment crisis through printing of money in the last months of 1998 had significantly eased the problem. At the beginning of 1999 the gross amount of non-payments was almost twice less than in January 1998.

The second part of Table 1.6 shows the effect, which the payment crisis had on the Russian industry. A year after the reform began 15.3% of Russian industrial enterprises was loss making. The total volume of losses suffered by all companies operating in the Russian economy was equal to 1.5% of their combined revenues. By the early 1999 already 49% of industrial enterprises were running at a loss. Their gross losses were larger than the total revenue of the Russian industry. In other words, in the course of six years of reform about half of Russian industrial enterprises became virtually bankrupt![10]

From a strategic perspective, post-Soviet industrial dynamics actually leave Russia with a very gloomy future. Since 1992 the country has been rapidly sliding into typical Third World production patterns with a few raw or semi-processed commodities becoming the most important items produced by the national economy. This process has been accompanied by sharp declines in the share of high-tech goods in overall industrial production. The largest falls in industrial production were recorded in the military-industrial complex where the 1996 volumes of military production totalled just 17% of the 1991 level. The falling output at Russian industrial enterprises was also accompanied by the development of an acute financial crisis, which in early 1997 made almost 50% of Russian industry insolvent.

These tendencies have greatly undermined Russian development potential in the modern, high-tech industries. The effects of the current crisis become even more disastrous when one takes into account the fact that all this is happening during the last decade of the 20th century when the rest of the world is undergoing an information technology revolution. That means that the technological gap between Russia and the developed world is increasing each year in a geometrical progression.

By the mid-1990s, the growing technological backwardness of the Russian economy had started to hit its major revenue-generating industry, the mining sector. Improving or even simply renewing the means of production in that sector was becoming increasingly problematic and dependent on imports of new equipment. This is the case, for example,

Table 1.7 **Depreciation of Capital in Russian Industry**
(share of obsolete equipment in the total volume of key assets, %)

	1990	1991	1992	1993	1994	1995	1996	1997
Electricity	40.6	40.1	42.3	43.4	43.4	45.7	47.4	48.3
Fuel	46.7	44.2	44.9	44.5	48.2	51.2	52.6	53.7
Ferrous metallurgy	50.1	45.7	46.0	47.1	44.8	46.9	48.9	50.2
Non-ferrous metallurgy	46.9	42.4	44.7	45.3	45.9	47.5	48.7	49.2
Chemical	56.3	52.1	55.1	53.1	53.9	57.4	59.7	60.9
Machine-building	47.5	42.7	45.5	45.7	45.4	47.5	50.1	51.3
Forestry and wood-processing	48.3	45.9	44.3	46.5	46.8	50.2	51.1	53.3
Construction materials	42.1	39.8	42.2	42.7	43.3	46.5	49.2	50.7
Light industry	40.2	38.8	42.9	43.5	42.8	47.7	51.8	53.7
Food-processing	40.7	39.0	40.6	42.1	41.1	42.8	45.7	46.1
All Industry	46.4	43.3	45.2	45.5	46.2	48.5	47.2	51.6

Sources:
Promyshlennost' Rossii. 1996, Moscow: Goskomstat 1996, p.64; *Rossiiskii statisticheskii ezhegodnik. 1998*, Moscow: Goskomstat, 1998, p.391.

with the modernisation of production facilities in the Russian oil-extracting and oil-refining industries. Even the largest exporting sector, the gas industry, has been experiencing a constant and accelerating decline in output since the start of the reform (Table 1.7).

The picture of the post-Soviet industrial decline in Russia becomes even more dramatic if we analyse it from a regional/local perspective.[11] The industrial specialisation of different geographical regions had always varied greatly in Russia. The major part of the country's manu-facturing facilities was traditionally concentrated in the Central region, the Urals and the North-Western economic region, while Siberia and the Far East account for a dominant share of Russian mining output.

Annual industrial production indices in Russia's 12 major economic regions reveal that since 1991 industrial output in real terms has been falling sharply in all of these regions (Table 1.8). The fastest growing economic regions during the late Soviet period were Central ChernoZem, the North Caucasus and Volgo-Vyatka, while the tradi-tional centre of Russian and Soviet heavy industry and the military-industrial complex, the Urals, had the lowest industrial growth rates.

In the majority of Russian economic regions critical tendencies in industrial production started to develop after 1990. However, in the main industrial areas (the Urals, the Far East and Eastern Siberia) indus-trial output began to fall earlier, in 1989. During 1991 industrial growth was recorded in only one economic region, the North-West. Since 1992

Table 1.8 Indices of Industrial Production by Economic Region,[a] 1990 = 100 (constant prices)

	1985	1988	1989	1990	1991	1992	1993	1994	1995	1996	1997	1998[b]
Northern	90.1	99.1	100.0	100	94.9	85.2	75.9	63.0	61.7	57.2	58.9	58.0
North-West	87.0	96.5	99.1	100	100.4	83.6	74.6	50.0	42.5	35.3	36.4	36.2
Central	87.0	97.4	99.1	100	97.4	75.4	66.4	48.4	42.1	32.5	33.2	31.0
Volgo-Vyatka	86.2	98.3	100.0	100	99.4	87.1	82.0	55.0	48.9	42.3	43.6	42.4
Central ChernoZem	83.3	95.8	99.2	100	96.6	84.7	77.0	57.7	56.6	50.8	51.3	50.1
Volga	87.7	99.1	100.0	100	97.2	85.1	77.8	58.3	53.1	50.1	52.1	49.4
North Caucasus	85.5	94.9	98.3	100	97.1	77.6	65.6	45.9	41.3	35.4	33.3	33.1
Urals	91.7	100.9	100.9	100	98.1	81.4	69.8	53.8	50.6	45.7	44.8	41.7
West Siberia	87.0	100.0	100.9	100	95.8	81.0	71.5	60.1	56.5	53.1	51.5	48.8
East Siberia	88.5	100.0	101.8	100	96.4	82.9	72.6	60.3	57.3	53.0	50.4	49.7
Far East	89.3	100.9	101.8	100	97.3	82.5	72.4	55.7	45.7	41.6	39.5	39.1
Kaliningrad	89.3	98.2	100.9	100	96.3	80.2	66.0	40.9	36.4	30.2	29.6	26.9
TOTAL RF[a]	87.7	98.2	100.0	100	92.0	75.4	64.8	51.2	49.6	47.2	48.1	45.6

NOTES:

[a] Regional statistics after 1991 include only large- and medium-sized enterprises, while national data series also include estimates of production at small businesses and joint ventures.

[b] Preliminary data.

Sourced and calculated from:

Narodnoe Khoziaystvo Rossiiskoi Federatsii. 1992, Moscow: Goskomstat 1992, pp.351–5; *Rossiiskaya Federatsiya v 1992 godu*, Moscow: Goskomstat 1993, pp.368–72; *Rossiiskii statisticheskii ezhegodnik. 1994*, Moscow: Goskomstat 1994, pp.613–5; *Rossiiskii statisticheskii ezhegodnik. 1995*, Moscow: Goskomstat 1995, pp.738–41; *Rossiiskii statisticheskii ezhegodnik. 1996*, Moscow: Goskomstat 1996, pp.966–9; *Sotsialno-ekonomicheskoe polozhenie Rossii. 1996 g.*, Moscow: Goskomstat 1997, pp.217–8; *Sotsialno-ekonomicheskoe polozhenie Rossii. 1998 g.*, Moscow: Goskomstat 1999, pp.329–30; *Rossiiskii statisticheskii ezhegodnik. 1998*, Moscow: Goskomstat, 1998, pp.380–1.

all Russian economic regions have been experiencing uninterrupted falls in their industrial production. Between 1990 and 1998 the largest falls (64–73% down from the 1990 level) in industrial output took place in the enclave area of Kaliningrad, in the centres of Russian manufacturing industry – the Central region and the North-West – and in the war-torn North Caucasus region. Marginally better off were those regions centred on mining – the North, Western and Eastern Siberia – with falls in industrial production over 40% from the 1990 level.

However, these agg regated regional data series often hide growing disparities in industrial performance between administrative areas that form one economic region. That problem becomes especially relevant for regions that incorporate major mining centres. For example, it is possible for industrial production in mining-dominated areas to experience marginal falls, while neighbouring areas lacking natural resources are in a state of deep recession.

In Table 1.9 we have shown two extremes (best versus worst) in industrial dynamics within the eleven major economic regions. This table demonstrates a rapidly growing gap in industrial performance within all regions. In most cases better performance was not linked to the share of one or another area in the overall Russian industrial output. For instance, the industrial output of Smolenskaya Oblast' is only a portion of that of Moscow, but the former showed significantly better development indicators than the latter. The same could be said about Tyumen' and Tomsk in West Siberia. By 1998 the largest difference in the rates of industrial decline had been recorded in the Far East (58 points), Volga region (55 points), North Caucasus (40), Central region (37), the Central ChernoZem region (31) and Western Siberia (30). In general, larger gaps occurred in remote regions in the east (Siberia and the Far East) and in the south (Caucasus), while smaller disparities were recorded in the European regions of Russia.

During the post-Soviet period all major Russian industrial areas (mining and manufacturing) have experienced significant falls in industrial output. The sole exception is the Sakha Republic where in 1996 industrial production amounted to 78% of the 1990 level and in 1995–96 was actually growing. This development can be explained by the unique position that Sakha occupies within the Russian Federation. This Far Eastern republic is the major Russian producer of diamonds and gold. After the collapse of the Soviet Union the Sakha government negotiated a special deal with the Russian central government, according to which the republic could reserve a certain share of the money received from diamond sales for its own use. This deal immediately put

Table 1.9   Annual Indices of Gross Industrial Output by Oblasts
(best vs. worst), 1990 = 100

	1990	1991	1992	1993	1994	1995	1996	1997	1998[a]
Northern									
Vologodskaya Oblast'	100	94	89	79	66	71.9	70.5	70.6	70.8
Karelia Republic	100	95	79	69	55	54.9	46.2	46.7	46.9
North West									
Novgorodskaya Oblast'	100	106	93	84	62	53.3	45.3	45.8	46.2
Pskovskaya Oblast'	100	95	76	69	41	32.8	27.2	25.3	23.4
Central									
Smolenskaya Oblast'	100	99	81	75	60	52.8	49.6	48.6	47.9
Ivanovskaya Oblast'	100	98	65	57	38	33.4	29.8	30.0	31.1
Volgo-Vyatka									
Nizhegorodskaya Oblast'	100	99.9	93.1	92	63	58	51	53.0	54.9
Chuvash Republic	100	99	76.5	66	41	33.6	26.9	27.4	27.5
Central ChernoZem									
Belgorodskaya Oblast'	100	99.5	88	85	72	73.4	65.4	69.3	70.4
Voronezhskaya Oblast'	100	97	85	74	46	43.7	36.3	37.0	38.8
Volga									
Ulyanovskaya Oblast'	100	104	96	98	86	72.2	65	74.8	88.2
Volgogradskaya Oblast'	100	97	77	65	45	39.6	35.6	34.5	33.1
North Caucasus[b]									
Krasnodarskii Krai	100	99	82	73	60	54.6	46.4	43.2	37.3
Dagestan Republic	100	85	65	51	24	17.3	14	14.4	14.2
Urals									
Orenburgskaya Oblast'	100	100	89	79	63	61.1	53.8	53.7	53.8
Kurganskaya Oblast'	100	96	72	67	44	39.2	32.5	32.2	31.9
West Siberia									
Tomskaya Oblast'	100	102	90	90	74	67.3	64.6	62.7	60.8
Altaiskii Krai	100	99.9	83	71	42	39.1	34.4	32.3	29.8
East Siberia									
Khakasiya Republic	100	109	98	97	81	74.5	67.8	67.1	67.6
Chitinskaya Oblast'	100	87	69	56	44	37.8	35.2	31.7	28.9
Far East									
Sakha Republic	100	98	78	75	75	76.5	78	74.1	71.0
Jewish Auton. Oblast'	100	95	71	47	33	22.4	17.1	14.4	13.3

NOTES:
[a] Preliminary data.
[b] Data for 1993–98 excluding Chechnya.

Sourced and calculated from:
Narodnoe khozyaistvo Rossiiskoi Federatsii. 1992, Moscow: Goskomstat, 1992, pp.351–5;
Rossiiskaya Federatsiya v 1992 godu, Moscow: Goskomstat, 1993, pp.368–72; *Rossiiskii statisticheskii ezhegodnik. 1995*, Moscow: Goskomstat, 1995, pp.738–41;
Sotsial'no-ekonomicheskoe polozhenie Rossii. 1995 g., Moscow: Goskomstat, 1996, pp.296–8;
Sotsial'no-ekonomicheskoe polozhenie Rossii. 1996 g., Moscow: Goskomstat, 1997, pp.217–8;
Sotsial'no-ekonomicheskoe polozhenie Rossii. 1998 g., Moscow: Goskomstat, 1999, pp.329–30;
Rossiiskii statisticheskii ezhegodnik. 1998, Moscow: Goskomstat, 1998, pp.380–1.

Graph 1.1 Best and Worst Regional Industrial Performers in Russia, 1990–98
(indices of industrial production in constant prices, 1990 = 100)

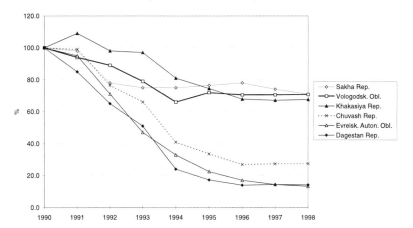

Sakha into an exclusive position within Russia and allowed its government to operate on a budget, which was proportionally significantly higher than that of any other Russian administrative area, except Moscow. That also allowed the Sakha authorities to continue subsidies to local industry and to invest in the establishment of new industries (food-processing, diamond-cutting, etc.).

In Graph 1.1 above we have put together the dynamics of regional industrial performance in six administrative areas of Russia: three with the lowest recorded falls and three with the largest industrial decline. With the exception of Vologodskaya Oblast' in the Russian North, all of these areas are ethnic autonomous regions. If we take Sakha out, the role that these regions played in Russian industrial development was traditionally low. Nevertheless, the graph demonstrates that there was a marked tendency in the way the crisis developed in "better-off" and "worse-off" regions. While in the former group industrial output declined sharply in the first years of reforms but stabilised somewhat after 1994, in the "worse-off" group output continued to decline uninterruptedly through to 1996. Thus, the gap in industrial dynamics between the regions started to grow from 1994, or after the changes that were introduced into the Russian decision-making system following the September–October 1993 confrontation between the parliament and the president and the election of a new parliament in December 1993. By

1996 the regional variations in industrial performance were stunning: while the gross output of Sakha's industry amounted to 78% of the 1991 level, industrial production in the North Caucasian republic of Dagestan totalled just 14% of what it was five years earlier.

The structural changes occurring within Russian industry in the 1990s could be summarised as the declining role of the manufacturing sector in the total industrial output and the growing importance of the resource sector. Although output fell in all industrial branches in the post-Soviet period, the rate of decline significantly differed between industries. In Table 1.10 we analysed the industrial performance of three groups of regions: those with predominantly mining, manufacturing or agricultural specialisation. Not surprisingly, in 1990–98 the manufacturing group of regions experienced the largest fall in its industrial production: the decline amounted to almost 63% down from the 1990 level which was significantly higher than the Russian

Table 1.10   Annual Indices of Gross Industrial Output by Groups of Regions

a) Dynamics of industrial output by group, 1990 = 100

	1990	1991	1992	1993	1994	1995	1996	1997	1998
Mining regions	100.0	93.1	78.9	71.0	64.6	63.0	60.4	61.6	60.5
Manufacturing regions	100.0	97.3	83.5	74.3	51.5	47.0	42.5	40.0	37.6
Agricultural regions	100.0	98.0	79.9	73.8	59.1	57.2	49.7	51.6	52.9

b) Share of groups in Russia's total industrial output

	1990	1991	1992	1993	1994	1995	1996	1997	1998
Mining regions	9.8	9.9	10.3	10.7	12.4	12.7	12.6	13.4	13.7
Manufacturing regions	7.7	8.1	8.6	8.8	7.8	7.4	7.0	8.4	8.3
Agricultural regions	2.7	2.9	2.9	3.1	3.1	3.2	2.9	3.0	3.2

NOTES:
Mining: Kemerovo, Tyumen' and Sakha only.
Manufacturing: St Petersburg, Samara and Khabarovsk only.
Agricultural: Belgorod, Krasnodar and Stavropol only.

Sourced and calculated from:
Rossiiskii statisticheskii ezhegodnik. 1995, Moscow: Goskomstat, 1995, pp.738–41;
Sotsial'no-ekonomicheskoe polozhenie Rossii. 1995 g., Moscow: Goskomstat, 1996, pp.296–8;
Sotsial'no-ekonomicheskoe polozhenie Rossii. 1996 g., Moscow: Goskomstat, 1997, pp.217–8;
Regiony Rossii. 1998, Vol.2, Moscow: Goskomstat, 1998, pp.330–1; *Sotsial'no-ekonomicheskoe polozhenie Rossii. 1998 g.*, Moscow: Goskomstat, 1999, pp.329–30.

national average (down 54 points). In administrative areas with mainly agricultural specialisation the decline in industrial output was less marked but still amounted to a dramatic fall of over 47%, while in mining areas the rate of decline was much lower (–40%). These developments were accompanied by changes in the share that the three groups had in the overall industrial production in Russia. Between 1990 and 1996 the share of the manufacturing group fell from 7.7% to 7%, during the same period the share of the mining group increased from 9.8% to 12.6%. The share of the agricultural group remained almost unchanged.

The picture of the regional dimension of the crisis of industrial production in Russia becomes much clearer if we present dynamics of industrial output in a chloropleth map (Map 1.1). In this map we have brought indices of regional industrial output in 1997 to the 1990 base level (100%) and then divided all regions into three major categories. In the first category we grouped regions where industrial crisis is most acute and, as result, where industrial output in the last seven years has declined by more than 50%. These areas are shaded in black and, as could be seen in Map 1.1, they cover significant part of Russia. Most of the European part of Russia – the country's traditional manufacturing base – was hit by the crisis. Other disaster areas include southern parts of Russia and the Caucasus, East Siberia and the Far East.

The second group of regions consists of areas where industrial output in 1990–97 has fallen between 30% and 49%. These areas are shown in dark grey shade and include northern parts of European Russia, Volga region and West Siberia.

Areas with the best levels of industrial performance constitute the third group. This group is shaded in light grey and includes only the following five administrative units: Nenetsk autonomous area in the North, Ulyanovskaya oblast' in the Volga region, Yamalo-Nenetskii autonomous area in West Siberia, and Sakha Republic and Chukotka in the Russian Far East. Nenetsk and Yamalo-Nenetsk areas, as well as Sakha, are major producers of primary commodities (oil, gas and minerals). Chukotka has entered the group of "best performers" after in 1997 it demonstrated an incredible industrial growth of 146% which primarily was the result of new mining projects started in the area. On the other hand, Ulyanovskaya oblast', where communist-dominated local legislature resisted all attempts to restructure the Soviet system of industrial management and continued to heavily subsidise the local industry, was an exceptional case for Russia.

Map 1.1   Indices of Industrial Output in Russian Regions in 1997, 1990 = 100

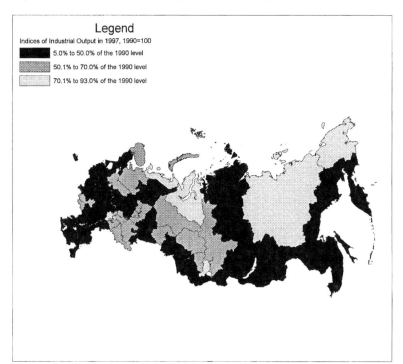

Map 1.1 also graphically demonstrates the emerging rift in industrial performance between neighbouring areas of which we spoke earlier (see Table 1.9). This rift is particularly striking in the East of Russia, where other Far Eastern areas, which are among those most hit by the industrial decline, surround "better off" Sakha and Chukotka. This "oasis"-type industrial model fosters the growth of inter-regional differences in population incomes and social conditions. The latter, in turn, brings new political contradictions into relations between the regions, creates more destabilising pressures and eventually leads to an increase in various forms of extremism and nationalism in the regions.

To conclude, reform attempts made by Russian leaders during the five years since the collapse of the USSR and aimed at restructuring the country's industrial potential, led to a significant decline in national industrial output. The decline was caused by a combination of factors; the most important of which included the structural crisis in the Soviet economy, which arose from its over-centralisation, poor management and inefficiency. The effects of this crisis were multiplied in the post-Soviet years by the gross lack of co-ordination in Russian reform strategies, the inexperience of the majority of Russian managers in the market economy, crime and corruption.[12] As a result, in the 1990s Russia significantly decreased production of the most sophisticated manufacturing products while the advanced, high-tech sectors of its economy were rapidly degrading and disintegrating. At the same time production of minerals and energy-carriers was falling at a significantly lower rate and, consequently, the share of primary industries in the GDP was increasing steadily.

In regional terms, Russia's major centres of manufacturing (the Central and North-Western regions) and the war-torn North Caucasus were the areas hit hardest by the industrial decline. Mining regions on average were only marginally better, while traditional agricultural areas where the role of industry had always been small, had the lowest rates of industrial decline. However, agricultural developments in post-Soviet Russia were also rather critical.

1.2 Crisis in agriculture

The economic crisis that Russia experienced in the post-Soviet period had possibly the most devastating effect on agriculture. Under Soviet rule agricultural production was considered a top priority; it was tightly state-controlled and heavily subsidised. In addition, local farming in the USSR was over-protected by the state from any competition whatsoever, whether domestic or foreign. Wholesale and retail prices for industrial and agricultural commodities were strictly regulated by the state and, consequently, were often rather artificial. In short, Russian agriculture as it developed in the Soviet period was not competitive and was unproductive and grossly dependent on state support.[13]

In this situation any attempt to decrease the level of state protection or support for agriculture was certain to have direct negative effects.[14] But what happened in Russia after 1991 was possibly the worst scenario that Soviet agricultural producers could have expected. Following the collapse of Soviet central planning and management, the post-communist Russian leaders announced that they were halting the earlier state practice of subsidising various branches of the economy through redistribution of wealth; they also opened the internal market to foreign competition and started to promote private enterprise in agriculture. All this was accompanied in January 1992 by price liberalisation, which immediately changed the ratio between industrial and agricultural prices and made many locally produced food commodities too expensive for the average Russian customer.

From the very beginning the Russian reform attempts were strongly and consistently opposed by the majority of agricultural producers. Agricultural producers were among the first and possibly the biggest losers from the transformation. They lost almost all of the substantial financial and material support, which they had previously received from the state at a time when the prices for industrial commodities for agriculture (machinery, fertilisers, etc.) were growing much faster than prices for foodstuffs. The opening of the Russian internal market following the decentralisation of foreign trade in early 1992 also resulted in the removal of former state protectionist barriers and forced the already weakened Russian agricultural producers into competition with foreign-produced foodstuffs.

The combined effect of these measures on agricultural production was extremely negative. Between 1990 and 1992 the gross agricultural output in Russia in constant prices decreased by 14% (Table 1.11b). The situation in agriculture continued to worsen throughout the first half of the 1990s, and by 1996 Russia was producing 38% less agricultural commodities than it produced in 1990.

During the 1990s the structure of agricultural production in Russia underwent a significant change. The Russian agricultural reform program had two main directions: privatisation of agricultural production and privatisation of land. While attempts by the Russian reformers to change the ownership of land were consistently opposed by the parliament, the restructuring of production resulted in a rapid growth of private farms in Russia. Between 1991 and 1994 the number of private farms increased from 4 400 to 270 000; in 1995–96 this number stabilised at the level of 279 000.[15] However, the share of these farms in the overall agricultural production in the 1990s did not exceed 3.1% (Table 1.11a).[16]

The most important structural changes in Russian agricultural output were the growth of ancillary sector and the decline of the enterprise sector (commercial farming). These two tendencies were directly related to one another.[17] As noted above, post-Soviet reforms put many large farms (both state-owned and collective) into an extremely hostile environment. That resulted in the continuous decline of production on large farms, which suffered the most from the increasing industrial prices, growing competition from foreign producers and lack of state financial support. Between 1990 and 1998 the volume of production at these farms fell by almost 65% (Table 1.11b).

Table 1.11 Structure and Indices of Gross Agricultural Production

a) Structure of agricultural production

	1990	1991	1992	1993	1994	1995	1996	1997	1998
All agriculture[a]	100.0	100.0	100.0	100.0	100.0	100.0	100.0	100.0	100.0
Enterprises[b]	73.7	68.8	67.1	57.0	54.5	51.5	50.8	49.9	46.2
Ancillary[c]	26.3	31.2	31.8	39.9	43.8	46.6	47.4	47.9	52.0
Farmers	0.0	0.0	1.1	3.1	1.7	1.9	1.8	2.2	1.8

b) Indices of gross agricultural production, 1990 = 100

	1990	1991	1992	1993	1994	1995	1996	1997	1998
All agriculture	100.0	95.5	86.5	82.7	72.8	67.0	63.6	64.4	56.5
Enterprises	100.0	89.2	78.8	64.0	53.8	46.8	43.8	43.6	35.4
Ancillary	100.0	113.3	104.6	125.5	121.2	118.7	114.5	117.3	111.6

c) Dynamics of Agricultural and Industrial Prices, 1990 = 1

	1990	1991	1992	1993	1994	1995	1996	1997	1998
Index of agricultural prices	1	2	15	122	366	1 206	1 427	1 555	2 208
Index of industrial prices	1	2	49	487	2 484	8 446	10 608	11 393	14 036
Ratio of agricultural and industrial prices	1 : 1.0	1 : 1.5	1 : 3.3	1 : 4.0	1 : 6.8	1 : 7.0	1 : 7.4	1 : 7.3	1 : 6.4

NOTES:
[a] All types of agricultural units: collective, state-owned and private.
[b] Category includes state enterprises (*sovkhozy*) and collective farms (*kolkhozy*).
[c] Production at ancillary agricultural plots of land of the rural population and country houses (*dachas*).

Sourced and calculated from:
Rossiiskii statisticheskii ezhegodnik. 1995, Moscow: Goskomstat, 1995, p.351; *Rossiiskii statisticheskii ezhegodnik. 1996*, Moscow: Goskomstat, 1996, p.376; *Sotsial'no-ekonomicheskoe polozhenie Rossii. 1995 g.,* Moscow: Goskomstat, 1996, p.74; *Sotsial'no-ekonomicheskoe polozhenie Rossii. 1996 g.,* Moscow: Goskomstat, 1997, pp.49, 110; *Rossiya v tsifrakh. 1996*, Moscow: Goskomstat, 1996, p.316; *Rossiiskii statisticheskii ezhegodnik. 1998*, Moscow: Goskomstat, 1998, p.443; *Sotsial'no-ekonomicheskoe polozhenie Rossii. 1998 g.,* Moscow: Goskomstat, 1998, p.8; *Sotsial'no-ekonomicheskoe polozhenie Rossii. 1998 g.,* Moscow: Goskomstat, 1998, pp.89, 183, 187.

While less and less locally produced foodstuffs were entering the Russian market, the majority of the Russian population could not afford to buy imported products which were also too expensive for the average consumer. In this situation many Russians were forced to seek alternative ways of providing themselves and their families with food. The result was an unprecedented growth of ancillary farming in Russia in the 1990s. Between 1990 and 1998 the share of private country gardens in the gross agricultural production almost doubled, reaching 52% (Table 1.11a). However, only a small proportion of this production was entering the retail trade chain; the bulk was consumed by producers and their families. The increased food self-sufficiency of the population has further intensified the crisis in the Russian commercial farming.

The changes that took place in the structure of agricultural production were also reflected in the dynamics of production of major agricultural commodities (Table 1.12). The production of commodities which generally require very little capital to produce and, therefore, can easily be produced in ancillary households – potatoes and vegetables – increased significantly during the early 1990s: in 1998 Russia produced more potatoes and vegetables than eight years earlier. At the same time production of all other commodities had fallen sharply: grain production in 1990–98 fell by almost 60%, meat – by 54%, milk – by 40% and eggs – by 31%. These dynamics clearly demonstrate that production in the ancillary sector was mainly limited to only a few commodities and did not generally expand into areas requiring industrial processing (e.g., grains and meat).

The structure of production of some major agricultural products in Russia is presented in Table 1.13. Analysis of this data reveals that grain production in post-Soviet Russia continued to be mainly concentrated at large farms (former *sovkhozes* and *kolkhozes*). During the early 1990s the share of the latter in the gross production of grain fell only marginally: from 99% in 1990 to 92% in 1998. During the same period changes in the structure of production of livestock products were much more pronounced: the share of large farms in the production of milk fell from 74% in 1990 to 50% in 1998 and meat – from 70% to 42%.

The continuous decline in production at large farms in Russia during the first half of the 1990s was only partly compensated by the growth of production by other categories of agricultural producers. The creation of private farms on a mass scale in the early 1990s had almost no effect on the structure of production. For instance, in 1996 Russia's 279 000 private farms had negligible shares in the production of major

Table 1.12 Production of Major Agricultural Commodities in Russia, 1985–98

a) Dynamics of production in physical volumes

	1985	1990	1991	1992	1993	1994	1995	1996	1997	1998[a]
Grain, mln t[b]	98.6	116.7	89.1	106.9	99.1	81.3	63.4	69.3	88.6	47.8
Potatoes, mln t	33.9	30.8	34.3	38.3	37.7	33.8	39.9	38.7	37	31.3
Vegetables, mln t	11.1	10.3	10.4	10.0	9.8	9.6	11.3	10.7	11.1	10.5
Meat, th t[c]	8 513	10 112	9 375	8 260	7 513	6 803	5 796	5 336	4 854	4 600
Milk, th t	50 169	55 715	52 000	47 236	46 524	42 176	39 241	35 819	34 136	33 200
Eggs, mlns	44 277	47 470	47 100	42 902	40 297	37 477	33 830	31 902	32 199	32 600
Wool, th t[d]	217.2	226.7	204.0	178.6	158.4	122.2	93.0	76.9	60.8	...

b) Indices of production, 1990 = 100

	1985	1990	1991	1992	1993	1994	1995	1996	1997	1998[a]
Grain	84.5	100.0	76.4	91.6	84.9	69.7	54.3	59.4	75.9	41.0
Potatoes	110.1	100.0	111.4	124.4	122.4	109.7	129.5	125.6	120.1	101.6
Vegetables	107.8	100.0	101.0	97.1	95.1	93.2	109.7	103.9	107.8	101.9
Meat	84.2	100.0	92.7	81.7	74.3	67.3	57.3	52.8	48.0	45.5
Milk	90.0	100.0	93.3	84.8	83.5	75.7	70.4	64.3	61.3	59.6
Eggs	93.3	100.0	99.2	90.4	84.9	78.9	71.3	67.2	67.8	68.7
Wool	95.8	100.0	90.0	78.8	69.9	53.9	41.0	33.9	26.8	...

NOTES:
[a] Preliminary data.
[b] Weight after processing.
[c] In slaughter weight equivalent, SWE.
[d] Physical weight.

Sources:
Selskoe khozyastvo SSSR. Statisticheskii sbornik, Moscow: Goskomstat, 1988, pp.282–9; *Narodnoe khozyastvo RSFSR v 1988 g.*, Moscow: Goskomstat, 1989, pp.455, 526; *Rossiiskaya Federatsiya v 1992 godu*, Moscow: Goskomstat, 1993, p.473; *Narodnoe khozyaistvo Rossiiskoi Federatsii. 1992*, Moscow: Goskomstat, 1992, pp.419–20, 472; *Rossiiskii statisticheskii ezhegodnik. 1995*, Moscow: Goskomstat, 1995, pp.362, 371, 804, 810; *Sotsial'no-ekonomicheskoe polozhenie Rossii. 1995 g.*, Moscow: Goskomstat, 1996, pp.75, 79, 344; *Sodruzhestvo Nezavisimykh Gosudarst v 1995 godu. Kratkii spravochnik*, Moscow: Statkom SNG, January 1996, p.89; *Rossiya v tsifrakh. 1996*, Moscow: Goskomstat, 1996, pp.319, 326; *Sotsial'no-ekonomicheskoe polozhenie Rossii. 1996 g.*, Moscow: Goskomstat, 1997, pp.50–3; *Rossiiskii statisticheskii ezhegodnik. 1997*, Moscow: Goskomstat, 1997, p.396; *Sotsial'no-ekonomicheskoe polozhenie Rossii. 1997 g.*, Moscow: Goskomstat, 1998, pp.92, 99; *Rossiiskii statisticheskii ezhegodnik. 1998*, Moscow: Goskomstat, 1998, pp.459–92; *Sotsial'no-ekonomicheskoe polozhenie Rossii. 1998 g.*, Moscow: Goskomstat, 1999, pp.90–7.

Table 1.13   Production of Major Agricultural Commodities by Category of Producers

a) Structure of production by category, % to all

	1991	1992	1993	1994	1995	1996	1997	1998[a]
Grain								
All agriculture	100.0	100.0	100.0	100.0	100.0	100.0	100.0	100.0
Enterprises	98.7	97.4	94.2	94.2	94.4	94.6	93.0	92.4
Ancillary	0.4	0.5	0.6	0.7	0.9	0.8	0.8	1.0
Farmers	0.9	2.1	5.2	5.1	4.7	4.6	6.2	6.6
Potatoes								
All agriculture	100.0	100.0	100.0	100.0	100.0	100.0	100.0	100.0
Enterprises	27.1	21.2	16.5	11.0	9.2	8.9	7.7	7.0
Ancillary	72.3	78.0	82.5	88.1	89.9	90.2	91.3	91.1
Farmers	0.6	0.8	1.0	0.9	0.9	0.9	1.0	1.9
Meat								
All agriculture	100.0	100.0	100.0	100.0	100.0	100.0	100.0	100.0
Enterprises	70.3	64.0	59.4	55.4	49.9	46.7	42.5	42.0
Ancillary	29.6	35.3	39.5	43.2	48.6	51.6	55.9	56.4
Farmers	0.1	0.7	1.1	1.4	1.5	1.7	1.6	1.6
Milk								
All agriculture	100.0	100.0	100.0	100.0	100.0	100.0	100.0	100.0
Enterprises	73.8	68.2	64.3	60.0	57.1	53.1	51.3	50.2
Ancillary	26.1	31.4	34.6	38.7	41.4	45.4	47.2	48.3
Farmers	0.1	0.4	1.1	1.4	1.5	1.5	1.5	1.5

b) Dynamics of production by category, 1991 = 100

	1991	1992	1993	1994	1995	1996	1997	1998[a]
Grain								
All agriculture	100.0	119.9	111.2	91.3	71.2	77.8	99.4	53.7
Enterprises	100.0	118.4	106.2	87.1	68.1	74.6	93.7	50.2
Ancillary	100.0	149.9	166.8	159.7	160.1	155.6	198.9	134.1
Farmers	100.0	279.8	642.7	517.1	371.6	397.6	685.1	393.4
Potatoes								
All agriculture	100.0	111.7	109.9	98.5	116.3	112.8	107.9	91.3
Enterprises	100.0	87.4	66.9	40.0	39.5	37.1	30.6	23.6
Ancillary	100.0	120.5	125.4	120.1	144.6	140.8	136.2	115.0
Farmers	100.0	148.9	183.2	147.8	174.5	169.2	179.8	289.0
Meat								
All agriculture	100.0	88.1	80.1	72.6	61.8	56.9	51.8	49.1
Enterprises	100.0	80.2	67.7	57.2	43.9	37.8	31.3	29.3
Ancillary	100.0	105.1	106.9	105.9	101.5	99.2	97.8	93.5
Farmers	100.0	616.7	881.5	1 015.9	927.4	967.6	828.4	785.1
Milk								
All agriculture	100.0	90.8	89.5	81.1	75.5	68.9	65.6	63.8
Enterprises	100.0	83.9	78.0	65.9	58.4	49.6	45.6	43.4
Ancillary	100.0	109.3	118.6	120.3	119.7	119.8	118.7	118.2
Farmers	100.0	363.4	984.2	1 135.5	1 132.0	1 033.2	984.7	957.7

NOTES:
[a] Preliminary data.

Sources:
Rossiiskii statisticheskii ezhegodnik. 1995, Moscow: Goskomstat, 1995, p.351;
Sotsial'no-ekonomicheskoe polozhenie Rossii. 1995 g., Moscow: Goskomstat, 1996, p.344;
Rossiya v tsifrakh. 1996, Moscow: Goskomstat, 1996, pp.320, 327; *Sotsial'no-ekonomicheskoe polozhenie Rossii. 1996 g.*, Moscow: Goskomstat, 1996, pp.51–3, 253, 255; *Rossiiskii statisticheskii ezhegodnik. 1998*, Moscow: Goskomstat, 1998, p.450; *Sotsial'no-ekonomicheskoe polozhenie Rossii. 1998 g.*, Moscow: Goskomstat, 1999, pp.90–8.

commodities: less than 5% for grain, less than 2% for meat and milk, and less than 1% for potatoes (Table 1.13a).

By the mid-1990s, it was the ancillary sector, not private farms that had become the major competitor of former state and collective farms. While between 1990 and 1998 the share of ancillary households in the production of grain remained at the same low level (0.5–1.0%), the increase in the share of production of other commodities was very significant: from 72% to 91% for potatoes, from 30% to 56% for meat and from 26% to 48% for milk. However, these dramatic changes were not a consequence of rapid growth in ancillary production; rather, they can be explained by a slump of production on large farms. Thus, while in 1990–98 the production of potatoes in ancillary households grew by 15%, on large farms it declined by more than 75% (Table 1.13b). Meat production in the ancillary sector in 1998 was 6.5% below the level reached in 1990, but at the same time it also fell by more than 70% on large farms. Milk production in Russia between 1990 and 1998 had increased by 18% in the ancillary sector but it fell by over 56% at former state and collective farms.

Tables 1.12 and 1.13 clearly show that gross agricultural production in Russia in the post-communist period continued to be driven by the production levels on large farms. An acute crisis in large-scale farming that in the early 1990s was greatly intensified by the collapse of the Soviet central management system, pushed Russian agriculture into deep recession. Attempts by the Russian reformist leaders to alleviate this situation through state support for the development of private farming had very little success. In the mid-1990s private farming remained at negligible levels. Ancillary households made up the only agricultural sector in Russia that recorded significant growth in its production levels during the 1990s. This sector expanded its production of potatoes and vegetables, but the bulk of these were produced for "in-house" (family) consumption. Levels of ancillary production of other commodities changed only marginally.

Dynamics of change in agricultural production also differed greatly between Russian economic regions (Table 1.14 and Map 1.2). The Volgo-Vyatka region was the only traditional agricultural area in Russia where decline in agricultural output was modest (–20% in 1990–97). Other major Russian agricultural areas (Chernozem, Volga and the North Caucasus) have demonstrated much steeper falls. Under the Soviet system these areas were highly dependent on central subsidies (and centralised re-distribution of resources); in the post-Soviet period when centralised funding was significantly reduced, all of these regions experienced an acute lack of local resources which could be diverted to support their agriculture. As a result, agricultural production in these regions in 1990–97 fell sharply (by 31–51%).

At the same time the resource-rich economic regions of the Russian North and Siberia were diverting a part of revenues from the sales of raw materials to support agriculture. Local subsidies helped agricultural producers in these regions to avoid large falls in the volumes of production: the decline in agricultural output in 1990–97 in these areas was between 27% and 32%.[18]

In the early 1990s the Russian enclave on the Baltic Sea, Kaliningrad, experienced the largest fall in its agricultural output. In Soviet times agricultural production in Kaliningrad was highly dependent on supplies of feed, fertilisers and other necessary components from other parts of the USSR. The collapse of the Soviet Union left the area isolated from mainland Russia, which immediately led to a sharp increase in transportation costs to the area. That made the local agricultural produce very expensive and low-competitive compared to the foodstuffs produced by

Table 1.14   Indices of Gross Agricultural Production by Economic Region, 1990 = 100

	1990	1992	1993	1994	1995	1996	1997
Northern	100	90	80	79	78	68	65
North-West	100	92	84	74	70	67	66
Central	100	91	84	82	77	79	71
Volgo-Vyatka	100	99	92	84	85	80	80
Central ChernoZem	100	83	84	72	65	64	66
Volga	100	89	84	81	70	69	79
North Caucasus	100	76	73	61	56	49	47
Urals	100	89	83	79	73	73	82
West Siberia	100	84	87	75	78	73	70
East Siberia	100	92	88	79	76	71	76
Far East	100	83	74	64	59	55	49
Kaliningrad	100	76	70	62	53	50	51
All Russia	100	86	83	73	67	62	63

Sourced and calculated from:
Ekonomicheskoe polozhenie regionov Rossiiskoi Federatsii, Moscow: Goskomstat, 1994, pp.150–1; *Sravnitelnye pokazateli ekonomicheskogo polozheniya regionov Rossiiskoi Federatsii*, Moscow: Goskomstat, 1995, pp.163–5; *Selskoe khozyaistvo Rossii. 1995*, Moscow: Goskomstat, 1995, pp.149–51; *Rossiiskii statisticheskii ezhegodnik. 1996*, Moscow: Goskomstat, 1996, pp.1004–6; *Rossiiskii statisticheskii ezhegodnik. 1997*, Moscow: Goskomstat, 1997, p.633; *Rossiiskii statisticheskii ezhegodnik. 1998*, Moscow: Goskomstat, 1998, pp.444–5.

Kaliningrad's neighbours (the Baltic States, Belarus and Poland), all of which had traditionally highly developed agricultural sectors.

The situation in the Russian Far East was to some extent similar to that of Kaliningrad. The Far East also imported from other areas of the Soviet Union most of the components it needed for agricultural production. Here, too, the rise in transportation costs in the post-Soviet period made local produce extremely expensive compared to imports. However, in addition to these factors the development of Far Eastern agriculture was also hampered by severe climatic conditions in the region, where very cold and long winters required massive inputs of energy to preserve the livestock while short summers and the lack of agricultural lands put strict limits on the production of other agricultural commodities. In the post-1991 period the removal of state subsidies to both agricultural and energy producers left Far Eastern agriculture without most of the energy,

Map 1.2 Indices of Agricultural Production in Russian Regions in 1997, 1990 = 100

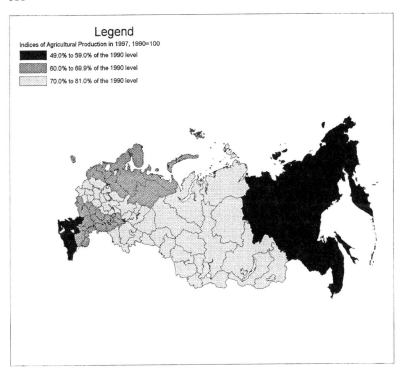

feed and financial support it used to receive. The result was a steep decline in agricultural output of 51% in 1990–97.[19]

Another Russian region, which also had a dramatic fall in agricultural production during the first half of the 1990s, was the North Caucasus. In Soviet times agriculture in this region was also highly dependent on state subsidies; the removal of state support also had an extremely negative effect on the output dynamics of agriculture. But the main reason behind the dramatic 53% fall in agricultural production in the region in 1990–97 was the destructive Chechen War that paralysed most of the region's economy during 1994–96.

In Table 1.15 we present dynamics of agricultural production in three categories of Russian regions which are grouped in accordance with their major economic profiles. In those regions where agriculture was not a dominant sector of the local economy (mining and manufacturing groups of regions) falls in agricultural production during 1990–97 were less dramatic than in the mainly agricultural regions. That tendency also led to a continuing decline in the share of agricultural regions in the Russian gross agricultural output: this share fell from 10.3% in 1990 to 7.9% in 1997 (Table 1.15b).

To summarise, since the collapse of the Soviet system of economic management agricultural production in Russia has been constantly declining. Agriculture, along with the military-industrial complex, was the branch of the national economy most dependent on the continuing flow of large state subsidies. Any disruption of this flow was certain to have an extremely negative effect on the level and dynamics of agricultural production. However, in the post-Soviet situation agricultural producers in Russia found themselves not only cut off from the state support they used to receive,[20] but generally in an economic environment which was extremely hostile to any form of agricultural business. Since 1992 real prices for agricultural commodities were continuously and rapidly falling behind industrial prices (Table 1.11c). By 1999 the majority of Russian agricultural producers – whether private farmers or collective farm workers – could not afford to purchase the necessary volumes of industrial products, including machinery, fertilisers, fuel and energy, etc.

The difficult financial situation in which many agricultural producers found themselves in the 1990s was further intensified by the need for them to compete on the Russian market with imported agricultural produce. Before 1992 local producers had no experience of market competition because wholesale and retail prices, internal trade and imports were all regulated by the state. The reduction of the volume of state support was in itself a heavy blow for many agricultural enterprises, but

Table 1.15   Annual Indices of Gross Agricultural Production by Groups of Regions

a) Dynamics of agricultural production by group, 1990 = 100

	1990	1992	1993	1994	1995	1996	1997
Mining regions	100.0	89.5	83.9	77.3	77.2	70.7	69.4
Manufacturing regions	100.0	90.3	77.1	71.4	66.4	64.4	70.7
Agricultural regions	100.0	77.0	77.3	64.9	60.2	54.3	53.0

b) Share of groups in Russia's gross agricultural production

	1990	1992	1993	1994	1995	1996	1997
Mining regions	4.3	4.4	4.3	4.6	4.9	4.1	3.9
Manufacturing regions	3.1	3.2	2.9	3.0	3.0	2.6	2.9
Agricultural regions	10.3	9.2	9.6	9.1	9.2	8.2	7.9

NOTES:
Mining: Kemerovo, Tyumen' and Sakha only.
Manufacturing: St Petersburg, Samara and Khabarovsk only.
Agriculture: Belgorod, Krasnodar and Stavropol only.

Sourced and calculated from:
Ekonomicheskoe polozhenie regionov Rossiiskoi Federatsii, Moscow: Goskomstat, 1994, pp.150–1; *Sravnitelnye pokazateli ekonomicheskogo polozheniya regionov Rossiiskoi Federatsii*, Moscow: Goskomstat, 1995, pp.163–5; *Selskoe khozyaistvo Rossii. 1995*, Moscow: Goskomstat, 1995, pp.146–51; *Rossiiskii statisticheskii ezhegodnik. 1996*, Moscow: Goskomstat, 1996, pp.1004–6; *Rossiiskii statisticheskii ezhegodnik. 1998*, Moscow: Goskomstat, 1998, pp.444–5; *Regiony Rossii. 1998*, Vol.2, Moscow: Goskomstat, 1998, pp.403–7.

that was also followed by a dramatic fall in the food consumption of the population and by the lifting of protection barriers on foreign trade. As a result the Russian agricultural sector was constantly reducing its production levels, while the country was becoming more and more dependent on food imports.[21]

It is no surprise that in the post-Soviet situation agricultural workers in general became very suspicious of the Russian government's reform policies. Their concerns were confirmed by the generally poor performance of the privatised agricultural units and by the extremely modest results achieved on private farms.

The falls in agricultural production were accompanied by a rapid decline in real incomes of the population. In real terms, in the post-communist period many foodstuffs became very expensive to buy for the majority of Russian families. These developments greatly stimulated growth in the ancillary sector, which by the mid-1990s became the only alternative to the collapse of large-scale agricultural production. However, the expansion of the ancillary sector was mainly limited to potato and vegetable production for family use. While this type of production became a very important channel of supply for many Russian families, its economic importance and general market influence in the production of some major agricultural commodities (e.g., grain and technical crops) were almost negligible. By the end of 1998 the Russian agriculture was as far away from any model of efficient and self-sustainable farming as it had been in 1990. The majority of farms continued to be highly dependent on an uninterrupted flow of state donations, despite the fact that the latter were significantly reduced. It can be argued that although attempts to reform this situation have caused serious disruption and damage to the old system of management in agriculture, they have generally failed to restructure it.

Notes

1. Janos Kornai, "Transformational Recession: The Main Causes", *Journal of Comparative Economics*, Vol.19, No.1, August 1994, pp.39–63.
2. Political behaviour and social psychology of Russian industrial managers are important factors in understanding the core of the managerial problem in the transitional Russia. A few recent publications were specifically devoted to the problem. See, for example, Simon Clarke (ed.), *Management and Industry in Russia: Formal and Informal Relations in the Period of Transition*, Aldershot: E. Elgar, (1995); Pavel H. Dembinski, *The Logic of the Planned Economy. The Seeds of the Collapse*, Oxford: Clarendon Press, 1991; Paul Gregory and Robert Stuart, *Soviet Economic Structure and Performance*, 4th Edition. N.Y.: Harper & Row, 1990; Ed A. Hewett, *Reforming the Soviet Economy: Equality versus Efficiency*, Washington, D.C.: Brookings Institution, 1988.
3. For more information about reforms on an enterprise level see M. Ernst, *Transforming the Core: Restructuring Industrial Enterprises in Russia and Central Europe*, Boulder, Colorado: Westview Press, 1996; S. Clarke (ed.), *Conflict and Change in the Russian Industrial Enterprise*, Cheltenham, UK: E. Elgar, (1996).
4. E. Duflo and C. Senik-Leygonie, "Industrial restructuring in Russia: early reactions of firms to the shock of liberalization", *The Economics of Transition*, Vol.5, No.1, May 1997, pp.45–62.
5. Stanislav Menshikov, "State Enterprises in Transition", *Transitions*, Vol.35, No.1, pp.125–48.
6. See: *Strategiya razvitiya Rossiiskoi ekonomiki i programma pervoocherednykh shagov*, Moscow: Institut ekonomiki, 1996.
7. For a detailed study of the Soviet and Russian military-industrial complex and problems of conversion in the post-Soviet period see: Julian Cooper, *The Soviet Defense Industry: Conversion and Economic Reform*, London: Royal Institute of Economic Affairs, 1991; Silvana Malle, *The Economic Organisation of War Communism*, Cambridge: Cambridge University Press,

1985; Alec Nove, *An Economic History of the USSR 1917–91*, Harmondsworth: Penguin Books, 1992; Ilya Bass, Leslie Dienes, "Defense industry legacies and conversion in the post-Soviet realm", *Post-Soviet Geography and Economics*, Vol.34, No.5, May 1993, pp.302–17; James H. Noren, "The Russian military-industrial sector and conversion", *Post-Soviet Geography and Economics*, Vol.35, No.9, November 1994, pp.495–521; Antonio Sánchez-Andrés, "Privatisation, decentralisation and production adjustment in the Russian defence industry", *Europe-Asia Studies*, Vol.50, No.2, March 1998, pp.241–55.

8. Crisis in the Russian military-industrial complex started to develop in the late Soviet period. It was significantly intensified by a series of government's attempts to convert Russia's military production into civilian output. For a recent discussion of the subject see K. P. O'Prey, *A Farewell to Arms? Russia's Struggle with Defense Conversion*, N.Y.: Twentieth Century Fund Press, 1995; C. G. Gaddy, *The Price of the Past: Russia's Struggle with the Legacy of a Militarized Economy*, Washington, D.C.: Brookings Institution, (1996).

9. For a good account of problem of enterprise debt in a comparative perspective see: David Begg and Ricjard Portes, "Enterprise Debt and Financial Restructuring in Central and Eastern Europe", *European Economic Review*, Vol.37, No.2/3, April 1993, pp.396–407.

10. The data in Table 1.6 refers to large- and medium-sized enterprises only and does not cover small businesses and joint ventures. However, large- and medium-sized enterprises produce between 75% and 85% of the total industrial output in Russia.

11. In statistical and economic terms Russia's 89 administrative regions (oblasts, territories and autonomous areas) are grouped into 11 economic regions: Northern, North-West (includes St Petersburg), Central (includes Moscow), Volgo-Vyatka, Central ChernoZem, Volga, North Caucasus, Urals, Western Siberia, Eastern Siberia and the Russian Far East. Kaliningrad (*Kaliningradskaya Oblast'*) is a separate administrative area that is also listed as the 12th economic region because of its enclave status. For a recent overview of Russian federal structure see Philip Hanson, "Russia's 89 Federal Subjects", *Post Soviet Prospects*, Vol.IV, No.8, August 1996.

12. D. Mario Nuti, "Russia: The Unfinished Revolution", *International Economic Outlook*, June 1994, pp.3–8.

13. See also David Sedik, Christian Foster and William Liefert, "Economic reforms and agriculture in the Russian Federation, 1992–95", *Communist Economies & Economic Transformation*, Vol.8, No.2, June 1996, pp.133–48.

14. For some recent discussion on the subject of Russian agrarian reform see D. van Atta (ed.), *The "Farmer Threat": the Political Economy of Agrarian Reform in Post-Soviet Russia*, Boulder, Colorado: Westview Press, 1993; K. Brooks, Z. Lerman, *Land Reform and Farm Restructuring in Russia*. Washington, D.C.: The World Bank, (1994); A. G. Zel'dner, *Agrarnyi sektor ekonomiki Rossii na poroge XXI veka*, Moscow: Institute of Economy, 1995.

15. *Rossiiskii statisticheskii ezhegodnik. 1996*, Moscow: Goskomstat, 1996, p.555; *Sotsial'no-ekonomicheskoe polozhenie Rossii. 1996 g.*, Moscow: Goskomstat, 1997, p.56.

16. The dynamics of the development of private farming in post-Soviet Russia has been analysed by Stephen K. Wegren and Frank A. Durgin in their

recent article "The political economy of private farming in Russia", *Comparative Economic Studies,*Vol.39, Nos.3–4, Fall–Winter 1997.

17. Richard Rose, Yevgeniy Tikhomirov, "Who grows food in Russia and Eastern Europe?", *Post-Soviet Geography and Economics*, Vol.34, No.2, February 1993, pp.111–26; Zvi Lerman, Yevgeniy Tankhilevich, Kirill Mozhin, and Natalya Sapova, "Self-sustainability of subsidiary household plots: lessons for privatization of agriculture in former socialist countries", *Post-Soviet Geography and Economics*, Vol.35, No.9, November 1994, pp.526–542; Stephen K. Wegren, "From farm to table: the food system in post-communist Russia", *Communist Economies & Economic Transformation,* Vol.8, No.2, June 1996, pp.149–84.

18. Local variations in the implementation of reforms, management experience of regional leadership and the level of its relations with the central power had also played an important role in the way the agricultural reform was pursued in different regions of Russia. See Peter R. Cramer, "Regional patterns of agricultural reform in Russia", *Post-Soviet Geography and Economics*, Vol.35, No.6, June 1994, pp.329–51; Kathryn Stoner-Weiss, *Local Heroes: The Political Economy of Russian Regional Governance*, Princeton University Press, 1997.

19. For more details on recent agricultural developments in the Far East see V.Tikhomirov, "Food Balance in the Russian Far East", *Polar Geography*, Vol.21, No.3, July–September 1997, pp.155–202.

20. In 1990 price subsidies and donations received by agricultural producers from the state budget totalled 27.5% of the cost of agricultural produce (33.8% in livestock breeding). In 1995 these subsidies fell to 9.4%. (*Ekonomika sel'skogo khozyaistva Rossii*, Moscow, 1996, No.11, p.9.) In 1995 expenditure on agriculture from the consolidated Russian budget (federal and local budgets taken together) was 20.4 trillion current roubles, or 1.2% of GDP. In 1996 it has declined to 14.1 trillion current roubles (0.7% of GDP). In constant prices the 1996 level equalled to just 47% of the 1995 level. (Calculated from: *Rossiiskii statisticheskii ezhegodnik. 1996*, Moscow: Goskomstat, 1996, p.416; *Sotsial'no-ekonomicheskoe polozhenie Rossii. yanvar' 1997 g.*, Moscow: Goskomstat, 1997, pp.140–41.)

21. In 1995 gross state expenditure on agriculture (including direct budgetary transfers and price subsidies) totalled 40.9 trillion roubles, which was less than the gross volume of imports of agricultural produce that equalled 59.1 trillion roubles (*Ekonomika sel'skogo khozyaistva Rossii*, Moscow, 1996, No.11, p.32). By 1993–94 in Russian public debates the issue of dependency on food imports was transferred into discussion of a broader question of Russia's food security. The most recent and full publication on the latter issue is E. N. Borisenko, *Prodovol'stvennaya bezopasnost' Rossii: problemy i perspektivy*, Moscow: Ekonomika, 1997.

2
State Finances, Banking Sector and Investment Flows

Developments on the Russian financial markets and, more broadly, the general financial situation in Russia have recently become one of the most discussed topics in the field of the post-Soviet Russian economy. Even prior to the August 1998 financial crisis, there were several reasons for this continuing interest. Firstly, since the start of Russian reform in 1992, the role of the financial sector in outlining general economic policy was growing rapidly. While in the Soviet period the area of finance was strictly controlled by the state with financial institutions playing only a secondary role in promoting and implementing general economic strategies, in the post-Soviet years this situation changed dramatically. The post-Soviet period was accompanied by galloping inflation, mass privatisation of state property, rapid capital accumulation, introduction of fluctuating currency exchange rates, and the restructuring of the whole banking sector. Within weeks of launching the reform, the Russian government proclaimed financial stabilisation to become the cornerstone of its reform strategy; that objective has remained high on its priority list ever since.

Secondly, the reformists' push towards a greater deregulation of the Russian economy and the reduction of the role of the state in economic management meant that financial markets and the banking sector in general were becoming more and more independent of state control. After 1992, the state no longer was playing the role of a sole or major investor in the economy. Non-state financial institutions were quickly moving into investment areas, particularly due to a rapid fall in the volumes of state capital investment.

Thirdly, Russian private banking – at least in its initial phase – was closely associated with export–import trade operations and other forms of quick and often semi-legal or even illegal accumulation of capital. In the years of reform, bankers in Russia formed the wealthiest group in society, a position that almost immediately put them into the spotlight of public, as well as the organised crime.

Despite its high public profile, Russian banking formed only one aspect of post-Soviet financial development in Russia. Other aspects included repeated efforts on part of consecutive Russian governments to reduce the deficit of the state budget, stabilise the national currency, improve tax collection and pay off massive wage arrears to state employees. The expenditure side of the state budget quickly came into the focus of Russian political struggles. Intensity of these struggles was rather high given the significantly decreased ability of the Russian state to fund (and subsidise) many non-profitable industries, agriculture, the military, social sphere and many other areas that were traditionally funded by the state during the Soviet years.

Price liberalisation that triggered the 1992 Russian reform put an end to the Soviet financial system. The latter was based on the principle of overall state control over all financial flows: investment, currency market, money circulation, foreign trade and pricing policies. The 1992 reform had effectively removed state regulation from pricing and trade areas. That immediately led to a "price race" between various branches of economy, industries, enterprises, service providers, etc. That also gave a boost to inflation and, consequently, undermined the stability of the national currency. During the first months of 1992, the Gaidar government was making desperate attempts to keep this situation under control, mainly through limiting the volume of money supply. However, not only did this policy fail to curb inflation, it also created a growing currency supply crisis.

At the same time, following the release of state controls over foreign trade flows, the Russian reformist government opened doors to a largely uncontrollable inflow of foreign currency onto the Russian market. That led to a considerable increase in the overall money supply in Russia. Due to their high attractiveness as an inflation-resistant instrument of savings, foreign currencies soon replaced the rouble as the main currency of choice for people's savings. This situation created a massive "internal capital flight" from the quickly depreciating rouble.

As a result of broad circulation of foreign currency on the Russian market, the link between prices and the supply of national currency became loose. Prices for goods in Russia were more and more frequently listed in dollars, while foreign currency shops ("dollar shops") were mushrooming across the country. This meant that the government's attempts to stop inflation through keeping the money supply under strict control had, in fact, a very limited effect on the consumer price index that continued to rise.

Another important factor that significantly undermined the planned reform in Russia was the monopolised structure of the Russian national economy. While price liberalisation can easily bring fast and astonishing positive results in a deregulated and non-monopolised economy, its effect, as was demonstrated by the Russian recent experience, can be rather modest or even negligible in a monopolised economy. The absence of real competition in the Russian economy meant that there was no incentive for Russian producers to lower prices. Instead, many of them chose either to increase prices for their products or to sell them on credit. In cases when the financial situation of these producers became really difficult, they preferred to put additional pressure of the government demanding increased state support, rather than to introduce changes into their marketing policies.

2.1   Federal budget, tax collection and dynamics of state borrowing in Russia

One of the immediate results of the 1992 price and trade reforms was the emergence of an acute cash crisis in Russia. By mid-1992, the government was forced to abandon its strict fiscal policies and bend to pressures from industrial and agricultural lobbies in parliament. In the second half of 1992, more money was printed and released onto the market, thus further increasing the inflation wave and, consequently, boosting internal (and external) capital flight. From that time on, the Russian government found itself fully engaged in attempts to bring budgetary deficit under control, walking a tightrope between tight monetary policies and a variety of lobbyist and regionalist pressures.

The dynamics of the Russian state budget are shown in Table 2.1. Between 1990 and 1992, the revenue structure of the budget had undergone significant changes. Decentralisation and deregulation of the Soviet economy was accompanied by restructuring of the taxation base: some forms of taxation (payments from profits, state duties on profits) typical of a state-run economy were abandoned with the start of reform, and new taxes were introduced (see Table 2.1a). Not only were the new taxes more numerous and complicated than the old ones, but Soviet-trained accountants and managers had no knowledge or experience of the way these taxes were calculated and collected. That created a great deal of uncertainty among both the public and the managerial elite in Russia, at least in the initial phase of reform

Table 2.1 Russian State Budget, [a] **1990–98**

a) In current prices (trillions current roubles)

	1990	1991	1992	1993	1994	1995	1996	1997	1998[b]
Gross revenue, incl.:	0.16	0.31	5.33	49.73	177.4	437.0	558.5	711.6	0.66
Turnover tax	0.05	0.07	–	–	–	–	–	–	–
Payments from profits by state enterprises	0.03	0.04	–	–	–	–	–	–	–
State duties on profits	0.02	0.09	–	–	–	–	–	–	–
Corporate tax	–	–	1.57	16.79	48.8	117.6	96.7	104.9	0.10
Value added tax	–	–	2.00	11.21	37.3	95.7	143.9	182.8	0.16
Income tax	–	–	0.43	4.40	17.5	36.6	56.6	75.2	0.07
Taxes on international trade and transactions	–	–	0.47	2.35	19.2	23.4	16.9	11.6	0.02
Excise duties	–	0.01	0.21	1.78	7.4	24.1	53.4	68.1	0.07
Natural resources use tax	–	–	0.18	1.46	4.7	12.3	21.2	37.2	0.01
Revenues from privatisation of state property	–	–	0.06	0.32	0.8	4.6	2.6	23.3	0.02
Other	0.06	0.10	0.41	11.43	41.7	123.2	167.2	208.5	0.22
Gross expenditure, incl.:	0.15	0.35	5.97	57.67	234.8	486.1	652.7	839.5	0.75
National economy	0.08	0.13	2.06	16.19	63.4	138.3	172.9	81.4	0.06
Social services and culture	0.07	0.10	1.38	14.37	55.3	129.1	188.4	270.5	0.24
Government management and law enforcement	0.00	0.01	0.35	4.20	18.5	37.5	56.4	88.0	0.07
Government management only	...	...	0.11	1.47	7.1	11.9	17.2	29.0	0.03
Defence	...	...	0.86	7.21	28.0	49.6	63.9	81.4	0.06
Foreign economic activities	0.00	0.01	0.42	2.77	5.0	21.5	26.7	2.6	0.11
Other	0.01	0.10	0.91	26.86	64.6	110.1	210.3	286.6	0.18
Surplus/deficit (–)	0.01	–0.04	–0.64	–7.94	–57.4	–49.1	–94.2	–127.9	–0.10
Surplus/deficit as % of GDP	1.3	–2.7	–3.4	–4.6	–9.4	–3.2	–4.3	–4.9	–3.6

Table 2.1 *continued*

(b) In constant prices (billions 1990 roubles)^c

Gross revenue, incl.:	159.5	135.7	146.7	138.5	121.2	113.4	100.8	110.1	93.4
Turnover tax	52.0	31.6	–	–	–	–	–	–	–
Payments from profits by state enterprises	31.2	–	–	–	–	–	–	–	–
State duties on profits	17.1	18.0	–	–	–	–	–	–	–
Corporate tax	–	40.2	43.1	46.8	33.4	30.6	17.5	16.3	13.7
Value added tax	–	–	55.0	31.2	25.5	25.0	26.1	28.5	22.4
Income tax	–	–	11.9	12.2	12.0	9.5	10.2	11.6	10.1
Taxes on international trade and transactions	–	3.4	12.9	6.5	13.1	5.2	2.6	1.5	1.9
Excise duties	–	–	5.8	5.0	5.1	6.3	9.7	10.6	9.7
Natural resources use tax	–	4.8	4.1	3.2	3.2	3.5	4.2	6.3	2.1
Revenues from privatisation of state property	–	–	1.7	0.9	0.5	1.2	0.5	3.6	2.5
Other	59.2	42.4	11.4	31.8	28.5	32.3	30.5	32.6	31.4
Gross expenditure, incl.:	151.0	152.1	164.3	160.6	160.5	127.4	118.9	131.2	108.1
National economy	75.8	56.8	56.7	45.1	43.3	36.2	31.5	12.7	9.1
Social services & culture	65.2	45.1	38.1	39.9	37.8	33.8	34.3	42.2	34.3
Government management & law enforcement	2.6	5.8	9.7	11.7	12.7	9.8	10.2	13.7	10.4
Government management only	...	...	2.9	4.1	4.9	3.1	3.1	4.5	4.3
Defence	...	...	23.5	20.1	19.1	13.0	11.6	12.7	8.1
Foreign economic activities	0.1	2.4	11.5	7.7	3.4	5.6	4.8	0.4	15.2
Other	7.3	41.9	24.9	74.8	44.2	28.9	38.4	44.9	26.6
Surplus/deficit (–)	8.5	–16.5	–17.7	–22.1	–39.2	–12.9	–17.2	–20.0	–13.8

Table 2.1 *continued*

(c) Budgetary dynamics (indices)

Gross revenue	100.0	85.1	92.0	86.8	76.0	71.1	63.2	69.0	58.6
Gross expenditure, incl.:	100.0	100.7	108.8	106.4	106.3	84.4	78.8	86.9	71.6
National economy	100.0	74.9	74.8	59.5	57.1	47.8	41.5	16.8	12.0
Social services and culture	100.0	69.2	58.4	61.2	58.0	51.8	52.6	64.8	52.6
Government management and law enforcement	100.0	223.1	373.1	450.0	488.5	376.9	394.1	527.4	399.8
Foreign economic activities	1.0	24.0	115.0	77.0	34.0	56.0	48.3	4.0	152.1
Other	100.0	574.0	341.1	1024.7	605.5	395.9	525.7	614.4	363.9
Surplus/deficit (–)	100.0	–194.1	–208.2	–260.0	–461.2	–151.8	–202.4	–235.7	–162.4

NOTES:

[a] Also referred to in Russian statistics as "consolidated budget" (the total of federal budget and regional/territorial budgets). Data for 1990–91 do not include Russia's share of payments to and subsidies from the USSR state budget.

[b] Preliminary data.

[c] Calculated using GDP deflators (see sources below).

Sources:

Rossiiskii statisticheskii ezhegodnik. 1995, Moscow: Goskomstat, 1995, pp.243, 273; *Rossiya v tsifrakh. 1996,* Moscow: Goskomstat, 1996, pp.164–8, 204–5; *Sotsial'no-ekonomicheskoe polozhenie Rossii, janvar'-iul' 1996 g.,* Moscow: Goskomstat, 1996, pp.9, 130–5; *Sodruzhestvo Nezavisimykh Gosudarstv v 1996 godu. Statisticheskii ezhegodnik.* Moscow: Statkom SNG, 1997, p.386; *Sotsial'no-ekonomicheskoe polozhenie Rossii, janvar' 1997 g.,* Moscow: Goskomstat, 1997, pp.138–40; *Rossiiskii statisticheskii ezhegodnik. 1997,* Moscow: Goskomstat, 1997, p.520; *Sotsial'no-ekonomicheskoe polozhenie Rossii, janvar' 1998 g.,* Moscow: Goskomstat, 1998, pp.152–7; *Statisticheskii byulleten' Statkoma SNG,* No.12 (196), June 1998, pp.135–7; *Rossiiskii statisticheskii ezhegodnik. 1998,* Moscow: Goskomstat, 1998, p.651; *Sotsial'no-ekonomicheskoe polozhenie Rossii, janvar' 1999 g.,* Moscow: Goskomstat, 1996, pp.200–1.

(1992–94), leading to a dramatic fall in the budgetary revenue base. In addition to these uncertainties caused by lack of knowledge, the difficult financial situation of many Russian enterprises in the post-1991 period pushed many of them to delay or even to stop paying taxes altogether.

As a result, the revenue base of the Russian state budget was shrinking rapidly: it fell from 160 billion roubles in 1990 to an equivalent in constant prices of just 93 billion roubles in 1998 (Table 2.1b). That was more than a fall of 40% in a period of eight years (Table 2.1c).

Such a situation led to a rapid growth of the budget deficit. In 1990 Russia had recorded a budgetary surplus of 1.3% of GDP. In 1991, when the spread of economic crisis throughout the Soviet Union became a reality, the Russian budget recorded a deficit equal to 2.7% of GDP. In the first three years of reform this deficit was increasing steadily and in 1994 it stood at 9.4% of GDP, the highest level since the collapse of the USSR (Table 2.1a).[1]

In 1994–95 the Russian government made a second attempt after 1992 to control the state budget.[2] This attempt coincided with the release of a large loan to Russia from the International Monetary Fund. One of the conditions under which this loan was made available to Russia was that the Russian government would keep the state budgetary deficit within agreed limits. However, in a situation when revenues to the state budget were continuing to fall, the only possible means of balancing the budget was a dramatic cut of state expenditure. In 1995, the state budgetary expenditure in Russia fell by more than 20% (Table 2.1b). Such austerity measures helped to bring the deficit down from 9.4% of GDP in 1994 to 3.2% of GDP in 1995.

In mid-1995 mounting political pressures associated with the approaching presidential elections, scheduled for June 1996, forced Russian leaders to abandon their austerity fiscal policy. Between September–October 1995 and July 1996 money supply had noticeably increased which, with a lag of two to three months, was followed by increase in the deficit of the state budget (Graph 2.1). However, immediately after the elections were over the government returned to the implementation of its earlier policy. In the period between July and October 1996 there was a negative money supply, and starting from September it had a visible effect on the overall dynamics of the budgetary deficit.

In addition to the use of strictly monetary methods, rapidly falling budgetary revenues were forcing the Russian government to introduce more and more cuts to budgetary expenditure. Between 1990 and 1997

Graph 2.1   Dynamics of Money Supply and Budgetary Deficit in Russia, 1993–97

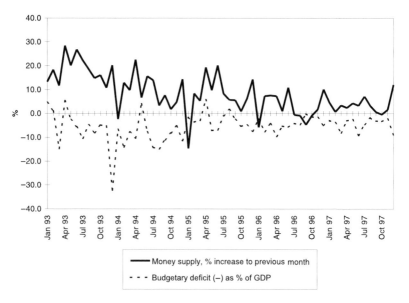

the volume of state budgetary allocations to the national economy (state capital investment, direct and indirect subsidies to enterprises, etc.) in real terms was reduced by almost two-thirds while the budgetary expenditure on social needs in the same period had more than halved (Table 2.1c). These cuts were in no contradiction to the government's original reform strategy, which put main emphasis on privatisation of state property and the consequent reduction of state intervention in the economy. This had to be accompanied by the gradual replacement of the Soviet-type expensive social protection system by market-driven and less costly social programmes.

Nevertheless, these cuts to economic and social spending were not followed by similar reductions of state expenditure on certain other major items. The most striking example has been the dynamics of state spending on maintaining of bureaucracy and law enforcement structures. In constant prices the Russian budgetary expenditure on state management and law enforcement has increased significantly in the post-Soviet period. In 1995 Russia was spending 3.8 times more on its bureaucracy and police than it did in the late Soviet period!

A partial explanation of this amazing tendency lies in the fact that in Soviet times Russia's bureaucracy was funded both from republican and USSR budgets. Union ministries often had much more power and a larger staff. When the Soviet Union collapsed, Russia absorbed most of Soviet state structures, with many all-union ministries being transformed into Russian institutions. Often this process did not entail any downsizing of these bodies; in some cases this change was even accompanied by additional staff increases. This explains the fact that after the Soviet Union had disintegrated and Russia assumed total control over its former state bodies, the budgetary spending on bureaucracy in Russia continued to grow rapidly up until early 1995. Between 1992 and 1994 the expenditure on state management in real terms had increased by 31%. It was only in mid-1995 that the Russian government, following its policy aimed at keeping the budget deficit under strict control, decided to significantly cut state spending on bureaucracy. However, in constant prices the level of spending in 1995 was still significantly higher than in 1990–92 (Tables 2.1b and 2.1c).

In general, at least as far as the first years of Russian reform are concerned, it would be more appropriate to speak about restructuring, rather than reduction, of state expenditure in Russia. In real terms budgetary expenditure only started to decline from its pre-reform level in 1995–96, i.e. five years after the revenue base of the budget started to shrink rapidly. Thus, while in 1994 the Russian government managed to collect only 76% of the 1990 budgetary income, in real terms it spent 6% more than in 1990! In other words, during the first years of the Russian reform the deficit of the state budget was increasing at an unprecedented speed. However, this deficit was only partially covered by increased money supply. As Graph 2.2 demonstrates, since early 1993 and until the August 1998 crisis the annual rate of inflation in Russia was actually falling.

The contradiction between the falling rate of inflation and the growing deficit of the state budget could only be resolved through a rapid increase in Russia's public debt. In accordance with the agreement on Soviet debt obligations reached by the former USSR republics in late 1991, Russia inherited 61% of all outstanding Soviet foreign debt liabilities. At the end of 1991, when the Soviet Union ceased to exist, its total outstanding external debt was equal to US$65.3 billion. Thus, Russia began its reforms with an external debt of approximately US$39.8 billion.[3] Six years later, at the beginning of 1997, Russia's external debt had almost tripled and totalled US$110 billion,[4] which meant that the accumulated state external debt had increased by more

Graph 2.2   Dynamics of CPI and Money Supply in Russia, 1992–97
(% of increase to previous month)

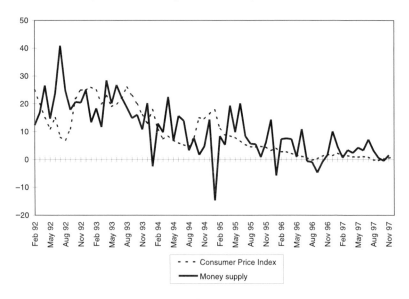

than US$10 billion per annum during the reform. During 1997 the state debt increased by a further 135 trillion roubles (US$26.7 billion). At the end of 1996, the Russian state debt was equal to 44.6% of GDP, a year later it constituted as much as 45.2% of GDP.[5] In November 1998 the overall foreign debt of the Russian government was already estimated at the level of US$150 billion, or almost US$15 billion more than the year before.[6]

Such a high pace of external borrowing was a spectacular development in itself. However, in addition to that, from 1993 the Russian government had started to actively borrow money on the internal Russian market through issuing short-term (GKO) and federal loan (OFZ) bonds. In 1995–96 the issuing of securities became one of the prime sources of non-budgetary revenue to the Russian government. In order to attract investment in purchases of these securities the Russian government was paying very high interest on GKO-OFZ, even if these securities were converted to foreign currencies.[7] However, this required even more funding which had to come through issues of new securities. The result was a build up of a pyramid investment scheme, coordinated and run by the government.[8]

The tempo of internal borrowing was increasing rapidly: in US dollar equivalence, in 1995 the Russian government borrowed four times more than in 1994, in 1996 – 2.5 times more than in 1995, and in 1997 – 1.2 times more than in the previous year (Table 2.2b). Between January 1994 and 17 August 1998 the gross volume of issued state bonds was equal to an astronomical sum of 972.5 billion denominated roubles or US$183 billion (Table 2.2). On 17 August 1998, when the GKO-OFZ market in Russia collapsed, the government net debt on bond issues stood at 387 billion roubles (US$67.6 billion). That was despite the fact that between 1 July and 17 August the Russian government had pulled all of its resources to repay outstanding state debt obligations and managed to reduce the debt by 11.3%.

If we compare the dynamics of Russian government's internal borrowing (GKO-OFZ issues) with the level of net revenues from sales of state bonds, the profitability of the whole bond scheme becomes

Table 2.2   Annual Dynamics of Internal State Borrowing in Post-Soviet Russia, 1994–August 1998

(a) In billion current roubles (1998 denominated roubles)

	1994	1995	1996	1997	Jan–Aug 1998	1994–Aug 98
Gross income from sales of GKO-OFZ bonds	12.9	106.2	297.3	386.5	169.6	972.5
Expenditure on servicing of GKO-OFZ bonds	7.2	95.2	282	379.6	209.5	973.5
Net budgetary revenue	5.7	11	15.3	6.9	–39.9	–1
Accumulated state debt[a]	11	77	237	384.9	387.1	387.1

(b) In billion current US dollars[b]

	1994	1995	1996	1997	Jan–Aug 1998	1994–Aug 98
Gross income from sales of GKO-OFZ bonds	5.9	23.3	58	66.6	29.6	183.4
Expenditure on servicing of GKO-OFZ bonds	3.3	20.9	55	65.4	36.6	181.2
Net budgetary revenue	2.6	2.4	3	1.2	–7	2.2
Accumulated state debt[a]	4.9	16.9	46.2	66.3	67.6	67.6

NOTES:
[a] Total amount of GKO-OFZ bonds in circulation at the end of the period.
[b] Calculated using average exchange rates of rouble to US dollar for the period stated.

Sourced and calculated from:
Rossiya-1997:Ekonomicheskaya kon'yuktura.Vypusk 1, Moscow: Tsentr ekonomicheskoi kon'yuktury, 1997, p.45; *Rossiya-1996:Ekonomicheskaya kon'yuktura.Vypusk 4*, Moscow: Tsentr ekonomicheskoi kon'yuktury, 1996, p.47; *Sotsial'no-ekonomicheskoe polozhenie Rossii, 1998 g.*, Moscow: Goskomstat, 1998, pp.257–61; *Sotsial'no-ekonomicheskoe polozhenie Rossii, janvar'-iyun' 1998 g.*, Moscow: Goskomstat, 1998, pp.191–4; *Sotsial'no-ekonomicheskoe polozhenie Rossii, janvar'-avgust' 1998 g.*, Moscow: Goskomstat, 1998, pp.193–5.

highly questionable. As Graph 2.3 demonstrates, monthly net revenues from bond sales since the time of their introduction in May 1993 never crossed the 5 billion rouble margin. That was despite the fact that in the period after mid-1995 sales of GKO-OFZ were growing rapidly and during 1997 and the first half of 1998 reached an equivalent of 40–60 billion of 1998 denominated roubles a month.

Although at the time the scheme was started in 1993–4 the share of net budgetary revenues from GKO-OFZ sales to their gross sales was quite high, since mid-1995 the budgetary effect of new bond issues was often more negative than positive. That occurred despite the huge expansion of bond issues that took place from mid-1995. As Graph 2.4 indicates, there was a visible change in government's attitude to bond issues in mid-1995. While one might argue that in the preceding period issues of GKO-OFZ bonds did constitute an important channel for funding of the state budget, since June 1995 their relative importance became extremely marginal. Moreover, even before the Asian crisis had struck world financial markets in mid-1997, the Russian bond market was showing worrying signs of decline. Since August 1997, or exactly one year before the Russian government had declared a default on payments of its internal debt, these signs were already transformed into a steady negative tendency.

Graph 2.3   Dynamics of the Bond Market (GKO-OFZ), May 1993–August 1998

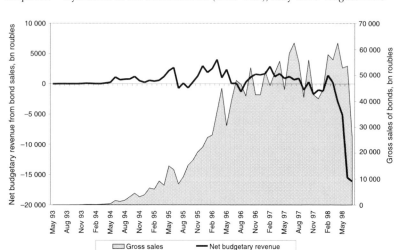

Graph 2.4   Budgetary Effectiveness of the GKO-OFZ Market
(monthly net revenues as % to gross sales)

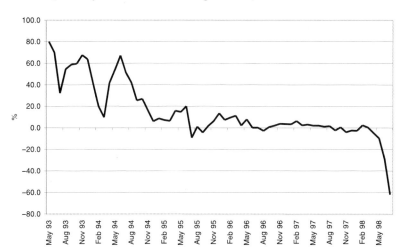

In other words, the 1998 Russian crisis was easily predictable. An indicator of the effectiveness of the Russian bond market, as presented in Graph 2.4, also shows that in reality the crisis had struck the market in March 1998 or almost half a year before the government had publicly declared its insolvency. Interestingly, this intensification of the crisis coincided with an unexpected decision made by President Yeltsin in March 1998 to sack Prime Minister Chernomyrdin. A few months later in the year, particularly following Yeltsin's attempt in August–September to reinstate Chernomyrdin, serious doubts arouse as to whether Chernomyrdin's sacking in March was a genuine decision by Yeltsin or rather a carefully devised plan by Chernomyrdin himself. In any case, it is hardly a pure coincidence that the Russian Prime Minister, who was responsible for bond issues since the whole scheme was introduced in 1993, stepped down exactly at a time when the bond market started to collapse.

The main conclusion that one can draw from this is that the scheme the Russian government chose for its internal borrowing was an extremely dubious exercise that had a very limited budgetary effect. It is clear that there should have been other, not only purely financial, reasons that prompted the Russian government to allow the GKO-OFZ market to grow to uncontrollable levels. I argue that the major underlying reason behind the expansion of the Russian bond market from

May 1993 to mid-1995 was an attempt on the part of the Russian government to simultaneously reach two contradictory goals: to stabilise the national financial market and to avoid dire social consequences of such action. In a sense, it was an experiment of implementing "shock therapy" without a shock. If it had occurred, such a shock would have been caused mainly by the cuts in state spending on social needs and on subsidies to loss-making enterprises. Instead, Russian leaders chose to avoid this shock through continued issuing of credits to industry and agriculture. However, since 1994 that was done not in the old "primitive way" of printing money (or issuing central bank credits to the government), but through a mass issue of state bonds. It comes as no surprise that the main buyer of these bonds was still the Russian Central Bank, which through this channel was continuing to indirectly credit the government.

Implementation of the GKO-OFZ bond scheme initially allowed the Russian government to get rid of its former anti-monetarist image and to change it to a much more respectable, pro-Western and monetarist one. And, more importantly, this was done without drastic cuts in subsidies to industry and agriculture. Due to the fact that in 1994–5 Russian reform experiments gained an appearance of "fiscal normality", they managed to receive support from some major international financial institutions, particularly the IMF. It is no surprise that a year after Russians started to expand their bond pyramid, the Fund approved its credit to Russia, the largest in its history. The change that occurred in the dynamics of the Russian GKO-OFZ market in mid-1995, almost immediately after Russia started to receive IMF funds, prompts me to conclude that the whole idea of introduction of these bonds might have been directly or indirectly related to Russia's external borrowing needs. While in 1993–4 there might have been a certain budgetary reasoning behind these bond issues, it seems that after May–June 1995 the government strategy on the bond market dramatically changed. The IMF credit allowed the Russian government to finance monetary stabilisation and to introduce the currency corridor using external sources, thus significantly decreasing the need for internal borrowing. While after mid-1995 the Russian government continued to issue GKO-OFZ bonds, the major goal of this policy seems to have been paying off the debt, which had already accumulated through previous issues. However, between late 1995 and mid-1996 net revenues from bond sales did register a certain rise, most probably as a result of increased funding needs for Yeltsin's presidential electoral campaign.

The dynamics of growth of Russian state indebtedness in the post-Soviet period reveal one important tendency: the tempo of growth of the Russian Federation's gross state debt started to increase dramatically after 1994 (Graph 2.5). In the first years after the collapse of the USSR (1992–93) Russia was mainly relying on external credits as means of balancing its budget. These were mostly loans from international financial institutions as well as some foreign governments' credits, mainly from Germany and the USA. Because these were primarily low-interest and long-term loans, their repayment was quite sustainable by the Russian budget.

However, in the post-1994 period the continuing slide of the Russian economy and the consequent fall in budgetary revenues resulted in a greatly increased pressure on the state budget. Despite the fact that the majority of Russian enterprises by that time were privatised, many of them were still overtly dependent on state funding, both in the form of direct and indirect state subsidies or low-interest loans. The only resolution to this paradoxical situation could come through large-scale closures of those industrial and agricultural enterprises that were consistently running at a loss. But the threat of highly negative political

Graph 2.5 Annual Dynamics of Growth of State Debt Accumulation (billion current US dollars; annual gross borrowing only, not net debt)

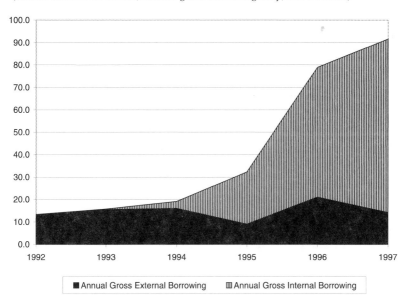

■ Annual Gross External Borrowing   ▥ Annual Gross Internal Borrowing

and social implications of such action stopped the Russian government short of doing that. That meant that, in a sense, the Russian economy continued to operate in accordance with the same principles, and at the same low level of profitability, as the collapsed Soviet centralised economy.

During the 1990s Russia's debt situation deteriorated significantly as a result of widespread and poorly organised privatisation and liberalisation of its economy. Withdrawal of state controls from trade and transfer into private hands of the major part of Russian resource industry had deprived the state of its most significant sources of budgetary revenues. In the post-Soviet period the Russian government had to rely increasingly on taxation as its major revenue base. However, that proved to be an unreliable source while gross volumes of tax collection were far below state spending needs. The choice that the government had to make in this situation was to either dramatically cut its spending, particularly on social needs and the national economy, or to borrow more money in order to fill in the growing gap. An attempt to print more money in 1992–93 had immediately provoked a huge inflation wave that the government found extremely difficult to control.

Thus, in late 1993, coincidentally soon after the violent closure of parliament, the Russian government started to dramatically increase its borrowing, both from internal and external sources. The rate of growth of Russia's debt was in direct relation to falling taxation revenue levels. The latter, in their turn, were indirectly related to the pace of Russia's privatisation campaign. As Graph 2.5 reveals, since 1995 the gross amount of Russia's annual borrowing was increasing in an almost geometrical progression. Issues of state bonds played a major part in that process, particularly because of the need to constantly feed the bond market with new borrowings with the only goal of repaying principal and interest on earlier issued bonds. The culmination of this borrowing spree came in 1997 when in one year the Russian government had borrowed from all internal and external sources a gross amount of over 90 billion US dollars!

Most of borrowed money went on servicing and repayment of previous debts. The remainder was spent on financial stabilisation (which was draining Russian state resources at the rate of up to 22 billion US dollars a month before the August 1998 collapse) and on subsidies to the national industry and agriculture. In this regard it is important to note that part of these subsidies was coming in a form of various tax breaks stimulating further falls in tax collection. All that meant that, in a sense, the Russian post-Soviet government was continuing to pursue the same economic policy as the Soviet government, but with a much more limited financial resource base. Moreover, as a result of the post-Soviet reforms, the Russian government's position has become even more difficult than that of the Soviet state. While the latter owned and controlled both revenue-generating and loss-making enterprises and could redirect investment flows between these two groups, the post-Soviet Russian government has largely abandoned its ownership and control of a significant part of the national economy. Therefore, redirecting of financial flows has become a very difficult task. The government's ability to provide support to bankrupt enterprises was directly dependent on the budgetary revenue base, which has continued to shrink. State borrowing has filled in the growing gap between the limitations of available financial resources and increasing political pressures from the ground.

At the start of reform in early 1992 the Russian state net public external and internal debt stood at approximately US$40 billion; five years later it was almost four times as large (US$156 billion). But what was worse was the fact that the major part of this borrowed money was spent on the continued subsidising of unprofitable enterprises, mostly through paying wages. The amount of money invested in the production sector was negligible. Instead of promoting structural reform aimed at development of income-generating industries, the government borrowed more and more money basically to preserve the status quo. This policy could not have any effect on the underlying factors that provoked the development of a large-scale economic crisis in Russia/the former USSR in the first instance.

However, promotion of this borrowing did bring the government some temporary benefits. It made it possible to postpone implementation of many difficult and unpopular reform measures, like massive closures of loss-making enterprises, elimination of state subsidies to agriculture and industries, etc. But, more importantly, this policy failed to halt the development of the economic crisis. The rapid growth of public indebtedness, which was a natural result of this policy, was accompanied by a significant increase in budgetary allocations for debt servicing.

By the mid-1990s debt repayments had become one of the Russian government's major financial problems. While at the start of reform Russia was spending about US$2–4 billion a year on the servicing of its foreign debt, by 1996 gross debt repayments totalled about US$8–10 billion. In the wake of the 1998 Russian financial crisis, it was reported that in 1999 Russia's payment obligations on foreign debt should already total US$17.5 billion.[9] The scale of the problem is expected to become much larger at the turn of the century. In 2000–2005 Russia will have to repay much of the money it has borrowed externally and internally during the first years of its reform attempts, including restructured Soviet and post-Soviet external debts as well as the internal GKO-OFZ debt. According to the Deputy Chairman of the Russian Central Bank, in 1998 alone Russia had to direct over 25% of its federal budget expenditure towards current payments on state debt.[10] That statement, of course, was made before Russia announced default on debt repayments on 17 August 1998. In January 1998 Russian debt repayments were already equal to 24% of all state expenditure,[11] provided the government was receiving all of its planned revenues. According to preliminary data, servicing of the state debt in 1998 constituted 14.2% of state budgetary expenditure or 4% of Russia's GDP. This was a significant increase from the 1997 figures when debt servicing equalled, respectively, 4.9% and 1.6%.[12]

The shrinking budgetary revenues and the consequent growth of public debt in post-Soviet Russia had one and the same cause: Russian taxpayers were paying less and less tax. In the mid-1990s, tax evasion became one of the most serious problems in the Russian economy. While this was a very serious problem in itself, the inability of the state to collect taxes also was directly linked to many other important political and economic issues, such as the direction and aims of Russian reform, the distribution of political power in Russia, the development of the shadow ("black market") economy, privatisation and restructuring of enterprises, etc. However, Russian officials often pointed out to falls in tax collection as the main evil that was independent of other problems and largely causing Russian economic distress. As a result, many of the government's efforts during reform years were aimed at improving tax collection through administrative measures; these included the establishment of special emergency bodies to oversee tax flows, the exertion of government pressure on tax debtors, a continuing increase of existing taxes, etc. These measures, however, failed to effect any significant change and the volume of tax non-payments continued to grow rapidly.

Problems with tax collection had appeared in Russia at the beginning of reform in 1992. Previously, under the Soviet system of economic management, taxes were automatically collected by the state, which was the sole owner of most properties. Under that former system, tax collection formed just another aspect of state regulation of the economy. The simplicity of this mechanism immediately became defunct after Russia embarked on the road of reform. Privatisation meant that a growing number of Russian enterprises were no longer obliged to report all of their financial operations to the state while liberalisation of prices and trade lifted state-imposed limits on profitability. The majority of Russians was not used to filling in tax declarations and had no experience in understanding tax legislation. All this made the collection of taxes from private citizens as well as businesses extremely difficult. In addition to that, gaps in the existing legislation and lack of experience in taxation services created numerous channels for widespread tax evasion.

However, in the first year of reform (1992) the problem of tax non-payments remained at a relatively modest level (Table 2.3). It was in 1993 and the following years that falls in tax collection started to reach critical levels. Although increased levels of privatisation did play a role in the acceleration of taxation problems because of a softening of state controls over activities of enterprises, it was the general crisis in the national economy that made tax collection an almost impossible task. The lifting of many foreign trade barriers that accompanied trade liberalisation in Russia opened up outdated and under-productive enterprises to foreign competition. High production costs put strict limits on the ability of Russian enterprises to compete, while high interest rates on internal financial markets (which were a result of high inflation levels in the first years of the Russian reform) made it impossible to borrow money for restructuring. As a result, Russian enterprises were rapidly losing to competition; their revenues were falling and their debts increasing. By the end of the first year of reform, the number of loss-making companies in Russia was 15%. Four years later the proportion had risen to 43%.

Falling company profits meant that Russian enterprises were paying less and less tax. At the same time, however, bankruptcies were very rare because in many cases closing of enterprises would have been socially and politically unacceptable. While enterprises were getting deeper and deeper in debt in order to pay off their workers (many of these loans came directly or indirectly from the state), they were paying less and less tax.

In essence, the problem of tax collection in post-Soviet Russia was closely linked to the problem of failed structural reform of the Soviet economy. The Russian government inherited an economy that was oversized, disproportional, ineffective and, in most cases, in desperate need of restructuring. These factors caused the collapse of the Soviet

Table 2.3   Growth of Tax Non-Payments to the Russian State Budget

	1992	1993	1994	1995	1996	1997	Jan–June 1998	1998[a]
Collected taxes[b]	4 380	35 630	116 700	364 300	473 000	593 400	225.5	517.7
Unpaid taxes[b]	83	2 572	15 100	55 000	110 500	181 800	228.0	259.0
Tax non-payments as % to:								
All planned tax revenues	1.86	6.73	11.46	13.12	18.94	23.45	50.28	33.35
GDP	0.44	1.5	2.47	3.37	4.9	6.8	19.2	9.6
Unpaid taxes[c]	200	3 357	3 595	12 043	21 545	31 334	37 354	12 542

NOTES:
[a] Preliminary data.
[b] In billion current roubles.
[c] In million US dollars. Calculated using average exchange rates of rouble to US dollar for the period stated.

Sources:

Rossiya-1993. Ekonomicheskaya konyuktura. Vypusk 4. Moscow: Tsentr ekonomicheskoi konyuktury, November 1993, p.45; *Rossiya-1994. Ekonomicheskaya konyuktura. Vypusk 1.* Moscow: Tsentr ekonomicheskoi konyuktury, March 1994, p.38; *Rossiiskii statisticheskii ezhegodnik. 1996,* Moscow: Goskomstat, 1996, pp.26, 418; *Sotsial'no-ekonomicheskoe polozhenie Rossii, janvar' 1997 g.,* Moscow: Goskomstat, 1997, p.139; *Rossiiskii statisticheskii ezhegodnik, 1997,* Moscow: Goskomstat, 1997, p.519; *Sotsial'no-ekonomicheskoe polozhenie Rossii, janvar' 1998 g.,* Moscow: Goskomstat, 1998, pp.153–5; *Sotsial'no-ekonomicheskoe polozhenie Rossii, janvar'-iul' 1998 g.,* Moscow: Goskomstat, 1998, pp.177–9; *Sotsial'no-ekonomicheskoe polozhenie Rossii, janvar' 1999 g.,* Moscow: Goskomstat, 1999, pp.201–3.

economy and, consequently, the political disintegration of the Soviet Union. However, the way the Russian post-Soviet governments approached these problems draws one to conclude that they did not learn the lessons of Gorbachev's failed reforms. Instead of creating (or developing) competitive sectors of the economy with the aim of transforming them into the main channel of revenues for stimulation of national growth, Russian reformists were mainly busy with the establishment of surface structures of a market economy (privatisation, banking, price liberalisation, currency convertibility, etc.). The unusual mixture of Soviet-type industrial and agricultural monsters with semi-developed and highly criminal market-type institutions, eventually created in Russia, proved to be incapable of introducing much-needed structural changes into the economy.

It can be stated that, with very few exceptions, the majority of Russian economic agents in the post-Soviet years have continued to act in almost the same way as they used to act during the Soviet period, and with the same negative consequences. The result has been continuation and, in fact, acceleration, of the general socio-economic crisis in the country. By 1994, crisis-stricken enterprises had begun to withhold from paying taxes on a mass scale. In early 1993 the gross volume of tax non-payments equalled 0.4% of Russia's GDP. On 1 July 1998 this figure already amounted to more than 19% of GDP (Table 2.3). According to the Russian Federal Tax Police, corporate tax evasion had become a widespread and growing problem: while in 1994 there were about 8 000 registered tax evasion cases, in 1995 there were already 13 000 cases, and during the first nine months of 1996 – 11 000 cases.[13] In late 1996 only 16.5% of all Russian enterprises and organisations were paying their taxes on time and in full, while 33.8% were not paying at all.[14] By the end of 1997 problems of tax collection in Russia were equivalent to a total state fiasco. In the first six months of 1998, just a few weeks before the Russian government had publicly announced that it could no longer continue to pay off its debts, the state managed to collect less than half of the planned tax levels!

Even the greatly increased dependency of the Russian government on non-budgetary sources of state revenue, mainly borrowing, did not provide enough funds to continue subsidies to the national economy at pre-crisis levels. The majority of Russian enterprises, whether private or still state-run, that continued to depend on state funding were faced with the necessity of cutting back on production. In this situation, a typical Russian enterprise was often operating at less than half its productive capacity, but continuing to employ most of its previous staff.

That meant that production costs had to grow considerably, even despite the fact that real wages were significantly reduced and not regularly paid. In addition to that, a build-up of inter-enterprise debts and a constant lack of credit and other resources forced a growing number of Russian enterprises to become less and less profitable.

The rapidly increasing numbers of loss-making enterprises had a "chain reaction" effect also on those Russian companies that continue to declare profits. By the mid-1990s, companies in the gas, electricity, oil and other traditional revenue-generating industries, also became tax debtors because they were not able to collect payments from their indebted customers. Many of the latter were state, military or community-oriented organisations like kindergartens and schools. Naming strategic or social reasons, the state often ordered that energy supplies to these customers be continued, however failing to provide any economic or financial base to ensure this. Paradoxically, at the same time the government continued to demand full payment of taxes from energy companies.[15]

The deteriorating economic situation was a major but not the sole reason for falling tax collection. Russian tax legislation provided numerous ways to avoid paying taxes. For instance, there was no provision in Russian law for forcing tax cheats to pay unpaid income tax.[16] Contradictory legislation allowed companies to choose whether to put priority on paying taxes or on paying salaries to their employees,[17] while large-scale business operations were often granted tax exemptions by special government decrees.[18] In most cases, criminals who were charged for tax-related offences, either managed to escape without punishment or were released from prison immediately after conviction.[19] In addition to tax exemptions, many regional authorities and some businesses often also received large customs privileges.[20] The Russian taxation system, with its 170 types of taxes and a tax burden of up to 95% of all business earnings,[21] was itself a major factor in forcing many businesses to seek ways of evading paying taxes. The State Taxation Service, established as recently as 1992, was extremely over-worked[22] and was itself often in desperate need of funds,[23] a situation which could not but provoke the spread of corruption among taxation officers.[24]

The Russian tax collection crisis also had an important regional aspect. Only a small number of administrative regions were fulfilling their tax obligations in full. At the same time, the number of Russian regions that found themselves unable to pay all taxes to the federal budget was constantly increasing. In 1996 only six of 89 regions were able to meet their tax obligations in full. Others paid taxes partially, while in 22 regions tax collection was lower than 30% of the projected levels. Ten Russian regions provided 60% of all taxes. These included Moscow and Moscow oblast', Tyumen', Tatarstan, St Petersburg, Samara, Omsk, Chelyabinsk, Sverdlovsk and Krasnodarskii Krai.[25] During the first five months of 1998 Moscow and Moscow oblast' alone already provided 28.5% of all state budgetary revenues in Russia.[26]

2.2 The emergence of private banking in Russia

The major feature of Russian financial developments in the years after the collapse of the Soviet Union was the rapid development of the private banking sector.[27] Until the end of the 1980s the Soviet banking system was totally owned and managed by the state. In formal terms this was a two-tier banking system consisting of the Central Bank and a variety of commercial banks – one national savings bank and a number of specialised (industry-based) banks. Financial flows between these banks were fully controlled by the government, which often used the population's savings as a temporary source for covering the budget deficit.

In the late Soviet period, the growth of non-state businesses sparked off the development of a number of financial institutions. Although these had a variety of forms, they mainly acted as mutual funds or other forms of co-operative finance. Most of these institutions were established as subsidiaries of private foreign trading companies. They often attracted their initial capital from private savings and investments of state and private companies.

In the early 1990s these prototype banks began to develop into proper banking organisations. They set up regional branches and established relations with other national and foreign banking institutions. In 1991 a number of national banking organisations were established, the largest of which was the Association of Russian Banks.

Following the collapse of the USSR and the beginning of mass privatisation in Russia, many former Soviet state-owned commercial banks were transformed into private banks.[28] The significant increase in the volumes of private trade that came immediately after the start of the Russian reform in 1992, was soon accompanied by a considerable growth in the number of private banks. Almost every medium to large trading company in Russia established its own bank. This process was made easy by the Russian legislation, which stipulated very small capital requirements for the opening of a new bank. The majority of these new banks were local and narrowly specialised and, as a rule, had either no, or very few, private accounts. Their major role was to act as financial intermediates in trading and other operations of their clients. Lack of capital did not allow these banks to invest in any large-scale or long-term projects.[29]

The decision taken in 1992 by the Russian government on the transfer of state accounts to private banks[30] placed a few Russian banking institutions (the so-called "authorised" banks) in a highly privileged position. Firstly, these banks received significant amounts of money that they could use for short-term crediting. The interest that they paid on state accounts was far below commercial interest rates, and sometimes even below the inflation rate. Secondly, via their business interaction with the state, these banks were able to establish special relations with many top Russian officials and to gain their continued patronage.

All these developments resulted in the creation of four main groups of the most influential banks:[31]

(1)   The large commercialised remnants of the former Soviet banking system (the former state-owned "specialised" banks).
(2)   Leading provincial banks that are politically well connected with local administrations and large companies and enjoy their support (and which were often established by these companies and administrations).
(3)   National industrial banks that serve whole industries and that were established by the leading corporations (monopolies) in these industries (mainly the oil and gas sectors).
(4)   Elite Moscow-based banks, most of which developed out of the co-operative and private structures set up by the Soviet state and political institutions in the last years of the existence of the USSR. The power and influence of these banks lies mainly in their political connections with either the federal government and its ministries, or regional and local authorities.

Of all the Russian banks, only one, the formerly state-owned savings bank *Sberbank*, can be called large by international standards. This bank holds about 72–73% of all private rouble deposits with total assets of around US$31 billion.[32] It is the only Russian bank listed among the world's top 200 largest banks. Sberbank is also the only bank whose deposits are guaranteed by the state, and is thus in a very different position to all other Russian commercial banks, which do not enjoy such a privilege and often do not have any deposit insurance whatsoever.

The extremely low international competitiveness of Russian banks not only limited their operations to the domestic market, but also forced them to seek state protection from foreign competition. The banking sector's fragility also became an important source of political leverage, because the collapse of Russian banks could easily undermine the government's position. The probability of an "Albanian scenario" occurring in Russia was greatly increased after the July 1994 collapse of the large investment company, MMM.[33] Although MMM's operations were based on a primitive financial fraud (the so-called "pyramid" scheme), its bankruptcy produced huge waves of political and social unrest across Russia. The government was forced to intervene by partially offsetting the losses of some clients and passing special legislation banning "pyramid" schemes.

In November 1993 lobbying from the banking sector resulted in a presidential decree which put a halt on the servicing of local clients by foreign banks.[34] Another government resolution limited the capital of all foreign banks operating in Russia to 12% of the total capital of the banking sector.[35]

In 1992 there were 1 700 private banks in Russia. The total volume of credits issued by those banks during 1992 was a mere US$23 billion or an average of US$13.5 million per bank (Table 2.4). The average Russian bank had only two branches. Despite the growth in bank numbers, the gross volume of credits in constant roubles fell from 178 billion roubles in 1990 to 141 billion in 1992 and to less than 55 billion roubles in 1998. The share of long-term projects in the overall volume of credits granted by Russian private banks was also falling: from 26.4% in 1990 to just 0.5% in 1992. By the mid-1990s it had grown to 6% which was still a very low level. In the last months of 1998, however, Primakov's government has made support for the national economy one of its top priorities. Through printing of money the government had significantly increased its investment into economy. That had an immediate effect on the structure of bank credits in Russia: according to the preliminary annual data for 1998, the share of long-term credits in the total volume of bank credits had jumped to 46%.

Despite these positive trends, the Russian banking sector in general remained very underdeveloped and economically weak with an extremely low level of capitalisation. For instance, at the end of 1995

Table 2.4 Russia's Banking Sector

a) Numbers of private banks (thousands)

	1990	1991	1992	1993	1994	1995	1996	1997	1998[a]
Private banks	...	...	1.7	2.0	2.5	2.6	2.6	2.6	2.5
Branches of private banks	...	...	3.1	4.5	5.5	5.8	5.1	6.4	4.5

b) Bank credits (billion current roubles)

	1990	1991	1992	1993	1994	1995	1996	1997	1998[a]
Total volumes of bank credits (state and private banks)									
Total credits to individuals and Companies	178	439	5 101.6	30 019	83 561	264 100	342 900	346 713	416.5
Including:									
Short-term credits[b]	131	397	4 835.3	28 982	79 285	168 700	212 900	265 935	224.5
Long-term credits[c]	47	42	266.3	1 037	4 276	32 500	21 700	10 375	192.0
Inter-bank credits	–	...	...	...	...	62 830	108 300	70 403	58.3

Table 2.4 *continued*

c) Total volumes of bank credit in constant prices

	1990	1991	1992	1993	1994	1995	1996	1997	1998[a]
In billion 1990 roubles[d]									
Total credits to individuals and Companies	178.0	192.1	140.5	83.6	57.1	69.2	57.1	49.5	54.7
including:									
Short-term credits[b]	131.0	173.7	133.1	80.7	54.2	44.2	35.4	37.9	29.4
Long-term credits[c]	47.0	18.4	7.3	2.9	2.9	8.5	3.6	1.5	25.1
Inter-bank credits	–	...	...	...	...	...	18.0	10.0	7.6
In billion US dollars[e]									
Total credits to individuals and Companies	278.1	7.4	23.0	31.2	36.7	57.8	66.9	59.8	42.9
including:									
Short-term credits[b]	204.7	6.7	21.8	30.1	34.8	36.9	41.5	45.9	23.1
Long-term credits[c]	73.4	0.7	1.2	1.1	1.9	7.1	4.2	1.8	19.8
Inter-bank credits	–	...	...	...	...	...	21.1	12.1	6.0

NOTES:
[a] Preliminary data.
[b] Less than one calendar year.
[c] Over one calendar year.
[d] Calculated using GDP deflators.
[e] Calculations based on annual average official exchange rate of rouble to USD.

Sources:
Rossiiskii statisticheskii ezhegodnik. 1994, Moscow: Goskomstat, 1994, p.274; *Rossiiskii statisticheskii ezhegodnik. 1995*, Moscow: Goskomstat, 1995, pp.279, 290; *Rossiya v tsifrakh. 1996*, Moscow: Goskomstat, 1996, pp.219, 222; *Sotsial'no-ekonomicheskoe polozhenie Rossii, janvar'-fevral' 1997 g.*, Moscow: Goskomstat, 1997, pp.150–2; *Rossiya-1997. Ekonomicheskaya konyuktura*. Moscow: Tsentr ekonomicheskoi konyuktury, June 1997, pp.37–8; *Rossiiskii statisticheskii ezhegodnik. 1998*, Moscow: Goskomstat, 1998, p.656; *Sotsial'no-ekonomicheskoe polozhenie Rossii, janvar'1999 g.*, Moscow: Goskomstat, 1999, pp.244–7.

the total banking assets in Russia amounted to US$132 billion, or 34% of the GDP. In the Czech Republic, for example, a comparable figure was 155%.[36]

The majority of projects financed by these banks were trade operations, short-term credit to industry and agriculture, and inter-bank loans. The latter constituted an important part of the activities of many banks, given their very low capitalisation level.[37] In fact, many Russian banks have fully re-profiled their business to inter-bank borrowing and lending of money. The boom on the inter-bank credit market that Russia experienced between late 1992 and mid-1995 was based on and could only have happened under the conditions of high inflation that existed at that time. Banks that were holders of large state or commercial deposits found it very profitable to lend those funds as short-term credits to other banks at high interest. Often refinancing was done on a "chain" principle, whereby money was transferred from one institution to another several times, each time with increased interest, before ending up in the hands of the true credit seeker.[38]

When the Russian government decided to take control of the inflation rate and introduced a currency corridor in May 1995, the inter-bank credit market started to shrink. In August 1995 this market collapsed, leaving some large and many smaller banks on the brink of bankruptcy. Soon afterwards the Russian Central Bank announced its intention to raise the minimum capital requirements for banks to 5 million ECU from January 1999. At the end of 1996 only 100 (3.8%) out of 2 600 Russian banks have surpassed that level.[39] At that stage 36.3% of Russian banks were stable while all others were categorised by the Central Bank as "problem banks".[40]

The 1995 crisis on the inter-bank market, although it was triggered more by the change in government policy than by any other factor, was the first symptom indicating that the general economic crisis in Russia was spreading into the banking sector. The build-up of problems in Russian banking during 1995–96 indicated that banks were becoming more and more affected by the growing insolvency of their corporate clients. In this situation many banks were forced to seek close partnerships with larger and more stable banking institutions. This tendency, in its turn, considerably strengthened consolidation and re-centralisation tendencies in the banking sector. A growing number of smaller banks were either liquidated or merged, while private and corporate clients were increasingly shifting their accounts to banks they could trust – even if that meant lower interest rates on their deposits.

In early 1997 57.8% of all assets in the sector were controlled by the 20 largest banks,[41] while five banks (Sberbank, Vneshtorgbank, Oneksimbank, Inkombank and Menatep) held 40% of the joint capital of the Russian banking system.[42]

This process was accompanied by the growth of national influence of the large Moscow-based banks, which were well connected politically. These included offshoots from former Soviet state-owned banks and the newly established "industrial" and "elite" banks. In 1995–96 Moscow banks opened new regional branches throughout Russia, often replacing merged or liquidated regional banks. By the time the cash privatisation of the largest state-owned industrial properties started to take off in 1995–96, Moscow banks emerged as the only national organisations that could put up any significant sums of money for the tenders.[43]

In April 1995 Moscow banks presented the Russian government with an initiative offering 9 trillion roubles (US$2 billion) in exchange for control of the state shares of several partially privatised companies. Initially the Russian government was reluctant to agree to this proposal. However, after the inter-bank credit crash in August placed Russia's fragile financial system under great strain, the Central Bank was forced to make multi-million dollar interventions in order to stabilise the situation and to prevent the fall of the rouble. This greatly increased the government's need for money, prompting President Yeltsin to sign a decree[44] later in August ordering the implementation of what became known as "loans-for-shares" deals. Tenders for control of state property that took place in November–December 1995 were organised by crediting banks and it was no surprise that these banks eventually won them. The big winners of these auctions were Oneksimbank and Menatep.[45]

The "loans-for-shares" scheme has been widely criticised in the Russian press, mainly because of the way in which these tenders were organised. The banks involved ended up paying extremely low sums of money, exchanging a payment equivalent to 1–2 years' worth of revenues of newly controlled companies for control over a period of up to 10 years. This scheme was also one of the first events to attract public attention to the issue of relations between the Russian banking sector and the state.

In the late Soviet period and during the first 2–3 years after the start of the Russian reform, there were very few instances of direct interrelation between the state and the banks. Although Russian bankers did support Yeltsin during the August 1991 putsch and, as a pay-back measure, the Gaidar government introduced a system of "privileged banks" in 1992, in the initial phase of reform the nature of state–bank relations was usually kept secret. The influence that banks had over the implementation of state policy was still low, which was the consequence of the relatively low level of the economic crisis and the fact that the government had access to many other funding sources at that time. In later years, however, the spread of the crisis, which was accompanied by drying up of financial flows to the state budget, put the Russian government under increasing pressure to seek new sources of finance. The "loans-for-shares" scheme was the first case of Russian banks offering financial assistance to the state in return for certain privileges. Since then, the involvement of Russian banks in the drafting and implementation of state policies has been growing rapidly.

In the first half of 1996, when Russia was engaged in the political battles preceding the June presidential elections, Russian banks, which had previously refrained from joint and public involvement in electoral politics, announced their support for Yeltsin. This announcement was accompanied by generous funding of Yeltsin's re-election campaign.[46] Following Yeltsin's victory in the elections, Vladimir Potanin, the president of one of the most "privileged" Russian banks – Oneksimbank, was appointed first deputy prime minister.

Potanin's appointment demonstrated that, in the mid-1990s, the secrecy characterising relations between the state and banks during the first stages of the Russian reform, was gone. Banks came into the open not only as important funding sources for the state, but also as distinct political players. This open involvement in politics was soon followed by a series of events showing that the banking community was far from united and often supported different, even opposing, political forces.

Without going into much detail,[47] the political positions of Russian banks and their relations with the state can be classified into three general ategories. First, there are the "court" banks, the most privileged commercial banks that have long-standing and close relations with the top members of Russia's ruling elite. These include several large former state-owned banks, industry-based banks (mainly connected to the oil and gas sector) and a few banks that were created in the process of reform. All of these banks exercise a significant degree of leverage on the federal government and its ministries, either through direct involvement in state policy (Potanin) or through providing credits to the government in exchange for new privileges. The influence of these banks is mainly limited to federal government structures by means of which they pursue their policies nationally. Because this group of banks has the closest relations with the present government, it has the strongest interest in preserving this government in power.

Second, there are many other large and influential banks that for historical or other reasons failed to establish close relations with the government. These banks support a variety of opposition forces, both in the democratic and nationalist camps. They often have a significant degree of leverage over federal and regional leaders and have established close links with various lobby groups in the parliament. However, at the federal government level their interests are often disregarded in favour of the first group.

And, thirdly, there are all the other banks, which either have no clear political preferences or which support local political leaders. These are mainly small to medium banks. With increasing frequency, these banks are falling victim to the corporatisation of the Russian banking sector, and in many aspects those that still exist are dependent on larger banks (e.g., inter-bank credits). These small operators often have very limited financial resources at their disposal and therefore present very low interest to government and corporate fund-seekers.

The growing involvement of banks in politics in recent years is symptomatic of the general tendency towards polarisation in Russian politics. The overwhelming dependence of the course and outcome of the Russian reform on top political personalities pushed many large banks to take sides. This was an amazing development, demonstrating clearly that in many crucial aspects Russia's new economy (and financial sector as well) are totally dependent on the government. If the present government loses power, many "privileged" banks will be forced to change their modes of operation or even to close down altogether.

The fragility of this position has forced a growing number of Russian banks to seek ways of securing their future beyond the present government. Transfers of capital across the Russian border[48] were the obvious but not the only way of achieving this goal. Another option was for banks to become more involved in the economy. In the first 1–2 years after the start of the reform, besides providing credits to their corporate clients the majority of Russian banks showed very little interest in the economy. The first stage of privatisation ("voucher" privatisation) made it very difficult for outsiders to gain control of the privatised enterprises and, in addition, the volumes of funds that banks could use on privatisation were very small. At that stage banks were mainly crediting export–import operations and their most reliable state and private clients.

The political confrontation in Russia in 1993 demonstrated that the emerging Russian political system had serious internal contradictions and was far from stable. The Yeltsin's 1993 constitution remedied this situation slightly by placing enormous power in the hands of the president. At the same time, however, the new constitution strongly personalised the whole system and made the future of Russia directly dependent on the health of the current president and the outcome of the next presidential elections. In fact, this constitution provoked the growing involvement of banks in political life and by 1996 it had opened the way to the emergence of a corporate state in Russia.

In order to diversify the level of their dependency on politics, Russian bankers began to become more and more involved in the management of the economy or, to be more precise, the management of Russia's most profitable enterprises. The launching of the second stage of privatisation in mid-1994 (cash privatisation) made it possible for banks – both through the use of accumulated and/or borrowed funds and via their political connections – to acquire controlling shares in Russia's enterprises. The "loans-for-shares" scheme was one of the methods used in this privatisation. In 1995–96 scandals and revelations of fraud in the media followed almost every auction of state-owned property that had high revenue-generating potential. Nevertheless, the results of these auctions were very rarely revised as a result of these revelations.

In December 1993 Yeltsin signed a package of documents on the establishment of "financial-industrial groups" (FIGs) in Russia.[49] These groups enjoy special status in their relations with the state, including tax breaks, preferential tariff treatments, and so on. During the three years that followed this decree 62 FIGs were established in Russia, bringing together over 1 000 companies and more than 90 financial institutions. In 1996 the share of FIGs in the Russian GDP stood at 10%, a five-fold increase over the previous year.[50] The two most powerful of these groups were run by the largest Russian "court" banks: one group, "Interros", was created by Oneksimbank and the other, "Yukos-Rosprom", by Menatep.

The creation of the FIGs, which were modelled on Japanese and Korean conglomerates, was an important stage in the development of the Russian banking sector. It marked the end of the division of banks into "privileged" and "other" categories. Now the banks that had ensured their close relations with the state were aiming at establishing their control over revenue flows in the economy, thereby securing a future independent of the political situation. The rise of the FIGs was accompanied by intensification of the struggles between the "court" banks over privatisation issues. The mass media – by the mid-1990s fully controlled by rival banking groups – also became involved in these struggles. The result was a series of public scandals aimed not only against competing banks, but also against their government proteges.

The top government officials caught in the crossfire of the "bank wars", and even the president himself, publicly pleaded for peace, but were unable to halt this damaging political fighting. In late 1996 the Russian government decided in the interests of its political survival to decrease its dependency on the banking sector. In early January 1997 the government commission on monetary and credit policies recommended the transfer of all state accounts from commercial banks to the Central Bank.[51] This was followed by an announcement that the government was significantly raising the capitalisation requirements for registration of banks and was barring commercial banks from collecting customs duties.[52]

The collapse of the Russian bond market in August 1998 had greatly undermined already fragile positions of the Russian banking sector. In the same way as the collapse of the inter-bank loan market three years earlier, freezing of the bond market meant that many leading banks had lost one of their most important sources of revenue. Moreover, because in pre-crisis months all Russian large banks were heavily investing in Russian state bonds, they found it difficult, if not impossible, to service their clients' accounts. Thus, the August collapse provoked a deep and widespread crisis of the Russian banking sector. The appointment of Yevgenii Primakov as the new Russian Prime Minister in September 1998 had brought to power new government that was no longer dependent in its survival on support of bankers or any other business pressure groups. By the end of 1998 Russian bankers had lost much of their earlier political influence, while their business and economic future remained highly uncertain.

The development of the banking sector was probably the most spectacular aspects of the creation of market economy in Russia. Along with privatisation, this was generally seen as the largest achievement of Russian reformists. In the course of post-Soviet years, Russian banks have evolved from poorly organised and primitive structures, which had very limited influence on economic and political developments in the country, into the most significant group of industrial property owners, the largest internal creditors of the state and one of the dominant political forces in Russia.[53] The establishment of large financial-industrial conglomerates very soon was followed by corporatisation in the banking sector. Given the high degree of monopolisation of the still structurally unreformed post-Soviet economy of Russia, in the second half of the 1990s this process was increasingly taking shape of replacement of the former state-owned and state-managed monopolies by privately owned monopolies.[54] By 1997 it became clear that this structural change made the former Soviet state function of revenue redistribution between profitable and unprofitable industries/enterprises impossible, leaving the larger part of the Russian economy starved of investment and the state with very little financial resources at its disposal. By 1998 the confrontation between victors of privatisation, on the one hand, and the supporters of state regulation of the economy, on the other, was becoming increasingly intense. The collapse of the Russian bond market in August 1998 had greatly accelerated this process and led to a *de facto* political and economic defeat of the new Russian business elite. Now bankers were no longer seen as "grey cardinals" of Russian politics; instead, they frequently found themselves used as scapegoats responsible for all earlier faults of the Russian reform.

2.3   Capital investment trends[55]

The decline in post-Soviet Russian industrial and agricultural production was greatly intensified by a dramatic fall in the volume of capital investment in Russia's economy. As early as by the end of the first year of reform, the need to renew capital stock of enterprises, industrial and agricultural alike, had become a major factor in their survival. Realisation of this fact had led many managers and directors of these enterprises to publicly demand a revaluation of the government's policies in the area of capital investment. The "directors' lobby" very soon became a powerful factor in post-Soviet Russian politics. By mid-1994 the demands of this lobby group received a new boost following the election of Mr Viktor Chernomyrdin (former head of the state gas monopoly *Gazprom*) as the new Russian Prime Minister. However, despite these growing pressures, the critical economic situation put drastic limits on the financial resources available to the government. While pursuing a policy of cutting all state expenses, including subsidies and investment in industry and agriculture, Russian reformers hoped that the growing gap in investment funding would be filled in by domestic private investors and through FDI. Numerous attempts made by the state in the last few years aimed at redirecting of population's savings and accumulated private bank funds into investment in production have not proved to be successful.

The long-term dynamics of capital investment in Russia show that in the decade between 1980 and 1990 the volume of investment was rising slowly. However, since 1990 it has been in decline, with the most dramatic fall occurring in 1992 (Table 2.5). There were also significant shifts in the structure of investment by branch of economy. In 1980–85 investment in all areas with the exception of construction were growing steadily, with the most notable growth recorded in the fuel industry. Between 1986 and 1988 this growth continued. During that period the (industrial) construction sector experienced substantial growth, which came mainly as the result of cuts in funding to agriculture.

When the Soviet leadership announced in 1989 that an increase in agricultural output would top its economic priority list, investment strategy was clearly re-oriented towards agriculture (with a more than two-fold increase in investment in one year!). In the same year investment in housing also increased substantially. The growth in public funding of agriculture and housing was accompanied by falls in the volumes of capital investment in all other major sectors of the economy, mainly in transport and communications, as well as machine-building.

In 1990 this tendency was again reversed when the share of agriculture in the total volume of public investment was significantly reduced. However, in the following year, when the general economic and financial crisis started to develop in Russia, a lack of investment funds pushed the Soviet and Russian governments to further investment cuts in all sectors of the national economy, although at that stage funds allocated to agriculture and public housing were reduced only marginally (by 5–8%).

The change of government at the end of 1991 resulted in a reassessment of Russia's public investment strategies. Investment emphasis was now placed on the revenue-generating sectors of the economy (the minerals and fuel industries). Capital-intensive and loss-making sectors were moved to the bottom of the new priority list. As a result, agriculture, (industrial) construction, machine-building (including the military-industrial complex), transport and communications, and social spending experienced much greater cuts in public funding than the minerals industry. The dynamics of investment in the housing sector also demonstrated a relatively smaller decline than in other sectors of economy, mainly because of an increase in private funding of housing. The 1993–94 deregulation of prices for transport and communications services made it possible to slow down investment falls in these sectors. Between the early and mid 1990s the largest falls in funding were experienced by agriculture, (industrial) construction and industry in general.

Table 2.5 Dynamics of Capital Investment in Russia, 1980–98 (1990 = 100)

	1980	1986	1990	1991	1992	1993	1994	1995	1996	1997	1998[a]
By source											
Total	65.5	84.2	100.0	84.3	50.8	43.1	36.3	29.7	24.4	23.2	20.9
Public finance from all sources (federal and regional state funding)	159.4	200.6	100.0	66.3	40.9	43.5	29.2	25.3	12.3	11.9	9.8
Company funds (including bank loans and other borrowings)	0.0	4.5	100.0	89.4	68.9	48.1	42.7	36.2	31.5	27.8	25.3
All other sources (including FDI)	53.9	76.3	100.0	121.2	4.0	18.5	11.8	14.8	31.3	38.5	49.6
By branch of economy											
Industry	76.3	111.2	100.0	81.7	56.7	43.5	28.8	27.8	24.6	24.3	21.3
Agriculture	82.3	68.9	100.0	95.0	32.9	19.6	9.9	5.1	4.9	4.1	3.4
Construction	76.9	94.5	100.0	83.9	29.5	21.0	22.0	19.1	19.9	18.7	17.0
Transport and communications	88.2	118.6	100.0	67.3	37.6	38.6	33.8	36.5	28.1	31.3	27.3
Housing	67.5	91.1	100.0	92.4	70.0	62.1	52.4	46.3	40.0	30.6	26.3
By major industries											
Industry total including:	76.3	111.2	100.0	81.7	56.7	43.5	28.8	27.8	24.6	24.3	21.3
Oil and fuel	78.1[b]	140.8[b]	100.0	80.9	71.3	56.8	35.8	36.0	32.7	32.3	25.5
Machine-building	85.7[c]	125.8[c]	100.0	70.8	29.1	23.0	14.1	10.8	8.8	6.9	6.6
Chemical and forestry	107.4	113.6	100.0	87.9	55.9	32.3	23.8	24.8	18.9	18.0	16.1
Construction materials	317.0	372.4	100.0	102.8	55.1	27.9	24.7	21.3	11.7	9.5	6.4
Electricity production	–	–	100.0	103.6	110.1	94.8	67.4	68.5	77.3	92.4	88.1
Metallurgy	–	–	100.0	93.0	78.1	57.8	40.5	39.1	31.8	31.0	28.8
All other industries	51.8	66.8	100.0	76.4	37.5	30.3	19.6	18.4	14.1	13.0	12.8

Table 2.5 *continued*

	1980	1986	1990	1991	1992	1993	1994	1995	1996	1997	1998[a]
As % of GDP											
Capital Investment as % of GDP (current prices)	...	...	38.7	15.1	14.0	15.8	17.8	16.4	16.7	15.3	15.0

NOTES:

[a] Preliminary data.

[b] Including electricity production.

[c] Including metallurgy.

Sourced and calculated from:

Narodnoe khozyaistvo RSFSR v 1987 g., Moscow: Goskomstat, 1988, pp.326–8; *Narodnoe khozyaistvo RSFSR v 1988 g.*, Moscow: Goskomstat, 1989, pp.612–4; *Narodnoe khozyaistvo RSFSR v 1990 g.*, Moscow: Goskomstat, 1991, pp.522–7; *Narodnoe khozyaistvo Rossiiskoi Federatsii. 1992*, Moscow: Goskomstat, 1992, pp.537–42; *Rossiiskaya Federatsiya v 1992 godu*, Moscow: Goskomstat, 1993, pp.530–3; *Rossiiskaya Federatsiya v tsifrakh v 1993 godu*, Moscow: Goskomstat, 1994, pp.210–4; *Rossiya-1994. Ekonomicheskaya konyuktura. Vypusk 1*, Moscow 1994, pp.197–8; *Narodnoe khozyaistvo RSFSR v 1988 g.*, Moscow: Goskomstat, 1989, pp.612–4; *Rossiiskii statisticheskii ezhegodnik. 1995*, Moscow: Goskomstat, 1995, pp.378; *Sotsial'no-ekonomicheskoe polozhenie Rossii. 1995 g.*, Moscow: Goskomstat, 1996, pp.56–9, 66; *Rossiya v tsifrakh. 1996*, Moscow: Goskomstat, 1996, pp.228–9; *Sotsial'no-ekonomicheskoe polozhenie Rossii. 1996 g.*, Moscow: Goskomstat, 1997, pp.42–9, 233–6; *Sotsial'no-ekonomicheskoe polozhenie Rossii, yanvar' 1997 g.*, Moscow: Goskomstat, 1997, pp.42–9; *Rossiiskii statisticheskii ezhegodnik. 1996*, Moscow: Goskomstat, 1996, p.450; *Sotsial'no-ekonomicheskoe polozhenie Rossii, yanvar'-fevral' 1997 g.*, Moscow: Goskomstat, 1997, pp.84–8; *Rossiiskii statisticheskii ezhegodnik. 1997*, Moscow: Goskomstat, 1997, pp.59, 409–11; *Sotsial'no-ekonomicheskoe polozhenie Rossii. 1998 g.*, Moscow: Goskomstat, 1998, pp.81, 331; *Sotsial'no-ekonomicheskoe polozhenie Rossii, yanvar' 1998 g.*, Moscow: Goskomstat, 1998, pp.53–4; *Sotsial'no-ekonomicheskoe polozhenie Rossii, yanvar' 1999 g.*, Moscow: Goskomstat, 1999, pp.160–1.

For most of the 1990s the investment share of Russia's GDP in current prices remained stable at around 14–17% level after the dramatic fall in 1990–91. However, in real terms the investment dynamics shown in Table 2.5 indicates that the volume of gross capital investment in Russia was constantly declining since the early 1990s. By the end of 1998 finances allocated to capital investment from all sources amounted to a mere one-fifth of the 1990 level. Until 1997 investment in housing was experiencing lowest falls; however, in 1997–98 there was a sharp fall in housing investment, which decreased by almost 25%. At the same time large state allocations into transport and communications in 1998 put this branch of Russian economy in the best position if compared to the 1990 level (Table 2.5). On the other hand, the investment situation in Russian agriculture could be described as catastrophic: in 1998 the volume of capital invested in that sector in real terms amounted to just 3.3% of the 1990 level. In 1990–98 the volume of capital investment in Russian industry as a whole fell by almost 80%. This figure, however, masks huge disparities between the various branches of industry: while in 1998 in real terms investment in electricity production was equal to 88% of the amount invested in 1990, funding in machine-building (engineering) fell by more than 15 times during the same period.

Following attempts made by the former Soviet President Mikhail Gorbachev in late 1980s aimed at liberalisation and decentralisation of the Soviet economic system, the share of capital investment financed from company funds in the gross volume of capital investment was steadily increasing since 1986. This process was further boosted in 1991–92 after the collapse of central planning (and funding) in Russia. In the new environment all Russian companies (whether privatised and or still state-owned) were forced to rely more and more on their own financial resources and any external funding (domestic and foreign) that they were able to attract.

The privatisation of banks deprived the state of its former role as the main capital accumulator; deregulation and liberalisation of internal and foreign trade transferred the levers of control of financial flows from revenue-generating industries from state into private hands. As a result of the reforms undertaken in 1992–93, the Russian state effectively withdrew from its former role as the major (if not sole) redistributor of investment funds in the country. The share of public investment in gross capital investment in Russia fell from more than 90% in the mid-1980s to around 40% in the late 1980s and to about 20% in the mid-1990s (see Table 2.6).

Table 2.6 Structure of Capital Investment in Russia, 1980–98 (shares, %)

	1980	1986	1990	1991	1992	1993	1994	1995	1996	1997	1998ᵃ
By source											
Total	100.0	100.0	100.0	100.0	100.0	100.0	100.0	100.0	100.0	100.0	100.0
Public finance from all sources (federal and regional state funding)	94.1	90.4	37.2	29.2	26.9	34.3	26.0	21.8	20.1	19.2	27.4
Company funds (including bank loans and other Borrowings)	0.0	2.7	51.3	54.2	69.3	57.4	64.2	62.8	63.3	61.5	66.4
All other sources (including FDI)	5.9	6.9	11.6	16.6	3.8	8.3	9.8	15.4	16.6	19.3	6.3
FDI only	N/A	N/A	N/A	N/A	N/A	2.4	1.7	1.5	3.2	0.5	2.3
By branch of economy											
Total	100.0	100.0	100.0	100.0	100.0	100.0	100.0	100.0	100.0	100.0	100.0
including:											
Industry	41.8	47.4	35.9	34.7	40.9	37.0	32.3	34.4	34.8	36.8	39.9
Agriculture	19.9	12.9	15.8	17.8	10.8	7.9	5.0	3.5	2.9	2.5	3.3
Construction	5.3	5.1	4.5	4.5	2.6	2.4	3.3	2.5	4.0	4.0	3.4
Transport and communications	15.9	16.6	11.8	9.4	8.8	11.0	12.8	14.6	15.3	18.0	18.1
Housing	17.1	18.0	16.6	18.1	21.7	23.1	23.7	22.8	20.3	16.4	11.0
By major industries											
Industry total	100.0	100.0	100.0	100.0	100.0	100.0	100.0	100.0	100.0	100.0	100.0
including:											
Oil and Fuel	24.2	41.0ᵇ	32.4	32.1	40.8	42.3	40.3	41.9	43.1	42.8	40.4
Machine-building	25.9ᶜ	26.1ᶜ	23.1	20.0	11.9	12.2	11.3	8.9	8.3	7.8	7.8
Chemical and forestry	13.1	9.5	9.3	10.0	9.2	6.9	7.7	8.3	7.2	4.6	3.5
Construction materials	16.3	13.1	3.9	4.9	3.8	2.5	3.4	3.0	1.9	1.9	1.3
Electricity production	9.3	…	6.2	7.8	12.0	13.4	14.4	15.2	19.4	21.1	19.0
Metallurgy	…	…	8.1	9.2	11.1	10.7	11.4	11.3	10.4	9.6	10.8
All other industries	11.2	10.3	17.0	16.0	11.2	12.0	11.5	11.4	9.7	12.2	17.1

NOTES:
ᵃ Preliminary data.
ᵇ Including electricity production.
ᶜ Including metallurgy.

Sources: See Table 2.5.

In the same period the share of company funding in gross capital investment increased dramatically: from less than 3% in 1986 to almost two-thirds a decade later. In 1986–97 the share of non-state and non-company funding (see category "All other sources" in Table 2.6) more than tripled and reached 19%. The latter, however, was the result of a much less significant fall in expenditure on housing in 1990–97. By 1996 more than a third of all investment in housing came from the population's savings which was a three-fold increase since 1991.[56] Table 2.5 shows that in 1996 housing investment totalled 40% of the 1990 level. The decline in that sector was significantly lower than the fall in investment of up to 4% of the 1990 level experienced in agriculture.[57]

In the post-Soviet period there have also been important changes in the structure of gross capital investment in Russia. In 1990–98 the share of investment in industry in the total volume of investment remained relatively stable (32–41%). The share of investment in the spheres of transport and communications, after a fall in 1992–93, was steadily growing and stood at 18% in 1997–98. In the same period the share of investment in industrial construction declined from 4.5% to 3.4%. Once again, agriculture was the main loser: the share of that sector in gross investment fell from almost 16% in 1990 to just 3.3% in 1998.

The gross volumes of capital investment in post-Soviet Russia mask the disparities in investment flows within the country. In order to compensate for this it is necessary to analyse, at least briefly, the structure and dynamics of capital investment in different economic regions of the Russian Federation.

The regional structure of capital investment in Russia gives a more comprehensive picture of general investment flows and serves as an indicator of the economic priorities of the current Russian leadership. As can seen from Table 2.7, predominantly mining-oriented regions, as well as the politically important central areas, have always been on the top of the list of investment priorities of both the Soviet and post-Soviet Russian governments. These regions include Western Siberia (gas and oil), the Central region (which includes Moscow) and the Urals (the centre of the Russian metals industry). The combined share of these three regions in the total volume of capital investment in Russia was 47.6% in 1990. By 1998 this share had increased to 57%.

The three regional investment leaders also experienced the lowest falls in the volumes of real investment during the crisis years (1990–98). In 1998 the volume of investment in these regions and in the North-West amounted to 20–30% of the 1990 level. This differed

Table 2.7 Regional Structure of Capital Investment in Russia (%)

a) Shares of Economic Regions in Total Volume of Capital Investment (%)

	1985	1990	1991	1992	1993	1994	1995	1996	1997	1998[a]
Northern	4.7	5.1	4.9	5.3	4.4	4.7	4.4	3.9	3.8	3.3
North-West	4.3	4.6	4.5	3.5	3.2	4.2	4.2	4.6	4.2	5.7
Central	17.5	17.6	15.8	15.6	18.0	22.4	22.5	20.3	21.8	27.0
Volgo-Vyatka	4.7	4.8	4.9	4.2	4.8	3.8	3.9	3.5	3.7	3.7
Central ChernoZem	4.8	4.6	4.4	4.6	3.8	3.4	4.2	3.8	3.5	3.8
Volga	10.8	10.3	10.8	10.7	10.6	9.5	9.7	9.3	10.1	10.5
North Caucasus	7.4	7.6	8.0	6.9	7.0	6.9	8.3	7.4	6.6	6.1
Urals	12.0	11.9	12.7	14.8	13.7	13.2	14.1	14.2	13.9	12.3
West Siberia	18.7	18.1	18.6	23.3	21.1	18.9	15.2	21.1	21.6	17.7
East Siberia	7.0	7.1	6.9	3.6	5.9	5.9	7.6	6.5	5.5	4.6
Far East	7.6	7.8	7.9	7.1	6.9	6.5	5.8	5.1	5.1	5.0
Kaliningrad	0.5	0.5	0.5	0.4	0.5	0.5	0.2	0.3	0.3	0.3
All RF	100.0	100.0	100.0	100.0	100.0	100.0	100.0	100.0	100.0	100.0

b) Dynamics of capital investment by economic region, 1990 = 100 (constant prices)

	1985	1990	1991	1992	1993	1994	1995	1996	1997	1998[a]
Northern	70.3	100.0	80.3	53.2	36.9	31.4	25.2	18.3	15.8	12.8
North-West	72.5	100.0	82.1	38.4	29.7	31.3	26.7	24.0	22.7	23.4
Central	77.0	100.0	76.2	45.2	44.0	43.6	38.0	28.2	25.9	30.1
Volgo-Vyatka	75.6	100.0	86.3	44.1	42.9	26.9	24.0	17.6	14.4	13.5
Central ChernoZem	80.4	100.0	81.9	51.5	35.4	25.7	27.1	20.5	16.9	16.6
Volga	80.3	100.0	88.4	53.1	44.3	31.6	27.8	22.0	19.8	20.5
North Caucasus	75.3	100.0	89.2	46.3	39.7	31.1	32.7	23.8	19.8	18.9
Urals	77.9	100.0	90.5	63.4	49.6	37.8	35.2	29.1	25.5	20.3
West Siberia	79.5	100.0	86.7	65.7	50.1	35.6	25.0	28.4	27.6	20.9
East Siberia	76.5	100.0	82.9	25.6	36.0	28.6	31.7	22.3	17.0	13.6
Far East	74.8	100.0	85.6	46.2	38.0	28.1	22.0	15.7	13.2	11.9
Kaliningrad	73.1	100.0	83.6	39.7	45.9	33.8	13.1	14.4	11.4	11.5
All RF	77.1	100.0	84.3	50.8	43.1	36.3	29.7	24.4	23.2	20.9

Table 2.7 *continued*

c) Dynamics of capital investment by groups of regions, 1990 = 100

	1985	1990	1991	1992	1993	1994	1995	1996	1997	1998[a]
Mining regions	80.2	100.0	88.7	75.6	56.7	39.9	24.6	32.4	30.7	22.7
Manufacturing regions	82.6	100.0	85.9	50.8	46.0	37.9	32.5	26.9	25.8	26.1
Agricultural regions	70.2	100.0	90.9	51.5	44.5	33.8	28.3	24.4	20.8	22.4

NOTES:
[a] Preliminary data.

NOTES:
Mining: Kemerovo, Tyumen' and Sakha only.
Manufacturing: St Petersburg, Samara and Khabarovsk only.
Agriculture: Belgorod, Krasnodar and Stavropol only.

Sources:
Kapitalnoe stroitelstvo v Rossiiskoi Federatsii, Moscow: Goskomstat, 1994, pp.11–2; *Rossiiskii statisticheskii ezhegodnik. 1995*, Moscow: Goskomstat, 1995, pp.842–4; *Sotsial'no-ekonomicheskoe polozhenie Rossii. 1995 g.*, Moscow: Goskomstat, 1996, pp.339–41; *Sotsial'no-ekonomicheskoe polozhenie Rossii. 1996 g.*, Moscow: Goskomstat, 1997, pp.233–4; *Sotsial'no-ekonomicheskoe polozhenie Rossii. 1997 g.*, Moscow: Goskomstat, 1998, pp.331–2; *Sotsial'no-ekonomicheskoe polozhenie Rossii, yanvar' 1999 g.*, Moscow: Goskomstat, 1999, pp.379–80.

significantly from falls of up to 11.5% from the 1990 investment level in all other Russian economic regions.

Russian investment priorities become even clearer if we single out those territories that have a clear economic profile from the economic regions and group them together. For instance, the territories of Kemerovo (coal production) and Tyumen' (oil and gas) in the Western Siberian economic region are among Russia's major mining areas along with the Republic of Sakha (coal, gold and diamond production) in the Russian Far East. All three areas also have manufacturing and agriculture, but mining is the dominant orientation. For the same purposes of comparison we have grouped together mainly manufacturing areas of St Petersburg (North-West), Samara (Volga) and Khabarovsk (Far East) into the "manufacturing group", and Belgorod (Central ChernoZem), Krasnodar and Stavropol (both – North Caucasus) into the "agricultural group". It is worth mentioning that all nine areas used for comparison are among Russia's leading economic territories and in 1996 had a combined share in the country's population of 17.6%.

As illustrated by Table 2.7, the dynamics of change in investment flows to these groups of regions were different in the post-Soviet period. Predominantly agricultural and mining areas experienced huge falls in investment (down to 22–23% of the 1990 level), which was lower than the decline in manufacturing areas (26% of the 1990 level). In 1998 there was a visible shift in Russia's investment strategy: mining areas that since the fall of the Soviet Union mining industries have topped the Russian leadership's investment priority list, have experienced a significant drop from the 1990 investment levels (from 30% to 23%). In the same year agricultural regions have registered a relative growth in investment while investment levels in manufacturing regions remained largely unchanged.

Regional investment disparities in Russia are striking if we compare per capita volumes of investment by economic region to Russia's national average (Table 2.8). In 1985 per capita funding of investment projects in Russian regions varied between –35% and +88% of the national average. By 1998 the limits of variation had increased significantly: at a time when Kaliningrad was receiving per capita investment of less than half the Russian average, Western Siberian investment was 1.7 times higher than the national average. Table 2.8 also demonstrates that the change in investment policies came in 1991–92, or precisely at the time when the Soviet government in Russia was replaced by Gaidar's reformist government. During 1994–95 a section of investment flows to Western Siberia was re-directed,

Table 2.8   Indices of Per Capita Investment by Region
(Russian average = 100)

	1985	1990	1991	1992	1993	1994	1995	1996	1997	1998[a]
Northern	112.3	123.3	117.4	130.0	107.8	116.7	108.7	96.4	96.6	84.5
North-West	77.0	82.5	80.5	62.8	58.1	77.4	76.5	83.9	77.4	105.6
Central	84.7	85.5	77.4	76.3	88.5	110.7	111.4	101.1	107.9	134.4
Volgo-Vyatka	81.5	84.6	86.5	73.3	84.5	69.9	68.5	61.1	64.8	65.5
Central ChernoZem	89.4	87.4	84.9	88.3	71.4	65.1	78.3	72.0	65.6	71.9
Volga	96.3	92.5	96.6	95.8	94.2	84.0	84.5	81.5	88.0	90.9
North Caucasus	65.3	66.3	69.3	59.1	59.4	58.3	69.9	62.0	54.7	50.7
Urals	86.5	86.5	92.6	107.5	99.7	95.4	101.9	102.8	100.1	88.3
West Siberia	188.0	177.4	181.9	228.8	206.8	184.9	149.0	205.8	211.4	171.4
East Siberia	114.2	113.7	111.5	57.1	95.3	95.8	122.2	104.6	88.5	74.3
Far East	144.1	144.9	146.8	132.8	131.4	124.2	113.9	99.7	101.1	101.1
Kaliningrad	80.1	83.5	82.1	64.0	86.7	79.3	35.0	46.5	44.6	40.6
All RF	100.0	100.0	100.0	100.0	100.0	100.0	100.0	100.0	100.0	100.0

NOTES:
[a] Preliminary data.

Sources:
Kapitalnoe stroitelstvo v Rossiiskoi Federatsii, Moscow: Goskomstat, 1994, pp.11–12; *Rossiiskii statisticheskii ezhegodnik. 1995*, Moscow: Goskomstat, 1995, pp.842–844; *Sotsial'no-ekonomicheskoe polozhenie Rossii. 1995 g.*, Moscow: Goskomstat, 1996, pp.339–341; *Sravnitelnye pokazateli ekonomicheskogo polozheniya regionov Rossiiskoi Federatsii*, Moscow: Goskomstat, 1995, pp.119–121; *Ekonomicheskoe polozhenie regionov Rossiiskoi Federatsii*, Moscow: Goskomstat, 1994, pp.111–112; *Sotsial'no-ekonomicheskoe polozhenie Rossii. 1996 g.*, Moscow: Goskomstat, 1997, pp.233–236; *Sotsial'no-ekonomicheskoe polozhenie Rossii. 1997 g.*, Moscow: Goskomstat, 1998, pp.331–332; *Sotsial'no-ekonomicheskoe polozhenie Rossii. 1998 g.*, Moscow: Goskomstat, 1999, pp.435–6; *Sotsial'no-ekonomicheskoe polozhenie Rossii, yanvar' 1999 g.*, Moscow: Goskomstat, 1999, pp.379–80.

mainly to the Central region (Moscow), but in 1996–98 this tendency was again reversed.

Three other economic regions that in the mid-1990s were receiving per capita investment above or equal to national average level, were the Central region, the Urals and the Far East. During the years of reform, investment trends in East Siberia and the North-West were subject to significant fluctuations. In 1991–92 per capita investment in East Siberia fell from 112% down to 57% of the national average. Between 1993 and 1995 this trend was reversed. East Siberia is the major centre of Russian non-ferrous (particularly aluminium) industry and timber production. In the Soviet period this industry was a major supplier of metals and other materials to the military-industrial complex. After the collapse of central economic planning in 1991–92 and the huge falls in military production that followed, the Eastern Siberian metals industry found itself in an extremely difficult situation.

This changed somewhat in 1993 when the industry started to be transferred into private hands. Since 1994 East Siberia became an important export revenue-generating region of Russia. This also had a visible positive impact on the flow of capital into the area. In 1997–98, following falls in world metal prices, the volume of investment directed to that region declined, as reflected in the per capita ratios of investment. In 1998 North-Western economic region, along with the Central region, have experienced largest growth in its share of investment in relation to the national average. This trend can be explained by a marked growth in investment flows coming into the two Russia's largest cities – Moscow and St Petersburg.

Russian statistical series also allow us to analyse differences in investment flows between all the 89 administrative units that make up the Russian Federation. In order to make such an analysis easier and to produce clearer results, the Table 2.9 lists only 12 of these units (*oblasts* and republics) which fall respectively into categories of areas with the highest and lowest per capita investment in Russia. Among the six leading investment areas are Russia's capital (Moscow), four mining areas (Komi and Tyumen' – oil and gas; Sakha and Magadan – gold and diamonds) and the Far Eastern area of Kamchatka which is one of major centres of Russia's fishing industry. Although all of these six areas were continuously successful in attracting investment, on a per capita basis the disparities between them are striking.

Oil and gas-rich Tyumen' is the indisputable investment leader in Russia; per capita investment in Tyumen' industry during last decade was between 3.6 and 8.7 times higher than the Russian per capita average. In 1997 Tyumen's share in the gross national volume of investment was the highest in Russia and stood at 25.8%. The second investment leader in Russia is Moscow, which attracted 16.7% of all investment made during 1998 in the Russian economy. Moscow was also a clear winner after the change in government in 1991–92: since 1992 its share in the total volume of investment in Russia had greatly increased. By 1998 per capita investment in Moscow was almost three times higher than the Russian average; that was a remarkable change from the late 1980s level of 67–87% of the national average. In 1998 Tyumen' and Moscow's combined population was less than 9% of Russian population but the two regions accounted for more than 28% of total investment in the Russian economy. In the post-Soviet period there was a significant decline in investment in real terms in both areas. However, these falls were much lower than for the rest of Russia. For instance, while the gross investment in Russia fell by more than

Table 2.9   Indices of Per Capita Investment by Selected Oblasts

a) Areas with largest and lowest per capita indices of capital investment (Russian average = 100)

	1985	1990	1991	1992	1993	1994	1995	1996	1997	1998[a]
Komi Rep.	155.1	159.8	154.2	196.8	140.6	152.9	161.4	193.2	175.8	137.0
Moscow	87.7	77.5	67.0	78.9	115.2	189.0	196.9	204.5	222.6	285.2
Tyumensk. Obl.	630.2	487.5	503.6	739.7	647.2	523.0	360.3	676.9	867.0	525.4
Sakha Rep.	224.4	223.9	252.2	306.4	254.3	236.6	221.8	220.7	215.6	146.5
Kamchatsk. Obl.	140.9	134.4	129.1	109.9	210.8	165.2	116.5	92.2	94.8	84.7
Magadansk. Obl.	200.3	216.9	328.2	212.8	185.5	160.7	148.6	133.3	221.2	213.0
Ivanovsk. Obl.	60.9	65.4	71.4	53.2	38.5	38.6	35.3	28.1	27.0	46.1
Dagestan Rep.	44.8	44.6	46.3	41.8	46.6	41.6	30.0	41.7	60.6	28.1
Karachaevo-Cherkesia	63.8	76.7	75.7	67.6	54.2	44.6	40.6	54.2	47.2	45.6
North Osetia Rep.	60.8	50.7	56.9	40.1	41.5	41.5	39.5	40.6	36.5	41.6
Chechen and Ingush Rep.	48.1	46.3	47.4	14.0	...	...	230.5	107.9	16.5	124.5[b]
Tyva Rep.	72.9	84.2	84.5	53.3	43.7	42.4	25.8	12.0	17.8	24.0
All RF	100.0	100.0	100.0	100.0	100.0	100.0	100.0	100.0	100.0	100.0

b) Dynamics of per capita capital investment in areas with largest and lowest levels, 1990 = 100

	1985	1990	1991	1992	1993	1994	1995	1996	1997	1998[a]
Komi Rep.	76.2	100.0	81.3	62.6	37.9	34.8	30.0	29.5	25.7	21.6
Moscow	88.9	100.0	72.9	51.7	64.0	88.6	75.5	64.5	61.3	72.2
Tyumensk. Obl.	101.5	100.0	87.1	77.1	57.2	39.0	22.0	33.9	34.3	25.6
Sakha Rep.	78.7	100.0	94.9	69.5	48.9	38.4	29.4	24.1	18.1	11.7
Kamchatsk. Obl.	82.3	100.0	81.0	41.6	67.5	44.7	25.8	16.8	16.2	13.6
Magadansk. Obl.	72.5	100.0	127.6	49.9	36.8	26.9	20.4	15.0	19.5	16.6
Ivanovsk. Obl.	73.1	100.0	92.0	41.3	25.3	21.5	16.0	10.5	8.2	10.0
Dagestan Rep.	78.8	100.0	87.5	47.6	45.0	33.9	20.0	22.9	21.2	10.2
Karachaevo-Cherkesia	83.8	100.0	85.9	32.7	31.5	25.5	24.3	21.5	19.1	17.8
North Osetia Rep.	94.2	100.0	94.6	40.2	35.2	29.8	23.2	19.6	14.7	14.5
Chechen and Ingush Rep.	81.6	100.0	86.2	15.3	0.0	0.0	147.9	56.9	8.3	6.3[b]
Tyva Rep.	67.9	100.0	84.6	32.2	22.4	18.3	9.1	3.5	4.6	5.9
All RF	78.5	100.0	84.3	50.8	43.1	36.3	29.7	24.4	23.2	20.9

Table 2.9 *continued*

c) Shares of selected areas in all-Russia capital investment (%)

	1985	1990	1991	1992	1993	1994	1995	1996	1997	1998[a]
Komi Rep.	1.3	1.4	1.3	1.7	1.2	1.3	1.3	1.6	1.2	1.1
Moscow	6.6	6.0	4.0	4.7	6.8	11.8	11.5	11.9	11.4	16.7
Tyumensk. Obl.	11.3	10.4	10.7	15.6	13.7	11.9	7.7	14.6	25.8	11.6
Sakha Rep.	1.6	1.7	1.9	2.2	1.9	1.8	1.6	1.5	1.3	1.0
Kamchatsk. Obl.	0.4	0.4	0.4	0.3	0.6	0.5	0.3	0.3	0.2	0.2
Magadansk. Obl.	0.8	0.8	0.8	0.5	0.4	0.3	0.3	0.2	0.3	0.4
Subtotal largest	*22.0*	*20.6*	*19.1*	*25.0*	*24.6*	*27.6*	*22.7*	*30.1*	*40.3*	*30.9*
Ivanovsk. Obl.	0.6	0.6	0.6	0.5	0.3	0.4	0.3	0.2	0.2	0.4
Dagestan Rep.	0.5	0.6	0.6	0.5	0.6	0.6	0.4	0.6	0.7	0.4
Karachaevo-Cherkesia	0.2	0.2	0.2	0.2	0.2	0.1	0.1	0.3	0.1	0.1
North Osetia Rep.	0.3	0.2	0.3	0.2	0.2	0.2	0.2	0.2	0.1	0.2
Chechen and Ingush Rep.	0.4	0.4	0.4	0.1	..	..	1.8	0.8	0.1	0.3[b]
Tyva Rep.	0.1	0.2	0.2	0.1	0.1	0.1	0.1	0.0	0.0	0.1
Subtotal lowest	*2.1*	*2.1*	*2.3*	*1.6*	*1.4*	*1.4*	*2.9*	*2.2*	*1.4*	*1.4*
All RF	100.0	100.0	100.0	100.0	100.0	100.0	100.0	100.0	100.0	100.0

NOTES:
[a] Preliminary data.
[b] Ingush Republic only.

Sources: See Table 2.8.

79% from 1990–98, investment in Tyumen' fell by 74% and in Moscow by only 28%.

In 1998 the six leading investment areas attracted over 30% of all investment in Russia. In the same year the six areas with the lowest investment had a combined share of only 1.4% in the total investment in Russia. In 1985 the share of the six regional investment leaders was 10 times higher than that of the group with lowest regional investment; in 1997 it was already 22 times higher. With the exception of Ivanovo (the centre of Russia's textile industry) all of the latter group are predominantly agricultural areas. In the post-Soviet period only one of these areas experienced an increase in investment of any significance: this was Chechnya, where investment grew significantly during and immediately after the Chechen War. However, the volume of this investment was heavily outweighed by the losses that the Chechen economy suffered during that destructive war. In 1997 investment in Chechnya has fallen back to pre-war low levels.

The data in Tables 2.9 and 2.10 reveal another important development: due to the growing lack of investment funds, volumes of real investment were constantly falling in all Russian regions and areas since 1992. In the first one or two years of post-Soviet developments, investment in the majority of Russia's regions declined to the point where de-industrialisation became a reality and the political and social situation could easily begin to spiral out of control. Therefore, new cuts in investment funds in the following years of reform primarily affected the major investment-absorbing areas. Growing pressures from the latter coupled with existing financial constraints pushed the central authorities in Russia to balance these local demands by implementing a policy of "flexible" investment shares. This meant that additional public funds were allocated to those important economic areas where the need was most severe (or, alternatively, where political implications could be the most serious). These new allocations were made at the expense of other regions (areas) where additional cuts to funding were made. However, these cuts immediately provoked resistance and growing pressures from latter regions.

Since 1992 the Russian government was caught up in this circle of pressures trying to balance the demands for funding coming from different regions. In many cases the strength and political importance of these demands, and not the national investment strategies, have been the main factors forming the national investment policy. As a result, by the mid-1990s the Russian economy had become even more

Table 2.10 Dynamics of Foreign Investment in Russia (all investment excluding financial sector, mln US dollars)

	1990–93	1994	1990–94	1995	1996				1997	1998[a]	1990–98 %
					Jan–Mar	Jan–Jun	Jan–Sep	All year			
Net total[b]	1 679.9	1 053.4	2 733.3	2 796.7	884.0	2 005.4	4 496.8	6 506.1	12 295	11 773	100.0
USA	...	...	1 226.9	812.9	359.7	510.8	882.1	1 695.2	2 966	2 238	24.8
UK	...	...	833.0	161.4	120.2	261	372.4	486.4	2411	1 591	15.2
Germany	...	...	470.4	293.5	60.7	132.3	194.4	288.9	1647	2 848	15.4
France	...	...	501.0	95.9	17.5	21.3	34.8	41.7	209	1 546	6.6
Switzerland	...	...	98.9	419.8	5.0	281	968.1	1 323.4	1 756	411	11.1
Netherlands	...	...	237.4	83.3	31.8	301.9	954.1	979.6	540	877	7.5
Subtotal	...	...	3367.6	1 866.8	594.9	1 508.3	3 405.9	4 815.2	9 529	9 511	80.6
Other or outflow (–)[b]	...	...	–634.3	929.9	289.1	497.1	1 090.9	1 690.9	2 766	2 262	19.4

NOTES:

[a] Preliminary data.

[b] Russian statistics show only "accumulated foreign investment" to a certain date, which is the net sum of gross investment and outflow of foreign capital.

Sourced and calculated from:

O razvitii ekonomicheskikh reform v Rossiiskoi Federatsii. Dopolnitelnye dannye za yanvar'–sentyabr' 1993 goda, Moscow: Goskomstat, 1993, p.172; *Rossiiskii statisticheski ezhegodnik. 1994*, Moscow: Goskomstat, 1994, p.777; *Rossiiskii statisticheskii ezhegodnik. 1995*, Moscow: Goskomstat, 1995, pp.946–7; *Sotsial'no-ekonomicheskoe polozhenie Rossii, yanvar'–sentyabr' 1994 g.*, Moscow: Goskomstat, 1994, pp.53–4; *Sotsial'no-ekonomicheskoe polozhenie Rossii, yanvar'–oktyabr' 1995 g.*, Moscow: Goskomstat, 1995, p.95; *Sotsial'no-ekonomicheskoe polozhenie Rossii, yanvar'–fevral' 1996 g.*, Moscow: Goskomstat, 1996, pp.67–70; *Sotsial'no-ekonomicheskoe polozhenie Rossii, yanvar'–mai 1996 g.*, Moscow: Goskomstat, 1996, pp.68–70; *Kapitalnoe stroitelstvo v Rossiiskoi Federatsii*, Moscow: Goskomstat, 1994, p.35; "Russia: 1996 Investment Climate Statement from US Embassy, Moscow", *BISNIS Briefs*, 31 July 1996; *Rossiya v tsifrakh. 1996*, Moscow: Goskomstat, 1996, pp.244–5; *Sotsial'no-ekonomicheskoe polozhenie Rossii, yanvar'–avgust 1996 g.*, Moscow: Goskomstat, 1996, pp.72–5; *Ekonomika Rossii, yanvar'–noyabr' 1996 g.*, Moscow: Goskomstat, 1996, pp.53–6; *Sotsial'no-ekonomicheskoe polozhenie Rossii, yanvar'–fevral' 1997 g.*, Moscow: Goskomstat, 1997, pp.84–8; *Sotsial'no-ekonomicheskoe polozhenie Rossii, yanvar' 1998 g.*, Moscow: Goskomstat, 1998, pp.114–5; *Rossiiskii statisticheskii ezhegodnik. 1997*, Moscow: Goskomstat, 1997, pp.594–5; *Rossiiskii statisticheskii ezhegodnik. 1998*, Moscow: Goskomstat, 1998, pp.710–1; *Sotsial'no-ekonomicheskoe polozhenie Rossii, yanvar' 1999 g.*, Moscow: Goskomstat, 1999, pp.163–8.

Map 2.1   Capital Investment in Russian Regions in 1997 (per capita in current roubles)

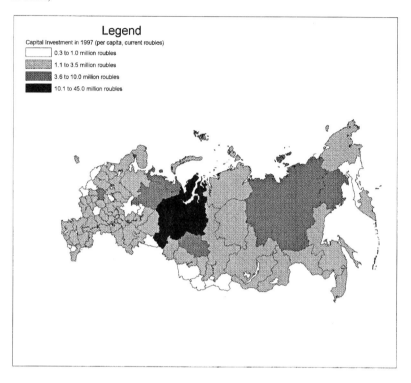

resource-oriented, while the development of capital-intensive industries and agriculture was seriously hampered.

Distribution of capital investment between Russian regions in 1997 is presented in Map 2.1 above. As could be seen on this map, striking differences exist in volumes of investment, which are directed to Russian region. Top levels of investment in 1997 were recorded in main oil- and gas-producing areas of Western Siberia. Yamalo-Nenetskii autonomous region had the highest level with an average of over 41 million roubles of investment per capita.[58] Other West Siberian areas with high investment levels included Khanty-Mansiiskii autonomous area (21 million roubles per capita) and Tyumen' (16.8 million roubles per capita).

The other group is made from Russian regions that in 1997 had levels of investment between 3.5 and 10.0 million roubles per person.

These are other major mining areas (Komi Republic, Nenetskii autonomous region, Sakha Republic and Magadan) and Moscow. The third group unites majority of Russia's administrative units where investment was below average (1 to 3.5 million roubles per capita). Regions with the lowest levels of investment (below 1 million roubles per capita) are presented on the map in the fourth group. These are mainly small ethnic areas where economic crisis is most acute. In 1997 the lowest level of investment in Russia was recorded in Chechnya and neighbouring Ingushetia (less than 0.4 million roubles per person). Other areas where investment levels are critical include Bryansk oblast' in the Central region, Komi-Permyatskii autonomous area in the Urals, and Tyva Republic and Aginsky-Buryatskii autonomous area in East Siberia. In these areas average per capita levels of investment were 50–60 times lower than in Yamalo-Nenetskii area.

2.4   Foreign investment in post-Soviet Russia

At the start of reform it was a common view among many Russian reformers that opening up of the Russian economy, its decentralisation and privatisation would be immediately followed by a large-scale foreign investment. When in the course of the first two years of reform it became clear that foreign investors were not prepared to bring large amounts of money into Russia, the government started to initiate various schemes aimed at attracting foreign capital through tax breaks, customs privileges, establishment of free trade and economic zones, etc. Despite these efforts, the level of foreign involvement in the Russian economy remained very low.

Between 1990 and 1996 the total volume of foreign investment in the non-financial sectors of Russian economy[59] amounted to $12 billion. This was six times less than the estimated need for investment in Russia during that period, and 25 times less than the investment that the People's Republic of China managed to attract in 1991–96.[60] Despite of the size of its economy, in 1996 Russia received less investment than Hungary and Poland, Russia's former allies in the ex-Eastern Bloc.[61] The share of foreign non-financial investment in Russia's gross volumes of investment from all sources in 1993–96 was between 2% and 4% (Table 2.6).

The dynamics of foreign investment in the non-financial sector of the Russian economy is shown in Table 2.10. According to these figures, US$5.5 billion were invested in Russia between 1990–95. In 1996 a further US$6.5 billion were brought into the country. The tendency has shown significant growth in 1997 when gross foreign investment amounted to an all-time peak of US$12.3 billion that was equal to all investment made by foreigners during the previous seven years. This indicates that since 1996 there was a significant change in the attitudes of foreign investors to Russia. It is interesting that in 1996 more than two-thirds of the annual volume of foreign capital was invested after the June 1996 presidential elections in Russia.[62]

Among the largest investors in the Russian economy are the United States,[63] the UK, Germany and Switzerland. Together these four nations accounted for almost two-thirds of all foreign investment in 1990–98. The rapid growth of investment from the Netherlands during 1996 and from Switzerland in 1996–97 could be largely attributed to the partial repatriation of the fugitive Russian capital through Swiss and Dutch banking systems.[64]

Of an estimated gross volume of $13.2 billion invested by foreigners in all sectors of the Russian economy during 1996, foreign direct investment[65] totalled just $2.4 billion, which was slightly up from $2 billion in 1995 (Table 2.11). The bulk of money invested in Russia during that year went into purchases of Russian state bonds and other securities ($6.7 billion). The next biggest item after investment in the financial sector was trade credits and bank deposits ($3.3 billion).[66] In 1997 portfolio investment in non-financial sectors of the Russian national economy still had a very small share of all non-financial investment – 5.5%. In 1998 it fell further to just 1.6%. In 1994–98 the share of FDI in the total volume of foreign non-financial investment declined from 52% to 29%. In the same period the share of foreign trade credits, bank deposits and other credits (see "Other" in Table 2.11) increased from less than a half to about 70%.

Since the beginning of reform in Russia significant changes have occurred in terms of the direction of foreign investment. At the start of the reform (1992–93) the major part of foreign investment was accumulated either as charter capital of various joint ventures with Russian enterprises (mainly in trade, oil exploration and processing, construction, metallurgy) or in the form of credits issued to Russian export–import companies.[67] This investment was generally aimed at facilitating export–import operations with Russian partners, at a time when most of the Russian economy was still owned by the state. The peak in "joint-venture" investment came in the first half of 1994, before the end of the first stage of Russian privatisation. At that time more than 80% of all foreign investment in the Russian economy

Table 2.11   Foreign Non-Financial Investment in Russia by Type, 1994–98

(a) In million current US dollars

	1994	1995	1996	1997	1998[a]
FDI	548.9	2 020	2 440	5 333	3 361
Portfolio	0.5	39	128	681	191
Other	504	924	4 402	6 281	8 221
Total	1 053.4	2 983	6 970	12 295	11 773

(b) As percent to total (%)

	1994	1995	1996	1997	1998
FDI	52.1	67.7	35.0	43.4	28.5
Portfolio	0.0	1.3	1.8	5.5	1.6
Other	47.8	31.0	63.2	51.1	69.8
Total	100.0	100.0	100.0	100.0	100.0

NOTES:
[a] Preliminary data.

Sources:
Rossiiskii statisticheskii ezhegodnik. 1996, Moscow: Goskomstat, 1996, p.466; *Sotsial'no-ekonomicheskoe polozhenie Rossii, yanvar'-fevral' 1997 g.*, Moscow: Goskomstat, 1997, p.85; *Sotsial'no-ekonomicheskoe polozhenie Rossii, yanvar' 1998 g.*, Moscow: Goskomstat, 1998, p.112; *Rossiiskii statisticheskii ezhegodnik. 1998*, Moscow: Goskomstat, 1998, p.710; *Sotsial'no-ekonomicheskoe polozhenie Rossii, yanvar' 1999 g.*, Moscow: Goskomstat, 1999, pp.164–5.

(excluding the financial sector) were directed towards industry. Half of the latter were invested in the fuel sector.

Privatisation of state-owned enterprises, many of which were turned into joint-stock companies in 1994–95, decreased the significance of "joint venture" investment. However, barriers on foreign ownership of Russian minerals companies that were imposed both by Russian legislation and by stockholders of the newly formed private enterprises, greatly limited the direct flows of foreign capital into the national economy. While direct investment in the production sectors of the economy have been declining steadily since mid-1994, the major part of foreign investment has been redirected into stock market operations, banking and finance. Thus, the share of industry in the total volume of foreign investment in Russia fell from 71% in 1994 to 32% at the end of 1998 (Table 2.12).

Table 2.12   **Structure of Foreign Investment in Russia, 1993–98**
(% to total, excluding stock market operations)

	1993	1994	1995	1996	1997	1998[a]
Investment in non-productive sector including:	12.0	6.0	29.0	56.5	60.8	53.4[b]
Credit, finance, insurance	...	...	18.5	52.4	57.4	5.1
Investment in productive sector including:	88.0	94.0	71.0	43.5	39.2	46.6
All industry, incl.:	54.0	71.0	43.3	32.7	29.3	31.7
Fuel	16.0	49.5	8.8	7.4	13.6	11.9
Chemical	6.0	6.0	5.8	1.5	0.7	1.5
Machine-building	23.0	4.1	6.6	2.8	2.2	3.5
Wood-processing	6.1	4.7	5.8	4.5	1.6	2.2
Food	2.0	2.4	9.9	11.2	5.7	7.7
Construction	5.0	9.8	7.3	1.4	2.2	1.6
Trade and catering	6.3	5.6	17.0	5.4	6.0	5.1
Total	100.0	100.0	100.0	100.0	100.0	100.0

NOTES:
[a] Preliminary data.
[b] The major part of this investment (45.6%) was directed to management structures of Russian large corporations, mainly the gas monopoly *Gazprom*.[75]

Sourced and calculated from:
See sources to Table 2.10; *Rossia-1995: Ekonomicheskaya kon'yuktura. Vypusk 1*, March 1995. Moscow: Tsentr ekonomicheskoi kon'yuktury, 1995, p.150; *Rossia-1997: Ekonomicheskaya kon'yuktura. Vypusk 4*, December 1997. Moscow: Tsentr ekonomicheskoi kon'yuktury, 1997, p.129; *Rossiiskii statisticheskii ezhegodnik. 1998*, Moscow: Goskomstat, 1998, p.710; *Sotsial'no-ekonomicheskoe polozhenie Rossii, yanvar' 1999 g.*, Moscow: Goskomstat, 1999, pp.164–5.

One of the major drawbacks in foreign investment in Russia is that a very small proportion of both direct and portfolio investment goes to productive sectors of the economy. Some current estimates put the share of such investment during the whole reform period at below $800 million.[68] And this was happening at a time when, according to the president of the US Overseas Private Investment Corporation (OPIC), there was at least $30 billion in new US investment just waiting to go into Russia.[69] Another recent estimate indicated that around $50 billion could be invested into the Russian fuel and energy sector alone.[70] However, this foreign money will start to come into Russia only after the existing Russian environment for foreign investors changes.

Foreign investors are put off from investing by the under-developed nature of Russia's market structures; existing tax burdens and the general instability of the taxation system; problems associated with the methods and outcomes of privatisation; outdated accounting practices;[71] frequent legal confusion arising from contradictory legislative acts; and widespread corruption in the bureaucracy and law-enforcement agencies. Added to that are frequent attempts undertaken by Russian legislators and companies aimed at limiting or even banning foreign participation in some areas of the economy.[72] The combination of all these factors explains the extremely modest scale of long-term foreign (direct) investment in the productive sector of the Russian economy. At the same time, attempts made by the Russian government in the recent years to attract foreign capital and credits, have opened up new opportunities for short-term but highly profitable foreign investment in Russia's emerging securities and stock markets.

The year 1996 saw the Russian stock markets booming. Billions of dollars of foreign portfolio investment were directed into purchases of Russian loans, state bonds and company shares, making Russia the most lucrative equity market in the Emerging Markets' group of countries.[73] Between mid-1995 and the end of 1996 the share of investment in banking and finance in the total volume of non-financial foreign investment increased by 2.5 times from less than 20% to 54%. During 1996 Russian statistics published volumes of foreign portfolio investment in "the financial sector" or stock market operations. According to these statistics, in the first half of 1996 the total volume of investment in that sector was 3.5 times larger than gross foreign investment in all other sectors of the Russian economy. After the results of the Russian presidential election became known, the flow of foreign capital into productive sectors of the economy increased, bringing the ratio between portfolio and all other types of investment down: in 1996 foreign investment in financial sector (purchases of state bonds and company shares) amounted to $6.7 billion, against $6.5 billion of investment in all other spheres of the national economy.

Although the 1996–97 "stock market boom" and the resulting flow of foreign investment into Russian financial markets largely helped to fund the government's program of short-term internal borrowing, this growth in the "financial" investment had a number of negative consequences. The rising attractiveness of Russian stock markets for foreign investors diverted significant amounts of funds from the productive sector of the economy. For instance, while in 1994 the share of foreign investment made in productive sectors of the economy was

94% of the total, two years later it fell to just 44% (Table 2.12). At the same time large dependency on readily manoeuvrable foreign funds made the Russian financial system even more vulnerable to fluctuations in domestic politics or on world financial markets. According to the chairman of the Russian State Bank, in November 1997, few weeks after the Asian financial crisis began, a major part of foreign capital (US$5 billion) has left the Russian bond market.[74] The effect of growing turbulence at world financial markets on Russia was greatly increased at the beginning 1998 with the start of the meltdown of the Russian bond market. The collapse of this market in mid-August 1998 has forced the Russian leadership to reassess its earlier economic strategy, including its investment policies.

The earlier shift in orientation of foreign investment flows in Russia from "joint-venture" to "finance" was also reflected in the regional structure of investment (Table 2.13). Resource-rich areas (Northern and Western Siberian regions) and key transport regions (Far East) were the main centres of foreign investment in the early "joint venture" period. However, in later years these areas largely lost their attractiveness to foreign investors: for example, between 1993 and 1998 the share of the Western Siberian region in the gross volume of non-financial investment fell from 15% to 8% and that of the Far East from 12% to 5%. During the same period the share of Tyumen' in the total volume of investment made by foreigners in the Russian economy declined eight-fold from 12% to 1.5%.

While investment in Russia's industrial regions were steadily falling in 1993–98, the country's capital city developed into the major centre for foreign investment in Russia, with its share in the gross foreign investment rising from less than 16% in 1993 to 69% in 1997. This spectacular development was mainly due to the fact that Moscow is home to the absolute majority of Russian national stock exchanges, banks and other financial institutions. Therefore, the bulk of foreign portfolio investment in Russia was naturally coming to Moscow. During 1998, particularly after the financial crisis of 17 August, a large volume of foreign investment has left Moscow. The result was a fall in the share of Moscow to 50% (Table 2.13b).

By 1996 Moscow had also become the absolute leader among Russian regions in attracting "joint venture" foreign capital. The larger part of this capital is now invested not in the production sectors, but in trade, services and financial structures.[76] In September 1996, of the total number of joint ventures in Russia 44.8% were based in Moscow; Moscow's JVs had a combined share of 43.4% in the gross exports

Table 2.13   Regional Structure of Foreign Investment in Russia (%)

a) Foreign investment by economic regions

	1993	1995	1996	1997	1998[a]
Northern	33.3	2.7	1.3	0.5	2.2
North-West	5.4	6.8	5.3	4.1	5.5
Central	17.4	57.9	73.0	71.1	59.1
Volgo-Vyatka	0.2	2.2	2.5	1.4	1.4
Central ChernoZem	0.6	0.2	0.4	1.0	1.6
Volga	7.9	9.6	2.8	7.1	8.6
North Caucasus	5.5	1.8	1.1	0.7	3.5
Urals	0.9	2.1	1.0	1.2	3.7
West Siberia	14.7	8.8	6.2	7.0	7.9
East Siberia	1.4	0.8	0.2	3.6	1.4
Far East	12.3	6.6	5.9	2.2	4.8
Kaliningrad	0.5	0.5	0.3	0.1	0.3
All RF	100.0	100.0	100.0	100.0	100.0

b) Areas with largest shares in foreign investment

	1993	1995	1996	1997	1998[a]
Moscow	15.9	46.9	65.5	68.9	49.8
Tyumensk. Obl.	11.6	3.5	3.7	1.8	1.5
St Petersburg	5.1	5.3	2.5	1.9	3.5
Moskovsk. Obl.	0.5	6.9	5.9	0.6	6.0
Tatarstan Rep.	2.4	5.4	1.3	5.7	5.8
Khabarovskii Krai	2.5	1.4	1.1	0.1	0.3
Primorskii Krai	2.5	1.8	1.4	0.8	0.7
Sakhalinsk. Obl.	4.2	1.7	0.6	0.4	1.2
Leningradsk. Obl.	0.1	0.7	2.2	1.4	1.6
Samarsk. Obl.	0.7	2.6	0.8	0.8	1.6
Nizhegorodsk. Obl.	0.1	2.0	2.5	1.3	1.3
Subtotal	45.5	78.1	87.5	83.7	73.4
All RF	100	100.0	100.0	100.0	100.0

NOTES:
[a] Preliminary data.

Sources:
Kapitalnoe stroitelstvo v Rossiiskoi Federatsii, Moscow: Goskomstat, 1994, pp.36–7;
Sotsial'no-ekonomicheskoe polozhenie Rossii, yanvar'-fevral' 1996 g., Moscow: Goskomstat,
1996, p.69; *Sotsial'no-ekonomicheskoe polozhenie Rossii, yanvar'-mai 1996 g.*, Moscow:
Goskomstat, 1996, p.69; *Rossiya v tsifrakh. 1996*, Moscow: Goskomstat, 1996, p.244;
Sotsial'no-ekonomicheskoe polozhenie Rossii, yanvar'-avgust 1996 g., Moscow: Goskomstat,
1996, pp.72–5; *Ekonomika Rossii, yanvar'-noyabr' 1996 g.*, Moscow: Goskomstat, 1996,
pp.53–6; *Rossiiskii statisticheskii ezhegodnik. 1996*, Moscow: Goskomstat, 1996, pp.466–7,
1096–8; *Sotsial'no-ekonomicheskoe polozhenie Rossii, yanvar'-fevral' 1997 g.*, Moscow:
Goskomstat, 1997, pp.86–7, 221–2; *Sotsial'no-ekonomicheskoe polozhenie Rossii, yanvar' 1998
g.*, Moscow: Goskomstat, 1998, pp.269–70; *Sotsial'no-ekonomicheskoe polozhenie Rossii,
yanvar' 1999 g.*, Moscow: Goskomstat, 1999, pp.381–2; *Regiony Rossii. 1998*, Vol.2,
Moscow: Goskomstat, 1998, pp.750–3.

made by joint ventures from Russia during the first nine months of 1996.[77]

The regional breakup of per capita levels of foreign investment in 1997 is shown in Map 2.2. In this map all Russian 89 administrative regions are grouped into four main categories. In the first category are regions where on average foreign investment in 1997 was between zero and US$10 per person. These regions include most of Russia's border areas in the Far East and Siberia, Caucasus ethnic republics and the majority of agricultural regions in the European part of Russia.

In the next group are regions with per capita levels of foreign investment between US$10 and US$83. These are the Far Eastern mining and fishing areas, oil- and gas-producing regions of West Siberia, and some of major manufacturing regions in Central Russia (Samara, Nizhnii Novgorod, Tula, Yaroslavl', St Petersburg).

Map 2.2   Foreign Investment in Russian Regions in 1997 (per capita, in current US dollars)

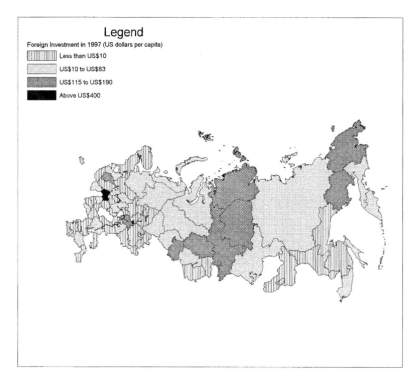

The third group is made of areas with relatively high levels of foreign investment. In per capita terms these regions have managed to attract between US$115 and US$190 in 1997. In all of these areas regions foreign investors are funding large projects, either in primary or manufacturing sectors. Included in this group are Magadan, Krasnoyarskii krai, Omsk and Tomsk oblasts, Tatarstan and Novgorod.

However, the fourth group in 1997 had levels of investment which were at least twice higher than in any other group. This group is made of Moscow and the neighbouring region which we have put together to make map presentation clearer. In 1997 there was an average of US$470 of foreign investment made per each person living in this combined area. If we list Moscow separately, then the difference in foreign investment levels between it and the rest of Russia becomes absolutely striking: during 1997, foreigners invested in Moscow an average of US$819 per capita as opposed to US$25 per capita for the rest of Russia, excluding Moscow.[78]

The profound social and economic crisis that has been developing in Russia since 1991 has had an extremely negative effect on public finance and investment. In the post-Soviet period, an acute financial crisis that almost paralysed the Russian national economy forced the government to make even larger sacrifices to its investment strategy. Increasing pressures from unpaid public employees, mounting state debts to internal and foreign creditors, shrinking state currency and gold reserves, and huge tax collection arrears put the already weakened financial system under great strain. It could be argued that short-term needs of political survival have largely replaced long-term economic and investment strategies on the current priority list of Russian reformists. During the last few years funding demands coming from a variety of political, social and regional quarters have been the main factors forming the national investment policy. In today's Russia, state investment policies (both with respect to the various branches of the economy and to the regions) are more and more reminiscent of the old Russian story about Trishka's coat ("Trishkin kaftan"): the continual appearance of new holes in a poor man's old coat means that he is forced to keep ripping off sections of the same coat.

By mid-1990s the need to cover the growing state budget deficit became the dominant objective of the Russian government's economic policy. Almost all of the government's other economic concerns were in one way or another subjugated to the achievement of this major aim (tax policies, foreign borrowing, demonopolisation and privatisation, state social and investment expenditures). In the decade between 1986–96 the Russian state to all its intents and purposes with-drew almost completely from pursuing any viable investment policy: during that period the share of public finance (federal and local) in the gross volume of investment fell from 90.4% to 18.8%. In 1996, in real terms, the total volume of all state investment in the national economy amounted to slightly more than 6% of the 1986 level.

Public investment cuts resulted in a rapid growth of the share of non-state investment in the gross volume of investment in the national economy from 2.7% in 1986 to over 66% ten years later. However, this growth cannot be attributed to an increase in the interest of private investors in funding of the Russian economy. In real terms, volumes of company investment in Russia fell by more than two-thirds over the past six years.

In the Russian economy the real volume of investment from all sources has fallen by more than four times in the post-Soviet period. In the last two years these greatly reduced flows of investment capital were mainly directed to the major Russian exporting industries (oil and gas extraction, timber, non-ferrous metallurgy), the city of Moscow and the post-war reconstruction of Chechnya. This has been done at the expense of funding all the other Russian regions and sectors of the economy. This investment policy has serious strategic implications for Russia's future:

(1)   It is leading to a rapid decline of the capital stock and to a further de-industrialisation of the economy (for instance, gross volumes of investment in engineering fell by over 90% in 1990–96).

(2)   Growing dependency on food and agricultural imports is becoming inevitable (during the last six years the share of agriculture in all investment declined from 16% to 3.2%, while in real terms money invested in that sector in 1996 was equal to less than 5% of agricultural investment in 1990).

(3)   The deterioration in investment funding of social needs (education, research and development, culture) will, in the long run, greatly undermine Russia's chances for the successful modernisation of its economy.

The deep crisis in the Russian financial system and economy is also reflected in the dynamics of foreign investment. The share of foreign investment in the total volume of all investment in Russia has never exceeded 4%. Since mid-1994 foreign investors have been directing less and less money into the production sectors of the Russian economy. At the same time, budgetary needs have forced the Russian government to borrow growing amounts of money by issuing internal and, since late 1996, external bonds. The interest rate on these bonds was significantly higher than the inflation rate and this immediately attracted both local and foreign investors. In 1996 the Russian equity market became the most lucrative area of investment in the financial sector in the non-Western world. During that year the volume of foreign investment in the Russian non-financial sector grew by 2.3 times over the 1995 level and exceeded the total sum of money invested by foreigners in Russia in the five previous years. However, of US$13.2 billion of 1996 foreign investment in all sectors of the economy, only US$2.4 billion were invested in Russian industry. The reminder was invested in purchases of Russian state bonds and debts or issued as trade and other credits to Russian companies and state agencies.

The collapse of state investment and the continuing decline in real private funding of the national economy has led to dramatic falls in Russia's industrial and agricultural production. Unless this adverse tendency is changed, it is hard to expect any substantial economic growth in Russia. Fundamental changes need to be made to the current Russian investment strategy without delay. Despite the acute shortage in state funds, there are massive and grossly under-utilised non-public financial resources available in Russia that are not being invested into the national economy. These include the population's not invested foreign currency savings (which are increasing by US$5 billion each month) and the capital that is invested abroad (at a rate of US$2 billion a month). Although there were signs in 1995–97 that some of this money was coming back into the national economy, only miserable amounts were invested in the production sector. The bulk of the money went into servicing export–import operations and purchases of state bonds.

It could also be argued that to a great extent it was the post-Soviet Russian government's actions that led to the situation where it is left with very inadequate financial resources and very limited means of controlling the development of investment in the country. Liberalisation of Russian foreign trade in 1992 opened up the main channel of capital flight out of the country and significantly reduced the funds available to the state, while the lifting of foreign currency controls led to a massive flight of the population's savings from quickly depreciating rouble into low-inflationary foreign currency. Privatisation of the state-owned economy resulted in the collapse of the system of state redistribution of funding between different branches of the economy. Thus, through losing control over revenue flows from export-oriented industries and foreign trade, the government cut itself from a major source of budgetary funding. At the same time the bulk of loss-making companies that in 1997 made up more than half of the Russian economy[79] remained dependent on state subsidies. But the state cannot declare most of these companies bankrupt, because this would effectively mean leaving millions of their employees without any source of income. The current financial crisis has left the Russian government without any resources that could be directed into paying unemployment benefits to these people. On the other hand, the deep investment crisis means that fewer new jobs are created each year.

It would be unrealistic to expect that this dilemma will solve itself without government intervention. At present all of the state's economic activities in Russia are directed towards increasing cash flows into the nation's shrinking budget. This, in my view, is a highly questionable policy because in the situation of major socio-economic crisis that exists in Russia the state has almost totally withdrawn from economic strategy and planning. Instead, the state's main efforts should be directed towards reversing negative trends in the national economy. Public investment policy should be the centre of such a strategy. Internal and external channels of capital flight should be, if not closed at all, at least state-controlled. If not, the government – if it continues to stand firm in implementing its current policies – will inevitably become even more isolated from the society and may resort to undemocratic (administrative and/or authoritarian) measures more frequently in pursuing its proclaimed strategic goals. And this would hardly bring the proclaimed objectives of democratisation and formation of the market economy in Russia any closer.

Notes

1. For a detailed account of the history of the current Russian budgetary crisis see S. Sinel'nikov, *Byudzhetnyi krizis v Rossii: 1985–1995 gody*. Moscow: Evraziya, 1995.
2. Jeffrey D. Sachs, "Russia's Struggle with Stabilisation", *Transition*, Vol.5, No.5, pp.7–10.
3. *Russian Economic Reform: Crossing the Threshold of Structural Change. A World Bank Country Study Report*. Washington: The World Bank, 1992, p.54.
4. According to the information released by First Deputy Chairman of the Russian Central Bank Sergei Aleksashenko. See "Russia's State Debt Hits $110B", *Interfax*, 5 June 1997.

5. *Russian Economic Trends*, March 1998.
6. Greg Myre, "Russia to restructure foreign debt", *Associated Press (AP)*, 12 November 1998. According to Deputy Finance Minister Mikhail Kasyanov, quoted in the same article, Russia inherited US$100 billion from the Soviet debt. However, this figure is highly questionable because it is 1.5 times larger than the World Bank's estimate of the total Soviet debt and not only its' "Russian part" that was made at the time of the collapse of the USSR (*Russian Economic Reform: Crossing the Threshold of Structural Change. A World Bank Country Study Report*. Washington: The World Bank, 1992, p.54.)
7. See V. Tikhomirov, "Russia: The Stock Market Boom", *Russian and Euro-Asian Bulletin*, Vol.6, No.1, January 1997, pp.10–4.
8. In the most recent *Transition Report* published by the European Bank for Reconstruction and Development this pyramid scheme is called "the Russian bubble". For the EBRD's assessment of the Russian financial crisis see *Transition Report 1998: Financial Sector in Transition*, London: EBRD, 1998, pp.12–9.
9. *Radio Free Europe/Radio Liberty Newsline*, Vol.2, No.214, 5 November 1998.
10. *Interfax*, 5 June 1997; "Coping with Huge Debt Repayments", *Reuter*, 16 June 1997; *RIA-Novosti*, 21 August 1997.
11. *Finansovye izvestia*, 2 April 1998.
12. *Sotsial'no-ekonomicheskoe polozhenie Rossii, janvar' 1999 g.*, Moscow: Goskomstat, 1999, p.201.
13. Valentin Kunin, "Tax Evasion on the Rise in Russia", *RIA-Novosti*, 5 December 1996.
14. *Trud*, 18 December 1996.
15. A good example of such case is the largest Russian company, the gas monopoly Gazprom. In June 1997 this company had to take a US$2 billion commercial loan in order to repay its outstanding tax debt. At the same time Gazprom was owed US$12 billion by delinquent domestic customers (*OMRI Daily Digest*, 22 April 1997 and 19 June 1997).
16. David Filipov, "Evasion schemes tax Russia's economy", *Boston Globe*, 28 October 1996.
17. *The Moscow Tribune*, 16 November 1996.
18. Among the most widely known cases are decrees allowing annual duty free imports of US$100–1,000 billion to the National Sports Foundation, the Russian Fund for Invalids of the Afghan War, the Russian Society of the Deaf and the Russian Orthodox Church (Carol Matlack, "Helping the Russian Mafia Help Itself. Tax Exemptions Have Become a Gold Mine... For Gangsters", *Business Week*, 9 December 1996).
19. *Trud*, 18 December 1996; "Tax Service Head Says Revenues Up 34%", *Interfax*, 6 February 1997.
20. According to the Russian Finance Minister, in 1996 tax exemptions cost around 160 trillion roubles (US$28 billion) to the Russian budget. About 100 trillion roubles out of that sum were exemptions granted to regional authorities (*Kommersant-Daily* (Moscow), 15 February 1997, p.1). A further 12.4 trillion roubles (US$2.2 billion) were lost as a result of customs privileges granted to individuals (*Segodnya*, 19 February 1997).
21. See Michael R. Gordon, "On the Road to Capitalism, Russia's Tax System Gets a Flat", *The New York Times*, 19 February 1997; Lidia Lukyanova, "Will

Russia Get a 'Smarter' Tax Policy?", *Prism* (The Jamestown Foundation), Vol.II, November 1996, Part 3.

22. In 1996 each tax inspector in Moscow was responsible for 200–300 businesses which meant that if proper inspections were done, a repeat inspection of the same business would be held each 30–35 years (Lidia Lukyanova, Ibid.).

23. In the beginning of 1997 the State Tax Service was owed 1.9 trillion roubles (US$340 million) from the federal budget (*OMRI Daily Digest*, 15 January 1997).

24. In 1996 101 tax officials were convicted of corruption, up from 54 in the previous year (*OMRI Daily Digest*, 11 March 1997).

25. *OMRI Daily Digest*, 7 November 1996 and 12 March 1997; *Monitor* (Jamestown Foundation), 14 November 1996. For an analysis of an important issue of fiscal relations between the centre and Russia's regions see Alastair McAuley, "The determinants of Russian federal-regional fiscal relations: equity or political influence?", *Europe-Asia Studies*, Vol.49, No.3, May 1997, pp.431–443; S. Lushin, "The fiscal and payments crisis", *Problems of Economic Transition*, Vol.40, No.5, September 1997, pp.36–48.

26. *Sotsial'no-ekonomicheskoe polozhenie Rossii, janvar'-iun' 1998 g.*, Moscow: Goskomstat, 1998, p.159.

27. This topic has been in the centre of a number of recent studies. See, for instance, Anders Aslund, "Russian banking: crisis or rent-seeking?", *Post-Soviet Geography and Economics*, Vol.37, No.8, October 1996, pp.495–502; William Tompson, "Old habits die hard: fiscal imperatives, state regulation and the role of Russia's banks", *Europe-Asia Studies*, Vol.49, No.7, November 1997, pp.1159–86; Pekka Sutela, "The role of banks in financing Russian economic growth", *Post-Soviet Geography and Economics*, Vol.38, No.2, February 1998, pp.96–105; Joachim Bald and Jim Nielsen, "Developing efficient financial institutions in Russia", *Communist Economies & Economic Transformation*, Vol.10, No.1, March 1998, pp.81–94.

28. The process of privatisation of Soviet state-owned specialised banks started in 1990–91, but was completed in 1992.

29. For more detail on the first stage of development of the Russian banking sector see R. Lamdany, *Russia: the Banking System During Transition*, Washington, D.C.: The World Bank, [1993]; Pekka Sutela, "The role of banks in financing Russian economic growth", *Post-Soviet Geography and Economics*, February 1998, Vol.39, No.2.

30. Jonas Bernstein, "Enter the corporate state", *The Moscow Times*, 19 September 1997.

31. Juliet Johnson, "High noon for Russia's banks", Loyola University, Chicago, 6 November 1997. Paper published in *Johnson's Russia List (JRL)*, 17 December 1997.

32. "Russia: foreign banks", *Oxford Analytica East Europe Daily Brief (OAEEDB)*, 17 January 1997; Julie Tolkacheva, "Russian banks face deadly competition from the West", *Reuter*, 5 September 1997.

33. For a detailed overview of MMM's collapse see Russian newspapers between end of July and mid-August 1994.

34. "Russia: foreign banks", *OAEEDB*, 17 January 1997.

35. Julie Tolkacheva, "Russian banks face deadly competition from the West", *Reuter*, 5 September 1997.

36. John Thornhill, "Russia: a quiet revolution", *The Financial Times*, 19 August 1997.
37. According to the president of Association of Russian Banks, Sergei Yegorov, the combined capital of Russian commercial banks as of 1 January 1998 totalled 112.3 billion new roubles (US$19 billion) which was 26.5% higher than a year earlier. This is an extremely low figure given the size of the Russian economy and the volume of savings of the Russian population. Lack of the public's confidence in the banking system is demonstrated by the fact that in early 1998 Russians preferred to keep some US$35 billion worth of foreign currency in cash rather than in banks (*Radio Free Europe/Radio Liberty News Line (RFE/RL)*, Vol.2, No.81, 28 April 1998).
38. According to some Russian expert estimates, up to 30% of all banks practically had no funds of their own (*Delovoi Mir*, 22–28 November 1996). Their liquidity was fully built up from the money they could borrow on the interbank credit market.
39. Juliet Johnson, Op.cit.
40. *Delovoi Mir*, 22–28 November 1996.
41. *RFE/RL*, 17 July 1997.
42. *Monitor*, 11 June 1997. In 1994–97 a total of 922 banks and lending institutions have lost their licences, 333 of them in 1997 alone. In addition to that, according to chairman of the RCB Sergei Dubinin, another 25% of Russian banks had "serious problems" (*RFE/RL*, Vol.2, No.81, 28 April 1998).
43. The process of the growth of influence of Moscow-based banks was a reflection of a more general tendency towards accumulation of all Russian financial resources in the nation's capital. Thus, by 1996, 85% of all financial resources in Russia were concentrated in Moscow. In addition, about 93% of the net revenue from Russian financial transactions remained in Moscow. The process of capital accumulation became more intense after the Russian government started to borrow money from internal sources on a large-scale through issues of state bonds, GKO-OFZ. However, 95% of money invested into these bonds came from other regions of Russia and not from Moscow (V. D. Marshak, "Mezhregional'nye finansovye potoki", *Region: ekonomika i sotsiologia* (Novosibirsk), No.1, 1998, p.147).
44. "Russia: banking lobby", *OAEEDB*, 20 January 1997.
45. Juliet Johnson, Op.cit.
46. Estimates of the size of the total funding vary between US$0.5 billion and US$1 billion (see, for instance, Juliet Johnson, Op.cit.; "Russia: banking lobby", *OAEEDB*, 20 January 1997).
47. For a good recent overview of the Russian banking sector see Mikhail K. Lapidus et al, *Understanding Russian Banking: Russian Banking System, Securities Market, and Money Settlements*, Kansas: Mir House, 1997.
48. On dynamics and ways of capital flight see V. Tikhomirov, "Capital flight from Post-Soviet Russia", *Europe-Asia Studies*, Vol.49, No.4, 1997, pp.591–615.
49. For the full text of these presidential decrees see *Dokumenty*, Moscow: Ekonomicheskie novosti, yanvar' 1994, pp.94–6.
50. *Rossiiskaya gazeta* (Moscow), 26 July 1997.
51. Mikhail Berger, "Place on secret bank list still proof of legitimacy", *St Petersburg Times* (St Petersburg), 26 January–2 February 1997.

52. *OMRI Daily Digest*, 5 March 1997; *RFE/RL*, 7 August 1997.
53. It is necessary to stress, however, that despite the significant political influence enjoyed by bankers in the contemporary Russia, Russian financial system remains extremely fragile. The lack of a sound independent economic base means that any negative political development in Russia, even the change of health of the Russian president, have immediate and strong effect on the positions of Russia's major banking institutions and financial markets in general. In this situation foreign credits play an important, if not central, role in ensuring the stability of the whole system. That also means that any serious fluctuations on the global financial markets are bound to have a devastating effect on the Russian financial market. This was clearly demonstrated in the late 1997 and in the early 1998, when, during the Asian financial crisis, the Russian government was forced to substantially increase its foreign borrowing in an attempt of preventing the fall of the Russian market. The fragility of the Russian financial and banking systems was stressed by many observers, starting from the first years of the reform. See: G. Khanin, "Kak rabotayut rossiiskie banki", *Eko*, No.6 (238), 1994, pp.49–53.
54. For an interesting discussion of the Russian corporate capitalism from a historical perspective see T. C. Owen, *Russian Corporate Capitalism from Peter the Great to Perestroika*, N.Y.: Oxford University Press, 1995.
55. This is an abridged and updated version of the chapter "Investment crisis in post-Soviet Russia" published in H. Shibata and T. Ihori (eds.), *Welfare State, Public Investment and Growth*, Tokyo: Springer-Verlag, 1998, pp.221–55. The author is grateful to Springer-Verlag Tokyo for granting a permission to reproduce this material.
56. *Sotsialno-ekonomicheskoe polozhenie Rossii. 1996 g.*, Moscow: Goskomstat, 1997, p.47.
57. After growing steadily in 1994–95 physical volumes of housing construction in Russia started to decline in 1996–97. In 1996 the total volume of housing construction fell by 10% from the 1995 level (*Rossiiskaya Gazeta*, 25 January 1997). And in 1997 housing in physical volumes experienced a further decline of 5% (*Sotsial'no-ekonomicheskoe polozhenie Rossii. 1997 g.*, Moscow: Goskomstat, 1998, p.81).
58. Data on per capita investment by region was calculated from: *Sotsial'no-ekonomicheskoe polozhenie Rossii. 1997 g.*, Moscow: Goskomstat, 1998, pp.331–332.
59. All investment minus mainly purchases of state bonds (GKOs) and state debts.
60. *Finansovye Izvestia*, 31 October 1996 and *Delovoy Mir*, 10–14 November 1996.
61. *Reuter*, 18 February 1997.
62. Also see S. Iovchuk and I. Kvashnina, "Foreign capital investment in Russia: status and outlook", *Problems of Economic Transition*, Vol.39, No.12, April 1997, pp.43–54.
63. In 1995 the bulk of US direct investment came from US tobacco and food companies: Phillip Morris, Master Foods, Pepsi Cola (*Nezavisimaya Gazeta*, 29 October 1996). By 1997 the US investment has shifted mainly to the Russian fuel industry (58.5% of all US direct investment in 1997)

(calculated from: *Sotsial'no-ekonomicheskoe polozhenie Rossii, yanvar' 1998 g.,* Moscow: Goskomstat, 1998, pp.113–115).

64. *Nezavisimaya Gazeta,* 29 October 1996.
65. Data on foreign investment in Russian statistical series is shown in accordance with the IMF methodology. FDI includes investment made by companies or individuals that own a Russian company or hold no less than 10% of its stock. Portfolio investment refers to purchases of shares in a company that amount to less than 10% of its total stock. (*Rossiiskii statisticheskii ezhegodnik. 1997.* Moscow: Goskomstat, 1997, p.594).
66. "Russia: foreign capital is $11 billion", *Associated Press (AP),* 27 December 1996; *OMRI,* No.32, Part 1, 14 February 1997.
67. Moscow-based joint ventures that were trade intermediaries made up 82.6% of all JVs operating in Russia in early 1990s (*Nezavisimaya Gazeta,* 29 October 1996).
68. Ibid.
69. Robert Lyle, "Russia: huge foreign investment hinges on reforms", *Radio Free Europe/Radio Liberty News Service,* 13 January 1997.
70. Bruce Clark, Chrystia Freeland, "Russia: $50bn awaits tax reform", *The Financial Times* (London), 7 February 1997.
71. Very often foreign investors reported as one of the major problems the so-called double accounting often practised by Russian companies which did not allow investors to keep track of cash flows at an enterprise. See Liam Halligan and Pavel Teplukhin, "Investment disincentives in Russia", *Communist Economies & Economic Transformation,* Vol.8, No.1, March 1996, pp.29–52.
72. For example, in February 1997 it was reported that the lower house of the Russian Parliament, the *Duma,* passed in the first reading amendments to the law on foreign investment banning foreign investment in many sectors of the economy, including telecommunications and electrical power distribution. Next month Russia's gas monopoly *Gazprom* blocked an attempt by foreign investors to buy its domestically traded shares ("Duma urges wide ban on foreign investment", *Reuters,* 21 February 1997; "Defensive Gazprom", *OAEEDB,* 3 March 1997).
73. For example, according to the data from the Emerging Markets Traders Association (EMTA) between end of 1995 and end of 1996 the average bid price on Russia's *Vneshekonombank*'s Yen loans changed by 141.67% making it the largest change on the EMTA's list (see V. Tikhomirov, "Russia: the stock market boom", *Russian and Euro-Asian Bulletin* (Melbourne), January 1997, Vol.6, No.1, pp.10–14.
74. *RFE/RL,* Vol.1, No.166, 24 November 1997.
75. See *Sotsial'no-ekonomicheskoe polozhenie Rossii, yanvar' 1999 g.,* Moscow: Goskomstat, 1999, p.164, note 3.
76. In January–September 1996 43% of registered joint ventures in Russia were operating in trade and catering (*Ekonomika Rossii, yanvar'-noyabr' 1996 g.,* Moscow: Goskomstat, 1996, p.79).
77. *Nezavisimaya Gazeta,* 29 October 1996 and *Ekonomika Rossii, yanvar'-noyabr' 1996 g.,* Moscow: Goskomstat, 1996, pp.79–80.
78. Calculated from: *Sotsial'no-ekonomicheskoe polozhenie Rossii. 1997 g.,* Moscow: Goskomstat, 1998, pp.269–270.

79. According to *Goskomstat*, in 1997 47% of industrial, 80% of agricultural, 59% of transport and 40% of construction companies were making losses. Out of the total number of all registered enterprises in Russia 60.4% were loss-making (*Sotsial'no-ekonomicheskoe polozhenie Rossii, yanvar' 1998 g.*, Moscow: Goskomstat, 1998, p.166).

3
The Russian Foreign Trade

The disintegration of the Soviet Union was accompanied in Russia by the collapse of the centralised system of foreign trade management.[1] When Russia embarked upon on the path of reforming of its economy in early 1992, one of the first measures taken was the liberalisation of foreign trade. Within a year (1992) thousands of new export–import companies were created in Russia while former state-run trade associations were restructured and privatised. Wholesale and retail trade chains were also transferred into private hands.

These developments resulted in significant changes in the organisation of Russian foreign trade. With a few significant exceptions, such as arms sales, most foreign trade turnover ceased to be state-controlled. Instead, by mid-1992 the Russian state had started to play an active role in the regulation of foreign trade flows through import duties, export quotas, etc. During the initial post-Soviet years, however, this new system of trade regulation was rather ineffective, due to of the absence of border and customs controls between Russia and many of the ex-Soviet states. In 1992 and 1993 massive unregistered flows of commodities took place across the Russian borders. Therefore, while official statistics showed a significant decline in the volume of Russian foreign trade in 1992, there were also large transfers of goods across the borders that were not registered officially.

3.1 Russian foreign trade with non-CIS countries

According to the official data, between 1990 and 1992 Russian exports to countries outside the former Soviet Union fell by over 40% and imports – by over 54% (Table 3.1a). This negative tendency in exports was reversed in 1993 and since that year Russian exports outside the

Table 3.1 Dynamics and Structure of Foreign Trade[a] with Non-CIS Countries

a) Annual volumes of Russian foreign trade

In million US dollars

	1985	1990	1991	1992	1993	1994	1995	1996	1997	1998[b]
Exports	57 635	71 148	50 911	42 376	44 297	53 001	65 607	70 975	69 954	59 000
Imports	56 395	81 751	44 473	36 984	32 807	36 967	44 112	49 125	55 808	45 800
Balance	1 241	−10 604	6 438	5 392	11 490	16 034	21 495	21 850	14 146	13 200

Indices, 1990 = 100

	1985	1990	1991	1992	1993	1994	1995	1996	1997	1998[b]
Exports	81.0	100.0	71.6	59.6	62.3	74.5	92.2	99.8	98.3	82.9
Imports	69.0	100.0	54.4	45.2	40.1	45.2	54.0	60.1	68.3	56.0

b) Structure of exports (%)

	1990	1991	1992	1993	1994	1995	1996	1997
Total exports including:	100.0	100.0	100.0	100.0	100.0	100.0	100.0	100.0
Minerals	45.4	51.7	52.1	46.7	43.1	40.2	46.1	46.5
Metals and precious stones	12.9	14.3	16.4	23.2	31.1	29.8	26.7	27.9
Chemicals	4.6	6.6	6.1	6.0	7.8	9.6	8.3	8.1
Machinery	17.6	10.2	8.9	6.5	6.0	8.1	7.9	8.1
Timber	4.4	4.7	3.7	4.2	4.1	5.9	4.3	4.6
Textiles	1.0	0.9	0.6	0.4	1.7	1.3	0.9	0.9
Food and agricultural raw materials	2.1	2.6	3.9	3.8	4.3	3.5	3.8	2.6
Other	12.0	9.0	8.3	9.2	1.9	1.6	2.0	1.3

Table 3.1 continued

c) Structure of imports (%)

	1990	1991	1992	1993	1994	1995	1996	1997
Total imports including:	100.0	100.0	100.0	100.0	100.0	100.0	100.0	100.0
Machinery	44.3	35.6	37.7	33.8	37.6	38.7	37.4	39.2
Food and agricultural raw materials	20.3	27.9	26.0	22.2	30.4	29.4	24.9	26.0
Chemicals	10.9	12.4	9.3	6.2	11.0	11.2	15.8	15.8
Textiles	9.3	9.9	12.2	13.9	7.6	4.7	4.3	3.3
Metals and precious stones	5.4	6.2	3.3	3.5	4.0	5.0	6.1	4.5
Minerals	2.9	2.9	2.7	4.0	2.9	2.9	2.8	2.7
Timber	1.1	1.1	1.2	0.5	1.7	3.0	4.3	4.3
Other	5.8	4.0	7.6	15.9	4.8	5.1	4.4	4.2

NOTES:
[a] Data includes estimates of "unorganised" ("shuttle") trade.
[b] Preliminary data.

Sources:
Rossiiskii statisticheskii ezhegodnik. 1994, Moscow: Goskomstat, 1994, p.421; *Rossiiskii statisticheskii ezhegodnik. 1995*, Moscow: Goskomstat, 1995, pp.429–30, 432; *Sotsial'no-ekonomicheskoe polozhenie Rossii. 1995 g.*, Moscow: Goskomstat, 1996, p.137; *Sotsial'no-ekonomicheskoe polozhenie Rossii, yanvar'-iyun' 1996 g.*, Moscow: Goskomstat, 1996, p.65; *Sotsial'no-ekonomicheskoe polozhenie Rossii, yanvar'-iyun' 1995 g.*, Moscow: Goskomstat, 1995, pp.66, 70; *Sodruzhestvo Nezavisimykh Gosudarstv v 1995 godu. Kratkii spravochnik*, Moscow: Statkom SNG, January 1995, pp.103, 107; *Rossiya v tsifrakh. 1996*, Moscow: Goskomstat, 1996, pp.142, 146–8; *Sotsial'no-ekonomicheskoe polozhenie Rossii, yanvar' 1997 g.*, Moscow: Goskomstat, 1997, p.76; *Sodruzhestvo Nezavisimykh Gosudarstv v 1996 godu*, Moscow: Statkom SNG, yanvar' 1997, pp.107, 115; *Rossiiskii statisticheskii ezhegodnik. 1997*, Moscow: Goskomstat, 1997, pp.577–81; *Sotsial'no-ekonomicheskoe polozhenie Rossii, yanvar' 1998 g.*, Moscow: Goskomstat, 1998, pp.96–109; *Sodruzhestvo Nezavisimykh Gosudarstv v 1997 godu. Kratkii spravochnik*, Moscow: Statkom SNG, 1998, pp.99, 107; *Sotsial'no-ekonomicheskoe polozhenie Rossii, yanvar' 1999 g.*, Moscow: Goskomstat, 1999, pp.134–6; *Rossiiskii statisticheskii ezhegodnik. 1998*, Moscow: Goskomstat, 1998, pp.745–9.

Commonwealth of Independent States (CIS) have been constantly on the rise. By 1996 Russia was exporting similar volumes of goods and commodities to the pre-reform period. Imports were also rising slowly, but in 1996 they were still slightly more than a half of what the country used to import in 1990.

As a result, in the post-communist period Russian trade with non-CIS countries had a large positive balance, which was a sharp turn around from the US$10.6 billion negative balance recorded by Russia in 1990. A negative foreign trade balance was also recorded during the first four months of 1992, but this has not been repeated since May 1992. In 1994–98 Russia was having a positive trade balance ranging between US$13 and 22 billion.

The structure of Russian exports to non-CIS destinations, both in the Soviet and the post-communist years, has been dominated by minerals, including oil and gas, which constitute the largest export item (40–50% of all Russian exports). The early 1990s saw a marked growth in Russian exports of raw materials and resources and a continuing decline in exports of machinery and other manufactured goods.[2] For instance, while the share of metals in overall exports increased from 13% in 1990 to 28% in 1997, the share of machinery in the same years fell twice from 17.6% to 8% (Table 3.1b).

The most significant category in Russian machinery exports is that of weaponry and other military hardware. The dramatic cuts in Russian military spending after 1991, which were mainly the result of the gross underfunding of the army by the state, opened up a growing niche for exports of advanced Russian-made weaponry to world markets, particularly to the Asian markets. Since 1993 Russia has been constantly increasing its annual volume of military exports, which in 1996 stood at the level of US$3.6 billion, or 20% of world arms sales. Arms exports grew by 65% in 1995 and by another 18% in 1996.[3] In the mid-1990s military aircraft accounted for about 55–60% of the gross volume of Russian arms sales.[4] It was reported in early 1997 that Russian arms exporters were planning to reach by the end of the century an annual level of exports of about US$10 billion,[5] reinstating Russia in the position, previously occupied by the Soviet Union, of one of the world's leading arms exporters.

The general export dynamics during the post-Soviet years have been directly related to the steep decline experienced by the Russian manufacturing sector. While the production of complicated, high-tech manufactured goods fell rapidly, minerals and metals were becoming a major source of foreign trade revenue. The rise in exports of the latter commodities was also accelerated by the continuing slump in Russian industrial production, which meant that local industry was able to absorb smaller quantities of raw materials, energy and metals than in previous years. In particular, the sharp decline in military production left large volumes of ferrous and non-ferrous metals unwanted by industry. The result was a rapid increase in Russian metal exports in the early 1990s.[6]

Between 1990 and 1997 Russia recorded a significant increase in two export categories: exports of metals increased by 1.8 times and exports of chemicals – by 1.7 times. Increased volumes of Russia's arms trade in the last few years were reflected in 1993–97 in an increase in the overall exports of machinery by 1.9 times (the latter, however, in 1997 still amounted to only 43% of the 1990 level). Another export category that had shown major growth between 1993 and 1997 were exports of textiles (3.5 times increase in 1993–97).

In 1990–92 the volume of Russian exports fell by over 40%, but since 1993 exports have been steadily increasing and by 1996 they had reached pre-crisis levels (Table 3.1a). Imports followed a pattern, although the fall in the volume of imports during the first years following the collapse of the Soviet Union was much sharper than the fall in exports. The improvement of import dynamics was also very modest, and in 1998 Russia's imports equalled slightly more than 56% of the 1990 level. Imports of all major commodities (in current dollars) fell significantly in 1990–96, but the trend was reversed in 1997 when imports increased by 14% over one year. The spread of the Russian financial crisis in 1998 and the rapid decline of the national currency exchange rate have had a direct negative effect on import dynamics. In the second half of 1998 Russian imports have declined sharply, bringing the overall annual volume to just 82% of the previous year's level.

Between 1990 and 1997 only in one import category the total volume of imports has become significantly higher: these were timber and wood products (including furniture). In 1997 Russia imported 2.4 times more timber than in 1990, or 13 times more than in 1993. The other two import categories that were constantly growing in the last few years were food items (in 1997 level of imports was equal to 82% of the 1990 level and 1.9 times higher than in 1993) and chemicals (89% of 1990 level and 392% of 1993). Between 1993 and 1997 Russian imports of machinery and metals (including precious metals) also increased significantly (by respectively 1.7 and 1.9 times), however in current dollars these amounted to only half of 1990 volumes.

Russia's major non-CIS foreign trade partners in the post-Soviet period have included Germany, USA, Italy, the Netherlands and China (Table 3.2). While Germany's share in Russian foreign trade turnover

Table 3.2   Russia's Major Non-CIS Foreign Trade Partners

a) Shares in exports (%)

	1990	1991	1992	1993	1994	1995	1996	1997
Total	100.0	100.0	100.0	100.0	100.0	100.0	100.0	100.0
Germany	10.1	20.3	14.0	11.5	12.0	9.2	9.9	9.4
USA	1.3	1.5	1.8	4.5	6.7	6.9	7.1	6.8
Switzerland	0.5	2.7	2.1	3.6	7.0	5.4	5.2	5.1
China	2.0	3.3	6.8	6.9	5.5	5.2	6.6	5.7
Italy	5.2	6.2	7.0	5.9	5.6	5.2	3.9	5.1
Japan	3.4	4.6	4.0	4.5	5.3	5.5	4.7	4.5
Netherlands	4.6	5.4	5.4	2.2	4.7	4.9	4.6	6.5
UK	4.5	2.8	5.5	7.6	8.0	4.7	4.5	4.1
Finland	4.3	4.0	3.8	3.1	3.6	3.6	3.7	4.0
Other	54.5	37.9	49.7	50.2	41.6	49.3	49.8	48.9

b) Shares in imports (%)

	1990	1991	1992	1993	1994	1995	1996	1997
Total	100.0	100.0	100.0	100.0	100.0	100.0	100.0	100.0
Germany	10.5	17.8	19.0	19.2	20.0	19.6	16.4	11.9
USA	4.6	7.6	7.8	8.6	7.3	8.0	9.2	7.3
Finland	3.8	1.9	3.4	2.7	5.7	6.2	5.3	3.4
Italy	3.6	5.4	8.3	4.1	5.6	5.6	7.4	4.7
Netherlands	0.7	1.5	1.1	1.6	5.7	5.0	3.2	2.2
Poland	8.4	4.0	3.7	2.0	3.3	4.0	2.9	2.4
UK	4.1	4.0	1.6	2.4	3.2	3.3	3.6	2.7
France	2.4	3.3	3.6	3.4	3.5	3.2	4.0	2.9
Other	61.9	54.5	51.5	56.0	45.6	45.2	48.1	62.6

c) Shares in foreign trade turnover

	1990	1991	1992	1993	1994	1995	1996	1997
Total	100.0	100.0	100.0	100.0	100.0	100.0	100.0	100.0
Germany	10.3	19.3	13.9	14.4	13.7	12.7	11.9	10.5
USA	2.8	4.0	4.6	6.0	6.8	7.0	7.7	7.0
Italy	4.5	5.9	7.0	5.3	5.3	5.2	5.0	4.9
Netherlands	2.8	3.8	4.1	2.0	4.9	4.9	4.2	4.6
Finland	4.1	3.2	3.6	2.9	4.5	4.5	4.2	3.7
China	2.2	3.6	5.9	7.6	4.7	4.3	5.6	4.2
Switzerland	1.3	2.4	1.8	3.2	5.2	4.3	4.1	3.2
UK	4.3	3.3	3.7	5.6	5.6	4.2	4.2	3.5
Other	67.8	54.6	55.4	53.0	49.4	53.0	53.2	58.4

NOTES:
Sourced and calculated from:
Rossiiskii statisticheskii ezhegodnik. 1995, Moscow: Goskomstat, 1995, pp.430–1; *Vneshnie ekonomicheskie svyazi SSSR i Sodruzhestva Nezavisimykh Gosudarstv v 1991 g.*, Moscow 1992, pp.152–3; *Sotsial'no-ekonomicheskoe polozhenie Rossii. 1995 g.*, Moscow: Goskomstat, 1996, pp.142, 144; *Rossiya v tsifrakh. 1996*, Moscow: Goskomstat, 1996, pp.142–4; *Rossiiskii statisticheskii ezhegodnik. 1997*, Moscow: Goskomstat, 1997, pp.577–8; *Rossiiskii statisticheskii ezhegodnik. 1998*, Moscow: Goskomstat, 1998, pp.745–6.

peaked in 1991 and has been falling ever since, the volume of Russian–US trade has been continuously rising up to 1996. With the exception of Germany, which had a share of more than 10%, the shares of all other countries in Russian foreign trade turnover were rather small. In general, Russia's foreign trade in the 1990s has been characterised by a high degree of geographic diversification.

In the post-communist period the balance of Russian foreign trade with non-CIS countries has been consistently positive; moreover, between 1993 and 1996 it was steadily growing. However, the dynamics of Russia's trade with its former Soviet counterparts have been quite different: since the collapse of the USSR the foreign trade balance has been falling and in the mid-1990s it even went into the red. This was mainly due to a significant increase in Russian imports from CIS countries. While exports to the CIS between 1992 and 1997 increased 1.5 times from US$11 billion to US$18 billion, imports in the same period tripled from less than US$6 billion in 1992 to US$17.6 billion in 1997 (Table 3.3a). The 1998 financial crisis led to a reversal of this trend leading to a fall in Russian exports to the CIS by 19% and imports from the CIS by 22% (Table 3.3).

3.2 Russia's trade with the Commonwealth of Independent States

After the Soviet Union collapsed there was a remarkable change in the structure of Russian exports to the CIS states. When the USSR was still in existence and the Soviet economy was centrally managed, Russia was one of the main suppliers of machinery and other manufactured goods to the other Soviet republics. The share of machinery in Russian exports was about one-third in the early 1990s. When the USSR disintegrated and the former Soviet economy was largely decentralised, the ex-Soviet republics were no longer bound by the necessity of buying exclusively (or mostly) Russian-made goods. That led to a rapid re-orientation of their trade preferences. As a result, Russian-manufactured commodities were finding less and less demand in the ex-Soviet markets.[7] Between 1990 and 1997 the share of machinery in Russian exports to the CIS fell almost twice from 35% to 19.5%. In 1990–97 the share of metals declined 1.5 times from 12.1% to 7.8% while the share of textiles dropped more than 5 times from 9.9% to just 1.9%. During the same period the share of minerals quadrupled to 54% in 1997 (Table 3.3b). In the mid-1990s Russia was the major supplier of raw materials and energy resources to almost all of the former Soviet republics.

Table 3.3   Dynamics and Structure of Russian Foreign Trade[a] with CIS States

a) Annual volumes of Russian exports[b]

	1988	1990	1991	1992	1993	1994	1995	1996	1997	1998[c]
Exports	61 402	67 344	124 056	11 229	15 349	14 541	15 489	17 624	18 298	14 900
Imports	62 068	60 736	95 896	5 987	11 497	13 551	16 833	19 703	17 652	13 700
Balance	−666	6 608	28 160	5 242	3 852	990	−1 344	−2 079	646	1 200

b) Structure of exports (%)

	1990	1991	1994	1995	1996	1997
Total exports	100.0	100.0	100.0	100.0	100.0	100.0
Machinery	35.0	30.5	17.3	18.4	18.5	19.5
Minerals	12.5	15.5	52.7	50.3	52.8	53.6
Chemicals	12.1	11.4	9.6	11.7	9.5	9.1
Metals	12.1	11.3	8.7	8.9	9.2	7.8
Timber	4.9	5.5	3.2	3.8	3.3	2.5
Textiles	9.9	13.7	2.9	2.3	1.8	1.9
Food and agricultural raw materials	3.8	2.5	3.7	2.8	3.2	3.6
Other	9.6	9.6	1.9	1.8	1.7	2.0

c) Structure of imports (%)

	1990	1991	1994	1995	1996	1997
Total imports	100.0	100.0	100.0	100.0	100.0	100.0
Food and agricultural raw materials	23.7	27.2	20.1	25.4	26.1	22.6
Machinery	30.5	24.6	28.6	21.8	19.8	24.1
Metals	11.1	12.2	14.4	16.7	17.9	14.2
Minerals	3.5	3.8	16.5	14.9	14.5	14.0
Chemicals	8.2	7.6	7.1	9.5	11.4	10.6
Textiles	16.4	18.4	8.7	7.6	5.8	8.1
Timber	1.0	1.3	0.8	0.9	1.1	1.5
Other	5.4	4.9	3.8	3.2	3.4	4.9

NOTES:
[a] Data for 1992–98 includes estimates of "unorganised" ("shuttle") trade.
[b] Data for 1988–91 in millions current roubles; for 1992–98 in millions current US dollars.
[c] Preliminary data.

Sourced and calculated from:
Rossiiskii statisticheskii ezhegodnik. 1994, Moscow: Goskomstat, 1994, p.423; *Rossiiskii statisticheskii ezhegodnik. 1995*, Moscow: Goskomstat, 1995, p.437; *Rossiiskii statisticheskii ezhegodnik 1996*, Moscow: Goskomstat 1996, pp.345–6; *Sodruzhestvo Nezavisimykh Gosudarstv v 1995 godu. Kratkii spravochnik*, Moscow: Statkom SNG, January 1995, pp.23, 101, 103, 107; *Sotsial'no-ekonomicheskoe polozhenie Rossii, yanvar'-iyun' 1996 g.*, Moscow: Goskomstat, 1996, p.65; *Rossiya v tsifrakh. 1996*, Moscow: Goskomstat, 1996, pp.141, 144; *Sotsial'no-ekonomicheskoe polozhenie Rossii, yanvar' 1997 g.*, Moscow: Goskomstat, 1997, p.76; *Sodruzhestvo Nezavisimykh Gosudarstv v 1996 godu*, Moscow: Statkom SNG, yanvar' 1997, pp.100–1, 106–7, 114–5; *Narodnoe khozyaistvo Rossiiskoi Federatsii. 1992*, Moscow: Goskomstat, 1992, pp.32–3; *Rossiiskaya Federatsiya v 1992 godu*, Moscow: Goskomstat, 1993, pp.38–9; *Sotsial'no-ekonomicheskoe polozhenie Rossii, yanvar' 1998 g.*, Moscow: Goskomstat, 1998, pp.96–111; *Rossiiskii statisticheskii ezhegodnik. 1997*, Moscow: Goskomstat, 1997, pp.577–8, 580–1; *Sodruzhestvo Nezavisimykh Gosudarstv v 1997 godu. Kratkii spravochnik*, Moscow: Statkom SNG, 1998, pp.99, 107; *Rossiiskii statisticheskii ezhegodnik. 1998*, Moscow: Goskomstat, 1998, pp.743–9; *Sotsial'no-ekonomicheskoe polozhenie Rossii, yanvar' 1999 g.*, Moscow: Goskomstat, 1999, p.137.

The changes in the structure of Russian imports from the CIS were less dramatic. Food and agricultural produce was the main group of commodities that Russia was importing from the CIS; between 1990 and 1997 the share of these imports has been stable at 23–27% (Table 3.3c). Imports of machinery and textiles from the CIS to Russia fell, while those of metals, minerals and chemicals increased. On the whole, Russia has been trading with the CIS less in manufactured goods and more in raw materials and agricultural produce.

The bulk of Russian trade with the CIS was taking place with just three post-Soviet states: Belarus, Kazakhstan and Ukraine. These countries had a combined share of 86.5% in 1997 Russian exports to the CIS and of 80.7% in imports from the CIS in the same year. This was higher than the 1990 level when these countries together accounted for 70% of Russian exports to the CIS and 67% of imports from the Commonwealth (Tables 3.4a and 3.4b). In contradiction to common perceptions, at least among Russians, in 1988–90 Russia had positive trade balances only with the Central Asian states and Ukraine. All the other republics in value terms were exporting more to Russia than they were receiving from it.

In 1997 this situation has changed, but not dramatically. With most of the ex-Soviet states Russia's trade was either in small surplus or in small deficit. The only exceptions were Moldova, which was exporting twice more to Russia than importing from it, and Ukraine. Between 1990 and 1994 Ukraine was having a negative trade balance with Russia, its major supplier of oil and gas. However, in 1995–96 the trend changed following a dramatic increase of food and machinery exports from Ukraine to Russia. In 1997, after Russia had imposed stricter customs controls and introduced protectionist measures against imports of some commodities which were traditionally imported from Ukraine (particularly spirits and wine), Ukrainian trade balance with Russia was back to negative figures, in fact largest in the last decade.

Table 3.5 gives a clear indication of the existing levels of dependency on the CIS and Russian markets in foreign trade of the ex-Soviet states. Among the CIS states Russia was the least dependent on trade with other ex-Soviet republics during the first half of the 1990s. At the same time in countries like Belarus, Kazakhstan, Kyrgyzstan and Moldova, about two-thirds of the total volume of export–import operations were made within the former Soviet Union (Table 3.5a). In the 1990s Russia remained an important trade partner for most of the CIS states. In 1997 it was still the main export destination for all of the ex-Soviet republics with the exception of Azerbaijan, Tajikistan and Turkmenistan.

Table 3.4   Geographical Distribution of Russia's Trade with CIS

a) *Export destinations (%)*

	1988	1990	1991	1992	1993	1994	1995	1996	1997
All exports	100.0	100.0	100.0	100.0	100.0	100.0	100.0	100.0	100.0
Azerbaijan	3.6	3.4	4.0	2.4	1.2	1.2	0.6	1.0	1.3
Armenia	2.6	2.6	3.4	1.1	0.5	1.1	0.9	0.7	0.4
Belarus	14.1	14.1	14.0	14.5	15.9	21.8	20.5	21.4	27.7
Georgia	4.3	4.0	4.1	1.1	0.3	0.4	0.3	0.6	0.8
Kazakhstan	14.1	13.6	13.9	24.9	17.2	15.3	18.5	16.4	14.9
Kyrgyzstan	2.1	2.3	2.1	1.9	1.5	0.7	0.7	1.0	1.0
Moldova	3.8	3.7	3.5	2.9	2.9	3.8	2.8	2.6	2.2
Tajikistan	2.2	2.2	2.1	1.3	0.7	1.0	1.3	0.9	0.5
Turkmenistan	1.9	1.9	1.8	2.2	1.4	0.8	0.6	0.6	1.4
Uzbekistan	9.3	8.8	9.2	7.7	5.3	5.8	5.7	6.8	5.9
Ukraine	42.0	43.3	42.0	40.0	53.1	48.0	47.9	48.0	43.9

b) *Sources of imports (%)*

	1988	1990	1991	1992	1993	1994	1995	1996	1997
All imports	100.0	100.0	100.0	100.0	100.0	100.0	100.0	100.0	100.0
Azerbaijan	6.2	6.1	6.6	3.4	2.1	1.4	0.8	0.9	1.7
Armenia	3.7	3.1	2.6	0.8	0.2	0.5	0.6	0.4	0.4
Belarus	17.0	16.4	12.9	15.4	22.8	20.3	14.5	18.2	30.6
Georgia	5.2	6.0	3.6	0.5	0.3	0.5	0.4	0.4	1.1
Kazakhstan	8.0	7.2	11.8	24.1	16.4	19.4	20.4	20.2	20.4
Kyrgyzstan	1.4	1.5	2.5	1.6	1.3	1.0	0.8	0.9	1.1
Moldova	5.3	5.8	5.2	2.7	1.3	4.6	4.7	5.5	6.0
Tajikistan	1.5	1.9	1.9	0.8	0.4	0.9	1.2	0.6	0.6
Turkmenistan	1.9	2.1	3.9	2.3	1.0	0.6	0.8	0.8	1.4
Uzbekistan	7.7	8.0	12.9	3.7	11.9	8.3	6.6	4.3	7.0
Ukraine	42.1	41.8	35.8	44.7	42.3	42.7	49.2	47.8	29.7

c) *Russia's exports as % of imports from CIS states (imports = 100)*

	1988	1990	1991	1992	1993	1994	1995	1996	1997
All CIS	98.9	110.9	129.4	186.7	133.0	109.6	93.4	96.6	117.8
Azerbaijan	57.5	61.0	77.5	131.8	76.0	97.8	70.4	107.3	90.1
Armenia	69.5	96.1	171.5	257.2	333.7	230.2	148.4	169.0	117.8
Belarus	82.1	95.3	140.4	175.8	92.8	117.8	131.7	113.6	106.6
Georgia	81.8	74.7	144.9	410.9	132.8	85.3	74.0	144.9	85.7
Kazakhstan	174.4	208.8	151.6	192.9	139.5	86.7	84.9	78.4	86.0
Kyrgyzstan	148.3	169.4	106.0	221.7	153.5	84.1	91.1	107.3	107.1
Moldova	70.9	69.8	86.0	200.5	296.7	90.4	54.8	45.7	43.2
Tajikistan	145.1	127.7	141.5	302.6	232.7	125.9	99.7	144.9	98.2
Turkmenistan	99.0	99.8	58.2	178.6	186.3	147.9	79.9	72.4	117.8
Uzbekistan	119.5	121.8	92.1	388.5	59.3	77.6	81.2	152.7	99.3
Ukraine	98.7	114.9	151.7	167.0	167.0	123.2	91.0	97.0	174.1

Sources: See Table 3.3.

In the same year Russia also had the largest share in imports of majority of member-states of the CIS, except the three Transcaucasian countries and the Central Asian states of Tajikistan[8] and Turkmenistan (Table 3.5b).

Table 3.5   Foreign Trade Orientation of the CIS States

a) Share of CIS in the gross volume of exports and imports (%)

	Exports				Imports			
	1994	1995	1996	1997	1994	1995	1996	1997
Azerbaijan	43	40	54	47	62	34	34	44
Armenia	73	62	41	41	52	50	34	34
Belarus	59	62	66	73	68	66	66	68
Georgia	75	63	65	55	82	41	39	36
Kazakhstan	58	53	56	45	60	69	71	54
Kyrgyzstan	66	66	80	53	66	68	56	62
Moldova	72	63	68	73	72	68	61	52
Russia	21	18	18	19	27	29	31	26
Tajikistan	23	34	44	40	42	60	59	63
Turkmenistan	77	49	69	64	47	55	28	54
Uzbekistan	62	39	23	...	54	41	32	...
Ukraine	55	52	44	39	73	63	43	59

b) Share of Russia in the gross volume of exports and imports (%)

	Exports				Imports			
	1994	1995	1996	1997	1994	1995	1996	1997
Azerbaijan	22	18	20	21	22	13	15	21
Armenia	40	33	32	30	37	20	16	16
Belarus	46	44	52	63	66	53	53	54
Georgia	...	37	29	28	12	18	20	15
Kazakhstan	44	42	45	34	49	49	56	46
Kyrgyzstan	17	26	25	16	28	22	23	29
Moldova	51	48	53	62	48	33	28	28
Tajikistan	11	13	10	8	16	17	11	15
Turkmenistan	2	2	9	...	12	10	12	11
Uzbekistan	29	19	14	...	34	26	20	...
Ukraine	40	43	35	26	64	51	39	47

Sourced and calculated from:
Sodruzhestvo Nezavisimykh Gosudarstv v 1994 godu. Statisticheskii ezhegodnik, Moscow: Statkom SNG, 1995, pp.56–7; *Sodruzhestvo Nezavisimykh Gosudarstv v 1995 godu. Statisticheskii ezhegodnik*, Moscow: Statkom SNG, 1996, pp.64–5; *Sodruzhestvo Nezavisimykh Gosudarstv v 1996 godu. Statisticheskii spravochnik*, Moscow: Statkom SNG, yanvar' 1997, pp.47–8, 97–101; *Sodruzhestvo Nezavisimykh Gosudarstv v 1996 godu. Statisticheskii ezhegodnik*. Moscow: Statkom SNG, 1997, pp.66–7; *Sodruzhestvo Nezavisimykh Gosudarstv v 1997 godu. Kratkii spravochnik*, Moscow: Statkom SNG, 1998, pp.89, 92–3.

Another important feature of trade dynamics between the ex-Soviet states in the 1990s was the constantly falling share of the CIS in their export–import operations. Between 1990 and 1997 only Belarus, Moldova and Tajikistan had retained (or increased) the shares of their exports to CIS. In the rest of the republics this share in 1997 was lower than in 1990, particularly in Armenia, Ukraine and Uzbekistan. Imports had a similar pattern. During the 1990s only in five CIS member-states the share of imports from the Commonwealth either remained unchanged or had grown (Belarus, Russia, Kyrgyzstan, Tajikistan and Turkmenistan).

To summarise, exports of raw materials and food imports were the two dominant features in the structure of post-Soviet Russia's foreign. In essence, Russia has been trading off its minerals and oil for food supplies. Exports of machinery and other high-tech products have fallen dramatically, particularly because of the general economic crisis crippling many Russian industrial enterprises, and the loss of the traditional markets for these commodities in Central and Eastern Europe and within the USSR. On the other hand, the rapidly falling agricultural production in Russia led to a significant increase in the local demand for imported food, mainly in the food-deficit areas of Russia.

Post-Soviet Russian foreign trade has mainly been oriented towards Western Europe (Germany), the US, the former USSR (the CIS) and China. Geographically Russian foreign trade remained highly diversified; in contrast to the majority of other CIS states, the larger part of this trade has been taking place outside the borders of the former Soviet Union. However, Russia has retained a prominent position in the trade preferences of all the ex-Soviet republics and for most of these it has remained also the main supplier of minerals and energy carriers, which gives Russia an important lever of economic pressure within the CIS. On a number of occasions Russian leaders have made attempts, albeit often unsuccessful, to use this lever as a tool in order to achieve political ends (notably in relations with Ukraine, Georgia and Armenia). This, however, pushed the ex-Soviet states to diversify their foreign trade and economic relations in order to lower the level of their dependency on Russia. The result has been a significant decline in the Russian share in the foreign trade of many of these countries in the 1990s. For instance, between 1994 and 1997 Ukraine decreased its dependency on Russian imports from 64% to 47%, Moldova – from 48% to 28%, Armenia – from 37% to 16%, etc. (Table 3.5b).

3.3   Regional patterns of foreign trade

The changes taking place in the structure of Russian foreign trade during the post-communist period had a direct impact on the regional distribution of foreign trade operations within Russia.[9] The increased share of raw materials in Russia's exports raised the importance of mining regions. For example, Western Siberia – Russia's major oil- and gas-producing region – more than doubled its share in Russian exports from 24% in 1990 to 59% in 1995 (Table 3.6a). This astonishing change was mainly the result of falls in the export shares of "manufacturing" regions (North-West, Central, Volga and the Urals) rather than of growth in the volume of oil and gas exports. In 1998, however, this trend was reversed when Western Siberia accounted for less than 20% of Russia's total exports.[10]

Russia's imports have traditionally been more diversified between the regions than its exports. In 1990 Moscow and the neighbouring areas within the Central economic region received one-third of Russia's gross imports. In the following years along with the decentralisation of foreign trade, however, the distribution of imports became more even. By 1993 the share of Central region had fallen 2.5 times to 12%, while the Volga region had become the largest gross importer among the Russian regions. Other large importers included the Urals, Western Siberia and the Central region (Table 3.6b). According to the recent official data,[11] in 1997 this situation has again changed dramatically. In that year the Central region has regained its former leading position as the major Russian regional importer, accounting for over 46% of all Russian imports. The other significant importing areas were North-West, Western Siberia and the Urals.

Making comparisons between the regions is rather complicated because of the uneven distribution of the population. Therefore, in Tables 3.6c and 3.6d we have presented the per capita dynamics of foreign trade at the regional level. In these tables we have taken the average per capita level of exports and imports for all Russia as a base (100). As Table 3.6c demonstrates, in per capita terms Western Siberia during the 1990s had the highest per capita levels of exports among all Russian regions: between 1.9 and 5.8 times higher than the national average level. By 1997 only two other regions (Central and Eastern Siberia) had per capita levels of exports higher than the Russian average. At the same time, per capita exports from regions like the North Caucasus, North-West, Central and Volgo-Vyatka made up only a fraction of the Russian average.

Table 3.6   Shares of Russian Economic Regions in Foreign Trade, 1990–97

a) Shares of economic regions in all-Russia exports (%)

	1990	1991	1992	1993	1994	1995	1997
Northern	9.0	8.4	5.8	9.6	9.2	4.8	5.8
North-West	4.4	4.3	2.6	2.4	2.3	1.1	4.4
Central	12.0	11.4	6.6	7.7	7.5	4.2	34.5
Volgo-Vyatka	3.9	4.4	2.7	3.1	2.8	1.4	1.7
Central ChernoZem	3.1	2.8	3.7	4.3	5.0	2.6	2.8
Volga	13.3	12.0	24.5	17.8	13.1	5.6	6.7
North Caucasus	4.6	5.1	2.7	2.2	1.7	0.9	1.8
Urals	11.5	12.1	17.2	14.6	17.5	9.6	12.2
West Siberia	24.2	24.8	20.0	22.4	26.2	59.2	19.1
East Siberia	8.0	8.6	8.1	9.2	8.0	6.8	8.0
Far East	5.3	5.4	5.5	6.3	6.1	3.2	2.5
Kaliningrad	0.8	0.9	0.7	0.4	0.6	0.4	0.4
All RF	100.0	100.0	100.0	100.0	100.0	100.0	100.0

b) Shares of economic regions in all-Russia imports (%)

	1990	1991	1992	1993	1997
Northern	3.5	6.7	7.0	7.2	2.4
North-West	11.7	7.2	2.9	1.7	9.6
Central	32.5	27.1	15.2	11.8	46.4
Volgo-Vyatka	3.8	4.7	4.2	3.9	1.8
Central ChernoZem	3.4	3.3	9.4	6.0	2.3
Volga	8.4	11.2	19.9	17.9	5.7
North Caucasus	8.0	6.4	3.4	6.5	5.8
Urals	8.6	10.3	10.0	13.6	7.0
West Siberia	8.6	8.4	10.9	13.2	8.2
East Siberia	5.1	7.5	10.1	9.3	4.0
Far East	5.9	6.6	6.2	8.0	4.4
Kaliningrad	0.6	0.6	0.8	0.8	2.5
All RF	100.0	100.0	100.0	100.0	100.0

c) Per capita shares in exports (all-Russia average = 100)

	1990	1991	1992	1993	1994	1995	1997
Northern	215.9	202.5	141.8	236.5	228.7	121.0	146.8
North-West	78.6	76.8	46.5	44.3	42.7	19.5	81.5
Central	58.2	55.5	32.4	38.0	37.1	21.0	170.8
Volgo-Vyatka	68.8	76.7	47.5	54.5	51.1	25.1	30.3
Central ChernoZem	59.5	53.0	71.0	80.9	94.8	49.8	52.9
Volga	118.9	107.1	217.9	157.4	115.2	49.1	58.5
North Caucasus	40.1	44.3	23.2	18.7	14.4	7.9	15.3
Urals	83.9	88.4	124.9	106.1	126.6	69.1	88.2
West Siberia	237.0	243.0	196.2	219.3	256.4	578.6	186.6
East Siberia	129.4	138.4	130.4	148.5	129.1	110.5	128.8
Far East	97.1	98.9	101.8	118.4	117.4	63.2	50.2
Kaliningrad	131.1	143.0	108.0	66.0	98.3	63.5	63.7
All RF	100.0	100.0	100.0	100.0	100.0	100.0	100.0

Table 3.6 *continued*

d) *Per capita shares in imports (all-Russia average = 100)*

	1990	1991	1992	1993	1997
Northern	83.1	163.0	169.4	176.3	60.4
North-West	209.3	129.7	51.9	31.2	176.4
Central	158.2	132.4	74.4	58.0	229.9
Volgo-Vyatka	65.8	82.2	73.3	68.6	31.0
Central ChernoZem	65.6	64.0	179.3	114.8	42.6
Volga	74.9	100.6	177.4	158.7	49.8
North Caucasus	69.6	55.2	29.1	55.6	48.0
Urals	62.6	74.8	72.8	98.7	50.2
West Siberia	84.2	82.1	106.5	129.4	79.8
East Siberia	82.6	120.0	163.1	149.8	65.3
Far East	108.4	121.9	116.3	152.2	88.4
Kaliningrad	102.5	94.4	140.1	124.9	398.5
All RF	100.0	100.0	100.0	100.0	100.0

Sourced and calculated from:
Rossiiskii statisticheskii ezhegodnik. 1995, Moscow: Goskomstat, 1995, pp.869–72; *Rossiiskii statisticheskii ezhegodnik. 1996*, Moscow: Goskomstat, 1996, pp.898–903; *Regiony Rossii. 1998*, Vol.2, Moscow: Goskomstat, 1998, pp.782–3.

Table 3.6 also shows that the differences in export potential between the various Russian regions started to grow dramatically after the collapse of the Soviet Union, following the declining importance of manufacturing goods in exports and the rising share of minerals in the export structure of Russian foreign trade. By the mid-1990s these differences had already been transformed into huge disproportions. For instance, while in 1990 per capita exports from the North Caucasus were 6 times less than that from Western Siberia, in 1995 these exports were already 73 times lower! In 1997 this situation became balanced when the gap between the two economic regions decreased to 12 times. Such disproportions formed the basis for growing political tensions between the regions, particularly when resource-rich regions started to object more and more insistently to the practice of redistributing the revenue from their exports between poorer regions. By the mid-1990s this imbalanced regional structure of Russian exports had become one of the most important factors undermining the federal basis of the Russian state.

Developments in regional per capita distribution of Russian imports were less critical. The difference in the level of import dependency on a per capita basis between the Russian regions remained unchanged in 1990–93 and did not exceed the factor of 3. After 1991, however, some important changes in per capita import distribution took place. In 1990, when Russia was still under the Soviet system of centralised management, the two largest cities – Moscow and Leningrad – and the neighbouring areas were receiving in per capita terms 1.6 and 2.1 times more imported goods than Russia on average (Table 3.6d). Two other food-deficit regions – the Far East and Kaliningrad – were importing at approximately the national average level, while all the remaining regions had per capita imports 17–35% below the national average. By 1993 the situation had changed. The largest per capita exporters (North, Western and Eastern Siberia) had also become the largest per capita importers. Levels of imports in the Far East and Kaliningrad remained high, but per capita imports to the Central region (including Moscow) and the North-West (including Leningrad/St Petersburg) had experienced large falls compared to the national average. Recently published data on regional distribution of Russian imports in 1997 has shown that by that year per capita import levels in Russian regions largely returned to pre-reform patterns. Central and North-West regions, along with Kaliningrad, were importing significantly larger volumes per head of their population that the rest of Russia. On the other hand, the least dependent on imports on a per capita basis were Central ChernoZem and Volgo-Vyatka regions.

The increased role played by minerals in the product structure of Russian exports was also reflected in the structure of regional exports (Table 3.7a). In 1994 minerals formed the major export item in the majority of regions. Even those regions without significant deposits of natural resources on their territory were exporting (or, rather, re-exporting) large volumes of minerals. Manufactured goods had significant shares in exports from those areas with a traditional manufacturing specialisation, while exports of agricultural products (mainly fish) were prominent in the Far East and Kaliningrad.

In 1994 the larger part of Russian exports of minerals came from Western and Eastern Siberia, the Urals and the North. Exports of manufactured goods mainly came from the Volga and Central regions, and the Urals, while exports of agricultural products came from the major fishing regions of the Far East and the North (Table 3.7b). The Central region also exported two-thirds of the gross volume of all other export items, which predominantly were exports of services from Moscow.

As one would expect, food and agricultural products were an important category of imports in the food-deficit areas of Russia (the Far East, Central and North-West regions, Kaliningrad), as well as in some major agricultural regions (Central Chernozem, North Caucasus). While the

Table 3.7 Structure of Foreign Trade by Economic Region

a) Regional export specialisation, 1994 (% to regional total)

	Food and agriculture	Minerals	Manufactured goods	Other	Total exports
Northern	10.7	77.5	11.6	0.2	100.0
North West	2.1	37.9	57.2	2.9	100.0
Central	2.3	37.5	40.2	20.0	100.0
Volgo-Vyatka	0.4	50.5	45.9	3.2	100.0
Central ChernoZem	0.6	86.2	12.8	0.5	100.0
Volga	2.2	27.7	69.4	0.7	100.0
North Caucasus	8.2	36.6	52.3	2.9	100.0
Urals	0.4	72.7	25.7	1.2	100.0
West Siberia	0.1	92.4	6.9	0.6	100.0
East Siberia	0.6	86.5	12.7	0.2	100.0
Far East	45.6	50.1	3.5	0.8	100.0
Kaliningrad	37.4	13.5	44.3	4.8	100.0
All RF	4.8	67.8	25.1	2.3	100.0

b) Shares in Russian total exports, 1994 (%)

	Food and agriculture	Minerals	Manufactured goods	Other
Northern	20.4	10.6	4.3	0.8
North West	1.0	1.3	5.3	2.9
Central	3.6	4.2	12.1	65.5
Volgo-Vyatka	0.3	2.1	5.1	3.9
Central ChernoZem	0.6	6.4	2.6	1.0
Volga	5.9	5.3	36.1	4.2
North Caucasus	2.9	0.9	3.6	2.2
Urals	1.4	18.7	17.9	8.9
West Siberia	0.6	35.7	7.2	6.4
East Siberia	1.0	10.2	4.0	0.8
Far East	57.6	4.5	0.8	2.2
Kaliningrad	4.7	0.1	1.1	1.3
All RF	100.0	100.0	100.0	100.0

Table 3.7 *continued*

c) Regional import specialisation, 1993 (% to regional total)

	Food and agriculture	Minerals	Manufactured goods	Other	Total imports
Northern	19.0	14.1	59.0	7.9	100.0
North West	29.8	3.9	61.5	4.9	100.0
Central	34.4	6.2	45.6	13.7	100.0
Volgo-Vyatka	22.1	2.3	66.2	9.4	100.0
Central ChernoZem	30.3	3.7	56.9	9.1	100.0
Volga	22.4	7.2	65.8	4.7	100.0
North Caucasus	27.6	5.7	43.8	22.8	100.0
Urals	17.9	5.3	69.0	7.8	100.0
West Siberia	11.5	17.8	61.4	9.2	100.0
East Siberia	18.8	23.7	42.4	15.1	100.0
Far East	41.8	2.6	45.4	10.2	100.0
Kaliningrad	32.9	33.5	23.8	9.8	100.0
All RF	23.8	9.5	56.6	10.1	100.0

d) Shares in Russian total imports, 1993 (%)

	Food and agriculture	Minerals	Manufactured goods	Other
Northern	5.7	10.6	7.5	5.6
North West	2.2	0.7	1.9	0.8
Central	17.1	7.7	9.5	16.1
Volgo-Vyatka	3.6	1.0	4.6	3.6
Central ChernoZem	7.7	2.4	6.1	5.5
Volga	16.9	13.5	20.8	8.3
North Caucasus	7.6	3.9	5.1	14.8
Urals	10.2	7.5	16.6	10.5
West Siberia	6.4	24.7	14.3	12.1
East Siberia	7.4	23.2	7.0	13.9
Far East	14.2	2.2	6.5	8.1
Kaliningrad	1.1	2.7	0.3	0.7
All RF	100.0	100.0	100.0	100.0

Sourced and calculated from:
Rossiiskii statisticheskii ezhegodnik, 1995, Moscow: Goskomstat, 1995, pp.869–72; *Sravnitelnye pokazateli ekonomicheskogo polozheniya regionov Rossiiskoi Federatsii*, Moscow: Goskomstat, 1995, pp.288–95; *Ekonomicheskoe polozhenie regionov Rossiiskoi Federatsii*, Moscow: Goskomstat, 1994, pp.253–60.

former were mainly importing food products, the latter were importing ingredients necessary for agricultural production and live animals. In 1993 manufactured goods (including consumer goods) were the largest import category in all Russian regions with the sole exception of Kaliningrad (Table 3.7c).

Between one-third and a half of all Russian exports comes from four areas: Moscow, Samara, Tyumen' and Primorskii Krai (Table 3.8a). Moscow is the main exporter of services, Samara is the leader in exports of manufactured goods, Tyumen' is the principal exporter of Russian oil and gas, while Primorskii Krai accounts for the largest share of Russian exports of agricultural produce (fish).

On Map 3.1 we have presented volumes of exports by region in per capita terms. This is the more reliable data, which refers to 1994 and was published by Goskomstat.[12] In that year only one region had a level of exports of about 3.2 million current roubles per person or 9 times higher than an average for Russia. That was oil- and gas-producing area of Tyumen' in Western Siberia. Other Russian regions with high level of exports included Vologda, Samara and Lipetsk, where per capita figures were in the range between 1.09 million and 1.8 million roubles per person. Regions with medium levels of exports (between 414 thousand and 898 thousand roubles per capita) included most of Western and Eastern Siberia, the Russian North, Primorskii krai and Sakhalin in the Far East, and few manufacturing areas in European part of Russia. All other Russian regions had very low export levels,[13] while, according to Russian official statistics, in 1994 exports from ethnic republics in the North Caucasus and Tyva Republic in Eastern Siberia were close to zero.

Between one-third and a half of Russian imports goes to 8 major importing areas. In 1993 Tatarstan, Samara, Primorskii Krai and Moscow had the largest shares in imports of foodstuffs; significant shares of minerals imports were delivered to Kemerovo, Irkutsk, Tyumen' and Samara (mainly energy carriers and metals); while manufactured goods were imported in large quantities by Samara and Tyumen' (mainly machinery).

Per capita distribution of Russian imports between regions in 1993 is shown on Map 3.2. The pattern here is much more balanced than in the case of exports. Leading importing areas of Russia were either areas of concentration of Russia's primary industries (Tyumen' and Karelia), centres of manufacturing industry (Samara and Lipetsk) or main fishing regions (Kamchatka and Murmansk).[14] In all of these areas per capita levels of imports were between 110 thousand and 186 thousand

Table 3.8   Areas with Largest Shares in Russian Exports and Imports (% to Russian totals)

a) Leading exporting areas

	Food and agriculture	Structure of exports in 1994			Share in Russia's exports	
		Minerals	Manufactured goods	Other	1994	1997
Moscow	1.6	0.5	1.3	21.8	1.2	29.3
Samarsk. Obl.	4.2	2.0	27.5	0.0	8.5	2.5
Tyumensk. Obl.	0.0	28.3	0.1	0.3	19.2	13.5
Primorskii Krai	31.3	0.6	0.6	1.0	2.1	0.8
Subtotal	37.1	31.5	29.5	23.1	31.1	46.1

b) Leading importing areas

	Food and agriculture	Structure of imports in 1993			Share in Russia's imports	
		Minerals	Manufactured goods	Other	1993	1997
Moscow	3.7	0.5	2.9	10.0	3.6	38.5
Tatarstan Rep.	6.8	1.4	4.6	1.7	1.3	1.3
Samarsk. Obl.	5.6	8.7	11.8	2.2	9.1	2.4
Rostovsk. Obl.	1.0	0.2	0.6	7.3	1.3	1.5
Kemerovsk. Obl.	0.7	13.8	1.6	0.9	2.5	1.1
Tyumensk. Obl.	1.4	9.0	8.0	4.8	6.2	4.4
Krasnoyarskii Krai	2.0	1.0	3.3	12.5	3.7	1.6
Irkutsk. Obl.	2.5	10.3	3.1	0.8	3.4	1.3
Primorskii Krai	5.5	0.1	0.5	2.1	1.8	1.6
Subtotal	29.1	44.9	36.4	42.4	32.8	53.8

Sources: See Table 3.6.

Map 3.1   Regional Distribution of Exports in Russia in 1994 (per capita, thousand current roubles)

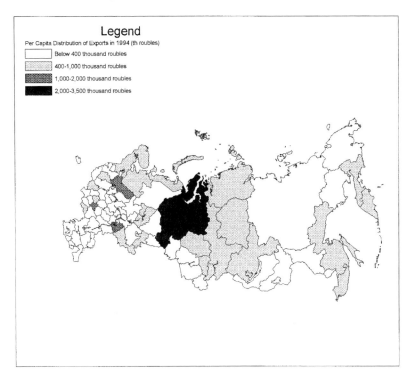

current roubles, or 2.5–4 times higher than the average Russian level. Areas with medium levels of imports were Far Eastern regions – Primorskii and Khabarovskii krais, and Sakhalin; other areas of Eastern and Western Siberia, the Russian North and few manufacturing regions in the European part of Russia. In the rest of Russia per capita imports were low (below 50 thousand roubles per person), while again, similar to export patterns, the lowest levels were recorded in Tyva and ethnic republics of the North Caucasus.

The existing regional distribution of Russian foreign trade flows means that those areas with a predominantly mining specialisation also have a leading role in exports of minerals, while the manufacturing regions dominate Russia's exports of manufactured goods (Tables 3.9a and 3.9b). However, the relation between exports of agricultural commodities and agricultural regions is not as simple. The

Map 3.2   Regional Distribution of Imports in Russia in 1993 (per capita, thousand current roubles)

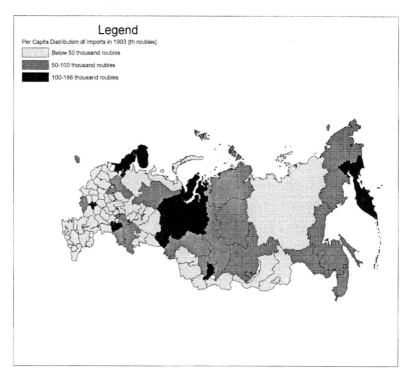

major part of Russian agricultural exports needs to be processed before exporting. That explains the fact that those regions producing agricultural goods have a significantly lower share in the gross exports of agricultural products than manufacturing regions (Table 3.9a).

The decentralisation and privatisation of Russian foreign trade that took place on a large scale during 1992, led to the central state's abandoning its former distributing and moderating role. In practical terms, this meant that those regions that had a higher exporting potential in the post-Soviet environment had more funds to spend on imports, than the regions with lower export levels. This is demonstrated clearly by the dynamics of imports by groups of regions presented in Tables 3.9c and 3.9d. While in 1993 mining and manufacturing regions had import levels generally higher than the Russian average, import dynamics in the agricultural group of regions were rather modest.

Table 3.9   Structure of Foreign Trade by Groups of Regions, 1993–94

a) Shares of groups of regions in total exports in 1994, %

	Food and agriculture	Minerals	Manufactured goods	Other
Mining regions	0.0	35.3	1.4	2.1
Manufacturing regions	6.0	4.8	29.3	0.9
Agricultural regions	1.2	2.6	2.6	1.4
All Russia	100.0	100.0	100.0	100.0

b) Ratio of per capita exports by group of regions to all-Russian average (latter = 100)

	Food and agriculture	Minerals	Manufactured goods	Other
Mining regions	0.0	711.7	29.0	41.9
Manufacturing regions	90.6	72.7	442.6	13.7
Agricultural regions	19.1	42.3	43.5	23.4
All Russia	100.0	100.0	100.0	100.0

c) Shares of groups of regions in total imports in 1993, %

	Food and agriculture	Minerals	Manufactured goods	Other
Mining regions	2.2	23.1	10.1	5.9
Manufacturing regions	9.6	9.3	14.1	5.8
Agricultural regions	6.9	3.1	5.6	7.4
All Russia	100.0	100.0	100.0	100.0

d) Ratio of per capita imports by group of regions to all-Russian average (latter = 100)

	Food and agriculture	Minerals	Manufactured goods	Other
Mining regions	43.7	465.3	202.8	118.5
Manufacturing regions	144.7	140.1	213.4	87.7
Agricultural regions	114.4	52.0	93.7	123.6
All Russia	100.0	100.0	100.0	100.0

NOTES:
Mining: Kemerovo, Tyumen' and Sakha only.
Manufacturing: St Petersburg, Samara and Khabarovsk only.
Agriculture: Belgorod, Krasnodar and Stavropol only.
Author's own calculations. For sources see Table 3.6.

One other important recent development in the area of Russian foreign trade warrants mentioning – the specifically post-Soviet phenomenon of "shuttle trade". Shuttle trade appeared in Russia on a mass scale immediately after the start of reforms in 1992 as a response from small businessmen to the rapidly changing and unstable economic environment. Price liberalisation led to a rapid depreciation of incomes for the majority of Russians. This, combined with galloping inflation, greatly increased the demand for cheaper consumer goods and foodstuffs. Another important factor in this connection was the disruption of the close economic ties between Russia and the other former Soviet republics, as well as within Russia itself, between its various regions and provinces.

In the situation of economic and legislative chaos that characterised the first months after the start of the reform in January 1992, differentiation in retail prices between the ex-Soviet republics, as well as between the Russian provinces, reached enormous levels. This situation prompted a massive increase in "shuttle trade" operations, whereby small traders (or their agents) bought products in other regions (republics) and then resold them locally with a certain profit margin. This type of primitive trade spread quickly across the nation, involving large numbers of people. Within a few months "shuttle trade" operations started to spread beyond the Russian borders and soon became one of the most popular forms of Russian foreign trade.

The underlying reason behind the rapid and massive growth of "shuttle trade" was the system of foreign trade taxation. While the trade operations of companies were subject to taxation and import duties, Russian legislation included a provision which allowed citizens to bring virtually unlimited quantities of goods into the country on an unlimited number of occasions per year, provided these goods conformed to the existing and very vague definition of "luggage". This meant that, given the high taxes on official imports, it was more profitable for a businessperson to buy a ticket abroad, pay for his/her overseas accommodation, purchase goods and bring them back as "luggage", rather than to import directly from a foreign wholesaler.

Another factor boosting the development of "shuttle trade" was the generally undeveloped nature of the Russian financial system. Many foreign companies and banks put little trust in letters of credit issued by Russian banks, while Russian legislation effectively prohibited businesses from opening accounts with foreign banks. Even these difficulties been overcome, the rate of interest that banks charged for their services was often too high for small businesses, while the need to pay transportation fees and customs duties made "official" foreign trade complicated, lengthy and unprofitable. But all of these difficulties were easily overcome by travelling person, dealing in cash, and bringing goods back for re-sale as "luggage".

While officially imported goods were registered with customs and thus automatically subject to taxation, goods that were imported through "shuttle trade" channels were in formal terms intended for private use and, therefore, their sale could easily be concealed from the taxation authorities.

According to various estimates, by the mid-1990s between 10 and 20 million Russian citizens were actively involved in "shuttle trade".[15] If one includes the other members of their families, then up to one-third of the Russian population was in one way or another dependent on income generated by "shuttle trade" business. The turnover of this business[16] was estimated at the level of US$10 billion in 1995 and between US$14 billion and US$20 billion in 1996.[17] If the latter figure is correct, then in 1996 about half of Russia's imports were brought into the country semi-legally and often duty-free. Moreover, it is highly likely that the taxes payable on the income received through the re-sale of these imported goods also went largely unpaid.

When the volume of "shuttle trade" reached enormous levels in 1993 the state reacted by officially limiting the quantities of various goods that could be imported by private citizens. New limits were imposed again in the following years until in August 1996 a Russian government decree stated that the value of duty-free goods that could be imported into Russia should not exceed US$1000 or 50 kilograms in weight.[18] Although that was twice as low as previous limits, it, nevertheless, failed to stop the spread of "shuttle trade" in Russia. The financial crisis that paralysed the Russian economy in August 1998 had led to a significant decline in the volumes of "shuttle trade". Continuing slide of rouble against US dollar made many of these trade operations unprofitable. In addition, measures that were taken by the Primakov government in late 1998 to limit the circulation of foreign currencies on the Russian market did not help small traders as well. It can be stated that by the end of 1998 "shuttle trade" has lost much of its earlier importance in Russian foreign trade operations.

To conclude, in the post-Soviet period Russian foreign trade has experienced a number of major structural changes. Firstly, it underwent mass privatisation and decentralisation. By the mid-1990s only arms exports and some gold, diamond, and oil and gas exports were still controlled by the state. Trade in all other commodities had passed over to private hands.

Secondly, privatisation of foreign trade significantly changed the pattern of regional distribution of revenue from foreign trade operations. While capital accumulation in the resource-rich (and top exporting) areas was increasing, all other areas of Russia were experiencing a constant and growing deficit in funds necessary to purchase goods abroad, be it foodstuffs, consumer goods or industrial intermediate goods. Often these goods had to be imported from richer areas in Russia at higher prices, which, in poorer areas, made the population's purchasing power even less. This situation stimulated the growth of political and economic tensions between the regions of the Russian Federation.

These changes in the structure of foreign trade also point out to the growing "Kuwaitization" of the Russian economy,[19] where the share of high value-added goods in the gross output was constantly falling, partly due to the collapse of traditional markets for Russian manufacturing exports in Eastern Europe and the former Soviet Union.

Thirdly, the privatisation of foreign trade helped to boost the development of the unofficial ("shadow") economy in Russia. It led to a mass spread of "shuttle trade" operations and consequent tax evasion in the retail trade, which became one of the major funding sources of the unofficial sector of the economy. Private foreign trade operations also provided the "shadow economy" with an important channel for covert transfers of funds across Russian borders. A series of measures taken by the Russian authorities aimed at limiting the negative consequences of this process did very little to stop the growth of corruption and the illegal capital formation which initially stemmed from the liberalisation of foreign trade.

And, fourthly, an important feature of the Russian foreign trade in the recent years was its growing trade diversion, which, however, had a rather negative strategic effect. As Peter Rutland explained, "it is important to distinguish between trade creation and trade diversion. The former contributes to economic growth; the latter just involves switching from one customer to another. Since 1991 Russia has seen more trade diversion than creation because the surge in exports to the West has coincided with a slump in trade with the other former Soviet republics and with the former Eastern European trading partners".[20]

During the 1990s Russia was actively seeking for new trade and economic partners, particularly those who will be willing to buy its manufacturing goods. This, however, proved to be an immensely difficult task. While some foreign buyers were interested in purchasing Russian armaments and military technologies, others – including ex-Soviet republics – were increasingly looking at Russia only as at a source of raw materials and energy supplies for their economies. This left very few grounds for optimism for Russian industrialists and forced them, along with local agricultural producers, to demand, more and more vocally, an active intervention from the state.

3.4   Capital flight: ways and volumes [21]

The issue of capital flight from Russia,[22] its origins, mechanisms and impact, has become a frequent theme of many publications and reports in recent years. Although a serious problem in itself, capital flight is also indicative of the general political and socio-economic processes that take place in the post-communist Russia. From that perspective capital flight might be viewed more as a consequence of these general developments than as a separate problem by itself. That means that any attempts to stop or limit capital flight would hardly be successful without eliminating these general factors that cause it. The latter include such major factors as the level of political stability in the society, development of taxation and economic management systems, investment legislation, property rights, and, above all, the question of the level of clarity in and the overall direction of general economic policies of the government. The fact that large amounts of capital are continuing to leave Russia is possibly the best indicator that business climate there is generally hostile to investments. We would expect that local businessmen would be the first to make use of opportunities in Russia if the investment climate were to change for the better. And at the same time it would be unrealistic to expect any breakthrough in foreign investments in Russia until the time when its local capital starts to return back. If now, almost five years after the start of the reform, that has not happened yet, probably means that Russia is following a wrong path in its attempt to reform.

While in the late Soviet period the problem of capital flight was hardly ever recognised officially, in the post-Soviet period its official interpretation has gone through a number of significant changes. It was in the first months after the collapse of the USSR that the problem of capital flight from Russia was officially raised. However, at that stage it was mainly linked to the activities of the Soviet Communist Party which, as it was officially claimed, has managed to transfer significant sums of money into secret accounts in foreign banks. However, these actions were extremely limited in their effects, which was mainly due to the fact that capital was exported from Russia through a number of complicated and generally covert ways.

Russian citizens and Russian businesses have no legal right to open accounts in foreign banks without special permission from a state body (bank, ministry). At the same time Russian commercial banks are not permitted to transfer abroad large amounts of money if that is not justified by a contract and/or has a permission (licence) from the Central Bank.[23] That means that for an attempt to export capital from Russia in a "civilised manner"[24] to be successful, Russians should have a foreign partner (or a Russian partner abroad). Such a requirement limits ways of exporting capital to areas where foreign activity is permitted in Russia, namely foreign trade and variety of investment projects (joint ventures, direct investments, shares in Russian companies, etc.). Due to complexities of registration and their openness to numerous bureaucratic controls, investment projects in the recent years were the least preferable option of exporting capital from Russia. That is also partly confirmed by the fact that the total volume of investments in Russia remains very low.[25]

The foreign trade became the major gateway for the capital flight from post-Soviet Russia. The dismantling of the Soviet system of centralised management of the economy in the first months of the start of the Russian reform led to a rapid privatisation of the area of foreign trade. Most of the former state-run trade agencies were privatised and a vast number of new trade companies were established. As early as by mid-1992 it was realised that through lifting of state controls over the country's foreign trade the Russian government deprived itself of one of the most important sources of hard currency revenues. With falling budget revenues the government attempted to re-establish its control over foreign trade through introduction of a variety of control, tax and licensing mechanisms in the area. These, however, failed to significantly improve the situation. In today's Russia foreign trade remains the most attractive option of exporting capital from Russia because of the easiness, speed and flexibility of trade operations, difficulties it creates for state taxation agencies in tracing the trade-related capital flight, and the look of "legality" and "respectability" that such operations have.

There are three main ways of exporting capital from Russia using foreign trade deals: (a) barter trade; (b) sham credits; and (c) double-invoicing (double-contracting). The barter trade boom occurred in Russia in 1991–93 when the country's financial and banking system was too underdeveloped to provide standard financial services for trade deals.[26] Constant delays in payments and bureaucratic hold-ups made it easier for many trading companies to directly exchange their export commodities for those commodities that they could easily sell on the local market. Often goods that were exported from Russia could be sold at a higher price on world markets than those imported. This meant that, except for a few cases of incompetence, Russian exporter was receiving an additional payment from his foreign partner, either through a money transfer to his private account in a foreign bank or through an unregistered (cash) payment in Russia.

Many of these barter trade deals involved a number of companies and often in different countries. Absence of proper customs and border controls between the former Soviet states in the first years after the collapse of the USSR greatly facilitated this process and made it possible on certain occasions even to smuggle large quantities of export commodities out of Russia.[27] Elaborate financial schemes and complex chains of traders, both in Russia and beyond, helped to mask these illegal operations.

With the development of the financial sector in Russia and the simplification of its currency rules barter trade deals were becoming more and more obsolete, at least for some of Russian companies.[28] Instead of a primitive exchange of goods new schemes of capital export were becoming during 1993 more widely used in Russia. One of such half-legal schemes was a "sham credit" when a Russian-based company either failed to receive payments for the commodities supplied to a foreign partner, or to receive goods from abroad after making all necessary payments. In both cases foreign partner (usually a small company established by Russian émigrés or by locals with the help of the Russian-connected capital) disappeared leaving the Russian company with "losses".[29]

Since 1993 the role of barter trade and sham credits in capital flight from Russia had significantly decreased as a consequence of the Russian government's actions aimed at introduction of more controls over barter operations and registration of companies involved in "shady" (i.e. illegal) financial and trade deals (including sham crediting). That pushed many Russian exporters of capital to abandon the use of these options in favour of what became known as "double-invoicing". This way of capital flight is also linked to foreign trade operations. It requires a close business partnership between Russian and foreign companies and is based on a high level of trust. "Double-invoicing" is in fact signing of two contracts for the same deal (or sending out two invoices for one delivery of goods). "Official" contract/invoice is used as a basis for reporting and taxation, while the second one ("unofficial") regulates the split of profit from the deal between the two contracting parties. "Double-invoicing" is used both in exports from and imports to Russia. In the first case, Russian traders sell goods at discounts, in the second case they buy at mark-ups. In both cases substantial excess earnings are provided to their foreign partners. The latter take part of these earnings as payment for their "services", while the larger part is transferred into accounts held by Russians in foreign banks.

In recent years, some Russian exporters, in order to avoid payment of taxes, have introduced a new form of capital exports: they simply stopped repatriating their export earnings. Tracing these payments was difficult because it usually involved a complicated scheme of intermediaries and affiliated companies.[30] Partly the blame for this rests with the Russian government itself, which failed to introduce an effective system of collection of information for taxation purposes. In 1997 the Russian Minister of Economy admitted, that the government had "practically lost" control over purchases of currency under contract. That led to a situation when "money was being taken out of the country in suitcases".[31]

A significant part of exported capital never returns back to Russia. It either helps to build up a personal financial base for its owners (or their families) when they later decide to emigrate from Russia, or it is invested into Western securities and/or real estate. However, some exported capital is also returned to Russia to be invested into prospective areas for capital exports.[32] Although Russian by origin, this capital is often brought back as a "foreign investment" of a third party (foreign company or a bank) or a company which was established by its owners abroad. Currently there are two major areas of re-investing of this capital in Russia: foreign trade operations and purchases of property. In the former case exported capital assists further exports of capital from Russia. In the latter case this capital is used in establishing of control over some Russian major producers of export commodities. Whatever the scheme, the major objective of such re-investments is to produce more capital for export and within a short period of time. Political instability, vast corruption, and continuing political, social and economic crises currently do not provide incentives for medium- or long-term investments into Russian economy.

The major part of capital flight from Russia goes through the following six Western European destinations: Cyprus, UK (London),

Switzerland (Zurich), Netherlands, Germany and Denmark. In each of these countries many Russian companies have opened their affiliates, established joint ventures with local businesses and created offshore companies.[33] A growing part of capital is also being illegally exported from Russia to the USA, especially through trade operations between resource-rich Russian Far Eastern regions and money-rich US West Coast states.[34]

Part of capital flight from Russia is also linked to money-laundering operations jointly organised by Russian criminals and criminals from other countries.[35] However, according to head of the Russian Bureau of Interpol Yu. Melnikov, this money formed only a small proportion of capital flight. Most of illegally exported capital was of Russian origin.[36]

Capital flight produces a number of negative effects on Russian developments. It is one of major reasons behind sharp revenue short-falls in Russia, both on federal and regional levels. It, therefore, deprives the country of much-needed funds for restructuring of its economy, social programs, and investments. The consequent lack of funds in Russia increases further its foreign debt. Although some of this capital is later re-invested into Russian economy, much of the return-ing money is used to fund illegal activities and is among the main factors that cause widespread corruption in the country. Because many of these capital-exporting operations are serviced by Russian commer-cial banks, many of these banks became associated with criminal and illegal activities both within Russian and abroad. This illegal accumula-tion of capital which is seen by many as a necessary stage in develop-ment of market economy, eventually undermines the belief in the reform process among broad sections of the population and leads to the development of large social and political tensions in the Russian society.

By mid-1990s ways of capital accumulation in post-Soviet Russia became almost inseparable from the foreign trade and inter-linked process of capital flight from Russia. Since most of the capital exported from Russia breached laws in at least two areas – tax evasion and break-ing the existing ban on foreign bank accounts for Russian nationals, it had a clearly criminal nature. Thus, capital flight also played one of the major roles in the growth of economic and related crimes in post-Soviet Russia. Part of this illegally acquired capital stayed in the country or later was invested back into Russia to fund a variety of legal and semi-legal business operations. Today almost every Russian com-mercial bank owes a substantial part of its capital to these illegal or semi-legal sources of finance.

Starting from the stage of *voucher* privatisation in 1992–94, revenues from foreign trade became the major source of funding the most lucrative privatisation deals. This process of redistribution of property opened new and even greater possibilities for accumulation of capital than the sphere of foreign trade, leading to an even greater interrelation between Russian businesses and the state. As a result, Russian bureaucrats responsible for directing and managing of privatisation became new targets for corruption.

By mid-1993 foreign trade-related capital also started to play a direct and increasingly important role in Russian politics through a variety of "lobbies" and "pressure groups". The majority of the most significant among these groups had their roots in and were directly related to exports of capital through foreign trade: these were either foreign trade lobbies of exporters or importers, or lobbies created by producers of the most important export commodities (oil, non-ferrous metals, gas, etc.). While some Russian businessmen even openly turned themselves into politicians, many others still preferred not to advertise their influence publicly. Despite that, their "donations" by 1994 became one of the major sources of funding of Russia's most influential political parties and leaders. This emerging unity of interests of semi-legal business and the corrupt state created a situation when the ability of the latter to make independent decisions started to become questionable.[37]

In the last two to three years and until August 1998 part of the fugitive capital returned back to Russia, attracted by high dividends that the Russian government was paying on its internal borrowings (GKO-OFZ bonds). As a result, in 1996 investment from countries like Switzerland, Cyprus and Liechtenstein had grown many-fold.[38] According to some estimates, in February–May 1997 this changed Russian net financial trends, which for the first time recorded a positive balance.[39] However, even if most favourable conditions existed, Russia could count on return of only portion of the fled capital. According to Viktor Melnikov, executive vice president of Tokobank and former head of the Department of Currency Regulation and Currency Control of the Russian Central Bank, about one-third of this capital was spent on purchases of real estate abroad, while another third was invested in securities, shares and bonds. The remaining third could come back and, in fact, part of it already started to come back in 1996–97 in the guise of foreign company investments.[40]

Since the time when the first estimates of the scale of the flight of capital from post-Soviet Russia started to appear in the Russian press in mid-1992, the issue of capital flight became one of the most heatedly debated in Russian politics. Accusations of direct or indirect involvement in the process of illegal exports of capital from the country were used as a major weapon in undermining popularity of political opponents by both sides in the March–October 1993 confrontation between the president and the parliament. Same tactics were again used in election campaigns of 1993, 1995 and 1996. For instance, in the 1996 presidential campaign each of the major candidates for the Russian presidency – Gennady Zyuganov,[41] Aleksandr Lebed,[42] Grigory Yavlinsky[43] and Vladimir Zhirinovsky[44] – with the notable exception of Boris Yeltsin,[45] made public statements promising to take decisive measures against capital flight, if elected.

The first estimates of volumes of capital flight from post-Soviet Russia were made public in July 1992. The source was the Russian Ministry of Internal Affairs which estimated that the total of US$20 billion belonging to enterprises, commercial organisations and individuals were lodged in Western banks.[46] From the end of 1992 a variety of estimates started to appear in the Russian press. The lowest were from the MFER, which assessed the volume of capital flight from Russia during 1992 at the level of US$2.5 billion.[47] However, according to the Bank for International Settlements (BIS), in 1992 depositors in the former USSR put US$5.8 billion into their bank accounts in the West.[48] Estimates for the same year from the International Bank for Reconstruction and Development (IBRD) were significantly higher and ranged between US$10 billion and US$15 billion.[49] While IBRD data corresponded to estimates made by IMF[50] and RCB,[51] information from the Russian Customs Committee claimed that the volume of capital illegally exported from Russia in 1992 was US$15–20 billion.[52] Some Western sources even put estimated capital flight in 1991–92 as high as US$40 billion.[53]

In 1993 a growing number of sources suggested that the scale of capital flight from Russia was much larger than recognised officially. By 1993 Russian commercial banks were reported to have deposits outside the country in the range of US$10–15 billion dollars.[54] OECD estimated Russian exports of capital in 1991–93 at US$20 billion[55] while the Russian Security Ministry – at US$26 billion.[56]

By 1994 variations in assessments of capital flight became even more striking. The lowest figure for the total amount of money illegally transferred from Russia abroad came from unnamed "Russian experts" cited by a governmental source (US$2.5–5 billion in 1994).[57] At the same time RCB estimated that only import-related capital flight amounted to losses of around US$300–400 million a month,[58] while, according to the Bank spokesman, in the period between 1990 and 1994 the total volume of capital flight stood at the level of US$30 billion.[59] That figure was only slightly lower than the data for the same period that came from the Russian Ministry of Economy (US$35 billion).[60] At the same time the European Bank for Reconstruction and Development (EBRD) estimated that total investments of Russian capital abroad during 1990–94 stood at US$43 billion,[61] while both the Russian Bureau of Interpol[62] and the State Investment Corporation[63] claimed that the gross volume of capital flight from Russia in the same period was US$80 billion. However, estimates coming from the Russian parliament were even higher. In May 1995 Duma Speaker Ivan Rybkin was quoted as saying that a total of over US$100 billion were illegally taken out of Russia in 1990–94.[64] Apparently Rybkin's estimates were based on the report by the Committee on Security and Defence of the upper house of the Russian parliament, the Federation Council. Committee's report which was published in February 1995, stated that the total amount of capital in foreign accounts of Russian private enterprises was between US$100 billion and US$300 billion including US$42.4 billion that has left Russia as part of minerals' exports in 1994.[65]

This striking ten-time difference in various estimates remained basically unchanged in the next year as well. For instance, while First Deputy Prime Minister Oleg Lobov assessed capital flight for 1990–95 as exceeding US$35 billion,[66] RCB and Customs estimated it to be about US$50 billion,[67] and the newly-appointed Secretary of the Security Council, Aleksandr Lebed, claimed that figure to be as high as US$400 billion.[68]

In 1996–97 estimates of capital flight from various sources became closer with most of observers agreeing that export of capital from Russia has stabilised at an annual level of US$12–15 billion.[69] At the same time, previous top estimates of gross capital flight since 1990 of around US$300–400 billion were generally recognised as unreliable while more moderate assessments of around US$150 billion of fled capital over the period of 6–7 years were cited most commonly.[70]

A summary of various estimates of annual levels of capital flight from Russia is presented in the Table 3.10. It is worth noting that most of the lower and the higher estimates come from Russia and basically from two sources – the Russian government and its Security Ministry/Ministry of Internal Affairs. While the former – for political reasons – in recent years was clearly trying to size down the scale of the problem, the spokesmen from Russian security establishment (which also has close links to the former KGB) were at the same time reporting flows of capital 3–16 times higher than reported by the other top Russian officials. According to a variety of Western banking and financial sources, as well as from RCB, volumes of capital flight from Russia registered in the West were at a medium level between these two extremes.[71]

Table 3.10   Variations in Estimates of Capital Flight from Russia, 1991–97 (in billions US dollars)

	1991	1992	1993	1994	1995	1996	1997	Total 1991–97
Minimum[a]	1.0[72]	2.5[73]	5.0[74]	2.5[75]	5.0[76]	10.0[77]	5.0[78]	**31.0**
Medium[b]	8.2[79]	13.0[80]	8.0[81]	17.0[82]	12.0[83]	12.0[84]	12.0[85]	**82.2**
Maximum[c]	15.5[86]	20.0[87]	17.0[88]	42.4[89]	30.0[90]	24.0[91]	20.0[92]	**168.9**
Difference between minimum and maximum estimates								
in times	*15.5*	*8.0*	*3.4*	*17.0*	*6.0*	*2.4*	*4.0*	***5.4***

NOTES:
[a] Minimum estimates came from the Russian Government, MFER and the Ministry of Economy.
[b] Medium estimates came from the Bank of International Settlements, the International Monetary Fund, the US Embassy in Moscow, the International Institute of Finance and the Russian Central Bank.
[c] Maximum estimates came from St Petersburg-based French banking consultants Eurosis Russie, the Russian Security Ministry, Russian Customs Committee, the OECD, the Duma, the Institute of Economy of the Russian Academy of Sciences and ABN-Amro economic news agency.

It is clear that such a sensitive issue as the issue of capital flight, which in Russia's situation is inter-linked with the general issue of the direction and goals of the post-communist reform process, is bound to be in the centre of political struggles. Therefore, views on the acuteness of the problem of capital flight, volumes and ways of exporting capital are dependent on political positions of those who express them. While the opposition might tend to exaggerate the size of the problem, the government is clearly trying to underestimate it. But even if we assume government's "conservative" estimates to be true, the scale of the problem of capital flight becomes quite worrying. According to the lowest estimates Russia in recent years lost in capital flight an equivalent of about one-third of its gross foreign debt[93] or an amount which is 6–7 times larger than the gross amount of foreign direct investments made into Russia by the end of 1995.[94]

One can make independent assessments of the volumes of capital flight from post-Soviet Russia through comparing Russian export/import prices to current world prices for the same commodities. The difference between these is indicative of capital flows from Russia that are linked to foreign trade deals ("double-invoicing"). Although this method does not include the capital that was exported using other ways (barter trade, sham credits/investments, etc.), it might still give us some idea of the scale of the problem and of whether the official Russian estimates reflect the reality.

The Table 3.11 lists *de-facto* volumes of Russian exports in US dollars of major commodities outside the Commonwealth of Independent States (CIS) and their equivalents in world prices. The export of these commodities amounted to about a half of Russia's total non-CIS annual exports. All of these commodities are qualified by the Russian government as "strategic goods" and, therefore, their exports were closely monitored by government bodies (MFER, customs, etc.). Despite all that, these data demonstrate the existence of a large difference between Russian export and world prices. Even if we disregard that (a) same commodities in large quantities are also exported by Russian traders to ex-Soviet republics[95] from where they later are partly re-exported to non-CIS destinations, and (b) that exports of other commodities of non-"strategic" nature are less rigidly controlled by the state (which gives capital-exporters even more space for manoeuvre), estimates of the capital flight from Russia only via exports of these "strategic" commodities still reach considerable amounts (Table 3.12).

Estimates of export-related capital flight also demonstrate that the dynamics of capital flight were in direct relation to the lifting of state control over exports of that or other commodity. For example, in 1992 when the major part of Russian crude oil exports[96] were still controlled by the state, Russia's revenues from exports of this product were US$89 million higher than they could have been if Russia exported crude oil at world prices. With the liberalisation of oil trade in the following years Russia was (as was recorded in official statistics) selling crude oil significantly lower than the world prices. On the other hand, re-introduction of the state control over nickel exports led in 1995–96 to an opposite change in the estimated dynamics of capital flight.

Due to the fact that Russia's imports are much more diversified than its exports it is much harder to make estimates of the total volumes of import-related capital flight. Moreover, specific features of the existing Russian taxation system when taxes on "official" (i.e. company) imports are significantly higher than that on "unorganised" (individual) imports led in recent years to the development of a situation when almost a quarter of the gross Russian imports are not registered at all.[97] All that makes any estimates of import-related capital flows from Russia

Table 3.11   Russian Exports of Major Commodities to non-CIS Countries, 1992–97 (in million US dollars)

a) De-facto exports

	1992	1993	1994	1995	1996	1997
Crude oil	8 545.0	8 370.0	9 245.0	11 000.0	14 063	13 011
Petroleum products	4 171.0	3 471.0	3 370.0	3 870.9	7 146	6 757
Coal	747.0	636.0	585.0	749.1	809.8	694.1
Natural gas	7 479.0	7 443.0	7 942.0	9 759.6	10 784	10 721
Aluminium	1 231.0	1 885.0	2 367.0	3 345.9	3 926	3 790
Copper	10.8	302.0	921.0	1 167.3	1 131	1 122
Nickel	715.0	432.0	677.0	1 232.7	1 214	…
Subtotal	**22 898.8**	**22 539.0**	**25 107.0**	**31 125.5**	**39 073.8**	**36 095.1**
Total annual exports	42 376.3	44 297.4	51 450.0	64 344.0	71 874.0	69 478.0
Subtotal as % of all exports	*54.0*	*50.9*	*48.8*	*48.4*	*54.4*	*52.0*

b) Equivalent in World Prices

	1992	1993	1994	1995	1996	1997
Crude oil	8 456	8 431	10 217	11 828	15 066	14 734
Petroleum products	4 813	4 743	5 518	5 399	…	…
Coal	743	708	624	886	862	759
Natural gas	7 843	7 205	8 827	10 911	13 248	12 083
Aluminium	1290	2540	3786	4245	3940	4323
Copper	14	294	1151	1346	1211	1216
Nickel	821	450	834	1202	1252	1538
Subtotal	**23 980**	**24 372**	**30 958**	**35 818**	**35 579**	**34 652**

NOTE:
Data in this table was calculated on the basis of (1) Russian average contract and average world prices for listed commodities published in the quarterly bulletin of the Russian government's Centre of Economic Analysis (Tsentr ekonomicheskoi kon'yuktury), and (2) official estimates of Russian exports of these commodities published in annual statistical handbooks of the Russian Statistical Committee (Goskomstat). It should be noted that the latter data does not include "unofficial" exports (direct unreported exports to non-FSU destinations and re-exports of Russian goods through former Soviet republics).

Sources:
Rossiya-1993: Ekonomicheskaya kon'yuktura. Vypusk 3, Moscow: Tsentr ekonomicheskoi kon'yuktury, August 1993, pp.272–273; *Rossiya-1993: Ekonomicheskaya kon'yuktura. Vypusk 4*, Moscow: Tsentr ekonomicheskoi kon'yuktury, November 1993, pp.280–281; *Rossiya-1994: Ekonomicheskaya kon'yuktura.1*, Moscow: Tsentr ekonomicheskoi kon'yuktury, March 1994, pp.242–243; *Rossiya-1994: Ekonomicheskaya kon'yuktura.2*, Moscow: Tsentr ekonomicheskoi kon'yuktury, June 1994, p.228; *Rossiya-1994: Ekonomicheskaya kon'yuktura.3*, Moscow: Tsentr ekonomicheskoi kon'yuktury, September 1994, p.193; *Rossiya-1994: Ekonomicheskaya kon'yuktura.4*, Moscow: Tsentr ekonomicheskoi kon'yuktury, December 1994, p.181; *Rossiya-1995: Ekonomicheskaya kon'yuktura.1*, Moscow: Tsentr ekonomicheskoi kon'yuktury, March 1995, p.194; *Rossiya-1995: Ekonomicheskaya kon'yuktura.2*, Moscow: Tsentr ekonomicheskoi kon'yuktury, June 1995, p.181; *Rossiya-1995: Ekonomicheskaya kon'yuktura.3*, Moscow: Tsentr ekonomicheskoi kon'yuktury, September 1995, p.159; *Rossiya-1995: Ekonomicheskaya kon'yuktura.4*, Moscow: Tsentr ekonomicheskoi kon'yuktury, December 1995, p.152; *Rossiiskaya Federatsiya v 1992 godu. Statisticheskii ezhegodnik*, Moscow: Goskomstat, 1993, pp.57–58; *Rossiiskii statisticheskii ezhegodnik. 1994*, Moscow: Goskomstat, 1994, p.438; *Rossiiskii statisticheskii ezhegodnik. 1995*, Moscow: Goskomstat, 1995, p.433; *Interfax Business Report*, 29 January 1996; *Rossiiskii statisticheskii ezhegodnik. 1997*, Moscow: Goskomstat, 1997, p.577–82; *Sotsialno-ekonomicheskoe polozhenie Rossii, yanvar' 1998 goda*, Moscow: Goskomstat, 1998, p.96–109; *Statisticheskii byulleten' SNG*, No.16 (200), August 1998, p.131; *Statisticheskii byulleten' SNG*, No.11 (195), June 1998, p.69; *BP Statistical Review of World Economy, 1998*. Oil: Spot crude prices (http://www.bp.com/bpstats/tables/oilpri1.htm); *McCloskey Coal Information Services Ltd.* (MCIS) (http://www.coal-ink.com/mcis_marker.htm); *World Bank Pink Sheet*, January 1998 (*http://www.worldbank.org/html/ieccp/pkjan98.html*).

Table 3.12   Estimates of Export-Related Capital Flight[a] from Russia by Commodity (in million US dollars)

	1992	1993	1994	1995	1996	1997
Crude oil	+89	−61	−972	−828	−1 003	−1 723
Petroleum products	−642	−1 272	−2 148	−1 528	...	...
Coal	+4	−72	−39	−137	−52	−65
Natural gas	−364	+238	−885	−1 152	−2 464	−1 362
Aluminium	−59	−655	−1 419	−899	−14	−533
Copper	−3	+8	−230	−179	−80	−93
Nickel	−106	−18	−157	+31	−38	...
Subtotal	−1 081	−1 833	−5 851	−4 693	−3 651	−3 776

NOTES:

[a] *De-facto* exports of major commodities less their equivalent in world prices. Negative values mean capital flight.

For sources see Tables 3.11a and 3.11b.

extremely difficult to make. However, many experts agree that capital flight through imports is even higher than that through exports.[98] For example, in July 1995 RCB estimated that breaches of import rules made by *registered* traders were costing Russia US$300–400 million a month.[99]

Available data on average contract prices of some major food commodities imported by Russia allow us to make some estimates of the import-related capital flight (Tables 3.13 and 3.14). Those data show that Russia was losing substantial amounts of money on buying foodstuffs above the average world price. Even if we make a discount on transportation costs that were not included in world prices, the ratio between contract and world prices indicates that substantial mark-ups were incorporated in Russian contracts or, in other words, that capital was also exported as part of Russia's imports. For instance, in 1992 Russia paid for its imports of wheat 7.5% more than the world price, a difference that could be attributed to the freight costs. But by 1995 this difference was already 43%. While such a dramatic growth of wheat import prices might still be attributed to a significant drop in volumes of grain imports, dynamics of imports of sunflower oil in 1992–95 indicated a substantial growth both in physical volumes and in the gap between import and world prices. Even though imports of the mentioned foodstuffs constituted only a minor part of Russian overall imports (11% in 1992 and down to just 1.1% in 1997), lack of a more detailed data on Russian imports[100] did not permit us to make a broader estimate of the level of mark-ups (capital flight) incorporated into Russian import prices.

Table 3.13   Russian Imports of Some Major Foodstuffs from non-CIS Countries,[a] 1992–97 (in million US dollars)

a) De-facto imports

	1992	1993	1994	1995	1996	1997
Wheat	2 563.0	75.1	161.0	163.0	120.5	41.7
Maize	827.0	60.7	179.0	...	33.6	51.4
Sunflower oil	104.0	38.7	59.2	160.0	67.3	180.2
White sugar	588.0	582.0	137.0	150.0	51.9	142.9
Subtotal	4 082.0	756.5	536.2	473.0	273.3	416.1
Total annual imports[b]	36 983.9	26 806.7	28 337.0	33 266.0	31 798.0	38 806.0
Subtotal as % of all[b] imports	*11.0*	*2.8*	*1.9*	*1.4*	*0.9*	*1.1*

b) Equivalent in world prices

	1992	1993	1994	1995	1996	1997
Wheat	2384	62	141	114	121	36
Maize	495	48	132	...	19	30
Sunflower oil	81	29	34	101	...	...
White sugar	386	403	132	145	100	234
Subtotal	3 346	542	439	360	240	300

NOTES:
[a] See note to Table 3.11.
[b] Data for 1992–95 excludes "unregistered" (shuttle) trade.

Sources:
Rossiya-1993: Ekonomicheskaya kon'yuktura. Vypusk 3, Moscow: Tsentr ekonomicheskoi kon'yuktury, August 1993, p.274; *Rossiya-1993: Ekonomicheskaya kon'yuktura. Vypusk 4*, Moscow: Tsentr ekonomicheskoi kon'yuktury, November 1993, p.282; *Rossiya-1994: Ekonomicheskaya kon'yuktura.1*, Moscow: Tsentr ekonomicheskoi kon'yuktury, March 1994, pp.244; *Rossiya-1994: Ekonomicheskaya kon'yuktura.2*, Moscow: Tsentr ekonomicheskoi kon'yuktury, June 1994, p.229; *Rossiya-1994: Ekonomicheskaya kon'yuktura.3*, Moscow: Tsentr ekonomicheskoi kon'yuktury, September 1994, p.194; *Rossiya-1994: Ekonomicheskaya kon'yuktura.4*, Moscow: Tsentr ekonomicheskoi kon'yuktury, December 1994, p.182; *Rossiya-1995: Ekonomicheskaya kon'yuktura.1*, Moscow: Tsentr ekonomicheskoi kon'yuktury, March 1995, p.195; *Rossiya-1995: Ekonomicheskaya kon'yuktura.2*, Moscow: Tsentr ekonomicheskoi kon'yuktury, June 1995, p.184; *Rossiya-1995: Ekonomicheskaya kon'yuktura.3*, Moscow: Tsentr ekonomicheskoi kon'yuktury, September 1995, p.163; *Rossiya-1995: Ekonomicheskaya kon'yuktura.4*, Moscow: Tsentr ekonomicheskoi kon'yuktury, December 1995, p.156; *Rossiiskaya Federatsiya v 1992 godu. Statisticheskii ezhegodnik*, Moscow: Goskomstat, 1993, pp.54–55; *Rossiiskii statisticheskii ezhegodnik. 1994*, Moscow: Goskomstat, 1994, p.436; *Rossiiskii statisticheskii ezhegodnik. 1995*, Moscow: Goskomstat, 1995, p.435; *Interfax Business Report*, 29 January 1996; *Rossiiskii statisticheskii ezhegodnik. 1997*, Moscow: Goskomstat, 1997, pp.577–82; *Sotsialno-ekonomicheskoe polozhenie Rossii, yanvar' 1998 goda*, Moscow: Goskomstat, 1998, pp.96–109; *Statisticheskii byulleten' SNG*, No.16 (200), August 1998, p.131; *Statisticheskii byulleten' SNG*, No.12 (196), June 1998, p.128; *BP Statistical Review of World Economy, 1998*. Oil: Spot crude prices (http://www.bp.com/bpstats/tables/oilpri1.htm); *McCloskey Coal Information Services Ltd*. (MCIS) (http://www.coal-ink.com/mcis_marker.htm); *World Bank Pink Sheet*, January 1998 (http://www.worldbank.org/html/ieccp/pkjan98.html).

The summary of estimates of foreign trade-related and total volumes of capital flight from Russia is given in the Table 3.15.

Even this raw assessment which, due to the lack of reliable data, is based on lower estimates of the volumes of capital flight from

Table 3.14   Some Estimates of Import-Related Capital Flight[a] from Russia by Commodity (in million US dollars)

	1992	1993	1994	1995	1996	1997
Wheat	−179	−13	−20	−49	+1	−6
Maize	−332	−13	−47	...	−14	−22
Sunflower oil	−23	−9	−26	−59	...	...
White sugar	−202	−179	−5	−5	+49	+91
Subtotal	−736	−214	−98	−113	−13	−28

NOTES:
[a] Equivalent in world prices less *de-facto* value of imports of major commodities. Negative values mean capital flight. Please note that available data on Russian average contract prices for imported goods is a CIF price, while world prices are given on a FOB basis. Therefore, transportation costs will form a part of the difference between contract and world prices. However, these transportation costs are unlikely to cover all of the difference because FOB world prices that are used here as a base for comparison are prices for the port of Rotterdam. Because of its closeness to major Russian European ports delivery costs from Rotterdam to Russia are relatively low and, in any case, are unlikely to cover all of the existing difference.

For sources see Tables 3.13a and 3.13b.

post-Soviet Russia, demonstrates the scale and acuteness of the problem. It shows that most of recent Russian government's estimates of capital exports were at least 3–6 times lower than the actual exports.[106] According to the above estimates, in the post-Soviet period Russia turned into a large investor into the Western economy with Russian private and company deposits in Western banks and financial institutions at least twice bigger than the gross investment into the Russian economy received via all channels from the West (direct, portfolio, official aid, multilateral, etc.). This happened at a time when Russia was hardly in a position to afford it: during 1990–95 Russian industrial production fell by 50%, its 1995 state budget deficit was over US$10 billion, while in early 1996 wage arrears stood at US$4.5 billion and non-payments by enterprises at US$28 billion. In 1995 about 26% of Russia's population had gross incomes below the official poverty line compared to 2–5% in the late Soviet period.[107] Our estimates also show that in 1995 the volume of exported capital was more than one third of the gross capital investment made from all sources into the Russian economy.[108]

Numerous attempts made by the Russian government to control and reduce the volumes of capital flight by bureaucratic means have failed to reach any significant results but instead lead to a wide spread of

Table 3.15 Estimates of Capital Flight from Russia in 1992–97: A Summary (in billion US dollars)

	1992	1993	1994	1995	1996	1997	1992–97
Exports[a]	2.0	3.6	12.0	9.7	8.2	8.9	44.4
Imports:	6.3	6.8	5.6	7.0	6.3	7.0	39.0
"Official"[b]	3.0	3.8	2.6	4.0	3.3	4.0	
Unregistered[c]	3.0	3.0	3.0	3.0	3.0	3.0	
CIS trade[d]	1.0	1.0	1.0	1.0	1.0	1.0	6.0
Barter trade[e]	1.5	1.2	0.6	0.3	0.3	0.4	4.3
Cash flows[f]	0.5	0.5	0.5	0.5	0.5	0.6	3.1
Total	11.0	13.1	19.7	18.5	16.3	17.9	96.8
Other estimates[g]	2.5~20.0	5.0~17.0	2.5~42.4	5.0~30.0	10.0~24.0	5.0~20.0	31.0~168.9

NOTES:
[a] Export-related capital flight is calculated on the basis of our earlier estimates of capital flight linked to exports of major commodities (Table 3.12) and the share of these exports in total Russian exports (Table 3.11a). It should be noted that while no data on average contract prices for commodities that are not listed in these tables are currently available, these commodities do not generally fall in the "strategic materials" group and, therefore, their exports were even more loosely controlled by the state. As a result, capital flight through exports of these "other" commodities was certain to be more significant.
[b] Data on selected "official" imports (i.e. through registered companies) in tables 3.13 and 3.14 shows the existence of import-related capital flight. However, these data are not sufficient to make estimates for overall Russian imports. Estimates given here are based on assessments of monthly capital flight through formal imports made by the Russian Central Bank in mid-1995.[101]
[c] In 1996 Russian annual unregistered ("shuttle") imports were *officially* estimated at a level of US$10 billion a year. Mark-ups on imported goods range between 30% and 60% of retail price. Part of capital accumulated through "shuttle trade" is later re-invested into other business operations inside Russia. However, a significant part of capital is also exported abroad. We assumed that annual unorganised trade-related capital flight in Russia was at a constant level of US$3 billion, which we deem to be a conservative estimate.
[d] These estimates cover both re-exports from "officially"-recorded and unregistered trade between Russia and CIS/FSU countries. Many Russian borders with the CIS' states still have no border and customs controls which means that our estimate of US$1 billion of annual capital exports through this channel is likely to be much lower than in reality. Volumes of Russian formal exports to the CIS were in 1994–95 in the range of US$13–14 billion and those of imports between US$10–13 billion.[102]
[e] The share of barter trade in overall foreign trade peaked in 1992 but since then has been steadily declining. Despite that volumes of barter trade remained high: barter operations accounted for US$8.2 billion in 1993 and US$4.2 billion in 1994, or respectively 10.7% and 5% of total annual foreign trade turnover.[103] We assumed that the levels of capital flight linked to the barter trade are unlikely be lower than those linked to official exports. These amounted to 8% of total exports in 1993 and to 23% in 1994 (see Tables 3.11 and 3.12). We assumed that the barter-related capital flight from Russia stood at an average level of 15% of the total volume of barter operations.
[f] There is an estimated US$20–25 billion circulating in cash inside Russia.[104] This is a conservative estimate. Some estimates of volumes of US dollars circulating in cash in Russia are twice as large: EBRD in late 1995 estimated that a total of US$43 billion was circulating in Russia.[105] It is no secret that a significant part of this money is later invested abroad (mainly in bank accounts or through purchases of real property). Almost all bank accounts opened recently by Russians in foreign banks were started with a cash deposit. We assumed that no less than 2–3% of the total turnover of US dollars within Russia are later exported. However, in reality the flow of capital via this channel is certain to be much larger.
[g] See Table 3.10.

corruption in the state sector. Thus, it might be argued that by mid-1990s economic crimes caused by illegally accumulated and exported capital became one of the major obstacles to the development of the Russian reform.

There is another major problem that has also played an important role in the growth of capital flight from Russia and that still largely remains intact. This is the problem of the level of public trust in the government and the consequent question of public endorsement of the current reform strategy. In the first days and months after the August 1991 putsch the victorious Russian government enjoyed an extremely high level of public trust which was based on mass expectations that the reform will bring changes for the better. However, starting from late 1992 to early 1993 the levels of political stability and of the popular trust in the Russian government fell dramatically and since that time continued to remain very low.[109] On the economic side, all this helped to create a political climate when the future of any significant investments into the Russian economy was extremely hard to predict. Chances that in the future the government might fall, re-nationalisation might occur, and legislation on taxation and other business activities would change were very high. In such a situation even Russian businesses preferred to export their capitals rather than to invest them at home. It is no surprise that no major foreign investments were recorded, with large investors continuing to keep themselves on a safe distance from these uncertainties, as well as crime and corruption that blossom in modern Russia. This mentality together with the increasing tendency of capital flight from Russia are unlikely to change significantly until the time when depositing money into foreign accounts will no longer be perceived by the majority of Russians (let alone foreigners) as a safer way of keeping money than investments into the Russian economy.

In this regard it is necessary to stress that to a large extent all of the negative factors that currently halt both local and foreign investors from investing into the Russian economy were themselves a consequence of the way post-Soviet reforms in Russia were conducted. The philosophy of post-communist Russian reformers based on the idealisation of a "pure market" that was seen as a remedy to most of Russia's ills, made them almost totally deaf to the social needs of the population. Even the notion of "economic crime" was considered by many decision-making Russian economists to become irrelevant with the development of a "pure market"; the terminology of "crime" in this sense was often replaced by a notion of "(self-) regulation". Such attitudes basically meant that, from the government's point of view, the problem of capital flight was no more than an excess in the necessary freedom of movement of capital and, for that matter, was symptomatic of the "natural" first phase of capital accumulation. However, after following this line of argument the Russian government was left with no effective means of halting the flow of capital from the country. Such "pure market" philosophy of "get rich now" – when pursued by the state – created the basis for a wide-scale corruption within the bureaucracy and, through that, very soon started to pose a serious threat to the very existence of the state and its ability to manage the country. By mid-1990s it became apparent that in their fight against crime many Russian leaders became captives of the crime monster they themselves helped to create earlier.

Opponents of the current government's policy – "new" communists probably the most vocal and organised among them – all argue that in the Russian situation of an over-centralised and highly monopolised economy which was inherited from the Soviet period, the government's attempts to bring to life the philosophy of a "pure market" simply cannot be effective. The existence and domination of monopolies leaves no ground for a fair competition. Therefore, in a situation like Russia's it is the task of the state to intervene and to use its levers and controls in order to redirect and change the system. But if, like in Russia, the state attempts instead to give these levers and controls away into private hands, it is essentially the state itself that opens gates for a rapid growth in variety of crimes, including capital flight and corruption. Intentionally or not, the policies of post-communist leaders of Russia had led to emergence of a typical (semi-) oligarchic state. It would be hard to expect any other result after the bulk of national wealth was "legally" transferred into the hands of very few "new riches" or is still totally controlled by a tiny group of top bureaucrats. At the same time with the majority of the Russian population the rest of state bureaucracy, including those dealing with law and order, became impoverished more than ever before, not least as the consequence of diminished state funds for capital investments, restructuring and social programs.

By mid-1990s the failure of the Russian leadership to take decisive actions to ensure that the transformation of the Russian society takes place in a democratic and fair manner, led to a growing alienation between the population and the establishment. This declining public trust in the government produced a political vacuum similar to the one that existed in the Soviet Union and, like before, it was also accompanied by a *de-facto* collapse of the state-supported ideology. In order to remedy the situation the government (also partly driven by 1995–96 election pressures) responded by moving the accent in its policy from the philosophy of "pure market" to a more "nationalistic" ("patriotic", anti-Western) rhetoric. At the same time its policies received a more "socially-oriented" façade. However, no significant moves were undertaken by the state that could seriously challenge the continuing spread of economic crimes in Russia. Recent political manoeuvring of Russian leaders significantly increased their chances for survival, as it was proved by the result of the 1996 presidential election. But with their socio-economic policies almost unchanged after the elections, the economic climate in Russia continued to remain largely criminal and hostile to investments while capital was uninterruptedly flowing from the country leaving its economic and social structures starving without finance.

Notes

1. The issue of organisation of foreign trade activities in Soviet and other socialist economies is well covered in Josef C. Brada, "The political economy of communist foreign trade institutions and policies", *Journal of Comparative Economics*, Vol.15, No.2, June 1991, pp.211–238, and Franklyn D. Holzman, *Foreign Trade Under Central Planning*, Cambridge, Mass.: Harvard University Press, 1974.
2. In addition to internal factors of Russian development, there were also important international trade and economic limits to the level and the nature of Russia's involvement in the world economy. See: Alan Smith, *Russia and the World Economy: Problems of Integration*, London and New York: Routledge, 1993.
3. Robin Ajello, "Why Moscow is selling advanced weapons to Asian friends ...and foes", *Asiaweek*, 7 February 1997; *Monitor: A Daily Briefing on the Post-Soviet States*, Vol.III, No.213, 13 November 1997.
4. Alexander Nikolayev, "Alligators' conquer arms market", *Panorama* (Moscow), 1997, No.4.
5. *Monitor*, Vol.III, No.23, 3 February 1997. In November 1997 the earlier official optimistic projections of the increase of Russian arms sales were significantly scaled down. See "Russian arms exports: the good and the bad news", *Monitor*, Vol.III, No.213, 13 November 1997.
6. In 1988 USSR exported 0.2 mln tonnes of aluminium to the West. In 1989 the figure remained the same, but in 1990 exports increased to 0.7 mln tonnes. In 1991 aluminium exports stood already at 1.0 mln tonnes and in 1992 CIS exports were 1.2 mln tonnes (*Delovoi Mir*, 21.05.93). In 1992 Russia alone exported about 1.0 mln tonnes of aluminium, i.e. more than 80% of CIS' total exports for the year. In 1993 Russian estimated aluminium exports were already 1.6 mln tonnes or 8 times more than total Soviet exports of the metal four years before that! (*Oxford Analytica East Europe Daily Brief (OAEEDB)*, 10.03.94; *Delovoi Mir*, 29.11.–05.12.93, p.11).

   Dynamics of growth of exports of other non-ferrous metals could be seen from the following figures: USSR/CIS exports of copper increased from 76 mln tonnes in 1989 to 300 mln tonnes in 1992 (4 times), exports of zinc during the same period – from 6 to 27 mln tonnes (more than 4 times), lead – from 6 to 80 mln tonnes (13 times!) (*Delovoi Mir*, 21.05.93).

Russian intervention into world metals' market left many foreign metal producers alarmed. The demands in the West for an increased protectionism from Russian exports grew simultaneously with the growth of exports from Russia, and already by 1993 70% of all Russian metals exports to the European Union were affected by quotas (*Monitor*, Vol.III, No.117, 16 June 1997). The latest of these protectionist measures was introduction by the European Commission of a 33% tariff on steel pipe imports from Russia in May 1997 (*Izvestia*, 14 June 1997).

7. Claudia Senik-Leygonie and Gordon Hughes, "Industrial profitability and trade among the former Soviet republics", *Economic Policy*, Vol.15, October 1992, pp.353–386; Robin A. Watson, "Interrepublic trade in the former Soviet Union: structure and implications", *Post-Soviet Geography and Economics*, Vol.35, No.7, September 1994, pp.371–408.

8. It should be noted that Tajikistan was also a recipient of large amounts of financial, military and humanitarian aid from Russia. These deliveries, however, were not recorded in the official foreign trade statistics. In general economic terms, Tajikistan had probably the highest level of dependency on Russia of all the former Soviet states in the mid-1990s.

9. See also Rolf J. Lamghammer, Matthew J. Sagers, Matthias Lucke, "Regional distribution of the Russian Federation's export earnings outside the former Soviet Union and its implications for regional economic autonomy", *Post-Soviet Geography and Economics*, Vol.33, No.10, December 1992, pp.617–634.

10. Calculations of regional shares in Russian foreign trade in 1997 as presented in the text and in Table 3.6 are based on Goskomstat's official statistical series. These, however, leave 8.3% of Russian exports (or US$7.3 billion) and 35.4% of Russian imports (US$26 billion) not distributed between the regions. Most probably, these are centralised exports and imports. Larger part of centralised exports is made of oil and gas supplies from Western Siberia. That means that the 1997 share of this economic region in overall Russian exports is likely to be larger than presented in Table 3.6. On the other hand, the larger part of non-listed imports might be Russian centralised food imports (mainly grain supplies) for the military, northern areas and other state needs. (See *Regiony Rossii. 1998*, Vol.2, Moscow: Goskomstat, 198, pp.782–3).

11. See note 10.

12. Data on per capita regional exports and imports was calculated from *Rossiiskii statisticheskii ezhegodnik. 1996*, Moscow: Goskomstat, 1996, pp.898–903. Russian statistical handbooks also published data on 1995 and 1997 regional exports. But that more recent data had left significant shares of Russia's total exports not distributed between regions, which made data for 1994 exports much more reliable and representative.

13. One area which incorrectly is shown as having low export levels is Sakha, Russia's major diamond-exporting region. Per capita export levels in Sakha should be one of the highest in Russia; however, Russian foreign trade figures include diamond sales only in overall trade series. Diamond trade continues to be the state monopoly, managed exclusively from Moscow.

14. On these maps, like on maps in other chapters of this book, for the purpose of a clearer presentation Moscow and St Petersburg are not shown separately, but are included in the neighbouring regions – respectively Moskovskaya oblast' and Leningradskaya oblast'. The figures used in map presentation are, therefore, an average for each city taken together with the surrounding region. The real importance of both cities in regional foreign trade patterns tends to be higher than indicated on the maps, which is certainly true for Moscow (see Table 3.8).

15. Interview with Vladimir Treml, *Voice of America*, 1 November 1996; Lidia Lukyanova, "If they get rid of the "shuttle traders", then who will feed and clothe Russia?", *Prism: A Monthly on the Post-Soviet States* (Jamestown Foundation), Vol.III, February 1997, Part 2.

16. All tables presented in this chapter already incorporate the official estimates of the "shuttle trade" operations.

17. *OMRI Daily Digest*, No.44, Part I, 4 March 1997; "Shadow economy: bigger than they think", *St Petersburg Times*, 16–22 June 1997.

18. Lidia Lukyanova, Op.cit.

19. See: Peter Rutland, "Russia's unsteady entry into the global economy", *Current History*, October 1996, Vol.95, No.603.

20. Peter Rutland, "Russia's unsteady entry into the global economy", *Current History*, October 1996, Vol.95, No.603.

21. This is a short and updated version of my paper on "Capital Flight from Post-Soviet Russia", *Europe–Asia Studies*, Vol.49, No.4, 1997, pp.591–615. I am grateful to Carfax Publishing Limited (PO Box 25, Abingdon, Oxfordshire OX14 3UE, UK) for granting a permission to reproduce this material.

22. In this chapter I analyse the so-called "external" capital flight or the flow of capital across the Russian border. However, the problem also has another aspect, "internal capital flight" or "dollarisation" of the Russian economy. The latter was and still constitutes an important feature of the post-Soviet developments in Russia. "Dollarisation" happens when the population uses foreign currencies (US dollar is the most preferable in Russia) as means of savings, particularly because of high inflation rates of local currency and/or as a result of lack of trust in the government. Some indication of the scale of this problem was given by the Russian Central Bank official who stated that in the beginning of 1997 there were approximately US$33 billion in circulation among the population compared to the gross Russian money supply of 125 trillion roubles or US$22 billion. In January 1997 Russians were spending nearly a quarter of their incomes on purchases of foreign currency, up from 14.3% in 1995 and 18.5% in 1996. During 1996 more than $8.7 billion were converted in Russia into dollars. Estimates of the total amount of cash savings, held on hands by Russian citizens at the end of 1997, range between $20 billion and $50 billion. (*OMRI*, No.60, 26 March 1997; Paul Goble, "Buying out Russia", *RFE/RL*, 4 March 1997; *Reuter*, 5 June 1997; Alan Philips, "Russia bled dry as $1bn a month is smuggled out", *The Electronic Telegraph* (UK), 6 June 1997; *The Los Angeles Times*, 11 October 1997; *St Petersburg Times*, 17–23 November 1997).

23. In September 1996 the Central Bank released data on Russian "official" investments abroad according to which Russian licensed foreign investments

in the period between March 1993 and March 1996 totalled US$416 million. During recent years the pace of Russian foreign investments grew rapidly: from $63 million in 1993 to $278 million in 1994 and $365 million in 1995. The largest projects cleared for exporting capital were carried out by Russian companies LUKoil ($126 million), Gazprom ($108.2 million), and Surgutneftegaz ($86.6 million). Main destinations for Russian "official" capital exports were Germany, the US and the UK (ITAR-TASS quoted in *OMRI*, 6 September 1996).

24. Some capital also leaves Russia in a "primitive" way, i.e. through cash amounts illegally taken across the border. It is practically impossible to make any reliable estimates of the levels of such capital flight, which, however, can reach considerable volumes. For instance, estimates of the total amount of US dollars circulating currently in Russia in cash vary between $15 billion and $25 billion.

25. At the end of 1995 the total volume of foreign direct investments in Russia was only US$5.53 billion, as estimated by the Russian Statistical Committee (quoted in *BISNIS Briefs*, 31 July 1996).

26. In September 1993 Russian Academician Leonid Abalkin stressed that barter operations were one of major routes of capital flight from Russia (*Finansovye izvestia*, 6 September 1993).

27. For instance, Baltic states (particularly, Estonia and Latvia) in 1992–93 became major centres for re-exports of smuggled and illegal exports of oil, petroleum products and non-ferrous metals from Russia. According to official statistics, Latvian 1993 exports amounted to two-thirds of its GDP, but in fact major part of these exports were re-exports of Russian oil and petroleum products (see "Latvia: economic outlook", *Oxford Analytica Eastern European Daily Brief (OAEEDB)*, 14 September 1994). Smuggling of non-ferrous metals through Latvia has in mid-1992 reached such a level that the Latvian government had to temporally ban all exports of these metals from the country (*RFE/RL*, 24 July 1992). Raw materials and other export commodities were illegally exported from Russia via other ex-Soviet republics, as well as through some of Russia's remote and semi-independent territories: Chechnya, the Far East, Murmansk, Kaliningrad, etc. Latter was even characterised by some observers as "smuggler's paradise" (see "Russia: smuggler's paradise", *OAEEDB*, 17 January 1995).

28. According to some recent estimates, some 70% of manufactured products shipped to customers were in 1997 still marketed via barter channels. The cash crisis that spread throughout the Russian economy in 1995–97, again increased the attractiveness of the barter trade. Thus, a survey which was conducted in early 1997 and covered 500 medium-size enterprises, revealed that their barter business increased from 6% in 1992 to 40% in 1996 (*RIA-Novosti*, 20 March 1997).

29. M. Sarafonov and N. Lirov, "Begstvo kapitala iz Rossii", *Ekonomika i zhizn'*, 1992, No.38, p.9.

30. See: Peter Henderson, "Russia brings new sophistication to tax chase", *Reuter*, 11 June 1997.

31. *Interfax-AiF*, No.29–30, 14–20 July 1997.

32. In 1993 it was estimated that only about US$300 million or less than 3% of the total estimated deposits of Russian commercial banks abroad was

lent by the banks to domestic Russian customers (see *OAEEDB*, 4 October 1993 and 8 November 1993).

33. In October 1994 it was reported that Cyprus alone was the home of 2,000 Russian companies with a further 11 Russian banks having their offices on the island (see "Russia: money-laundering", *OAEEDB*, 5 October 1994).

34. See "Russia: wild East", *OAEEDB*, 26 July 1995.

35. See "Russia: money-laundering", Op. cit.

36. *Megapolis-Express*, No.24, June 1995.

37. In itself this issue may be a topic for a major study. Numerous examples can prove inconsistency of post-Soviet economic policies in Russia. In short, almost every major decision taken by the Russian government which had a potential of limiting ways and revenues from exports of capital, was immediately followed by measures aimed at giving privileges to certain businesses (presumably, most "influential" ones). For example, just within a month after President Yeltsin signed a decree abolishing all existing privileges for exporters and importers (13 March 1995), new privileges and "special regulations" were introduced into the foreign trade' legislation on the same day the decree was signed (!) and then also on 14 March, 22 March, 23 March, 24 March, 29 March, 6 April and 13 April. (see *Dokumenty*, April–July 1995). On 15 April 1995 the Russian government gave large-scale privileges to US confectionery company, Mars Inc., but the text of the agreement was never made public (see note in *Dokumenty*, June 1995, p.263). Attempts to "speed up" the privatisation process in Russia two months before the December 1995 parliamentary elections (including the controversial loans-for-shares' deal) are among most recent examples of a highly dubious way the existing "inter-relation" between business and the state works in Russia (on privatisation see Russian central newspapers between October 1995 and January 1996). One of the major players in this new "privatisation" campaign, head of Oneksimbank Vladimir Potanin, following 1996 presidential elections finally became the vice-premier of the Russian government in August 1996. Interestingly, one of the official reasons for his appointment was that Potanin "may help reverse the capital flight" (!) (see comments in *Rossiiskaya gazeta*, 16 August 1996). For a recent interesting revelation of accumulation of capital via Russian aluminium industry see Julia Flynn, Patricia Kranz and Carol Matlack, "Grabbing a corner on Russian aluminium" in *Business Week*, 6 September 1996.

38. *St Petersburg Times*, 3–9 February 1997.

39. *Reuter*, 5 June 1997 and 4 September 1997.

40. *Interfax-AiF*, 22 July 1997.

41. The pre-election economic programme of the Russian Communist Party titled "From Destruction to Creation: Russia's Road to the 21st Century" directly addressed the issue of "preventing capital flight of US$20 billion a year" that could be achieved through a comprehensive audit of commercial banks and the blocking of existing channels of capital flight (see *Interfax Business Report*, 4 June 1996 and "Russia: Zyuganov economics", *OAEEDB*, 31 May 1996).

42. In mid-March 1996 Lebed suggested to create a federal commission with the aim of "tracking down and returning money that has been taken out

of Russia illegally" (*Interfax*, 13 March 1996). After the first round of elections and his deal with Yeltsin, Lebed, in his capacity as a newly-appointed head of Russia's Security Council, proposed a set of measures to stop Russia loosing "the currency that is stashed illegally abroad". Measures included introduction of profit ceilings for transactions, state price controls, a tougher regulation of foreign economic relations, increased fight against tax evasion, tax concessions for returning capital, etc. (*Interfax Report on Food & Agriculture*, 5 July 1996).

43. In his public statement in mid-May 1996 Yavlinsky promised voters "to close outlets for capital flight" if he was elected president (*Monitor*, 13 May 1996).

44. In his TV interview in April 1996 Zhirinovsky suggested a simple recipe to return capital from overseas: he promised to solve the problem "by arresting relatives of 'swindlers' who have sent their money abroad" (*OMRI*, 3 May 1996).

45. Although I have not managed to find any pre-election statements from Yeltsin on the problem of capital flight, Yeltsin's election programme calls for a better regulation of foreign trade. Also, during the time a number of officials of the Russian government made statements on the issue, but these statements could not be automatically interpreted as reflecting Yeltsin's position.

46. Russian Television, 10 July 1992, quoted in *RFE/RL*, 4 September 1992.

47. Interview with ex-Minister for Foreign Economic Relations Petr Aven in *Trud*, 12 January 1993. A year later these Russian government's estimates for 1992 were increased to US$4 billion (see "Russia: trade prospects", *OAEEDB*, 19 January 1994).

48. "Russia: capital flight", *OAEEDB*, 18 July 1994.

49. Wilfred Thalwitz from IBRD quoted in *The Wall Street Journal*, 15 November 1993, p.A8.

50. IMF estimate for 1992 was US$13 billion. See "Russia: capital flight", Op. cit.

51. Interview with Chairman of the Russian Central Bank Viktor Gerashenko, *Vlast' i ekonomika*, 14 June 1995.

52. "Russia: capital flight", Op. cit.

53. See *OAEEDB*, 19 May 1992 and 22 September 1993.

54. "Russia: debt rescheduling", *OAEEDB*, 4 October 1993, and "Russia: banking crisis", *OAEEDB*, 22 December 1993.

55. See "Russia: capital flight. Part 1: scope and consequences", *OAEEDB*, 8 November 1993.

56. Ibid.

57. *Rossiiskie vesti*, 29 March 1995 quoted in *Ezhenedelnyi informatsionnyi byulleten'*, No.10, March 1995 (published by the RF's Governmental Centre on Economic Reforms).

58. Acting RCB Chairman Tatyana Paramonova cited in *Interfax Business Report*, 31 July 1995.

59. *Segodnya*, 29 July 1995.

60. Interview of Minister of Economy Evgenii Yasin in *Post-Factum Weekly News Digest*, 15 February 1995.

61. EBRD report of 1 November 1995 cited in *Monitor*, 24 November 1995.

62. *Megapolis-Express*, No.24, June 1995.
63. See interview with head of the State Investment Corporation Yuri Petrov in *Ekonomika i zhizn'*, 1995, No.41, p.37.
64. Rybkin also estimated monthly levels of capital flight at US$2–2.5 billion (see interviews with Rybkin in *RIA Economic Daily News*, 4 May 1995, and *Rossiiskaya gazeta*, 2 June 1995). The difference in parliamentary estimates and that from government sources is be partly attributed to the fact that, as stated in the report by the Duma's Committee of economic policy (April 1995), parliamentary assessments were based on information from the State Statistics Committee and RCB and included estimated volumes of capital flight *and* unregistered imports (*RIA-Novosti*, 5 April 1995).
65. See *Post-Factum Weekly News Digest*, 15 February 1995.
66. *OMRI*, 9 August 1996.
67. Oleg Pavlov, chairman of FSCEC, quoted in *Interfax Business Report*, 4 April 1996.
68. Aleksandr Lebed quoted in Peter Reddaway, "Russia heads for trouble", *The New York Times*, 2 July 1996.
69. See: Peter Rutland, "Russia's unsteady entry into the global economy", *Current History*, October 1996, Vol.95, No.603; Russian Deputy Procurator General (*OMRI*, No.243, 18 December 1996); First Deputy Chairman of RCB (*RFE/RL*, No.47, 6 June 1997).
70. See, for instance: *Delovoi Mir*, 2 April 1997; Louise I. Shelley, "The price tag of Russia's organized crime", *Transition: The Newsletter About Reforming Economies*, Washington: The World Bank, February 1997; *RIA-Novosti*, 23 September 1997.
71. It should be noted that Western data is predominantly based on bank records and does not include most of cash-based operations involving Russians, like cash transfers from Russia, cash-based purchases of properties in the West, etc. These, however, constitute a significant part of capital flows from Russia.
72. *RFE/RL*, 10 September 1992.
73. *Trud*, 12 January 1993.
74. *OAEEDB*, 19 January 1994.
75. *Rossiiskie vesti*, 29 March 1995; *Interfax Business Report*, 24 March 1995.
76. *Interfax Business Report*, 21 November 1995.
77. *Interfax Business Report*, 16 December 1996.
78. *Interfax-AiF*, No.29–30, 14–20 July 1997.
79. *OAEEDB*, 18 July 1994.
80. *OAEEDB*, 18 July 1994.
81. *OAEEDB*, 18 July 1994.
82. *BISNIS Briefs*, 31 July 1996.
83. *Delovoi mir*, 12 April 1995; *OAEEDB*, 3 May 1996.
84. *RFE/RL*, 6 June 1997.
85. *RFE/RL*, 6 June 1997.
86. *OAEEDB*, 8 November 1993.
87. *OAEEDB*, 18 July 1994 and 8 November 1993.
88. *OAEEDB*, 8 November 1993.
89. *Post-Factum Weekly News Digest*, 15 February 1995.
90. *RIA Economic News*, 4 May 1995; *Segodnya*, 20 October 1995.

91. *RIA-Novosti*, 21 February 1997.
92. *Reuter*, 5 June 1997.
93. The Russian gross foreign debt in May 1996 was estimated at the level of US$107 billion, of which US$11.4 billion were owed to international financial institutions, US$62.1 billion to foreign governments, US$20.3 billion to commercial banks and US$13.2 billion to other private creditors. (See "Russia: debt rescheduling", Op.cit.)
94. In July 1996 the Russian Statistical Committee (Goskomstat) released data according to which the total volume of foreign direct investment in Russia in 1995 was a mere US$1.9 billion. Goskomstat's assessment of overall accumulated stock of foreign direct investment at the end of 1995 was US$5.53 billion. The Russian government's estimate of the total accumulated investment to the same date was about US$6.2 billion. See "Russia: investment climate statement from the US embassy in Moscow", *BISNIS Briefs*, 31 July 1996, and *Ekonomika i zhizn'*, 1995, No.41, p.37.
95. For example, in 1995 Russian exports of crude oil to the CIS totalled 25.5 million tons, or 26.3% of non-CIS exports. In the same year over one-third of the total Russian exports of natural gas (in physical volumes) were directed to the CIS (*Sotsial'no-ekonomicheskoe polozhenie Rossii. 1995*, Moscow: Goskomstat, 1996, p.140).
96. Exports of petroleum products were liberalised in early 1992.
97. The so-called "shuttle trade" or "unorganised" imports were estimated by the government's Centre of Economic Analysis (Tsentr ekonomicheskoi kon'yuktury) at levels of 24% of gross imports from non-CIS countries in 1994 and 20.2% in 1995. "Unorganised" trade accounted for 23.9% of overall imports from the CIS in 1994 and 19.9% in 1995 (calculated from *Rossiya-1995: Ekonomicheskaya kon'yuktura.4*, Moscow: Tsentr ekonomicheskoi kon'yuktury, December 1995, p.154). The total volume of "shuttle trade" is reported to be over $10 billion a year; this trade involves between 10 and 30 million people in Russia (or up to one fifth of its total population) (*Kommersant-Daily*, 24 July 1996).
98. See Mikhail Lyubskii, "Valyutnoe regulirovanie..."; *Interfax Business Report*, 22 November 1995; *OAEEDB*, 28 November 1995.
99. Acting Chairman of RCB Tatyana Paramonova cited in *Interfax Business Report*, 31 July 1995.
100. About one-third of Russian overall "official" imports falls under category of machinery and equipment. However, this category is highly diversified. In addition to machinery and commodities that were not listed in Tables 3.13 and 3.14, other significant import categories include beverages, beef and pork, metals, tubes, poultry, and clothes (*Rossiya-1996: Ekonomicheskaya kon'yuktura.1–2*, Moscow: Tsentr ekonomicheskoi kon'yuktury, June 1996, p.151).
101. See *Interfax Business Report*, 31 July 1995.
102. *Sodruzhestvo Nezavisimykh Gosudarstv v 1995 godu. Kratkii spravochnik.* Moscow: Statkom SNG, January 1996, p.23.
103. *Sotsial'no-ekonomicheskoe polozhenie Rossii. 1994*, Moscow: Goskomstat, 1995, p.76.
104. See *Vek*, 3 January 1995, p.6; *Finansovye izvestia*, March 1995, No.13; *Economica Weekly Press Summary*, 9–15 September 1995, No.35.

105. *OMRI Economic Digest*, 16 November 1995.
106. This, however, might be a consequence of a wrong interpretation of the existing data when capital flows via *one* channel were taken for a summary of flows through *all* channels.
107. See Vladimir Tikhomirov, "Stabilisation in Russia? A brief analysis of Russia's socio-economic performance", *Russian and Euro-Asian Economics Bulletin*, June 1996, pp.14–23.
108. Capital investments from all sources in 1995 were 250,200 billion roubles. Average annual currency exchange rate in the same year was 1 US dollar to 4 554 roubles. Therefore, capital investments in US dollar equivalent were US$54.9 billion against estimated capital flight for the year of US$18.5 billion (*Sodruzhestvo Nezavisimykh Gosudarstv v 1995 godu. Kratkii sprav-ochnik*, Moscow: Statkom SNG, January 1996, p.208; *Sotsial'no-ekonomich-eskoe polozhenie Rossii. 1995*, Moscow: Goskomstat, 1996, p.13).
109. Most of the observers of the 1996 Russian presidential elections agreed at least on one thing: in these elections the overwhelming majority of Russian voters clearly demonstrated their disagreement, if not rejection, of many aspects of Yeltsin's reform course. Thus, re-election of Yeltsin for a second term of presidency was widely interpreted not as an endorsement of his socio-economic policies, but as a sign of theoretical and tactical weaknesses of opposition. The cleverly (but not fairly) mastered election campaign played an extremely significant role in boosting of Yeltsin's public image; the same effect also came from his pre-election manoeuvring (Chechnya, Lebed, wage re-payments, etc.). However, probably the most significant reason for Yeltsin's election victory lies in the fact that by the time of elections Russian opposition was not able to come up with a popular (even charismatic) opposition leader who was capable of produc-ing an alternative democratic strategy that would be clear and understand-able to voters, would easily win their sympathies and at the same time would seriously challenge the status quo without returning to the unde-mocratic experiences of the Soviet past. In mid-1996 Russia the time was possibly still not right for such an opposition to emerge.

4
Social Development and Income Distribution

4.1 Dynamics of population and employment growth

In the post-Soviet period Russia has been experiencing a serious demographic crisis. Since the reforms in January 1992 the Russian population has been steadily declining. In net terms between 1992 and 1999 Russia lost 2.4 million people (Table 4.1). The population fall of 480 000 recorded in 1996, was at the time the steepest decline in any single year since World War II.[1] By 1998 the annual rate of population decline was already more than three-quarters of a million.

To a large extent this decline was the result of dramatic drops in the birth rate from about 17 births per 1 000 people in the mid-1980s to nine per 1 000 ten years later.[2] During the same period, the death rate increased significantly, reaching almost 16 deaths per 1 000 people in early 1995, but then falling to less than 14 in 1998–99. Between 1991 and 1998 the birth rate fell by over one-third while the death rate increased by 23%. The death rate increment was caused by many factors, among the most important of which were the extremely high death rate among men, increasing death rates among people capable of work and the general deterioration of the health of the population.[3]

In the early 1990s infant mortality in Russia was also on the increase, but since 1995 it has been gradually decreasing which was mainly due to falls in the birth rate. According to recently published data, in 1997 infant mortality level in Russia was the lowest during the 1990s. However, the 1997 level of 16.7 deaths per 1 000 population was still very high, even for developing countries: in 1996 among the countries of Europe, Asia and America only Afghanistan and Cambodia had recorded higher rates.

Table 4.1 General Demographic Indicators
In millions unless stated otherwise

	1 Jan 91	1 Jan 92	1 Jan 93	1 Jan 94	1 Jan 95	1 Jan 96	1 Jan 97	1 Jan 98	1 Jan 99	% of change 1991–98
Population	148.54	148.7	148.67	148.37	148.31	147.98	147.5	147.1	146.3	–1.0
Birth rate[a]	13.4	12.1	10.7	9.4	9.6	9.3	8.9	8.6	8.8	–35.8
Death rate[a]	11.2	11.4	12.2	14.5	15.7	15	14.2	13.8	13.6	22.9
Life expectancy[b]	69.2	69.0	67.9	65.1	64.0	64.6	65.9	66.7	...	–3.0
Male[b]	63.8	63.5	62.0	58.9	57.6	58.3	59.8	60.8	...	–4.7
Female[b]	74.3	74.3	73.8	71.9	71.2	71.7	72.5	72.9	...	–1.2
Infant mortality[c]	17.4	17.8	18	19.9	18.6	18.1	17.4	17.2	16.7	–1.4
Net migration [–]	0.18	0.02	0.25	0.44	0.81	0.5	0.34	0.35	0.30	93.9
Migrants [–]	–0.73	–0.68	–0.67	–0.48	–0.34	–0.34	–0.29	–0.23	–0.21	–67.9
Immigrants [+]	0.91	0.69	0.93	0.92	1.15	0.84	0.63	0.58	0.51	–35.9

NOTES:
[a] Per 1 000 population.
[b] In years.
[c] Under age of one per 1 000 births.

Sourced and calculated from:
SNG: *Statisticheskii byulleten'*, No.13 (149), July 1996, Moscow: Statkom SNG, p.36; *Rossiiskii statisticheskii ezhegodnik. 1994*, Moscow: Goskomstat, 1994, p.43; *Rossiiskii statisticheskii ezhegodnik. 1995*, Moscow: Goskomstat, 1995, pp.29, 38, 42–3; *Rossiya v tsifrakh. 1996*, Moscow: Goskomstat, 1996, pp.25, 28–30; *Sotsial'no-ekonomicheskoe polozhenie Rossii.1996 g.*, No.12, Moscow: Goskomstat, 1997, pp.207–8; *Rossiiskii statisticheskii ezhegodnik. 1996*, Moscow: Goskomstat, 1996, pp.50, 59; *Voprosy statistiki*, Moscow, No.3, 1997, pp.54–8; *Sotsial'no-ekonomicheskoe polozhenie Rossii.1997 g.*, Moscow: Goskomstat, 1998, pp.290–3; *Sotsial'no-ekonomicheskoe polozhenie Rossii. yanvar' 1998 g.*, Moscow: Goskomstat, 1998, pp.219–24; *Rossiiskii statisticheskii ezhegodnik. 1997*, Moscow: Goskomstat, 1997, p.86; *Rossiiskii statisticheskii ezhegodnik. 1998*, Moscow: Goskomstat, 1998, pp.156–64; *Sotsial'no-ekonomicheskoe polozhenie Rossii. 1998 g.*, Moscow: Goskomstat, 1999, p.435; *Sotsial'no-ekonomicheskoe polozhenie Rossii. yanvar' 1999 g.*, Moscow: Goskomstat, 1999, pp.291–9.

The most shocking indicator of the contemporary demographic crisis in Russia, however, is the average life expectancy. By the mid-1990s the death rate among working-age Russians was higher than a century ago, in tsarist times. From 1991 to 1995 deaths in the 20–29 age group increased by 61%, 30–39 years – by 75% and 40–49 years – by 73%.[4]

In 1994–95 male life expectancy fell to the lowest point ever in the Russian post-war history; the resultant gap between male and female life expectancy in Russia – 13 years – was the largest recorded in the world.[5] In a recent article Russian demographers stated that an average of 12.6 males per 1 000 working-age male population dies in Russia compared to 3.0 per 1 000 female population.[6] There has been a gradual improvement in male life expectancy since 1995, but this was mainly the result of a reduction in exogenous causes of death.[7]

The demographic crisis in post-Soviet Russia is directly related to steep falls in living standards over the past six years, shrinking employment opportunities, inadequate health service, and the political and social instability in the country. In the Soviet Union the job market, wage levels and movements of the labour force were all controlled and regulated by the state. Central planning meant that there was no official unemployment in Russia before 1991. Every Russian citizen was required to have a job or to face criminal charges. This led to a situation where the job market became artificially oversized; it created the phenomenon of "hidden" unemployment with companies and organisations employing many more people than actually required. "Hidden" unemployment was an internal feature of the Soviet economic system and it was the major underlying cause of the extremely low productivity rates in the USSR.[8]

The last years of the Soviet reform were characterised by growing deregulation of the labour market. Private businesses, co-operatives and other forms of non-state enterprises were allowed to operate. In the mid-1990 unemployment registration was established in the Soviet Union, although the number of unemployed was still negligible at that stage.

When the Russian reform was launched in early 1992, it was anticipated that unemployment would rise many-fold as a result of cuts in over-staffed companies, closures of obsolete or highly unprofitable businesses, etc.[9] However, this did not happen. In early 1999 the officially registered unemployed in Russia numbered less than 2 million people, or 2.6% of the economically active population. Estimates of total unemployment figures which were calculated using the ILO methodology did not exceed 10–12% (Table 4.2).

Table 4.2 Employment Indicators
All data as at the end of the year stated

	1990	1991	1992	1993	1994	1995	1996	1997	1998[a]	% of change 1990–97
Employment (mln)										
Economically active population	...	...	75.67	75.01	73.96	72.87	73.23	72.82	72.20	...
Total employment,[b] including in:	75.29	73.81	72.07	70.85	68.48	66.44	65.95	64.64	63.30	–14.1
Industry	22.81	22.41	21.32	20.81	18.58	17.18	16.37	14.89	...	–34.7
Agriculture and forestry	9.97	9.97	10.34	10.35	10.53	10.00	9.51	8.83	...	–11.4
Construction	9.02	8.49	7.89	7.14	6.79	6.21	5.88	5.65	...	–37.4
Transport and communications	5.82	5.75	5.63	5.41	5.35	5.25	5.22	5.12	...	–12.0
Trade	5.87	5.63	5.68	6.37	6.48	6.68	6.80	8.71	...	48.4
Services	3.22	3.16	2.99	2.98	3.02	2.98	3.20	3.36	...	4.3
Medicare	4.24	4.31	4.23	4.24	4.39	4.45	4.53	4.41	...	4.0
Education and culture	7.23	7.27	7.52	7.24	7.38	7.32	7.31	7.14	...	–1.2
R&D	3.13	3.08	2.31	2.24	1.83	1.69	1.51	1.43	...	–54.3
Banking and finance	0.40	0.44	0.49	0.58	0.75	0.82	0.80	0.78	...	95.0
State management	1.60	1.53	1.36	1.51	1.53	1.89	2.66	2.58	...	61.3
Other	1.98	1.77	2.31	1.98	1.85	1.97	2.16	1.74	...	–12.1
Unemployment (mln)										
Total unemployed[c]	...	...	3.59	4.16	5.48	6.43	6.73	8.06	8.90	...
Registered unemployed	...	0.06	0.58	0.84	1.64	2.33	2.51	2.00	1.90	...
Strikes										
Participants, mln	0.10	0.24	0.36	0.12	0.16	0.49	0.66	0.89	0.53	787.0
Total work-days lost, mln	0.21	2.31	1.89	0.24	0.76	1.37	4.01	6.00	2.88	2 757.6

NOTES:
[a] Preliminary data.
[b] Excluding students.
[c] Classified as unemployed in accordance with the ILO methodology that also takes into account hidden unemployment.

Sourced and calculated from[7]:
Rossiiskii statisticheskii ezhegodnik. 1995, Moscow: Goskomstat, 1995, p.54; *Rossiiskii statisticheskii ezhegodnik. 1994*, Moscow: Goskomstat, 1994, pp.26, 60–1; *Rossiya v tsifrakh. 1996*, Moscow: Goskomstat, 1996, pp.33, 36, 40, 47; *SNG: Statisticheskii byulleten'*, No.13 (149), July 1996, Moscow: Statkom SNG, p.36; *Narodnoye khozyaistvo RSFSR v 1990 g.*, Moscow: Goskomstat, 1991, pp.109, 121; *Short-term economic statistics. Commonwealth of Independent States, 1980–93*, Moscow: Statkom SNG, 1993, p.128; *Rossiiskaya Federatsiya v 1992 godu*, Moscow: Goskomstat, 1993, p.132; *Narodnoye khozyaistvo Rossiiskoi Federatsii. 1992*, Moscow: Goskomstat, 1992, p.131; *Rossiiskii statisticheskii ezhegodnik. 1996*, Moscow: Goskomstat, 1996, pp.81, 84; *Sotsialno-ekonomicheskoe polozhenie Rossii. 1996 g.*, Moscow: Goskomstat, 1997, pp.179–81; *Rossiya-1997. Ekonomicheskaya konyuktura, Vypusk 1*, Moscow: Tsentr ekonomicheskoi konyuktury, 1997, p.161; *Sotsialno-ekonomicheskoe polozhenie Rossii. 1997 g.*, Moscow: Goskomstat, 1998, pp.283–9; *Sotsialno-ekonomicheskoe polozhenie Rossii. yanvar' 1998 g.*, Moscow: Goskomstat, 1998, pp.208–15; *Rossiiskii statisticheskii ezhegodnik. 1997*, Moscow: Goskomstat, 1998, p.111; *Rossiiskii statisticheskii ezhegodnik. 1998*, Moscow: Goskomstat, 1998, pp.173–98; *Sotsialno-ekonomicheskoe polozhenie Rossii. 1998 g.*, Moscow: Goskomstat, 1999, p.288; *Sotsialno-ekonomicheskoe polozhenie Rossii. yanvar' 1999 g.*, Moscow: Goskomstat, 1999, pp.272–3.

These levels were strikingly low, given, for instance, the slump in industrial production.[10] But if one looks closer at the Russian reform and the way it was carried out, one might find clues that help to explain this puzzling situation. The major emphasis in the 1992–97 Russian reform was placed on financial stabilisation, free trade and privatisation of state property. At the same, time modernisation and the reconstruction and/or restructuring of the national economy was put at the end of priority list of the Russian government. But even less attention the state devoted to stimulation of job creation. The official process of unemployment registration was extremely bureaucratic, unemployment benefits were low and payments were often delayed. This meant that in an absolute majority of cases the closure of an obsolete enterprise was in practice equal to throwing its employees out onto the street basically without any means of subsistence.

These grave social consequences of almost any reform or restructuring at the microeconomic level paralysed reforms on most Russian enterprises. In this situation managers of both state-owned and privatised companies preferred to borrow money from banks or the state and to continue unprofitable operations, rather than to restructure (or close) their companies. By the mid-1990s the absolute majority of Russian companies, formerly or currently owned by the state, were heavily in debt, in desperate need of modernisation and incapable of competing on an open market.

However, this reluctance of managers or state authorities to close loss-making firms also meant that the formal unemployment in Russia remained very low. Five years after the collapse of the Soviet system "hidden" unemployment (or, to be more accurate, over-employment at (ex-) state enterprises) remained the major feature of the Russian labour market, although continuation of such practice was now motivated more by social factors than government political strategies.[11]

The past few years have seen a number of interesting developments in the employment situation in Russia. The most dramatic of these was the two-fold increase in the number of people employed in the banking sector and a drop of almost 50% in the numbers employed in R&D (Table 4.2). While the former is a reflection of the high wages in the booming Russian financial sector, the critical financial situation in research and academia has stimulated a large outflow of people from these areas into other sectors, mainly education, health and the private business sector. As noted earlier, the falls in the number of people employed in industry, agriculture, construction and transport were much smaller than the corresponding falls in production in these areas.

Apart from banking, the other areas experiencing growth in employment over the past five years have been the public service, trade, health and community services. Interestingly, in 1997 there were almost one million more state bureaucrats in Russia than in 1990, during the communist rule. This development raises serious doubts about the nature and effectiveness of the Russian reform, particularly when the earlier dynamics towards the gradual reduction in the numbers of state bureaucrats was dramatically reversed in 1996–97.

The 48% growth in the number of people employed in trade in 1990–97 reflects the changes that had taken place in the so-called "formal" or "organised" trade structures. These include officially established retail and wholesale trading outlets. It needs noting, however, that these statistics do not cover the recent phenomenon of "shuttle" trade. "Shuttle" trade spreads over private internal and external trade, open market and street sales, and shadow economy trading operations. In the post-Soviet years this informal trade has been one of the truly blossoming areas of the Russian economy. It was estimated that between 20 and 40 million people were engaged in "shuttle" trade in the mid-1990s[12] and that this sector accounted for about 63% of all trade operations.[13] If we include people employed in formal trade as well as in the informal trade, then this sector of the Russian economy will become the largest job provider in the country that accounted for approximately 50% of the total economically active population in the mid-1990s!

In recent years, particularly since early 1995, there was an alarming increase of labour unrest and general strike activity in Russia. This growth was a direct response to the deterioration of Russia's social and economic situation, and the inability of the government to improve the situation. A large proportion of these strikes was caused by wage arrears, a problem that greatly undermined the stability of Russian labour market in 1995–98.

In 1997 the number of participants of strikes in Russia was 6.6 times higher than in 1990. In 1996–97 there was a marked increase in the duration of strikes, particularly when during 1996 three times as many working days were lost in strikes as in 1995.

4.2   Current crisis in health services and in education

Table 4.3 gives some general indication of the tendencies and the current state of health of the Russian population and the medical service provided in the country. The data show that in the 1990s the number of doctors per 10 000 population remained relatively stable (the Russian level is among the highest in the world); at the same time, the number of other medical professionals (nurses, technicians, etc.) was declining rapidly. The latter was the result of a substantial decline in incomes for these professions as well as of the deterioration in working conditions and the social status enjoyed earlier by the medical personnel.

With the adoption in 1993 of two laws, one transferring ownership of many medical facilities from the federal to the regional level and the other establishing a system of compulsory medical insurance, the federal government significantly reduced the level of its involvement in funding of the medical sector.[14] However, regional authorities were unable to fill the emerging gap in public health funding, while the ability of private medical insurance funds to attract additional financial resources were grossly limited by the falling incomes of the Russian population. As a result, in the post-Soviet period Russian public health has experienced significant cuts in funding and investment, leading to large reductions in the construction of new hospitals and other medical facilities. Reduced funding for medical services has also meant that many existing hospitals have been experiencing acute shortages of

Table 4.3 Health and Medical Services

	1990	1991	1992	1993	1994	1995	1996	1997	1998[a]	% of change 1990–97
Doctors[bc]	45.0	42.6	43.0	43.4	43.3	44.5	45.7	46.2	46.9	2.7
Medical personnel[b]	124.5	115.8	115.3	113.1	109.7	111.0	112.7	111.5	111.1	–10.4
Hospital beds[b]	137.5	134.8	130.8	129.4	127.4	126.1	123.9	121.0	119.0	–12.0
Morbidity[de]	651.2	665.8	615.6	654.3	653.2	678.8	648.5	674.2	...	3.5
Disabled persons[b]	51.7	61.5	75.7	77.7	76.5	91.1	79.9	77.7	...	50.3

NOTES:
[a] Preliminary data.
[b] Per 10 000 population.
[c] Including dentists.
[d] Per 1 000 population.
[e] Registered for the first time.

Sourced and calculated from:
Rossiiskii statisticheskii ezhegodnik. 1995, Moscow: Goskomstat, 1995, p.165; *Rossiya v tsifrakh. 1996*, Moscow: Goskomstat, 1996, pp.97–98, 100; *Sotsial'naya sfera Rossii*, Moscow: Goskomstat, 1995, pp.138, 143, 155; *Sotsial'no-ekonomicheskoe polozhenie Rossii.1996 g.*, No.12, Moscow: Goskomstat, 1997, p.194; *Rossiiskii statisticheskii ezhegodnik. 1996*, Moscow: Goskomstat, 1996, pp.58, 204–223; *Rossiiskii statisticheskii ezhegodnik. 1997*, Moscow: Goskomstat, 1997, pp.231, 233, 239, 249; *Sodruzhestvo Nezavisimykh Gosudarstv v 1997 godu. Statisticheskii spravochnik*. Moscow: Statkom SNG, 1998, p.256; *Rossiiskii statisticheskii ezhegodnik. 1997*, Moscow: Goskomstat, 1997, pp.295, 299,304, 314; *Sotsialno-ekonomicheskoe polozhenie Rossii. 1998 g.*, Moscow: Goskomstat, 1999, p.302.

drugs; in many cases hospital equipment is either completely worn-out or obsolete.[15]

Deterioration of medical services has had a grave effect on the health of the Russian population. Infant and adult death rates have been increasing, as has morbidity, while the birth rate has been falling. The number of disabled persons increased almost by more than 50% between 1990 and 1997.

The decline in the quality of medical services has been supplemented by a significant lowering of the levels of health awareness. In the mid-1990s Russian per capita alcohol consumption reached the highest level in the world and was nearly double the danger level drawn by the World Health Organisation.[16] In 1990–95 the incidence of heart and blood disease increased 2.1 times, infectious diseases – by more than one-third, and diseases of the nervous system – by 27%. According to Russian medical sources, in 1995 over 70% of the population were living in the conditions of severe emotional and social stress.[17]

Dramatic falls in the volume of financial resources at the government's disposal has had an extremely negative impact, not only on general social developments in post-Soviet Russia, but also on education and research. Since 1992 strikes by unpaid school and university teachers have become so common that they often go unreported in the news. Obviously this has affected the quality and availability of education, particularly in isolated areas. Even in Moscow, St Petersburg and the major Russian provincial capitals many state-run schools are finding it more and more difficult to retain qualified teaching personnel and to upgrade their facilities. But the degradation of the education system is most apparent in the provinces, where the lack of textbooks, modern teaching facilities, salary funds, etc. creates a major obstacle to the teaching process.

Despite the severe and constant lack of funds experienced in recent years by Russian educational institutions, Russia has managed to retain a well-developed education system. As shown in Table 4.4, literacy levels in Russia, as in the former USSR, remain among the highest in the world. Since the start of reforms in Russia Soviet achievements in the educational sphere have been further enhanced by the outflow of highly-qualified personnel from research institutions to schools and universities where salaries have become higher, wage delays less frequent and working conditions generally better. This tendency is clearly demonstrated in Table 4.5: whereas the number of school students in Russia increased by more than 6% between 1990 and 1997, the student/teacher ratio in the same period actually fell from 14.3 to 12.4.

Table 4.4   Education Level of the Russian Population, %
All population aged 15 and older

	1989	1994
Full higher education[a]	11.3	13.3
Uncompleted higher education[b]	1.7	1.8
High education[c]	46.6	50.4
Other school education	33.9	30.2
Illiterate/no formal education	6.5	4.3
Total	100.0	100.0

NOTES:
[a] Those who successfully completed full course and received a degree (diploma).
[b] Those who completed full 2–4 years of higher education.
[c] Those who completed 8–11 years of secondary school and received school certificate.

Source:
Rossiiskii statisticheskii ezhegodnik. 1995, Moscow: Goskomstat, 1995, p.119.

While student numbers at schools have been constantly increasing throughout the 1990s (though it was predicted that these numbers will start to fall later in the decade when the effects of the current demographic crisis hit the education sector), university enrolments experienced a decline in the first years of the Russian reform. Student numbers at Russian universities were falling since the early 1980s, but then these numbers stabilised at the beginning of the 1990s at the 2.8 million level.[18] Between 1991 and 1994 student numbers fell to 2.5 million (Table 4.5). However, in 1995–97 this tendency reversed with a sharp increase in student numbers to pre-crisis levels. In 1997 and, according to the preliminary data, in 1998[19] numbers of university students in Russia were at their highest levels since the early 1980s.

The latter development was a consequence of the general change in public mentality and employment market in Russia. The chances of making a good living out of primitive, primarily trade, "market" operations that opened certain opportunities in the early years of the reform, had almost disappeared by the mid-1990s. The growing complexity of business operations in Russia, increased dealings with foreign companies and reforms in the taxation and accounting systems greatly increased the demand for legal and accounting specialists, economists, computer programmers, etc. who had knowledge of foreign languages and Western accounting standards and who, at the same time, were conversant in the rapidly changing and highly complicated area of Russian internal legislation. As a result of these changes on the Russian

Table 4.5 Science and Education in Russia

	1990	1991	1992	1993	1994	1995	1996	1997	% of change 1990–97
Schools									
Total number of students, mln	20.9	20.9	21.0	21.1	21.6	22.1	22.2	22.2	6.2
Students per 1 teacher	14.3	13.8	13.3	12.8	12.8	12.9	12.4	12.4	–13.3
Universities									
Total number of students, mln	2.8	2.8	2.6	2.5	2.5	2.7	2.8	3.1	10.7
Students per 10,000 population	190	186	178	171	172	179	190	208	9.5
Science and Research[a]									
Number of research institutions	4 646	4 564	4 555	4 269	3 968	4 059	4 122	4 137	–11.0
Research personnel, thousands	1 227.4	1 079.1	984.7	778.8	640.8	620.1	572.6	535.4	–56.4
including:									
Doctors of sciences	15.5	16.2	17.4	18.2	18.1	19.3	19.5	20.2	30.3
Candidates of sciences (PhD)	127.0	118.0	111.4	105.2	97.3	97.2	93.1	89.9	–29.2
Post-graduate students[b], thousands	64.9	61.1	53.6	52.0	55.4	64.5	77.5	91.4	40.9
Successful graduates (PhD), thousands	3.5	3.1	3.1	3.2	2.7	2.6	2.9	3.6	2.9
Successful graduates (Doctor)	71	430	247	194	168	137	200	226	218.3
State expenditure on R&D									
in constant prices, 1990 = 100	100.0	36.5	17.6	14.7	11.9	8.2	7.2	9.2	–90.8
As % of federal budgetary expenditure	10.70	3.90	2.62	3.11	1.96	1.99	1.80	2.47	–76.9
As % of GDP	2.50	0.96	0.54	0.49	0.46	0.35	0.33	0.41	–83.6

NOTES:
[a] Data exclude universities and other higher education institutions.
[b] Seeking candidate's (PhD) and doctor's degrees.

Sourced and calculated from:
Nauka v Rossiiskoi Federatsii. Moscow: Goskomstat, 1995, pp.5, 11, 45–6; *Rossiya v tsifrakh. 1996.* Moscow: Goskomstat, 1996, pp.75, 77, 87–8; *Sotsial'naya sfera Rossii,* Moscow: Goskomstat, 1995, pp.166, 172, 184, 188; *Rossiiskii statisticheskii ezhegodnik. 1994,* Moscow: Goskomstat, 1994, pp.57, 143; *Rossiiskaya Federatsiya v 1992 godu,* Moscow: Goskomstat, 1993, p.358; *Rossiiskii statisticheskii ezhegodnik. 1995,* Moscow: Goskomstat, 1995, pp.119, 149, 274; *Economica Weekly Press Summary,* Moscow: Analytica, Vol.2, No.37, 23–29 September 1995; *Segodnya,* 28 March 1996, p.5; *Rossiiskii statisticheskii ezhegodnik. 1996,* Moscow: Goskomstat, 1996, p.473; *Rossiiskii statisticheskii ezhegodnik. 1997,* Moscow: Goskomstat, 1997, pp.188, 207, 501–8, 519–20; *Rossiiskii statisticheskii ezhegodnik. 1998,* Moscow: Goskomstat, 1998, pp.263, 268, 284, 623, 626, 629, 634–5.

job market, a substantial increase in demand for university degrees was registered since 1995.

While the central importance of the education sector for the general development of society has largely helped to protect it from a total degradation during the "transition" period, the situation in the "unprotected" areas of research and development has been catastrophic. In the research infrastructure inherited by Russia from the Soviet Union, higher education institutions traditionally played a very limited role. The bulk of the country's research potential was concentrated in specialised research institutions, including those affiliated with the Russian Academy of Sciences, various ministries, enterprises and companies, as well as independent research bodies. Many of these institutions played a central role in Soviet technological development. Traditionally, most scientific research groups were also directly or indirectly affiliated with the military-industrial complex. The economic crisis that paralysed the Russian economy in the post-Soviet period has had a direct and adverse effect on the country's research potential. But this effect has been much less visible than in education.

It should be noted that the significance of the current critical situation in research is strategic rather than tactical.[20] When teachers strike, this sends an immediate political signal to the local community and to the society as a whole, but strikes of researchers have an extremely limited political effect. The lack of political power together with the dramatic decline in their social status has stimulated many researchers, particularly the younger generation, to seek alternative, mainly not research-oriented, employment opportunities.

The consequences of the current "brain-drain" from Russian scientific and research institutions will only start to make itself felt in one or two decades, when Russia's prospects for modernisation and independent technological development will inevitably become more obscure and uncertain. These negative changes are taking place in Russia at a time when the importance of R&D potential in global economic development is becoming crucial, particularly in the new industries where the information and technological revolution is currently under way. Therefore, the neglect of R&D needs in Russia may well create a much more serious problem of general technological backwardness throughout the whole country, consigning Russia to the developing group of countries for years to come.

The gap in technological development between the West and the Soviet Union started to grow in the 1970s; by the mid-1980s it had become so obvious that, together with other factors, it pushed the

Soviet leadership onto the reform track. The decline of Gorbachev's power in the late 1980s was to a large extent a result of his failed attempts to modernise the Soviet economy. However, in the post-1991 period, the economic crisis that crippled the Russian economy, forced the government to move the issue of Russian technological restructuring and modernisation to the bottom of the reform priority list. The result was the catastrophic decline of Russian science.

It is hard to measure the extent to which the Russian R&D potential has been devastated in recent years. The available data, disturbing as they are, still give only a very approximate picture of the real situation. For example, the data in Table 4.5 show that from 1991 to 1997 the research staff of Russian research institutions fell more than twice. However, these data do not indicate the fact that such unprecedented decline was mainly a result of dramatic falls in the numbers of young researchers. Data on the age structure of Russian research personnel are currently available only for 1994. These figures indicate that in 1994, 66.8% of researchers were over 40 years of age.[21] This compares rather negatively with the corresponding data for the Soviet Union as a whole in 1988, when researchers over 40 years of age comprised 54% of all research staff.[22]

A mass outflow of young Russian researchers from science and R&D is also demonstrated by falls in the number of first post-graduate degree holders in 1990–97. Russia has a two-tiered system of post-graduate degrees, with the lower degree of *"kandidat nauk"* (approximately equivalent to a Western Doctor of Philosophy) and the higher level of *"doktor nauk"* (equivalent to or higher than a Western Doctor of Science). In most cases those seeking a *doktor's* degree already hold a *kadidat* degree. The majority of first degree (*kandidat*) holders received their degree before reaching the age of 30. As can be seen from Table 4.5, the number of candidates of sciences in Russian academia fell by more than a quarter in 1990–97, while until 1997 the number of successful post-graduate students was constantly falling. During the same period, however, there was a dramatic increase in numbers of holders of higher post-graduate degrees (*doktor*): their numbers increased by 30%, while the number of successful graduates receiving *doktor's* degrees increased more than two times.

The latter development requires some explanation. Firstly, it should be noted that the official data on the number of successful graduates receiving *doktor's* degrees in 1990 are much lower than was actually the case. This is because in the Soviet period the academic councils, which examined the doktor's theses, were not necessarily located in the same republic as the actual graduates. Thus, many Russian researchers obtained their degrees in other republics, while many non-Russian holders of *doktor's* degrees received their qualifications in Russia. This fact also explains a sudden increase (by more than six times) of new holders of *doktor's* degrees in 1991. Secondly, in recent years the outflow of highly qualified personnel from Russian academia has caused a significant decline in general research standards. In this connection, the requirements for obtaining a *doktor's* degree have been also substantially eased.

Possibly the best indicator of the critical situation in Russian science is the data on R&D expenditure (Table 4.5). In 1990–97 state expenditure in that area in constant prices fell by almost 11 times; the budgetary share of R&D expenditure shrunk from 10.7% in 1990 to just 2.5% in 1997. At the same time no significant alternative sources of R&D finance have been created inside the country. It is no surprise that by the end of the decade Russian science found itself in a situation of deep crisis.[23]

4.3 Changes in national and regional food consumption patterns

Another important indicator of the negative impact of the post-1991 developments on the Russian society is the change in the food consumption patterns of the population. The dramatic falls in living standards of the Russian people affected the quality and quantity of the food they consumed almost immediately, which, together with the degradation of health and medical services, had an adverse impact on the demographic development, as discussed above.

The data for annual per capita food consumption indicate that in 1990–93 there was a significant fall in consumption of all basic food products, except potatoes and bread (Table 4.6). This process was reversed somewhat in 1993–94, with the average consumption of meat, milk, sugar and vegetables rising slightly above the low 1992–93 levels. However, in 1995–97 the consumption of milk, meat and eggs again dropped significantly. In 1997 the average Russian citizen was consuming 20% less fish, 26% less meat, 42% less dairy products, 19% less fruit and 9% less vegetables than in 1990. On the other hand, until 1996 per capita consumption of bread remained higher or at the same level as in 1990 while consumption of potatoes was significantly higher.

According to some independent estimates, in the post-Soviet years overall per capita food consumption in Russia dropped to 40% of the

Table 4.6   Food Consumption in Russia
In kilograms per capita

	1990	1991	1992	1993	1994	1995	1996	1997	% of change 1990–97
Fish and fish products	15	14	12	11	9	9	9	12	–20.0
Milk and milk products	378	348	294	305	305	249	235	219	–42.1
Meat and meat products	70	65	58	57	58	53	48	52	–25.7
Fruits and berries	37	35	29	31	30	30	31	30	–18.9
Eggs (pcs)	231	229	243	236	210	191	173	...	...
Sugar and confectionery	32	29	26	29	28	27	26	33	3.1
Vegetables	85	87	78	77	71	83	78	77	–9.4
Bread and bakery products	97	101	104	107	101	102	97	93	–4.1
Potatoes	94	98	107	112	113	112	108	...	...

Sources:
Rossiiskii statisticheskii ezhegodnik. 1995, Moscow: Goskomstat, 1995, p.103; *Rossiiskii statisticheskii ezhegodnik. 1997*, Moscow: Goskomstat, 1997, p.175; *Sotsial'naya sfera Rossii*, Moscow: Goskomstat, 1995, p.58; *Rossiiskii statisticheskii ezhegodnik. 1998*, Moscow: Goskomstat, 1998, p.249.

1991 level, or, in other words, the population was forced to turn the clock back 20 years in this respect.[24] These dramatic changes in food consumption patterns were directly related to post-Soviet social developments. For instance, significant falls in the consumption of meat and dairy products came as a result of falls in population incomes that made these products (whether locally produced or imported) unaffordable for many Russians.[25] The huge drop in the 1990s in the consumption of fish products was also the outcome of falling incomes and the rise of prices for these products. Extremely high costs of transportation pushed prices for fish produced in the Baltic States and the Russian Far East (the major fishing areas of the former USSR) beyond the reach of many Russians.

Unable to consume expensive food products, many Russians were forced to change their consumption patterns towards increased shares of potatoes and bread. In addition to that, a significant part of the population became dependent, more than ever before, on food which they have grown themselves on private plots of land in the countryside (*dachas* and ancillary households). According to a recent report prepared by the Russian Academy of Sciences, in 1996 between 70% and 80% of the population listed their "fruit and vegetable gardens" as an important additional source of food supply.[26]

However, changes in food consumption patterns have varied greatly across the different regions of Russia. The vastness of Russia's territory, the general underdevelopment of its infrastructure, and regional differences in the levels of industrial and agricultural production meant that the purchasing powers of salaries in the various regions and oblasts of Russia have always differed greatly.[27] For instance, while in the Soviet days workers in the Far Eastern region of Magadan received much higher wages than those in central European areas, food prices in Magadan were also significantly higher because of huge transportation costs and the almost total non-viability of local agricultural production in that remote area of Russia. Therefore, although an average per capita income in Magadan was always much higher than Russian national average, the amount of food that could be purchased on that income was, in fact, the same or even lower than in other areas of the country.

In 1992, decentralisation of state food distribution structures led to disproportionate development in food supply and food pricing in Russia. Prices for foodstuffs and consumer goods, previously established and controlled centrally, became regulated solely by primitive market forces. This immediately resulted in growing differences in prices between various regions. While in traditional agricultural areas prices for foodstuffs increased only marginally (compared to average per capita incomes in these areas), in the predominantly manufacturing and mining regions falls in the purchasing power of the population's incomes were much more pronounced.

These new variations in food consumption patterns do not show up in Russian national statistics. The Graph 4.1 shows the dynamics of change in the share of a monthly basket of basic food products[28] for consumption by one adult in the average per capita monthly income in Russia. According to this graph, in the first months of the Russian reform there was a dramatic increase in food prices: between December 1991 and January 1992 the price of the food basket increased 4.5 times and reached more than 90% of an average income. Huge price fluctuations continued until mid-1993 when the cost of this basket stabilised; since then it has remained within a very high range of 30–40% of an average monthly income. Another interesting development that comes out clearly on the graph is that despite the common view that the August 1998 financial crisis had a severe negative effect on the living standards of the Russian population, according to dynamics presented on Graph 4.1 between June and December 1998 the share of food basket in an average per capita income remained very stable at around 28–30%. That meant that before the end of 1998 most Russians have still not yet experienced any significant negative consequences of the collapse of the national banking system.

Graph 4.1   Share of Food in the National Average Income, %
(food basket for one adult as % of national per capita income, monthly data)

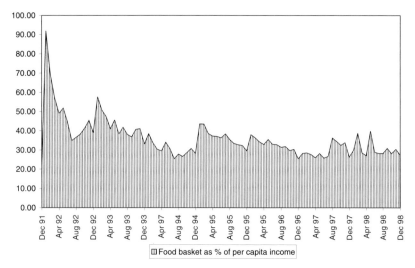

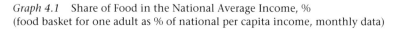

This national picture becomes more complicated if we try comparing local food prices and local incomes in different regions of Russia. Food-income ratios are one of the most reliable indicators of differences in inter-regional social development. The data on regional incomes and prices for major food products allow us to analyse the dynamics of changes in population incomes in various areas of Russia.

On the basis of the information on retail prices for food products in Russian cities which is regularly collected by the Russian Ministry of Agriculture and published in Russian newspapers, we have calculated the average prices for four basic food products in various regions, oblasts and major cities of Russia. Then, by dividing monthly incomes by the average prices in the regions, we calculated indices of purchasing power of regional incomes, represented in the volume of a food product that a given income can buy. Comparing the latter to the national average data, we then determined deviations from the national average in the purchasing power of incomes in various regions. Table 4.7 summarises the results of these calculations.

As indicated in Table 4.7a, there are significant differences in the purchasing power of average regional incomes between the various economic regions. On average, real ("product-deflated") per capita

Table 4.7   Purchasing Power [a] of Regional Incomes in Russia, 1994–96

a) Index of food products that could be purchased on an average regional income, Russian national average = 100

	Beef		Milk		Butter		Sunflower oil	
	Mar 94	Mar 96	Mar 94	Mar 96	Mar 94	Mar 96	Mar 94	Mar 96
Northern	124.4	106.2	103.7	78.7	135.4	107.8	130.1	103.6
North West	98.9	96.5	91.8	88.7	104.8	96.1	108.0	106.1
Central	115.8	105.9	127.4	107.4	108.9	105.2	142.9	104.4
Volgo-Vyatka	84.8	71.1	109.5	85.8	73.0	69.2	79.9	70.9
Centr.ChernoZem	96.0	80.2	100.2	81.0	62.6	65.7	108.0	93.3
Volga	105.2	83.9	127.4	109.6	83.7	74.1	109.2	71.7
North Caucasus	71.7	78.9	70.0	69.9	62.8	69.1	97.5	100.9
Urals	99.3	80.3	86.7	76.2	88.8	71.7	74.5	79.3
Western Siberia	131.7	91.1	124.1	89.9	124.2	83.9	111.1	70.5
Eastern Siberia	109.6	93.8	93.6	98.0	85.3	97.8	67.6	78.3
Far East	83.9	84.7	72.3	83.8	129.6	130.2	97.4	95.3
Russia total	*100.0*	*100.0*	*100.0*	*100.0*	*100.0*	*100.0*	*100.0*	*100.0*

b) Disparities in purchasing power of average incomes in selected areas, Russian national average = 100

	Beef		Milk		Butter		Sunflower oil	
	Mar 94	Mar 96	Mar 94	Mar 96	Mar 94	Mar 96	Mar 94	Mar 96
Rich Areas[b]								
Moscow	185.1	298.6	178.4	242.4	220.1	310.6	193.1	280.1
Sakha Republic	101.7	99.3	206.5	120.3	186.8	167.2	132.9	115.6
Murmansk	175.9	130.1	97.5	98.1	192.3	119.9	161.2	123.4
Poor areas[b]								
Pskov	82.4	69.3	109.3	65.5	85.7	67.6	104.6	70.2
Chuvashia	58.3	70.8	90.6	89.1	52.4	57.1	70.9	62.4
Ryazan'	82.8	63.3	61.1	67.9	74.4	61.9	93.4	60.2
Russia total	*100.0*	*100.0*	*100.0*	*100.0*	*100.0*	*100.0*	*100.0*	*100.0*

In March 1994 the product equivalent of an all-Russia average per capita monthly income was 27.7 kg of butter, 68.3 kg of vegetable oil, 235.8 kg of milk or 42.9 kg of beef. In March 1996 the purchasing power of an average per capita income in Russia was equal to 35.0 kg of butter, 74.8 kg of vegetable oil, 242.3 kg of milk or 56.6 kg of beef.

NOTES:

[a] All data are estimates for the stated period based on average retail prices in regional capitals and average per capita incomes in the corresponding regions.

[b] Samples only. Published data on prices are currently available only for selected cities and regions, and exclude some of the poorest areas where price/income ratios are even more dramatic than in those areas represented in the table above.

Calculated from:
Krestyanskie vedomosti, Moscow, 14–20 March 1994, 04–10 April 1994 and 18–24 March 1996;
Sotsialno-ekonomicheskoe polozheniye Rossii, janvar'-mart 1994, Moscow: Goskomstat 1994, pp.281–2;
Sotsialno-ekonomicheskoe polozheniye Rossii, janvar'-aprel' 1996, Moscow: Goskomstat 1996, pp.97, 235–6.

incomes were highest in the Central and Northern regions and lowest in the North Caucasus, the Chernozem region and the Urals. Between 1994 and 1996 the purchasing power of average incomes experienced a sharp decline in all regions of Russia. In some of the regions (Western Siberia and the Volga region) incomes fell below the national average in 1996, while only two years earlier they had been above the average. By March 1996 incomes in purchasing power terms were below the national average already in almost all regions. This meant that the purchasing power of incomes and, accordingly, the consumption of food products were distributed unevenly across Russia.

Table 4.7b provides an explanation for this. From the published price and income data series we have selected six Russian areas with the highest and the lowest levels of average income purchasing power. As this *oblast*-level analysis reveals, averages for an economic region tend to level out the huge disparities in real incomes that exist within certain economic regions, just as the Russian national average hides the disparities between the 12 economic regions. For example, the relatively high average living standards in the Central region largely can be attributed to a high-income level in the city of Moscow. In 1996 an average Muscovite could afford to buy 3 times more beef and butter, 2.8 times more sunflower oil, and 2.5 times more milk than an average Russian citizen. But within a distance of just a few hundred kilometres, in the same Central economic region, we find one of the poorest areas in Russia, Ryazan'. In 1996 the average per capita income in Ryazan' could purchase 10–40% less some of major foodstuffs than the average Russian income.

Between 1994 and 1996 the purchasing power of an average Muscovite's income had grown 1.5 times. In the same period the purchasing power of incomes in all poor areas, as well as in two traditionally high-income areas (the Far Eastern Republic of Sakha and the Northern city of Murmansk), has dropped significantly. On average, in 1996 Muscovites could purchase 4–5 times more of the listed foodstuffs on their average income than people living in the poor areas of Russia could. These striking inequalities in wealth distribution become even more worrying when one takes into account the fact that prior to 1992, when all salaries and food prices were controlled by the state, the gap in purchasing power of regional incomes was only marginal.

Some of the latest available figures on purchasing power of regional incomes and Russian population's consumption patterns are presented in a graphical format on Map 4.1.[29] The map lists shares of a monthly basket of 25 major foodstuffs in average per capita incomes in Russian administrative units. For presentation purposes, we have grouped these units into three main categories: high-income areas where the cost of the basket is between 10% and 23% of an average income; medium-income areas (23–35%) and low-income areas (more than 35%).

In December 1997 highest incomes in purchasing power terms were registered in Russia's main oil- and gas-producing areas: Tyumen', Komi Republic, Magadan, Krasnoyarskii krai, Irkutsk and Sakha. The majority of other areas of Russia fell into a medium-income group, while population of North Caucasian ethnic republics and some industrially depressed central regions (Ivanovo, Ryazan', Tula) had the lowest incomes. Disparities in purchasing power of regional incomes were rather alarming: while in the late 1997 an average person living in Tyumen' could afford to buy on his income an equivalent of 8.6 food baskets, per capita income in Ivanovo was equal to the cost of only 1.8 food baskets.

Map 4.1   The Cost of Food Basket as a Share in an Average Per Capita Salary by Region, December 1997

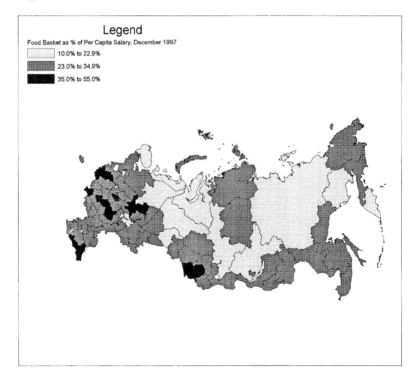

Such an immense difference in purchasing power of *average per capita* regional incomes is indicative of the process of polarisation, which was taking place within the Russian society since the start of the reform. Polarisation of incomes – and living standards – was taking place both on a social level, between various strata of the society, and on a regional level, between rich and poor oblasts. Map 4.1 and Table 4.7 clearly demonstrate that in contemporary Russia geographical income distribution and food consumption have become very disproportionate: there is currently only a handful of high income areas which rise well above the rest of the country. These are either financial and bureaucratic centres, or mining areas. On the other hand, among the remaining areas of Russia traditional agricultural areas and ethnic autonomous republics form the lowest income zone.

4.4   The widening gap between rich and poor

The major crisis that almost paralysed the Russian economy in the 1990s had a direct impact on the country's social development. For the majority of the Russian population, the effect of this crisis was multiplied by the growing disproportions in income distribution. While a small part of the population was gaining financially from the reform, at least until the August 1998 crisis, the remainder suffered immensely. Within just five years, income distribution in Russia had taken on a structure that was practically the diametrical opposite of that which prevailed under Soviet rule.

Table 4.8 shows general terms the interrelation between dynamics of inflation (consumer price index), average incomes, nominal and real salaries. The last year of existence of the Soviet Union (1991) and the first two years of the Russian reform (1992–93) were a period of rapid impoverishment of the Russian people. During that time consumer prices were growing much faster than the average per capita income. This process peaked in 1992 when the CPI grew 3.7 times faster than incomes.[30] After 1994, following Russian government's attempts to curb inflation and bring some stability into the national financial system, the process somewhat reversed and by 1997 annual index of CPI in constant (1990) prices was 1.5 times higher than that of the real average income. However, as the August financial crisis has shown, this stability was extremely fragile and based on massive government borrowings. The preliminary data for 1998 demonstrated a significant rise in the CPI/income ratio, almost to 1992–93 levels. Much of this second impoverishment of the Russian population has

Table 4.8 Dynamics of Average Income and CPI (indices, 1990 = 100)

	1990	1991	1992	1993	1994	1995	1996	1997	1998[a]
Gross current average income	100	217	1 853	20 419	95 193	245 885	359 437	424 855	447 945
Consumer price index	100	260	6 786	63 788	200 934	462 147	562 895	624 813	1 152 155
Ratio = CPI/average income	1	1.2	3.66	3.12	2.11	1.88	1.57	1.47	2.57
Real average income	100	116	61.5	71.3	79.9	69.8	69.8	72.2	59.1
Real average salary[b]	100	97.0	65.0	65.2	60.0	43.2	45.4	54.3	46.8
Real average salary paid[c]	100	97.0	64.9	64.8	59.2	42.2	42.1	43.9	42.1
Gap in incomes between rich and poor (in times)[d]	4.4	4.5	8.0	11.2	15.0	13.5	13.1	13.5	13.4

NOTES:
[a] Preliminary data.
[b] Data for average salaries is based on Tables 4.11 and 4.13 (see below).
[c] Deflated average salary less average wage arrears.
[d] Total incomes of 10% of population with lowest incomes compared to total incomes of 10% of population with highest incomes.

Sourced and calculated from:
Rossiiskii statisticheskii ezhegodnik. 1994, Moscow: Goskomstat, 1994, pp.84, 284; *Rossiiskii statisticheskii ezhegodnik. 1995*, Moscow: Goskomstat, 1995, pp.77, 294;
Sodruzhestvo Nezavisimykh Gosudarstv v 1995 godu. Kratkii spravochnik, Moscow: Statkom SNG, January 1996, pp.37, 47;
Sotsial'no-ekonomicheskoe polozhenie Rossii, yanvar'-iyun' 1996 g., Moscow: Goskomstat, 1996, pp.95, 155–6, 160; *Sotsial'no-ekonomicheskoe polozhenie Rossii. 1995 g.*, Moscow: Goskomstat, 1996, pp.255–7, 262; *Rossiiskii statisticheskii ezhegodnik. 1996*, Moscow: Goskomstat, 1996, p.116;
Sotsial'no-ekonomicheskoe polozhenie Rossii. 1996 g., Moscow: Goskomstat, 1997, pp.164, 182, 189; *Sotsial'no-ekonomicheskoe polozhenie Rossii. 1997 g.*, Moscow: Goskomstat, 1998, pp.7–8, 266–72; *Sotsial'no-ekonomicheskoe polozhenie Rossii. 1998 g.*, Moscow: Goskomstat, 1999, pp.260–8.

happened in the last four months of 1998 that followed the August financial collapse.

In the first year of the Russian reform (1992) real per capita income in Russia fell dramatically: by almost 40% from the 1990 level. In the next two years real incomes were growing steadily reaching on average almost 80% of the 1990 level, but in 1995 they sharply decreased again. This decline mainly resulted from renewed attempts by the Russian government aimed at controlling inflation and money supply in the country. According to *Goskomstat* data for 1996–97, real per capita incomes in 1996 remained at the 1995 level and in 1997 have again started to increase gradually. The August 1998 crisis had caused a total reversal in these trends. During 1998 the annual average per capita income in Russia in real terms had fallen to its lowest level in the 1990s, or to just 59% of its 1990 equivalent.

From a general social perspective, 1992 was the most critical year in recent Russian history when around 90% of the population within a very short period of time, practically overnight, suffered huge financial losses. Surprisingly, however, there were no significant political crises that year. A number of factors can explain that. The most important are:

(1)   High level of expectations of the future change among the population, with many people willing and prepared to sacrifice immediate material gains for the sake of prosperity in the future.

(2)   Hopes for a successful (albeit painful) reform were at the time significantly strengthened by negative and vivid memories of the last days and months of Communist rule, particularly towards the end of 1991 when acute food shortages became an everyday reality across Russia.

(3)   Despite these shortages, many families still held relatively large reserves of food and other commodities that were accumulated during the last years of the Soviet era and which later helped many Russians to survive truly dramatic falls in income.

The dynamics of nominal and *de facto* (i.e., actually paid) salaries show that the importance of wages in the structure of overall incomes of the population was constantly falling in the 1990s. In real terms nominal salaries in the national economy fell in 1990–98 by 53%; however, if we take into consideration delays in wage payments, then in 1998 the real (paid) salary was equal to just 42% of what it was in 1990. However, during the same period per capita average income in real terms had decreased less rapidly, to just 59% of its 1990 level.

Falls in incomes and salaries have been significantly greater for certain social groups and classes than for an average Russian employee. The gap between rich and poor in Russia has been growing rapidly in the early 1990s: between 1990 and 1994 this gap increased from 4.4 times to 15 times. Since 1995 the gap stabilised at a slightly lower but still comparatively very high level of 13 times (Table 4.8). These large income disproportions show that during the years of reform income polarisation and poverty in Russia were on the rise.[31]

The dynamics of change in the income distribution among the Russian population, as presented in Table 4.9, are also indicative of these alarming tendencies. According to these data, between 1990 and 1998 the proportion of the population with gross earnings below half the average national per capita income (current roubles) increased almost three times from 11% to 32%. However, the dynamics of non-deflated incomes in Russia show that, in fact, in the period before 1998 the share of the population with incomes higher than the national average income was on an increase but following the August 1998 crisis it fell to an approximately pre-reform level.

The picture of income distribution in Russia becomes different if we deflate incomes of the population and compare annual dynamics using one criterion. In Table 4.9b we took the average income of 1990 as a base and then broke up population incomes in the following years into three major categories: (a) those with a gross income of less than half of the 1990 average income; (b) Russians with incomes between half and full average 1990 income; and (c) high-income earners (above the 1990 average income). The result is quite stunning. The trend towards income polarisation in Russia during the 1990s becomes apparent: while in 1990–98 the share of "the poor" (incomes below 50% of the 1990 average level) increased by 4.6 times, the share of "the rich" (with income levels above the 1990 average) had fallen by 6.9 times.

Another important conclusion that can be drawn from these figures is that between 1990 and 1992, in the first years of the Russian reform, there was a dramatic fall in incomes which was only partially offset by changes in the following years.

The process of impoverishment of the population was accompanied by a narrowing of the share of Russian mid-income earners. While in 1991 people with incomes between 0.5 and 1.0 of an average 1990 income constituted 57% of the Russian population, in 1995 their share in the population fell to just 33%. By 1997–98 this share increased to above 40% level. However, income trends that developed in the period

Table 4.9 Russia: Income Distribution of Population

a) Income levels of population, current roubles (shares of population in %)

	1990	1991	1992	1993	1994	1995	1996	1997	1998[a]
% of population with incomes:									
lower than 0.5 av. income	11.4	13.4	26.5	16.6	35.0	31.7	25.3	24.6	32.1
between 0.5 and 1.0 av.income	53.2	60.2	40.0	42.3	36.0	28.4	39.3	31.2	34.3
over 1.0 av.income	35.4	26.4	33.5	41.1	29.0	39.9	35.4	44.2	33.6
All population	100.0	100.0	100.0	100.0	100.0	100.0	100.0	100.0	100.0

b) Real income levels of population (shares of population in %)

	1990	1991	1992	1993	1994	1995	1996	1997	1998[a]
% of population with incomes:									
lower than 0.5 av. 1990 income	11.4	3.9	49.6	35.5	39.2	47.4	47.7	39.4	52.2
between 0.5 and 1.0 av. 1990 income	53.2	57.2	39.3	38.7	35.5	33.1	36.0	48.0	42.7
over 1.0 av. 1990 income	35.4	38.9	11.1	25.8	25.3	19.5	16.3	12.6	5.1
All population	100	100	100	100	100	100	100	100	100

NOTES:
[a] In December 1998.

Calculated from:
Rossiiskii statisticheskii ezhegodnik. 1994, Moscow: Goskomstat, 1994, pp.93–5; *Rossiiskii statisticheskii ezhegodnik. 1995*, Moscow: Goskomstat, 1995, pp.77, 85–7; *Sotsial'no-ekonomicheskoe polozhenie Rossii. 1995 g.*, Moscow: Goskomstat, 1996, pp.261–2; *Sotsial'no-ekonomicheskoe polozhenie Rossii. 1996 g.*, Moscow: Goskomstat, 1997, pp.188–9; *Rossiiskii statisticheskii ezhegodnik. 1996*, Moscow: Goskomstat, 1996, p.117; *Sotsial'no-ekonomicheskoe polozhenie Rossii. 1997 g.*, Moscow: Goskomstat, 1998, pp.266–72; *Sotsial'no-ekonomicheskoe polozhenie Rossii. 1998 g.*, Moscow: Goskomstat, 1999, pp.268–9.

after the August 1998 crisis are in the future likely to result in a further narrowing of the mid-income strata.

If we consider a middle level of incomes to be one of the major attributes of a middle class, then the post-Soviet changes in income distribution are indicative of a process of gradual disappearance of the Russian (Soviet) middle class. This process had a number of extremely negative political consequences. Income polarisation, both at social and geographical levels, significantly destabilised political and social situation in Russia. Mass support that the policy of Russian reformers attracted in the first months after the start of reform was quickly disappearing. Instead, the majority of Russian people were becoming increasingly indifferent to reform endeavours of the government, as well as to the earlier ideals of freedom and political democratisation. By the mid-1990s this indifference was becoming gradually transformed into growing popularity of various extremist and nationalist forces.

If we present the changes in income distribution in a graphic format, the disappearance of the middle class becomes even more striking. Graph 4.2 shows that in 1990 Russia had an income structure in the form of a pyramid with its top cut off. Many developed societies have similar income structures. This pattern remained mostly unchanged in 1991, but in the following years the shape of this structure was almost totally transformed. By 1998 the income structure of the Russian population was a complete reverse of the late Soviet model. The larger part of the population in that year have found themselves in a low-income group while a tiny proportion of Russians had incomes higher than the 1990 average income. This structure put Russia far behind the developed nations and closer to income distribution patterns in many developing countries of Africa, Asia and Latin America.

Although income changes were always secondary to more general problems of economic transformation and the strategy of reform, their effect for many Russians was more visible and, in most cases, more painful than any other recent development. There is little doubt that such changes as massive growth in poverty and disappearance of the middle class are bound to have far-reaching political effects. The rapid spread of poverty across Russia intensifies local separatism and significantly weakens Russia's federal base. This is disturbing in immediate terms because it leads to the growth of political extremism and of various forms of nationalism in Russia. However, the strategic importance of these processes is yet to be analysed.

One of the first transformations initiated by the Russian reformers was the removal of the state-controlled currency exchange rate. This

Graph 4.2   Change in Real Income Distribution in Russia, 1990–98
(by main income groups of population; average per capita income in 1990 = 1)

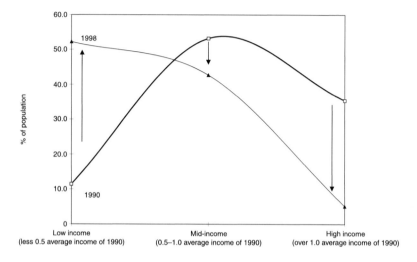

led to a fast demonopolisation of the foreign currency market and to disappearance of the black market for currency exchange that existed in the Soviet times.[32] The earlier artificial exchange rates were replaced by market rates, which, however, in real terms were significantly lower than in the Soviet period. This was mainly due to a dramatic fall in demand for foreign currency as a result of falls in real incomes of the people. Currency exchange rates in the post-Soviet period became largely determined by the interests of large groups of Russian trading organisations (exporters and importers) and national banks. Increased business and other communications between Russia and the rest of the world meant that foreign cash became much more readily available on the internal market than ever before in Soviet times.

All these factors created an amazing situation: while the average real income of the population during 1992 fell by 47%, in current US dollar terms it in fact increased by 5.2 times (Table 4.10). According to data from the Moscow Centre of Economic Analysis, between December 1991 and December 1996 the real average wage in the Russian national economy fell by almost two-thirds; during the same period the national average wage in US dollar equivalent increased by 24.5 times! In other words, in the five years between late 1991 and the end of 1996 the purchasing power of the US dollar in Russia had decreased by more than 70 times (see Graph 4.3).

Table 4.10 Dynamics of the Average Salary in the National Economy, 1991–98

	Dec 91	Dec 92	Dec 93	Dec 94	Dec 95	Dec 96	Dec 97	Dec 98
Salary in current roubles	1 195	16 071	141 218	354 236	735 500	1 017 100	1 214 800	1 390
Salary in constant roubles (Dec.1991 prices)	1 195	634	735	823	719	719	744	608
Salary in US dollars (MIBEX exchange rate)	7.5	38.8	113.9	103.9	159.1	183.8	203.8	67.3[a]

NOTES:

[a] Calculation based on the official rate of the Russian Central Bank.

Sourced and calculated from:

Rossiya-1997. Ekonomicheskaya kon'yuktura. Vypusk 4. Moscow: Tsentr ekonomicheskoi kon'yuktury, December 1997, p.166; *Sotsial'no-ekonomicheskoe polozhenie Rossii. 1998 g.,* Moscow: Goskomstat, 1999, pp.263–5.

Graph 4.3   Dynamics of Average Wage in Russia
(constant prices and current US dollars)

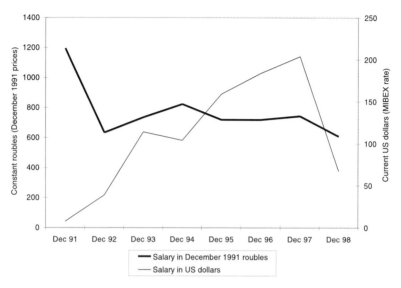

The artificial character of this trend was fully demonstrated by the August 1998 crisis. The collapse of the Russian financial market had left many major Russian buyers of foreign currency (banks, private importers) without any or with substantially reduced funds. Those who still had rouble funds under their control rushed to exchange them into foreign currencies in an attempt to save their reserves from fast depreciation. That led to a sharp fall in the rouble exchange rate. However, the larger part of population had no savings or any spare funds that had to be protected against inflation and could be invested into foreign currency. Within a short period of five months the average salary in Russia in US dollar equivalent had fallen by 2.6 times: from US$177 in July 1998 to just US$67 in December 1998.[33]

4.5   Shifts in occupational wages

Changes in the average national wage in Russia, dramatic as they are, fail to reflect the significant shifts that occurred in occupational incomes in the last five years.[34] Table 4.11a demonstrates that in 1990–98 ratios between the average salary in all national economy and average salaries in various occupational groups were subject to significant changes. If we take the last year of the Soviet era (1991) as a base year, then in the period between 1991 and 1997–98 the ratio of average wage to the national average salary had fallen in the following branches of the economy: agriculture, trade, health, education, arts and culture, and R&D. By far the most dramatic fall of all was recorded in agriculture. In the same period the ratio between sectoral and national wages had increased significantly in the public service, transport, communications, construction, and in banking and finance.

The average salary of public service workers in Russia had started to grow considerably in the mid-1990s. While in 1991 Russian bureaucrats were on average receiving a salary equal to the national average salary, by 1998 the ratio between these salaries was already 1:1.4. Increase in bureaucratic incomes may serve as a good indicator of the weakness of the Russian ruling elite, because each pay rise in the public sector coincided almost exactly with increased social and political tensions in the country. Thus, monthly statistics demonstrate that the average public servant's salary increased significantly in 1989–1990,[35] and then again in January–March and in September–October 1993. In 1995, as a result of attempts by the Russian government to stabilise the financial situation in the country, there was a relative fall in salaries of Russian bureaucrats. However, this trend was reversed in the following years, particularly on the eve and in the aftermath of the 1996 Russian presidential election.

After the collapse of the command economy and the decentralisation of business operations, those who could control the country's infrastructure became one of the major beneficiaries of the reform. Given the size of its territory, in Russia transport and communications are destined to play a crucial role in the normal functioning of the national economy. In the Soviet period, infrastructure always had a special status, which greatly facilitated monopolisation tendencies in this area. In the post-Soviet period, the existence of monopolies in transport and communications, inherited from the Soviet system, created vast new opportunities for often unjustified increases of revenues in these sectors. In the post-1991 period, tariffs for transport and communications services had risen dramatically, soon followed by rises in the sectoral average wage.

While salary rises in the spheres of transport and communications were made possible mostly as a result of the Soviet economic heritage, an increase in the sectoral-national wage ratio in the other sector, the building industry, was directly linked to the initial post-Soviet boom in

Table 4.11 Average Salaries in the Russian National Economy by Occupational Groups

a) Average salaries in current roubles by occupational groups relative to an average salary in the national economy

	1990	1991	1992	1993	1994	1995	1996	1997	1998[a]
Average salary in economy	1.00	1.00	1.00	1.00	1.00	1.00	1.00	1.00	1.00
Industry	1.03	1.11	1.18	1.08	1.04	1.12	1.10	1.11	1.19
Agriculture	0.95	0.84	0.66	0.61	0.50	0.50	0.48	0.46	0.41
Construction	1.24	1.27	1.34	1.33	1.29	1.26	1.22	1.28	1.35
Transport	1.15	1.20	1.46	1.51	1.50	1.56	1.44	1.41	1.41
Communications	0.85	0.91	0.91	1.07	1.23	1.24	1.30	1.43	1.38
Trade and catering	0.85	0.86	0.81	0.80	0.79	0.76	0.77	0.79	…
Information services	0.95	0.93	0.82	0.92	1.06	0.87	0.99	1.22	…
Communal services	0.74	0.80	0.82	0.92	0.96	1.02	1.06	1.07	…
Medicare and sports	0.67	0.76	0.66	0.76	0.76	0.74	0.77	0.70	0.66
Education	0.67	0.71	0.61	0.68	0.69	0.65	0.70	0.65	0.60
Arts and culture	0.62	0.67	0.52	0.62	0.62	0.61	0.65	0.62	0.60
R&D	1.16	0.94	0.64	0.68	0.78	0.77	0.83	0.94	0.95
Banking and insurance	1.35	1.80	2.04	2.43	2.08	1.63	1.93	1.77	1.99
Public service (state management)	1.20	0.99	0.94	1.15	1.17	1.07	1.20	1.31	1.43

Table 4.11   *continued*

b) Dynamics of change in real average salaries by occupational groups, 1990 = 100

	1990	1991	1992	1993	1994	1995	1996	1997	1998[a]
Average salary in economy	100.0	97.0	65.0	65.2	60.0	53.4	56.1	58.9	51.0
Industry	100.0	104.5	74.6	68.8	60.7	58.2	61.7	65.5	60.7
Agriculture	100.0	85.2	45.3	42.0	31.8	28.1	27.1	27.2	20.9
Construction	100.0	99.1	70.3	69.9	62.2	54.2	68.7	75.7	68.7
Transport	100.0	100.7	82.5	85.3	78.1	72.3	80.9	82.9	72.0
Communications	100.0	104.1	69.7	82.6	87.2	78.1	72.7	84.1	70.5
Trade and catering	100.0	97.9	62.0	61.1	55.5	47.9	43.2	46.3	...
Information services	100.0	94.8	56.0	63.3	66.9	48.5	55.6	72.2	...
Communal services	100.0	105.6	72.1	81.3	78.3	73.9	59.3	63.0	...
Medicare and sports	100.0	109.9	63.7	74.1	68.2	58.8	43.3	41.5	33.5
Education	100.0	102.8	59.5	66.6	61.9	52.2	39.2	38.2	30.7
Arts and culture	100.0	105.3	54.4	65.2	60.2	52.2	36.3	36.3	30.8
R&D	100.0	78.5	36.0	38.0	40.3	35.6	46.7	55.1	48.4
Banking & insurance	100.0	129.0	97.9	117.2	92.5	64.2	108.1	104.4	101.5
Public service (state management)	100.0	79.6	51.1	62.7	58.2	47.5	67.4	76.9	73.1

NOTES:
[a] Preliminary data.

Sourced and calculated from:
Rossiiskii statisticheskii ezhegodnik. 1994, Moscow: Goskomstat, 1994, p.88; *Rossiiskii statisticheskii ezhegodnik. 1995*, Moscow: Goskomstat, 1995, pp.77, 80; *Sotsial'no-ekonomicheskoe polozhenie Rossii. 1995 g.*, Moscow: Goskomstat, 1996, pp.268–71; *Sotsial'no-ekonomicheskoe polozhenie Rossii. 1996 g.*, Moscow: Goskomstat, 1997, pp.191–2; *Sotsial'no-ekonomicheskoe polozhenie Rossii, yanvar' 1996 g.*, Moscow: Goskomstat, 1996, p.78; *Rossiiskii statisticheskii ezhegodnik. 1996*, Moscow: Goskomstat, 1996, p.121; *Rossiiskii statisticheskii ezhegodnik. 1997*, Moscow: Goskomstat, 1997, p.144; *Sotsial'no-ekonomicheskoe polozhenie Rossii, yanvar' 1997 g.*, Moscow: Goskomstat, 1997, pp.175–6; *Sotsial'no-ekonomicheskoe polozhenie Rossii, yanvar' 1998 g.*, Moscow: Goskomstat, 1998, pp.204–5; *Rossiiskii statisticheskii ezhegodnik. 1998*, Moscow: Goskomstat, 1998, pp.208, 224; *Sotsial'no-ekonomicheskoe polozhenie Rossii, yanvar' 1999 g.*, Moscow: Goskomstat, 1999, pp.262–4.

construction and renovation of office buildings, and in privately-funded housing construction.

In Table 4.11b we put together the dynamics of change in real (deflated) sectoral salaries. In the post-Soviet period in only one branch of the Russian economy the real average wage was equal or higher than its 1990 level. This was banking and finance. Despite the recent Russian financial crisis, during 1998 average salaries in this sector of the economy in real terms remained higher than in 1990. Like in the case of bureaucracy, the dynamics of change in the average salary in this sector are indicative of a close interrelation between economics and politics in modern Russia. In the first three years of reforms (1992–94) real salaries in banking experienced certain fluctuations which, however, were rather marginal compared to a continuing fall in real wages in all other branches of the economy. The end of the first stage of privatisation in mid-1994 had deprived many banks and financial institutions of one of their major source of revenues – trading in privatisation cheques (vouchers). That coincided with government attempts to increase the fiscal discipline in the country in 1995. The result was a considerable decline in the real salary in banking during 1995.

The approaching presidential elections forced the Russian leadership to seek political and financial support from the Russian business community. Special relations between bankers and the state were established, while the former managed to secure a number of lucrative deals for themselves. In the course of the 1996 election year the real average wage in banking increased dramatically – by more than 68% (Table 4.11b).

These rises in real wages of bureaucrats, monopolists and bankers were largely offset by a continuing decline in occupational salaries in all other branches of the Russian economy. The falls were most pronounced in agriculture,[36] R&D, trade, information services, arts and culture, and in education. By 1998 real salaries in these sectors were between 21% and 48% of the 1990 level. These rates of fall were significantly higher than in the other areas of the Russian economy.

Changes in real incomes of different occupational categories are a reflection of more general developments in the country's economy since 1990. These changes indicate that there was a significant and continuing decline in the basic sectors of the Russian economy (industry and agriculture) and in the most important of the social services (health, education, and science). According to data in Table 4.11b, in 1996–97 the real average wage in industry was rapidly rising. However, this rise masked large disproportions between various branches of industry, just as the national average salary significantly levels out income disparities between different occupational groups.

The ratios of industrial wages to the national average salary (Table 4.12a) show growing wage disparities between the various sectors of Russian industry. While in three branches (electricity production, oil and fuel complex, and ferrous metallurgy) post-Soviet wages have risen to a level considerably higher than the national average, employees in most of the other sectors have experienced a sharp decline in their incomes, if compared to the national average salary. Changes in the industrial wage have, in fact, reflected a more general process of re-orientation of the post-Soviet Russian economy towards resource-based industries (mineral and oil extraction, ferrous and non-ferrous metallurgy). During the same period the output in all manufacturing industries had been falling rapidly. Wage ratios, as shown in the Table 4.12, generally reflected this process.

While the average industrial wage was constantly falling in 1990–95, during 1996 and 1997 it experienced a slight rise (Table 4.12b). The dynamics of this process have varied greatly from industry to industry. In the first year of the reform (1992) real wages fell far below their 1990 levels in all but three industries – oil extraction, non-ferrous metallurgy and electricity production. In the next year (1993) the real average wage in non-ferrous metallurgy also fell beyond the 1990 level, real wages in oil industry followed in 1994 and in electricity production – in 1995. However, in 1997 real salaries in the latter two industries had increased significantly (respectively, by 24% and 17% in one year) which brought average salaries in these sectors to approximately 1990 levels. In the same year workers in all other industries were in real terms paid salaries which were far below 1990 levels, while in the light industry the average wage was equal only to about one-third of what workers were paid in 1990.[37]

These trends confirm the general tendency of the Russian post-Soviet economic development, which we outlined in the previous chapters. The Russian economy in the 1990s was rapidly becoming re-oriented towards production of minerals and raw materials. While the share of primary industries in the overall output was constantly rising, the share of value-subtracting activities was rapidly falling. Changes in occupational and sectoral wages were a direct reflection of this process. For instance, the dramatic decline of average salaries in the machine-building sector is clearly a reflection of the critical situation in the military-industrial complex, while the acute falls in salaries of workers in light industry are a rather alarming indicator of the current crisis in the

Table 4.12 Average Salaries by Branches of Industry

a) Average salaries in current roubles by branches of industry relative to an average salary in the national economy

	1990	1991	1992	1993	1994	1995	1996	1997	1998[a]
Oil and fuel	1.48	1.83	2.90	2.55	2.37	2.56	2.42	2.44	2.35
Electricity	1.21	1.67	2.21	2.10	2.05	2.09	2.04	1.98	1.89
Machine-building	1.01	0.96	0.87	0.83	0.80	0.85	0.83	0.85	0.86
Ferrous metallurgy	1.17	1.27	1.70	1.43	1.21	1.36	1.46	2.02	2.04
Non-ferrous metallurgy	1.45	1.77	2.50	2.16	1.97	2.24	2.07	1.40	1.26
Chemical	0.97	1.08	1.28	1.01	0.94	1.08	1.06	1.09	1.07
Forestry and wood-processing	1.02	1.07	1.10	0.90	0.83	0.95	0.87	0.85	0.88
Construction materials	1.04	1.18	1.16	1.15	1.14	1.11	1.03	1.02	0.95
Light industry	0.82	1.05	0.85	0.71	0.54	0.56	0.50	0.51	0.52
Food-processing	1.03	1.19	1.27	1.30	1.22	1.18	1.17	1.15	1.22
Average in industry	1.03	1.11	1.18	1.08	1.04	1.12	1.10	1.11	1.19
Average in all economy	1.00	1.00	1.00	1.00	1.00	1.00	1.00	1.00	1.00

Table 4.12 continued

b) Dynamics of change in real average salaries by industry branch, 1990 = 100

	1990	1991	1992	1993	1994	1995	1996	1997	1998[a]
Oil and fuel	100.0	120.0	127.6	112.6	96.2	92.8	89.3	94.6	78.7
Electricity	100.0	134.2	118.8	113.0	101.6	92.2	91.5	93.2	77.0
Machine-building	100.0	92.9	56.2	53.5	47.6	45.3	42.9	46.5	40.6
Ferrous metallurgy	100.0	105.7	94.9	80.1	62.3	62.4	65.8	67.4	59.0
Non-ferrous metallurgy	100.0	117.8	111.8	97.2	81.4	82.5	75.4	75.7	59.1
Chemical	100.0	108.1	86.2	68.4	58.4	59.6	58.0	62.7	53.1
Forestry and wood-processing	100.0	102.3	70.3	57.6	49.3	50.2	50.3	51.6	46.5
Construction materials	100.0	110.2	72.0	72.1	65.4	56.7	53.2	55.2	44.2
Light industry	100.0	124.1	67.5	56.1	39.2	36.6	35.0	37.6	33.5
Food-processing	100.0	111.9	80.0	82.3	70.9	61.0	64.8	66.9	61.5
Average in industry	100.0	104.5	74.6	68.8	60.7	58.2	61.7	65.5	60.7
Average in all economy	100.0	97.0	65.0	65.2	60.0	53.4	56.1	58.9	51.0

NOTES:

[a] Preliminary data.

Calculated from:

Promyshlennost' Rossii. 1995, Moscow: Goskomstat, 1995, pp.61–2; *Rossiiskii statisticheskii ezhegodnik. 1996*, Moscow: Goskomstat, 1996, p.123; *Rossiiskii statisticheskii ezhegodnik. 1997*, Moscow: Goskomstat, 1997, pp.144, 146; *Sotsialno-ekonomicheskoe polozhenie Rossii, yanvar' 1998 goda*, Moscow: Goskomstat, 1998, pp.204–51; *Rossiiskii statisticheskii ezhegodnik. 1998*, Moscow: Goskomstat, 1998, pp.224–5; *Sotsialno-ekonomicheskoe polozhenie Rossii, yanvar' 1999 goda*, Moscow: Goskomstat, 1999, pp.262–3.

consumer goods market in Russia. On the other hand, producers of energy-carriers have generally managed to maintain or even increase their average real income levels, despite significant falls in output. Successes achieved by the leaders of this group in lobbying Yeltsin's cabinets and regional governments demonstrate the fact that it has become a major force framing post-Soviet Russian state policies in the political as well as the economic arena.

4.6   Wage arrears and changes in regional per capita incomes

Another important post-Soviet development that has become one of the most acute issues in Russian contemporary politics is the problem of wage arrears. This problem was virtually unknown in the Soviet times, when wages were paid on time and in full. Delays in salary payments started to occur almost immediately after the beginning of reforms in the early 1992, and by the end of the same year the issue had taken on political significance.

Although frequently viewed by Russian officials as a stand-alone issue, the problem of wage arrears has its roots and is in direct consequence to a more general issue of the content of the Russian economic reform and the manner in which it was implemented. Reforms in Russia began with the liberalisation of prices and trade and were soon followed by the first stage of ("voucher") privatisation. The lifting of state control over prices was interpreted by the overwhelming majority of domestic producers as granting them total freedom in price regulation. This produced a large wave of inflation prompting producers of various industrial and agricultural commodities to increase prices for their produce on a daily basis. However, their attempts to overcome inflationary pressures have created even higher inflation rates.

Already by mid-1992 this vicious circle of inflation put many Russian enterprises in a difficult situation. The first to suffer were those enterprises where state regulation of prices was still in place (for example, the military-industrial complex), as well as those companies that produced intermediate goods and were therefore dependent on payments from other producers. Price hikes made all domestic products much more expensive, while liberalisation of foreign trade made a great portion of local produce uncompetitive. Many Russian factories became overstocked with unsold produce and, as a result, cash-stripped. By the late 1992 almost every Russian enterprise was a *de facto* bankrupt. In an attempt to overcome this crisis, many enterprises started either to enter into barter trade deals with other companies or to sell their produce abroad, where cash payments for deliveries normally came promptly and in full.

The Russian state's inability to control the financial situation in the first years of reform and to establish an effective system of social security placed the majority of both state-run and formerly state-owned enterprises in a difficult situation. The absence of social security network and job vacancies greatly contributed to a growing reluctance of Russian managers to make significant staff cuts or to declare their companies bankrupt. Instead, they preferred to take out commercial credits (or, if possible, state credits) and in most cases continued to run their enterprises in the same inefficient way as they did it under the Soviet system. Growing delays in payments between enterprises and the rapidly increasing incompetitiveness of the majority of Russian companies (particularly in the manufacturing sector) led to the appearance of the problem of delays in wage payments.[38]

At the end of the first year of reform (1992) gross wage arrears in the Russian economy totalled 70 million US dollars, which was equivalent to 2.5% of the national monthly salary fund. Between 1993 and 1995 this share had grown 10 times, while arrears reached 2.9 billion US dollars at the beginning of 1996. Then, in 1996 alone, the volume of wage arrears tripled, both in US dollar terms and as a percentage of the gross monthly fund in the national economy.[39] Despite Russian government's active search to the solution of this problem during 1997, wage arrears remained at the same level as in 1996. In early 1998 the average working Russian citizen was not receiving the equivalent of almost one full monthly salary payment per year (Table 4.13).[40]

A dramatic depreciation of the Russian national currency, the rouble, that accompanied the spread of financial crisis since August 1998, has led to a significant reduction in the gross amount of wage arrears in US dollar terms. At the beginning of 1999 wage arrears in Russia totalled US$3.7 billion, which was 2.4 times lower than in January 1998. However, in rouble terms wage arrears had actually increased. In January 1999 each Russian employee was on average not paid an equivalent of almost 110% of his month's salary, while a year before that the figure was 84%. This later development contradicts a common view that after Primakov government came to power it had significantly reduced the volume of wage arrears through printing of money. The official Russian statistics show that at least up until early 1999 this was not the case and that wage arrears in Russia continued to grow.

Table 4.13 Russia: Wage Arrears in National Economy

	1 Jan 93	1 Jan 94	1 Jan 95	1 Jan 96	1 Jan 97	1 Jan 98	1 Jan 99
Cumulative arrears:							
in billion current roubles	29.0	766.1	4 199.8	13 380.0	47 151.0	52 637.0	77.0
in million current US dollars[a]	69.9	614.4	1 183.0	2 883.6	8 494.1	8 831.7	3 729.6
Arrears as % of gross average monthly salary fund in the national economy (est.)	2.5	7.7	17.3	27.1	85.7	83.9	109.5

NOTES:

[a] Calculations are based on the exchange rate of rouble to US dollar for the date stated.

Sourced and calculated from:

Sotsial'no-ekonomicheskoe polozhenie Rossii (monthly statistical bulletins from Goskomstat), 1993–99.

Tables 4.14a and 4.14b show that the industrial sector of the Russian economy accounted for the larger part of wage arrears, comprising between 50% and 60% of the gross volume of delayed salary payments in 1993–98. It is interesting to note that until 1995 there were no wage arrears recorded on transport, which placed that sector in a privileged position. In addition to that, real salaries of transport workers had also fallen by a much lower margin than in other branches of the economy (Table 4.11b). Between 1993 and 1998 the share of agriculture in the gross volume of wage arrears had fallen sharply – from 38% to 17%. This, however, can be mainly attributed to the growth in the overall volume of unpaid wages. Between early 1993 and early 1999 wage arrears in agriculture in US dollar equivalent had increased 24 times from $26.2 million to $630.3 million.

According to Table 4.13, the sharpest rise in the gross volume of wage arrears in real terms took place during 1996. In Table 4.14c we put together indices of monthly dynamics of change in wage arrears during 1996. These dynamics show that during that politically crucial year for Russia the tempo of accumulation of wage arrears varied significantly between sectors of the national economy. On the whole, in 1996 salary delays in agriculture, industry and construction were growing more slowly than in the social sectors (education, health, culture and arts). In all sectors of the national economy the growth of wage arrears was significantly lower in the first half of the year, or before the presidential elections: while between January and early July the gross amount of unpaid wages in current roubles increased by 45.9%, until late December it had grown by a further 58.1%.

The growing social stratification of Russian society, as demonstrated by increasing income disparities between the various occupational groups, is also supplemented by the process of geographical (regional) income differentiation.[41] Because of the existing differences in economic development, specialisation and resource potential, the various Russian regions receive rather different shares of the generated national income. If we compare this income share with the population share of a particular region, the picture that emerges is that one of rapidly growing inequality in regional income distribution in Russia.

In Table 4.15 we analysed the dynamics of per capita incomes in the 12 Russian economic regions and the relation of the average per capita incomes to the national average. Table 4.15a demonstrates that between 1990 and December 1997 only two economic regions managed to increase their shares in the gross population income. These were the Central and Western Siberian regions which host, respectively, Russia's

Table 4.14 Russia: Wage Arrears by Sectors of Economy

a) *Wage arrears by major sector of economy (% to total)*

	1 Jan 93	1 Jan 94	1 Jan 95	1 Jan 96	1 Jan 97	1 Jan 98	1 Jan 99
All major branches of economy	100.0	100.0	100.0	100.0	100.0	100.0	100.0
Industry	47.5	51.6	57.8	59.9	57.4	58.3	58.3
Construction	15.0	17.4	14.5	16.1	16.8	16.4	17.2
Agriculture	37.5	31.0	19.2	14.9	15.3	17.5	16.9
Transport	0.0	0.0	8.5	9.0	10.4	7.8	7.6

b) *Wage arrears in all economy in 1996 (% to total)*

	20/1/96	25/3/96	6/5/96	10/6/96	8/7/96	12/8/96	23/9/96	14/10/96	11/11/96	9/12/96	23/12/96
All economy	100.0	100.0	100.0	100.0	100.0	100.0	100.0	100.0	100.0	100.0	100.0
Industry	50.9	50.9	52.0	49.4	50.0	49.8	49.2	48.4	46.9	46.6	47.0
Construction	14.4	14.3	14.6	13.3	13.5	12.9	13.7	13.2	13.0	13.1	13.7
Agriculture	15.0	13.0	12.7	11.9	12.4	12.8	13.0	12.8	12.8	12.5	12.5
Transport	8.1	8.2	7.8	7.2	7.5	7.6	8.5	7.8	8.1	8.1	8.5
Education	6.8	7.2	7.2	10.7	9.0	8.4	7.3	8.8	10.1	10.5	9.5
Medicare	4.0	4.2	3.5	4.9	5.0	5.8	5.5	6.0	6.1	6.0	5.4
Culture and Arts	0.8	0.7	0.7	1.0	1.0	1.0	0.9	1.1	1.2	1.2	1.0
R&D	...	1.5	1.5	1.7	1.6	1.7	1.8	1.9	2.0	2.1	2.3

Table 4.14 *continued*

c) Dynamics of wage arrears in 1996 (current roubles, January 1996 = 100)

	20/1/96	25/3/96	6/5/96	10/6/96	8/7/96	12/8/96	23/9/96	14/10/96	11/11/96	9/12/96	23/12/96
All economy	100.0	119.0	116.7	140.4	145.9	168.0	196.9	209.0	215.8	223.4	230.7
Industry	100.0	119.0	119.1	136.4	143.4	164.3	190.5	198.6	198.7	204.4	213.0
Construction	100.0	118.8	118.7	130.2	136.7	151.0	188.3	192.6	195.1	203.6	220.4
Agriculture	100.0	102.9	99.1	111.5	121.0	143.4	170.5	179.0	184.1	185.7	193.0
Transport	100.0	120.7	111.9	123.7	135.5	157.7	206.7	199.8	214.6	223.6	242.3
Education	100.0	124.7	123.4	219.1	191.2	205.7	209.7	270.0	317.7	341.8	319.5
Medicare	100.0	124.9	100.2	170.6	179.3	241.2	269.9	310.6	325.4	331.2	311.9
Culture and Arts	100.0	105.8	112.3	180.6	196.8	226.5	237.4	295.5	329.0	352.3	311.0

Sources:
Rossiya v tsifrakh. 1996, Moscow: Goskomstat, 1996, p.216; *Sotsial'no-ekonomicheskoe polozhenie Rossii, yanvar'-iyun' 1996 g.*, Moscow: Goskomstat, 1996, p.137; *Sotsial'no-ekonomicheskoe polozhenie Rossii, yanvar' 1996 g.*, Moscow: Goskomstat, 1996, p.81; *Sotsial'no-ekonomicheskoe polozhenie Rossii, yanvar'-aprel' 1996 g.*, Moscow: Goskomstat, 1996, p.139; *Sotsial'no-ekonomicheskoe polozhenie Rossii, yanvar'-iun' 1996 g.*, Moscow: Goskomstat, 1996, p.139; *Sotsial'no-ekonomicheskoe polozhenie Rossii, yanvar'-iul' 1996 g.*, Moscow: Goskomstat, 1996, p.150; *Sotsial'no-ekonomicheskoe polozhenie Rossii, yanvar'-sentyabr' 1996 g.*, Moscow: Goskomstat, 1996, p.157; *Sotsial'no-ekonomicheskoe polozhenie Rossii, yanvar'-oktyabr' 1996 g.*, Moscow: Goskomstat, 1996, p.163; *Sotsial'no-ekonomicheskoe polozhenie Rossii, yanvar'-noyabr'' 1996 g.*, Moscow: Goskomstat, 1996, p.158; *Sotsial'no-ekonomicheskoe polozhenie Rossii. 1996 g.*, Moscow: Goskomstat, 1997, pp.164–5; *Sotsial'no-ekonomicheskoe polozhenie Rossii, yanvar' 1998 g.*, Moscow: Goskomstat, 1998, p.186; *Sotsial'no-ekonomicheskoe polozhenie Rossii. 1998 g.*, Moscow: Goskomstat, 1999, pp.240–1.

financial and business centre (Moscow) and the country's major oil-producing area (Tyumen'). These increases were accompanied by falls in the shares of almost all other economic regions. The financial crisis of 1998 has left the Central region (Moscow) as the sole beneficiary of post-Soviet changes in the regional income distribution in Russia.

The same data recalculated as a ratio of regional average income to the national average (Table 4.15b) give basically the same picture: until 1997 this ratio had increased only in Central and Western Siberian economic regions, while in the course of 1998 only Central region has managed to retain its leading position. Our calculations show that the ratio of the Western Siberian average per capita income to the national average increased from 1.16 in 1990 to 1.29 in late 1997 but then fell to 1.10 in 1998, while in the Central region it jumped in 1990–97 from 1.17 to 1.56 and in 1998, despite the financial crisis, it increased further on to 1.71. In the same period average incomes fell in relation to the national average in all other economic regions of Russia. While in 1990 seven out of 12 economic regions had average per capita incomes higher than the national average, in December 1998 this number had reduced to just four.

The dynamics of change in per capita incomes in constant prices (Table 4.15c) give us even a more dramatic picture. According to these data, in the 1990s the income situation in the Central region differed noticeably from the situation in the rest of Russia: it was the only region of Russia where the average per capita income in real terms had came close and even exceeded its pre-reform levels in the 1992–98 period. The second best region in terms of income situation was Western Siberia, but during 1998 the combined effect of Russia's financial crisis and drop in world oil prices has led to huge fall in the average per capita real income this region. Economic regions where per capita incomes fell by more than half in the past eight years were the war-stricken North Caucasus, the Russian enclave of Kaliningrad on the Baltic Sea, the predominantly agricultural regions of Volgo-Vyatka and ChernoZem, and the traditional centre of Russian manufacturing, the North-West. Russia's financial crisis of 1998 had a direct negative effect on real income dynamics in all regions. However, regions where falls in average income were most significant were Volgo-Vyatka (30% decline in real per capita income during 1998), Western Siberia (–28%), Eastern Siberia (–26%) and the Urals (–22%).

The underlying economic factors framing the process of regional income diversification in post-Soviet Russia become more visible if we

Table 4.15 Regional Distribution of Income

a) Shares of regions in gross volume of incomes in Russia (%, current prices)

	1990[a]	Dec 92	Dec 93	Dec 94	Dec 95	Jun 96	Dec 96	Dec 97	Dec 98
Northern	4.6	5.4	5.4	5.1	4.3	4.2	4.0	4.2	4.2
North-West	5.9	4.5	4.8	5.3	5.7	5.7	5.5	4.7	5.2
Central	22.8	21.4	22.6	28.8	33.2	29.9	33.2	30.2	33.5
Volgo-Vyatka	5.0	4.5	4.5	4.0	3.7	3.9	3.6	3.8	3.2
Central ChernoZem	4.5	4.0	4.1	3.6	3.4	3.9	3.6	3.5	3.8
Volga	10.0	10.1	9.4	8.4	8.1	8.2	8.5	8.9	8.7
North Caucasus	9.7	8.1	8.1	7.6	7.0	7.3	6.9	7.7	7.7
Urals	12.3	14.0	13.1	11.1	10.3	11.0	11.0	11.3	10.6
West Siberia	11.2	13.1	13.0	12.0	11.6	12.3	11.6	12.7	11.0
East Siberia	6.2	7.3	6.7	6.3	5.9	6.4	5.7	6.2	5.4
Far East	7.3	7.3	7.8	7.2	6.3	6.7	6.1	6.4	6.1
Kaliningrad	0.6	0.5	0.5	0.5	0.5	0.4	0.4	0.4	0.5
All RF	100.0	100.0	100.0	100.0	100.0	100.0	100.0	100.0	100.0

b) Relation of per capita income by region to Russian average (all Russia = 1)

	1990[a]	Dec 92	Dec 93	Dec 94	Dec 95	Jun 96	Dec-96	Dec 97	Dec 98
Northern	1.17	1.39	1.39	1.32	1.11	1.11	1.06	1.11	1.11
North-West	1.10	0.84	0.92	1.01	1.10	1.09	1.05	0.91	0.99
Central	1.17	1.10	1.17	1.48	1.71	1.54	1.70	1.56	1.71
Volgo-Vyatka	0.92	0.82	0.83	0.73	0.67	0.70	0.65	0.69	0.58
Central ChernoZem	0.91	0.79	0.81	0.71	0.66	0.76	0.70	0.69	0.74
Volga	0.95	0.93	0.87	0.77	0.74	0.75	0.77	0.80	0.78
North Caucasus	0.89	0.73	0.71	0.67	0.60	0.64	0.60	0.66	0.69
Urals	0.94	1.06	0.99	0.84	0.78	0.83	0.82	0.85	0.79
West Siberia	1.16	1.34	1.33	1.23	1.18	1.25	1.17	1.29	1.10
East Siberia	1.05	1.23	1.13	1.06	0.99	1.08	0.95	1.04	0.90
Far East	1.41	1.43	1.57	1.46	1.29	1.38	1.25	1.32	1.26
Kaliningrad	1.02	0.79	0.90	0.78	0.82	0.68	0.68	0.70	0.73
All RF	1.00	1.00	1.00	1.00	1.00	1.00	1.00	1.00	1.00

Table 4.15 *continued*

c) Dynamics of real per capita incomes by economic region, 1990 = 100 (constant prices)

	1990[a]	Dec 92	Dec 93	Dec 94	Dec 95	Jun 96	Dec 96	Dec 97	Dec 98
Northern	100.0	72.9	85.0	90.2	66.4	58.7	63.3	68.9	58.1
North-West	100.0	47.0	59.4	73.2	69.4	61.2	66.4	59.4	54.9
Central	100.0	57.7	71.3	101.2	102.1	81.5	102.0	96.3	90.0
Volgo-Vyatka	100.0	54.9	64.6	63.7	50.8	47.4	49.3	54.3	38.7
Central ChernoZem	100.0	53.6	63.0	62.6	50.7	51.4	53.8	54.6	49.7
Volga	100.0	60.6	65.2	65.1	54.5	48.8	56.6	61.3	50.4
North Caucasus	100.0	49.9	57.0	59.5	47.1	43.9	46.5	53.6	47.2
Urals	100.0	69.2	75.0	70.7	57.3	54.2	60.8	64.6	51.0
West Siberia	100.0	70.8	81.8	84.3	70.7	66.3	70.6	80.5	58.0
East Siberia	100.0	72.0	77.0	81.1	66.3	63.7	63.4	71.7	53.0
Far East	100.0	62.2	79.0	82.7	63.7	60.3	61.9	67.3	54.6
Kaliningrad	100.0	47.4	63.0	61.3	55.7	41.4	46.6	49.6	43.7
All RF	100.0	61.5	71.3	79.9	69.8	61.7	69.8	72.3	59.1

NOTES:
[a] Average monthly income for all of 1990.

Calculated from:
Rossiiskii statisticheskii ezhegodnik. 1994, Moscow: Goskomstat, 1994, pp.510–2, 711–3; *Pokazateli sotsialnogo razvitiya Rossiiskoi Federatsii i ee regionov*. Moscow: Goskomstat, 1993, pp.105–7; *Uroven' zhizni naseleniya Rossii. 1996*, Moscow: Goskomstat, 1996, pp.65–7; *Sotsial'no-ekonomicheskoe polozhenie Rossii, yanvar'-iiul' 1996 g.*, Moscow: Goskomstat 1996, pp.261–2; *Sotsial'no-ekonomicheskoe polozhenie Rossii. 1996*, Moscow: Goskomstat 1997, pp.317–8; *Sotsial'no-ekonomicheskoe polozhenie Rossii, yanvar' 1997 g.*, Moscow: Goskomstat 1997, pp.265–6; *Sotsial'no-ekonomicheskoe polozhenie Rossii, yanvar' 1998 g.*, Moscow: Goskomstat 1998, pp.293–4; *Sotsial'no-ekonomicheskoe polozhenie Rossii, yanvar' 1999 g.*, Moscow: Goskomstat 1999, pp.397–8.

group nine out of the 89 Russian administrative regions (*oblasts, krais* and autonomous republics) into three categories based on their dominant economic profile – mining, manufacturing or agriculture (Table 4.16). This analysis shows that by the end of 1997 in predominantly mining regions per capita incomes in real terms were back to their 1990 levels, while their ratio to the national average income increased from 1:1.4 in 1990 to 1:2 in 1997. During 1998, however, the average per capita real income in this group of regions fell by almost 27%, which brought it to about 75% of the 1990 level. Nonetheless, this still was significantly higher than in the two other groups of regions with agricultural and manufacturing specialisation. According to these data, in the course of reform period agricultural group of regions suffered the most with an average per capita income in December 1998 equal to only 70% of Russia's average and in real terms to just 47% of what the average income was in 1990.

Although grouping Russia into economic regions is often useful for comparative purposes, this method of analysis tends to mask striking disproportions within economic regions. We mentioned earlier that the relatively low falls in average incomes in the Central and West Siberian economic regions can be attributed to significantly higher incomes in money-rich Moscow and oil-rich Tyumen'. Table 4.17 confirms this hypothesis. In that table we selected three Russian administrative areas with the highest per capita incomes and three areas with the lowest incomes. (Interestingly, two in the latter group are located in the North Caucasus.) While in real terms incomes in Moscow and Tyumen' considerably increased between 1990 and 1997, they fell in all other selected areas (Table 4.17b). Interestingly, the data show that the August 1998 financial meltdown in Russia had only a marginal effect on the dynamics of real average income in Moscow. At the same time in other areas effects of this crisis were much more pronounced. While in December 1998 average per capita income in Moscow in real terms was only 1.3% less than a year before, in Kalmykia it fell by 52%, in Kamchatka – by 38% and in Tyumen' – by 32%. In December 1998 the gap between the average per capita income in Moscow and the area with the lowest per capita income was 12.5 times, far above the difference of 2.7 times registered times in 1990.

At the end of 1998 the average Muscovite was earning 4.3 times as much as the average working Russian (Table 4.17a). Table 4.17c demonstrates the striking scale of current income disproportions in Russia: between 1990 and 1998 the average real income in Moscow increased by 156% while in the rest of Russia excluding Moscow it fell

Table 4.16 Income Dynamics in Selected Groups of Regions

a) Relation of per capita income by groups of regions to Russian average (all Russia = 1)

	1990[a]	Dec 92	Dec 93	Dec 94	Dec 95	Jun 96	Dec 96	Dec 97	Dec 98
Mining regions	1.41	1.98	2.08	2.05	1.77	1.97	1.86	2.01	1.73
Manufacturing regions	1.13	0.96	1.02	1.01	1.18	1.16	1.15	1.08	1.19
Agricultural regions	0.92	0.84	0.86	0.79	0.74	0.73	0.69	0.75	0.70
All RF	1.00	1.00	1.00	1.00	1.00	1.00	1.00	1.00	1.00

b) Dynamics of real per capita incomes by groups of regions, 1990 = 100

	1990[a]	Dec 92	Dec 93	Dec 94	Dec 95	Jun 96	Dec 96	Dec 97	Dec 98
Mining regions	100.0	86.3	105.3	115.9	87.6	86.2	92.1	102.7	75.3
Manufacturing regions	100.0	52.3	64.4	71.9	73.4	63.8	71.4	69.5	65.1
Agricultural regions	100.0	55.8	66.9	68.2	56.1	48.6	51.9	58.4	46.8
All RF	100.0	61.5	71.3	79.9	69.8	61.7	69.8	72.3	59.1

NOTES:
[a] Average monthly income for all of 1990.

NOTES:
Mining: Kemerovo, Tyumen' and Sakha only.
Manufacturing: St Petersburg, Samara and Khabarovsk only.
Agriculture: Belgorod, Krasnodar and Stavropol only.

Sources:
See Table 4.15.

Table 4.17 Income Dynamics in Russia's Areas with Highest and Lowest Per Capita Incomes

a) Relation to the Russian average income

	1990[a]	Dec 92	Dec 93	Dec 94	Dec 95	Jun 96	Dec 96	Dec 97	Dec 98
Moscow	1.67	1.79	1.73	3.10	4.11	3.46	4.31	3.66	4.25
Tyumen'	1.63	2.57	2.67	2.73	2.17	2.63	2.53	2.67	2.14
Kamchatka	1.95	2.11	2.24	2.12	2.31	2.24	1.96	2.38	1.72
Karachaevo-Cherkesia	1.04	0.80	0.63	0.68	0.49	0.51	0.57	0.58	0.47
Kalmykia	1.16	0.84	0.64	0.62	0.41	0.48	0.45	0.60	0.34
Dagestan	0.62	0.54	0.58	0.63	0.40	0.35	0.44	0.44	0.45

b) Dynamics of real incomes, 1990 = 100 (constant prices)

	1990[a]	Dec 92	Dec 93	Dec 94	Dec 95	Jun 96	Dec 96	Dec 97	Dec 98
Moscow	100.0	65.7	73.9	147.7	171.5	127.6	179.6	157.8	155.8
Tyumen'	100.0	97.0	116.8	134.0	93.1	99.7	108.6	118.5	80.7
Kamchatka	100.0	66.6	81.9	86.8	82.9	70.9	70.3	88.1	54.3
Karachaevo-Cherkesia	100.0	47.2	43.0	51.8	32.8	30.3	38.2	40.0	27.7
Kalmykia	100.0	44.4	38.9	42.6	24.3	25.5	27.0	37.0	17.9
Dagestan	100.0	53.6	66.7	81.1	44.6	34.7	49.1	51.2	43.9
Ratio between highest and lowest regional per capita income (in times)	2.7	3.3	3.0	4.9	10.3	9.9	9.8	8.3	12.5

Table 4.17 *continued*

c) Comparison of income dynamics in Moscow, Tyumen' and the rest of Russia, 1990 = 100 (constant prices)

	1990[a]	Dec 92	Dec 93	Dec 94	Dec 95	Jun 96	Dec 96	Dec 97	Dec 98
Moscow	100.0	65.7	73.9	147.7	171.5	127.6	179.6	157.8	155.8
Russia minus Moscow	100.0	61.1	71.1	72.6	58.9	54.7	58.0	63.1	49.0
Moscow and Tyumen'	100.0	73.7	84.9	144.1	150.9	120.3	160.9	147.4	135.6
Russia minus Moscow and Tyumen'	100.0	59.6	69.3	70.1	57.5	52.8	55.9	60.8	47.7

NOTES:
[a] Average monthly income for all of 1990.

Sources: See Table 4.15.

by 51%! Income dynamics show that in 1994 there was a sharp rise in the average income in Moscow, which rapidly transformed the Russia's capital city into an "oasis of prosperity". There was a slight decrease in Muscovites' incomes in the first half of 1996, which can be directly attributed to the (temporary) redistribution of funds between the Russian provinces in the lead-up to the June 1996 presidential elections. In late 1996 and in 1997–98 real income dynamics in Moscow have again returned to high levels. In the post-Soviet period, these large income disproportions have played a significant part in straining of relations between the Moscow city authorities and regional leaders from other parts of the country, as "rich Muscovites" were viewed with a large degree of hostility in almost all Russian provinces.

Until the 1998 financial crisis Moscow and Tyumen' were headed the list of Russian administrative areas where the average per capita income is above the national average. If we group the top seven of these areas into a "high-income" category, the seven poorest – into a "low-income" category, and the remaining 75 Russian administrative areas into a "middle-income" category, the following dynamics emerge (see Graph 4.4).

In real terms, incomes of the population in the low-income group of Russian areas (4.5% of the total population) have undergone the

Graph 4.4   Growth of Income Disproportions Between 89 Russian Areas (indices of change of per capita income by group of areas, Russian national average = 1)

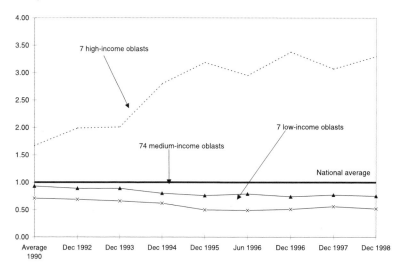

sharpest falls: by the end of 1998 people in these areas were on average receiving just 45% of their 1990 incomes. Incomes in the medium-income group comprising 75 areas and 85% of the population fell almost to the same level (46% of the 1990 levels). In December 1998 the ratio of per capita average incomes in these two groups of areas to the Russian national average income was 1 to 0.5–0.8 (Table 4.18b).

On the other hand, between 1990 and 1998 average incomes of those living in the seven areas grouped into high-income category increased dramatically. Even the August 1998 crisis had very limited effect on income dynamics in these regions. In late 1998 the average real income in this group was 121% of the 1990 level, or 3.3 times higher than the national average. Besides the 1998 crisis, there was also another notable deviation from this upward income trend when between December 1995 and June 1996 the average income in the high-income group fell by almost 20%. This phenomenon was directly linked to the state policy of redistribution of income in the moths preceding the 1996 presidential election campaign.

A graphic presentation of income dynamics in Russia in the 1990s is given in Map 4.2, where regional average per capita incomes in 1997 are shown in real terms as a share of their 1990 levels. All administrative areas were grouped into four categories. In the lowest group are areas with the most significant falls of 50–90% from the 1990 level: these are Chechnya and Ingushetia in the North Caucasus and agricultural centres in the European part of Russia. The second group (30–50% falls) unites majority of areas in the European part, the Urals and the Far East.

The remaining two groups include Russian areas where the situation with population incomes was significantly better. In the third group (falls in incomes less than 30% from the 1990 level) are the centres of primary industries in the Far East (Sakha, Kamchatka), Eastern Siberia, Sverdlovsk in the Urals, Samara in the Volga region, and most of areas in the North. The only two areas where income levels in 1997 were higher than in 1990 (fourth group) were Moscow and Tyumen'. The map clearly demonstrates the astonishing differences in income distribution, particularly in the European Russia. By 1997 Moscow was the only area in that part of Russia where real per capita incomes remained high, while in all the surrounding areas population incomes were below 70% of their 1990 equivalent.

During the late Soviet period (1985 to 1991) the Russian central government actively pursued a policy aimed at equalising regional income disparities through transfers of funds from the "rich areas" (national centres of mining industry and trade) to the "poor" areas (predominantly

Table 4.18 Growth of Regional Income Disproportions in Russia

a) Dynamics in constant prices, 1990 = 100

	1990[a]	Dec 92	Dec 93	Dec 94	Dec 95	Jun 96	Dec 96	Dec 97	Dec 98
High income areas	100	73	86	134	133	109	142	133	121
Medium income areas	100	59	68	69	57	52	55	60	46
Low income areas	100	60	66	70	49	43	50	57	45
All RF	100	61	71	80	70	62	70	72	59

b) Relation of per capita incomes to the Russian average

	1990[a]	Dec 92	Dec 93	Dec 94	Dec 95	Jun 96	Dec 96	Dec 97	Dec 98
High income areas	1.67	1.99	2.01	2.80	3.19	2.95	3.38	3.07	3.30
Medium income areas	0.93	0.89	0.89	0.80	0.76	0.79	0.74	0.77	0.75
Low income areas	0.71	0.69	0.66	0.62	0.50	0.49	0.51	0.56	0.52
All RF	1.00	1.00	1.00	1.00	1.00	1.00	1.00	1.00	1.00

Table 4.18 *continued*

c) Shares in gross income and in total population (%)

	1990[a]	Dec 92	Dec 93	Dec 94	Dec 95	Jun 96	Dec 96	Dec 97	Dec 98
Income									
High income areas	18.0	21.0	21.1	29.1	32.8	30.3	34.8	31.5	34.1
Medium income areas	79.0	75.9	76.0	68.1	64.9	67.5	62.9	65.9	63.5
Low income areas	3.1	3.0	2.9	2.8	2.3	2.2	2.3	2.5	2.4
All RF	100.0	100.0	100.0	100.0	100.0	100.0	100.0	100.0	100.0
Population									
High income areas	10.8	10.6	10.5	10.4	10.3	10.3	10.3	10.3	10.3
Medium income areas	84.9	85.0	85.1	85.2	85.2	85.2	85.2	85.2	85.2
Low income areas	4.3	4.4	4.4	4.5	4.5	4.5	4.5	4.5	4.5
All RF	100.0	100.0	100.0	100.0	100.0	100.0	100.0	100.0	100.0

NOTES:

[a] Average monthly income for all of 1990.

High: Moscow, Tyumen', Kamchatka, Sakha, Magadan, Murmansk, Sakhalin.
Low: Dagestan, Kalmykia, Karachaevo-Cherkesia, Marii-El, Adygeya, Ivanovo, and Kursk.
Medium: All other areas of RF.

Sources:
See Table 4.15.

Map 4.2   Dynamics of Change in Real Per Capita Incomes in Russian Regions, 1990–97 (%, 1990 = 100)]

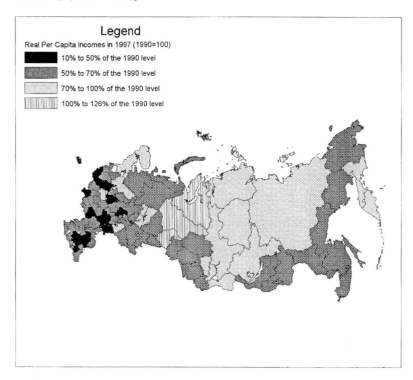

agricultural areas). This policy was made possible by a situation in which prices and salaries were centrally controlled. However, the liberalisation of prices in 1992, which was accompanied by the granting of increased autonomy in economic management to Russia's local governments, made continuation of the old policy impossible. After the start of the reform in 1992 the policy of income redistribution was in practice abandoned by the central government, while state controls over salary levels, particularly at the budget-funded enterprises, remained in place. This meant that while the central government continued the Soviet practice of formally guaranteeing a certain wage for state employees, it had given away most of its levers of income redistribution. This situation created a growing gap between the obligations and possibilities of the Russian state, one of the major consequences of that was the problem of wage arrears.

Another important result of the post-Soviet socio-economic reform was acceleration of the growth of income disproportions within society – both structurally and geographically. The national per capita income structure was reversed (Graph 4.2) with the bulk of the population in the mid-1990s finding themselves in the low-income group. At the regional level a few administrative areas – mostly Moscow and major mining regions – have been rapidly getting richer while the rest of the areas have been sliding further into poverty. While in 1990 one-tenth of the Russian population living in the high-income group of administrative areas had a share in the gross national population's income of 18%, in December 1998 this share was already as high as 34% (Table 4.18c).

It should be noted that during the post-Soviet political crises the Russian government made limited attempts aimed at containing the rapid income and regional diversification. This was the case in September–December 1992 when the Gaidar cabinet halted its reforms; exactly a year later, during and immediately after the clash between President Yeltsin and the Russian parliament; and again during the January–June 1996 election campaign. The fall of the Kirienko government after the August 1998 crisis had brought to power a much more moderate and less reform-radical government headed by Yevgenii Primakov. The latter also attempted to reverse or at least to halt some of negative social effects of previous reforms but, as 1998 data had shown, with little success.

A warning sign development that emerges from the above analysis is the one that signals of an increasing fault-line dividing the Russian society. In occupational terms, the split occurred between, on the one hand, bankers, oil workers and state bureaucrats, who gained financially (and politically) from the post-Soviet changes, and, on the other, peasants, manufacturing workers and intellectuals, who lost most of their incomes during the change. Between 1990 and late 1997 two regional centres – one bureaucratic (Moscow) and the other oil-producing (Tyumen') – on average have seen a 150% increase in their population's incomes, while in the rest of the country the average per capita income fell by almost 40%. But it was only Moscow that had managed to retain its high level of income after the August 1998 crisis.

Among areas hit hardest by the reforms was North Caucasus, where in December 1998, the population was receiving on average 47% of the 1990 income. It is no surprise, therefore, that the North Caucasus has become one of the most politically and socially unstable regions in post-Soviet Russia.[42]

Notes

1. Michael Specter, "Deep in the Russian soul, a lethal darkness", *The New York Times*, 8 June 1997. See also Michael Ellman, "The increase in death and disease under 'katastroika'", *Cambridge Journal of Economics*, 1994, Vol.18, pp.329–355; Timothy Heleniak, "Economic transition and demographic change in Russia, 1989–1995", *Post-Soviet Geography and Economics*, Vol.36, No.7, September 1995, pp.446–456.
2. "Russian population plummeting, U.S. group says", *Reuters*, 3 February 1997.
3. *The Guidelines of the Programme for the Medium Term Social and Economic Development of Russia. The Report of the Russian Academy of Sciences prepared for Duma Hearings.* Part One: The Concept of Overcoming of Recession, Moscow, May 1997; *Strategiya razvitiya Rossiiskoi ekonomiki I programma pervoocherednykh shagov.* Moscow: Institute of Economics, 1996.
4. B. Brui, I. Zbarskaya, A. Volkov, "O sovremennom sostoyanii I prognoze smertnosti naselenia Rossiiskoi Federatsii", *Voprosy statistiki*, Moscow, No.3, 1997, pp.54, 56.
5. Michael Specter, "Deep in the Russian soul, a lethal darkness".
6. Working age in Russia for men is between 16–59 years of age, for women – 16 to 54 years. (Brui, B., Zbarskaya, I., Volkov, A., p.56.)
7. Murray Feshbach, "Comments on current and future demographic and health issues", *Johnson's Russia List*, 10 June 1997.
8. See G. Standing, *Russian Unemployment and Enterprise Restructuring: Reviving Dead Souls*, N.Y.: St. Martin's Press, 1996.
9. Tito Boeri, "Transitional unemployment", *The Economics of Transition*, Vol.2, No.1, March 1994, pp.1–25.
10. Employment in all the major sectors of Russian economy was declining by a much slower rate than the output. Thus, while in 1996 industrial production in constant prices was 46.7% of the 1990 level, the number of employed in that sector was 73.1% of the 1990 figure. The gap in similar figures for agriculture is even more striking (62% output and 99.5% employment) which also indicates that a substantial portion of rural population was in fact employed outside the formal economy ("shadow" economy, ancillary sector). For data comparisons see Tables 1.1 and 1.11.
11. According to Russian minister Yevgenii Yasin, the existing difference between the unemployment rate and the decline in the economy is mainly covered by the growth in the small business sector which compensated for this decline. Yasin also warned that, if Russia continues restructuring its industry in the future, unemployment will rise dramatically (*ITAR-TASS*, 24 June 1997).
12. *Voice of America (VOA)*, 1 November 1996; Lidia Lukyanova, "If they get rid of the 'shuttle traders', then who will feed and clothe Russia?", *Prism: A Monthly on the Post-Soviet States*, Washington: Jamestown Foundation, February 1997, Vol. III, Part 2.
13. "Shadow economy: bigger than they think", *St Petersburg Times*, 16–22 June 1997. For a discussion of that issue see also Chapter 5.
14. V. Shkolnikov, "Zdorovie naselenia Rossii", *Voprosy statistiki*, Moscow, No.3, 1997, p.74.

15. D. Chernichovsky, H. Barnum and E. Potapchik, "Health system reform in Russia: the finance and organization perspectives", *The Economics of Transition,* Vol.4, No.1, May 1996, pp.113–134.

16. Michael Specter, "Deep in the Russian soul, a lethal darkness".

17. For a detailed study of health situation in Russia see: V. Shkolnikov, "Zdorovie naselenia Rossii", pp.68–75.

18. Between 1980 and 1990 numbers of university students in Russia fell from 3.0 million to 2.8 million (see *Sotsialnoe razvitie Rossiiskoi Federatsii v 1992 godu,* Moscow: Goskomstat, 1993, p.157).

19. In 1998 there were 3.35 million university students in Russia (*Sotsial'no-ekonomicheskoe polozhenie Rossii. 1998 g.,* Moscow: Goskomstat, 1999, p.304).

20. John H. Moore, "Science, technology and Russia's future: two legacies", *Communist Economies & Economic Transformation,* Vol.9, No.1, March 1997, 43–60.

21. Calculated from *Nauka v Rossii. 1996,* Moscow: Goskomstat, 1996, p.32.

22. *Nauchno-tekhnicheskii progress v SSSR. Statisticheskii sbornik,* Moscow: Goskomstat, 1990, p.22. However, Russia had the largest proportion in the total number of researchers in the USSR: in 1988 it was 67.8% (*Narodnoe khozayistvo SSSR v 1988 g. Statisticheskii ezhegodnik,* Moscow: Goskomstat, 1989, p.278).

23. While in the Soviet period budgetary donations made up only a part of the gross R&D funding, by the mid-1990s they had become the only viable source of funds for Russian science. That meant that the scale of cuts in research funding from non-state sources was significantly higher. Information from the Russian Academy of Sciences gives some indication of the real scale of R&D's funding crisis: according to Academy's recent report, in 1992 alone funding of scientific work proper from all sources in the Russian Academy of Sciences dropped fifty (50!) times (*The Guidelines of the Programme for the Medium Term Social and Economic Development of Russia. The Report of the Russian Academy of Sciences prepared for Duma Hearings.* Part Two: The Development Prospects of National Economy Sectors, Moscow, May 1997).

24. *The Guidelines of the Programme for the Medium Term Social and Economic Development of Russia. The Report of the Russian Academy of Sciences prepared for Duma Hearings.* Part One: The Concept of Overcoming of Recession, Moscow, May 1997.

25. According to a recent report of the Russian Academy of Sciences, in the mid-1990s about 40% of the Russian population, including two-thirds of children and one-third of elderly people, were consuming amounts of food which were less than the official minimum subsistence level. (Ibid.)

26. Ibid. The role of ancillary sector in post-Soviet Russian agriculture is discussed in more detail in Chapter 2.

27. See N. V. Petrov, S. S. Mikheyev, L. V. Smirnyagin, "Regional differences in the Russian Federation: social tensions and quality of life", *Post-Soviet Geography and Economics,* Vol.34, No.1, January 1993, pp.52–58; Barbara Severin, "Observations on regional aspects of food availability in Russia", *Post-Soviet Geography and Economics,* Vol.36, No.1, January 1995, pp.41–57.

28. Based on Goskomstat series. Until the end of 1996 the basket comprised 19 basic products, since early 1997 – 25 products.

29. Data used in Map 4.1 was reconstructed using indices and national figures published in *Sotsial'no-ekonomicheskoe polozhenie Rossii. 1997 g.*, Moscow: Goskomstat, 1998, p.178 and *Sotsial'no-ekonomicheskoe polozhenie Rossii. Yanvar' 1998 g.*, Moscow: Goskomstat, 1998, pp.202, 301–302.

30. See also Vincent Koen and Steven Phillips, *Price Liberalisation in Russia: Behavior of Prices, Household Incomes and Consumption During the First Year*, Washington, DC: International Monetary Fund, Occasional Paper No.104, July 1993.

31. Statistics show that the average wages of the 10% best-paid workers were 22 times higher than the average wages of the 10% worst-paid workers in December 1994 and 26 times higher in December 1995 (in most market economies, this difference is usually no more than five-fold) (Olga Menshikova, "Novye bednye na rynke truda", *Moya Gazeta*, 30 October 1996). See also Olga Kryshtanovskaya, "Rich and poor in post-communist Russia", *The Journal of Communist Studies and Transition Politics*, Vol.10, No.1, March 1994, pp.3–24; Tat'iana Iarygina, "Poverty in rich Russia", *Problems of Economic Transition*, Vol.37, No.8, December 1994.

32. Under the strict currency control that existed in the Soviet Union, there were two parallel currency exchange rates – the official one and the "black market" or street rate. The difference between the two would often reach 10 or more times. While the official rate was established by the government and was mainly used in state-run trade operations and currency exchange with foreign tourists, the unofficial rate reflected the actual demand/supply of foreign currency in the hands of the population, and was mainly dependent on the activities of small-scale traders.

33. Calculated from: *Sotsial'no-ekonomicheskoe polozhenie Rossii. 1998 g.*, Moscow: Goskomstat, 1999, pp.259, 264–5.

34. See Hans Aage, "Russian occupational wages in transition", *Comparative Economic Studies*, Vol.38, No.4, Winter 1996.

35. No monthly data are available for 1991, but we can assume that this growth continued up until August 1991, i.e. until the beginning of the process of *de-jure* disintegration of the Soviet Union.

36. Alfred B. Evans, Jr., "The decline of rural living standards in Russia in the 1990s", *The Journal of Communist Studies and Transition Politics*, Vol.12, No.2, June 1996.

37. Some observers link the recent decline in Russian light industry to the growth in cheap imports of consumer goods from mainland China, Taiwan, Turkey, Thailand and Hong Kong. These imports made locally-produced goods uncompetitive, leading to significant falls in domestic production.

38. However, Russian government officials have continuously denied the existence of a direct link between state reform policies and wage arrears. For instance, Prime Minister Chernomyrdin in early 1997 stated that "the main causes of non-payments in the Russian economy are irresponsibility of enterprises and organisations with regard to their specific obligations and poor budget performance, as a result of which the state becomes the main culprit for non-payments". Thus, according to the Russian Premier, enterprises, not the state, were to be blamed for the mounting delays in salary payments (*Delovoi Mir*, 24 January 1997).

39. According to a poll carried out in late 1996 by the All-Russia Centre for the Study of Public Opinion (VTsIOM), only 29.5% of respondents received their wages in full and on time, down from 52% in 1993. In October 1996 about 65–67 million Russian citizens were waiting (sometimes for several months) for the money due to them. Residents of small towns and villages were the most likely to be paid late in October (70% of those surveyed), while Muscovites were in the best position. Of the residents of the Russian capital surveyed, 64% were paid on time and only 18% suffered wage delays. Those who were paid on time and in full were most often managers and employees in the management sphere, white-collar workers with no special education and on the whole residents of Moscow and St Petersburg and the inhabitants of Russia's European north. Those paid least often were workers and generally inhabitants of rural settlements and small towns, in Siberia and the Far East (*Segodnya*, 11 December 1996; *Izvestia*, 26 November 1996; *OMRI*, No.229, 26 November 1996; *Trud*, 11 December 1996).

40. Attempts undertaken by the Russian government towards solving the problem of unpaid wages are discussed in Chapters 3 and 9.

41. See also Denis J. B. Shaw, "Russia's division into 'rich' and 'poor' regions", *Post-Soviet Geography and Economics*, Vol.34, No.5, May 1993, pp.323–325.

42. Some Russian observers had recently warned that income inequalities can even lead to the breakup of the Russian Federation. See V. Litvinov's article in *Ekonomika i zhizn'*, 1998, No.16, p.29.

5
The Evolution of Modern Russian Capitalism

In this chapter I will attempt to briefly analyse the evolution of the Russian reform strategy, its main achievements and faults. This is a topic that in the last years was attracting most of attention in political studies of contemporary Russia,[1] often provoking heated debates among academics inside Russia and abroad. This is also a favourite topic for many journalists that cover Russia, because it is often directly linked to many events that make top news world-wide: crime, big money, shady deals, political crises, etc.

The Russian "new capitalism" started to develop many months before the collapse of the USSR. In fact, many of its features the post-Soviet Russian capitalism were directly inherited from the Soviet economic system. Another important characteristic of the Russian "new capitalism" is that from the start it had a somewhat artificial nature: its development was initiated from "above", by the Soviet ruling elite, while the majority of the Russian population was left mainly with a role of an outside watcher of what was generally seen as a new "grand experiment". These two main features of the Russian "new capitalism" have played a crucial role in its future development.

The economic structure of contemporary Russia started to evolve from the Soviet system in the mid-1980s. By that time the Soviet Union already had a dual economy: one, state-owned and controlled, which was extremely monopolised, inflexible and inefficient, and the other, small-scale and private, which was often treated by the state as semi-legal or illegal and, therefore, was often highly criminalised. The role of the private sector in various branches of the Soviet economy differed greatly. While in agriculture private farming (or production in ancillary households and private gardens) was relatively developed and even enjoyed a certain degree of legal recognition, in industry the scale of private enterpreneurship was very modest and very rarely legal. Only a small share of retail trade and services was in private hands, while foreign trade, banking and finance were fully controlled by the state.

The reforms that were started in 1985 by Soviet leader Mikhail Gorbachev opened a new broader niche for private enterpreneurship. By the late 1980s private ventures (many of which were established as co-operatives) boomed in the areas of small-scale production, retail trade and services. State control over medium to large industrial enterprises became softer which boosted the growth of the "shadow" (i.e. illegal) economy. The flow of resources between the state and private sectors of the economy increased substantially, provoking growing criminalisation of state economic management and law enforcement structures.

In the late 1980s and early 1990s the emerging private sector had overgrown its initially assigned limits: at that time within the structures of Komsomol, the youth branch of the ruling Communist Party, first prototype foreign trade and banking private ventures started to appear. Creation of these structures was an extremely important development. First, these ventures could not appear without a certain degree of support and protection from the state. While in many other areas the growth of capitalism was limited to small business operations in "traditional" areas and was more or less spontaneous in character, foreign trade private operations were performed by well-connected (young) bureaucrats, enjoyed special protection from certain state structures and were mainly Moscow-based. Second, these "elite" capitalist ventures were among the most successful and profitable private enterprises ever to appear in the late Soviet history. These business operations were based exclusively on the existing gap between internal and world prices, on existence of a fixed (and artificial) currency exchange rate and the deficiency of the internal Soviet market. Due to their privileged position these "elite" capitalist ventures managed to accumulate significant (by Soviet standards) amounts of capital within an extremely short period of time.

It was in this environment of the crumbling state hold of the economy and the growing formal and informal private sector that the Russian economic reform was launched at the start of 1992. Between 1992 and 1998 this reform has passed several stages which I will analyse in more detail below. The stages included: (a) Gaidar reforms; (b) the confrontation; (c) Chernomyrdin's stalemate; and (d) the Chubais reform. The current, post-Chubais period, which has started in

September 1998 with coming to power of the Primakov government, was seen by many observers as a gradual retreat from the earlier reform strategy. Despite changes of the government during 1999 the essence of this policy remained largely unchanged. In contrast to earlier years this policy was characterised by a growing role of the state and its institutions in economic management and implementation of the general economic policy. However, a detailed study of post-Chubais reforms falls beyond the scope of this book.

5.1 Gaidar reforms (1991–92)

In January 1992 the Russian reformist government headed by the Acting Prime Minister Yegor Gaidar launched its reform programme. The major objective of this programme was to transfer the Russian planned and heavily centralised economy into a market-type economy within a relatively short period of time. It was envisaged initially that reforms would start to bring fruit in one to two years' time. Both Gaidar and President Yeltsin publicly acknowledged that the first months of the reform will be difficult and accompanied by significant falls in the living standards of the population but that already by the end of the first year of reform the Russian economy will start to pick up.

The Gaidar's reform strategy was aimed predominantly at loosening of the state control over the economy. This was to be achieved by a variety of means: the privatisation of state property, lifting of state control over prices, decentralisation of state management of the economy, creating conditions for development of market institutions and infrastructure in Russia. There were only few economists that disagreed with the necessity of all these measures. However, the sequence of reforms and their priority status right from the start were subject to heated debates.

The fundamental mistake made by the Gaidar government was that it chose a strategy based on achieving fast results. That was often done at the expense of the longer-term strategies. Thus, more difficult, time-consuming and capital-intensive tasks of restructuring and demonopolisation of the Soviet economy in the reform strategy were replaced by measures aimed primarily at softening and elimination of the existing state control. Although the latter task was much easier and faster to implement (given state powers inherited from the Soviet system), this was a profound mistake that in the later years have significantly undermined chances for the ultimate success of the Russian reform. This reform strategy left basically untouched such major features of the Soviet economic structure, as its heavy militarisation, high dependency of many sectors on state credits, general inflexibility and hostility to innovation, the huge bureaucratic component, and monopolisation of all basic industries. In the event the release of levers of state control over the economy during the first years of reform had greatly accelerated the crisis tendencies that were already evident in the 1980s without offering any practical alternatives.

Among the first reform steps taken by the Gaidar government were lifting of state controls over retail prices and the deregulation of foreign trade. These measures helped to overcome the deficiency of the retail market, which in the last months of 1991 reached critical levels. Within two–three weeks after reforms were announced the shops that earlier had empty shelves were again full of goods. However, the removal of price controls led to a significant increase in retail prices, which, in turn, provoked a large inflationary wave. Just a month after the reform was started, the Russian government was fully occupied by the task of keeping the inflation under control. Implementation of all other objectives – including those of macroeconomic restructuring and stimulating investment – had to be postponed until a much later stage.

Price and foreign trade reforms also had another important consequence. These reforms mainly targeted those areas of business, which were already controlled by young "elite" capitalists. Therefore, it is no surprise that the latter turned out to be the major beneficiaries from the early Gaidar reforms. The removal of the state monopoly in the area of foreign trade made it possible for them to significantly expand their businesses. Accumulation of large financial resources in internal and foreign trade during 1992 also boosted the development of Russian non-state banking and financial institutions. Within a year these institutions have evolved from semi-business party-run structures to independent and increasingly aggressive advocates of the new Russian capitalism.

An interesting feature of the Gaidar price and trade reform was its unfinished character. On the one hand, this reform led to a liberalisation of retail prices for the larger part of consumer commodities (with exception of some socially important commodities such as bread and milk, prices for which were continued to be partially controlled by the state). On the other hand, this reform did not affect most of industrial commodities prices for which continued to be state controlled. This in turn, created a growing imbalance between prices for consumer and industrial products, and between internal and world prices for Russia' major export commodities, such as oil and oil products, non-ferrous metals, timber, rare metals, etc.[2]

In a short period of time after the start of reform a significant part of the flow of primary goods between Russia's mining and manufacturing industries was re-directed to external markets. While the local industry was receiving less and less of necessary components, Russia's private direct and indirect exports boomed. Networks of semi-legal and illegal export chains were quickly established between managers (directors) of oil and mining enterprises, transportation firms, export companies, private banks, customs officials and medium and top-level state bureaucrats. Because many export deals were associated with high risks but even higher revenues, they also often involved elaborated chains of dealers.

The growing criminalisation of economic environment in Russia during the first months of reform was greatly facilitated by the *de facto* absence of border/customs controls with other former Soviet republics. Transfers of commodities from Russia to other republics were often continued to be viewed as "internal supplies" (as was the case in the USSR), but further re-exports of these commodities were already beyond the control of Russian authorities.

The reform opened ways for quick and virtually unlimited enrichment for that part of the Russian elite, which either had access to or control over export production and distribution, or ran established and efficient foreign trade businesses. It was mostly during this period between 1992 and 1993, that young Russian "elite" capitalists quickly evolved from petty traders into bankers, financiers or heads of successful trading houses and commodity exchanges. They managed to accumulate significant financial resources part of which was used to build new or to strengthen the existing "contact networks" within the state bureaucracy.

In order to halt the massive outflow of resources from the country, the Gaidar government moved in by establishing export quotas for major goods. However, these measures had only temporary effect. Moreover, these measures were often interpreted by corrupt Russian bureaucrats as yet another reason to demand even higher bribes for their "services".

While Russian private exports boomed, the retail market and the local manufacturing industry were quickly sliding into a deep recession. Inflationary wave, that followed the liberalisation of prices, wiped off all of population's savings and significantly undermined the trust in the national currency. The internal and external flight of capital increased while an acute lack of investment brought the economy to a standstill.

The means that the Gaidar government chosen to fight the inflation in the first half of 1992 were mainly aimed at limiting the money supply in a hope this would eventually halt the inflation and bring prices into balance. However, this policy led to an acute cash crisis in the country but failed to stop the growth in retail and wholesale prices. At the same time the government quickly found itself under growing pressures from producers and the parliament to increase the money supply. In the summer of 1992 the government eventually gave up to parliamentary pressures. The result was new and even stronger wave of inflation. In order to keep the budgetary deficit within limits, the government had to greatly increase its external borrowing.

It was in this critical situation that in late 1992 the government decided to start mass privatisation of the state property. Each citizen of the Russian Federation received a voucher, which entitled him or her for an equal share of the state property. Vouchers were distributed in October 1992 and two months later first sale auctions of state enterprises already took place. By the end of 1992 18 mid-sized and large companies and 46.8 thousand small shops were privatised. Another 3.5 thousand industrial enterprises have been leased.[4]

In December 1992, following the refusal of the Russian parliament to approve Yegor Gaidar as prime minister, the first Russian post-Soviet reformist government had to step down. This effectively ended the initial stage of the Russian reform (Table 5.1).

Probably the main result that the Gaidar government managed to achieve during the time it was in office was a significant destabilisation of the Soviet system of economic management. However, no alternative system was created. The strategic objective of macroeconomic restructuring of the Russian economy had quickly lost its priority under pressures from growing internal monetary and political problems. The diminishing state control over the economy was accompanied by large falls in the state revenue base and by the rise in the flow of capital from the country. All that led in 1992 to an acute investment crisis in Russia. Due to inflation, population's savings were depreciated within days after the start of reform soon followed by significant falls in the living standards of the people. Privatisation of foreign trade operations put local producers under a double pressure: while trying to adapt themselves to the new inflationary situation, they were also forced to compete with an increasing supply of low quality but cheap imported goods. At the same time the government, by means of

Table 5.1   Gaidar Reforms: Social and Economic Results, 19923
(indices; constant prices)

	1992 as % of 1991
GDP	81%
Budget deficit in 1992, % of GDP	8%
Non-payments of taxes, % of gross federal budgetary expenditure in 1992	...
Industrial production	82%
Agricultural production	90.6%
Inter-enterprise debts at the end of year, % of GDP	15.7%
Capital investment	60.3%
Foreign investment, billion US dollars	0.81[a]
including financial only	−
Real average income of the population	53%
Inflation (CPI)	2610%
Life expectancy, male	98.4%
Life expectancy, female	99.7%
Unemployment as % of economically active population (ILO methodology)	4.8%
Unpaid wages at the end of year, % of GDP	0.15%
Annual external borrowing, billion US dollars	13.3
Annual internal borrowing, billion US dollars	−
Estimated capital flight, billion US dollars	11

NOTES:
[a] In 1990–92.

leaving controls over prices for primary goods intact while opening the trade borders, effectively switched its policy of subsidies from the former direct support for industry and agriculture to indirect subsidies of private traders.

Russia's financial situation would have been much worse if Russian foreign debts were not rescheduled. In 1992 the Russian government paid only US$2.1 billion (21%) in principal and interest repayments on foreign credits out of US$9.9 billion which were due that year.[5]

5.2   The confrontation (1993)

The strategy of reform pursued by the Gaidar government was from the start met with a growing degree of hostility by the Russian legislature. By the end of 1992 the conflict between the government and the parliament resulted in the change of the cabinet. Gaidar was replaced in the post of prime minister by the former head of the large gas monopoly and an influential bureaucrat, Viktor Chernomyrdin.

Despite the fact that Chernomyrdin's view on the reform was significantly more moderate than Gaidar's, the conflict between executive and legislative branches of the power continued to develop into 1993. Chernomyrdin, whom many Russian parliamentarians initially expected to pursue a different policy from Gaidar, chose instead to join forces with the latter by giving him first a ministerial post and later in the year making him the first deputy premier.

The confrontation between the two branches of power was growing throughout the most part of 1993. In September the conflict reached its culmination when Yeltsin decided to dissolve the Russian parliament. This was followed by two weeks of open confrontation with the parliament until Yeltsin finally ordered a military attack against the rebels.

The breaking up of parliamentary resistance in early October 1993 removed the largest stumbling block on the way of the Russian reform. The adoption of the new constitution in December and new parliamentary elections led to the creation of the new legislature with had significantly fewer powers than the disbanded parliament. While pro-government factions in the new parliament were clearly in the minority, the president could now virtually force its selection of the government on the parliament. This situation made it possible to continue the reform; however, it did not resolve the earlier conflict between the president (and his government) and the legislature.

Despite the growing resistance to its policy throughout the year, the government in 1993 continued with implementation of its earlier reform strategy. "Voucher privatisation" was well under way, attempts to bring the inflation under control also continued (mainly through reducing federal budgetary expenditures on social needs and on subsidies to the economy), while the "informal" foreign trade was still on the rise. The negative consequences of the reform were also becoming more evident. Russian industrial and agricultural producers were becoming less competitive even at their home market. Exports were almost totally reoriented towards sales of minerals. Restructuring of the economy still remained to be a distant objective.[6]

During 1993 the task of balancing the budget was on the top of government's priority list. While credits of the Russian Central Bank (or printing of money) continued to be the major source for covering the growing budget deficit, the need to curb the inflation put dire limitations on the level to which the government could use this source.

Therefore, starting from early 1993 the Russian government in its fiscal policies was relying more and more on external sources of budgetary revenues. The most important among those were taxes and borrowing.

During 1992–93 the system of taxation in Russia underwent a number of significant changes. The Soviet tax system where the state not only owned and controlled all major economic developments but also was automatically collecting taxes from most of its businesses and employees, was effectively dismantled. While a declining number of enterprises and employees that were still under state control continued to pay their taxes in the old way, many new businesses and privatised enterprises were no longer subject to the system of automatic taxation. The activities of the latter were taxed through a system of federal and local taxes, many of which contradicted or overlapped each other. The total tax burden was so heavy that it almost immediately forced many non-state enterprises to find ways for tax evasion, thus pushing them into a "shadow" or "informal" economy. As a result of widespread tax evasion and continuing decline in industrial and agricultural output, state revenues from taxation started to fall rapidly. The government responded by introducing more taxes that made bureaucracy even more powerful but in the end failed to stop massive tax evasion.

The growing weakness of internal sources of budgetary revenue led to an increase in government's reliance on borrowing, which was gradually becoming one of the main sources of state revenues. Between 1992–94 the gross amount of the money that the Russian government was receiving through foreign loans and credits was constantly increasing. However, this money could only partially balance the budget. However, the spread of economic crisis in Russia in 1993 put many new enterprises on the edge of bankruptcy and forced their managers to seek state support, either on federal or local level. The pressure on the state financial system was increasing daily and very soon it became obvious that foreign borrowing could not remedy this situation.

In May 1993 the Russian government announced the first issue of "state short-term bond notes" (GKO). This opened a new and increasingly important channel of balancing the state budget – internal borrowing. At that time the gross amount of internal borrowing constituted a small proportion of budgetary revenues. The major ways, through which the government was balancing the budget were (a) new cuts to the existing budgetary spending, (b) the printing of money, and (c) foreign credits. In 1993 the deficit of the federal budget reached its highest level in the post-Soviet period (10.7% of the GDP). The largest creditor of the government was the Russian Central Bank which covered 86.7% of the deficit; another 12.4% were covered by foreign credits and 0.9% by internal borrowing. Such heavy reliance on printing of money kept the rate of inflation high: in 1992 CPI increased by an astronomical 2 610% and by further 940% in 1993.

Sharp cuts that Gaidar's and Chernomyrdin's governments introduced to the expenditure side of the budget, particularly to funding of enterprises, provoked a new problem which in the later years has almost totally paralysed Russian industry. Many enterprises that were left without state crediting immediately found themselves incapable to pay for intermediate goods. The result was the growth of inter-enterprise debts that by the end of 1993 reached an unprecedented level of more that one-third of the country's GDP (Table 5.2).

The confrontation between the executive and legislative powers in Russia that characterised most of developments in 1993, did not, however, break the decisiveness of Russian reformers to continue with

Table 5.2   The Confrontation: Social and Economic Results, 1993 (indices; constant prices)

	1993 as % of 1992
GDP	88%
Budget deficit in 1993, % of GDP	10.7%
Non-payments of taxes,	
% of gross federal budgetary expenditure in 1993	7.5%
Industrial production	83.8%
Agricultural production	96%
Inter-enterprise debts at the end of year, % of GDP	34%
Capital investment	85%
Foreign investment, billion US dollars	0.87
including financial only	...
Real average income of the population	116%
Inflation (CPI)	940%
Life expectancy, male	95%
Life expectancy, female	97.4%
Unemployment as % of economically	
active population (ILO methodology)	5.6%
Unpaid wages at the end of year, % of GDP	0.47%
Annual external borrowing, billion US dollars	15.5
Annual internal borrowing, billion US dollars	0.23
Estimated capital flight, billion US dollars	13.1

the reform. "Voucher privatisation" continued and by the end of the year 8 500 mid-size and large companies and 80 500 small shops were transferred into private hands.[7] Activities of private foreign traders, non-state banks and small businessmen have also significantly expanded.

The breakup of parliamentary opposition and the adoption of the new constitution that significantly expanded powers of the president and, in effect, moved the executive power away from the control of legislature, opened a new stage in the development of Russian new capitalism at the end of 1993. Soon after it was elected the new parliament approved Chernomyrdin as the Russian prime minister.

5.3   Chernomyrdin's stalemate (1994–95)

The victory achieved in acute political struggles in the late 1993 enabled President Yeltsin and the Russian government to continue its reform attempts. However, fresh memories of the parliamentary resistance and a real possibility of the emergence of a new crisis of power (opposition parties retained dominating positions in the new parliament) pushed the Chernomyrdin government to take a gradual and non-confrontational approach to the reform. While the earlier reform strategy was not abandoned, implementation of reforms was made by small and cautious steps and, if possible, with the approval of the parliament.

In the absence of political resistance, the major obstacle to the continuation of reforms was inflation. Extremely high rates of inflation that Russia was experiencing in 1992–93, undermined almost any serious attempt to reform, as well as the confidence of local and foreign investors. In the core of the problem of inflation was the established practice of covering the budget deficit through central bank credits. In the course of 1994 the Chernomyrdin's government began to gradually cut its dependence on central bank funding: while in 1993 central bank credits covered 86.7% of the budgetary deficit, in the next year these credits accounted for 73.7%.[8]

In 1993–94 the government also made a number of steps aimed at restructuring the expenditure side of the state budget. In the second half of 1993 Russia has stopped providing subsidies to the other ex-Soviet republics and some of the USSR's former allies. Funding of some major military and research programs was also halted. This enabled the government to receive additional financial resources that were directed towards fighting the inflation and reducing the state debt to the enterprises.[9] These measures helped to bring down the level of the gross inter-enterprise debt[10] and to significantly reduce the rate of inflation in 1994.

Partial achievements in stabilising of the national economy in 1994 did not stop the decline in the living standards of the population. Despite the fact that in 1994 the real per capita income slightly increased, it was still far beyond the late Soviet 1991 levels. During 1994 delays in payment of wages to state employees became a regular and widespread phenomenon; in late 1994 gross volume of wage arrears reached 0.7% of the GDP. Unemployment also increased: at the end of the year it stood at the level of 7.4% of the economically active population (Table 5.3). Falls in the real income of the population led to negative changes in food consumption patterns; these together with cuts to the funding of health and social services resulted in a dramatic decline in the life expectancy of the population.

Table 5.3   **Gradual Reform – Year One: Social and Economic Results, 1994** (indices; constant prices)

	1994 as % of 1993
GDP	87.4%
Budget deficit in 1994, % of GDP	10.4%
Non-payments of taxes,	
% of gross federal budgetary expenditure in 1994	6.1%
Industrial production	79%
Agricultural production	91%
Inter-enterprise debts at the end of year, % of GDP	15.7%
Capital investment	74%
Foreign investment, billion US dollars	1.053
including financial only	...
Real average income of the population	112%
Inflation (CPI)	324%
Life expectancy, male	97.8%
Life expectancy, female	99%
Unemployment as % of economically	
active population (ILO methodology)	7.4%
Unpaid wages at the end of year, % of GDP	0.67%
Annual external borrowing, billion US dollars	16
Annual internal borrowing, billion US dollars	3.1
Estimated capital flight, billion US dollars	19.7

Pursuing of an active anti-inflationary policy led to a growing dependency of the government on external credit resources. In 1994 internal borrowing becomes an important source of budgetary funding. In order to make investment in state bonds attractive, the government starts to pay extremely high interest rates on its bonds, thus diverting flow of investment from production to financial markets. In 1994 the issue of internal state bonds already helped to cover 9% of the federal budget deficit; another 15% were covered through foreign loans and credits. In addition, a further 25.4% Russia's foreign debt repayments were rescheduled during 1994.[11]

An improvement of the financial and budgetary situation did not halt the development of negative tendencies in the production sphere. In 1994 industrial and agricultural output in Russia recorded largest annual falls in the post-Soviet period. This resulted in the growth of the deficiency of the internal market and, consequently, in an upsurge in the Russian imports. However, because exports of primary commodities also continued to grow, Russia registered a 1.5 times increase of its trade balance, which at the end of 1994 reached US$25 billion.

On 1 July 1994 the "voucher privatisation" in Russia was formally ended. By that time a total of 16 500 enterprises employing about 21.8 million became private companies. In 1994 already 62% of Russia's GDP was produced in the private sector of the economy.[12] Despite official assurances that were made at the start of this privatisation and according to which all of state property was to be privatised through voucher auctions, by June 1994 a little more than half of Russia's industrial potential was privatised that way. The remaining property – which included some of the most profitable state companies in mineral and energy sectors, and in telecommunications – the government was intending to privatise at cash auctions during the later, second stage of privatisation. This decision rose serious doubts about the credibility and fairness of the government's reform strategy.[13]

Another major result of the "voucher privatisation" was the creation of a large proportion of insider-controlled private firms in Russia. The legal framework for "voucher privatisation" was formed by the law "On the Privatisation of State and Municipal Enterprises in the Russian Federation" that was passed by the Russian parliament back in July 1991. However, by the time this law came into force, the parliament and the government introduced a number of significant changes.[14] When voucher auctions started to take place in the late 1992, there were three possible models for privatising state companies. In accordance with Option 1, 40% of the shares of a company undergoing privatisation could be sold to its workers, while 60% were to be sold at the auction or held by the state for later stage. Under Option 2, 51% of the shares were to be sold to workers and the remaining 49% were held by the state or sold at an auction. Option 3 was applicable only to medium-sized enterprises and allowed a managing group that promised to restructure the firm, to buy 30% of the shares, while workers and managers of the company under privatisation could buy 20% of the shares. The latter option could be chosen only with the approval of all the workers employed at the company.

At the end of the "voucher privatisation" 73% of enterprises were privatised under Option 2, 25% under Option 1 and only 2% under Option 3.[15] That meant that the majority of privatised companies in Russia ended up in the hands of their employees. In most cases this hampered any further restructuring of newly privatised companies, particularly in the area of reshaping and downsizing of staff.[16] The way it was implemented, "voucher privatisation" did not lead to any significant changes in the management of these companies, which remained in the hands of their formerly state-appointed directors. Thus, the first stage of privatisation failed to reach some of its most important goals, like raising budgetary revenues, attracting increased investment and improving the performance of enterprises.

Vague and often contradictory character of the privatisation legislation did not help to overcome existing ambiguities. In the end many important decisions on privatisation were taken by local and federal authorities, which created new opportunities for the spread of corruption. In the process of voucher privatisation new criminal networks were established between the holders of large amounts of vouchers (banks, voucher funds), privatisation officials and managers of enterprises that were undergoing privatisation. In the end, regardless of the privatisation method used, the process of transfer of state property into private hands led to a considerable ownership consolidation and to prevalence of institutional over individual shareholders.[17] It can be argued, therefore, that privatisation did not correlate the fundamental fault of the Soviet economy – the high level of centralisation and generally low level of efficiency of its management. In the course of privatisation a highly corporate private management replaced the central state management of the economy. The latter was mostly made up from former Soviet managers (directors), state bureaucrats and a small but influential groups of new Russian businessmen, mainly bankers. Although in formal terms these new property owners were no longer controlled by the state, like their Soviet predecessors they were mostly interested in maintaining and expanding of their grip over the economy, but had not in its restructuring and higher efficiency.

The critical situation that developed in the Russian economy in 1994 by the end of the year started to undermine Russia's chances of getting new foreign credits, much needed for keeping its financial system in a balance. While the state budget deficit reached dangerous levels, production in the major sectors of the economy was rapidly falling. The end of the voucher stage of privatisation was immediately followed by the government push for cash privatisation, which opened new ways for filling the shrinking state budget. However, staging of new privatisation auctions proved to be a difficult task because of growing demands on part of the parliament and the public to give the whole process a more transparent and fair character. In December 1994 even the newly appointed chairman of the State Privatisation Committee, Vladimir Polevanov, stated that privatisation course needs "alternations" while "wrongly privatised" state property might be re-nationalised.[18]

Failure to secure uninterrupted flow of foreign credits and loans, that at the beginning of 1995 were covering half of the state budget deficit in Russia, forced the Chernomyrdin government to introduce significant changes to its economic policy. In April 1995 the International Monetary Fund approved a US$6.25 billion standby loan to Russia.[19] This loan, however, was conditional on Russia managing to stabilise its financial system and to cut its budgetary spending.

In May 1995 the Russian government introduced a "currency corridor" which imposed limits within which the exchange rate of the national currency to foreign currencies was allowed to fluctuate. This step was backed by significant financial interventions of the Russian Central Bank; the result was that within few weeks the inflation rate in Russia started to go down dramatically.[20] This policy was effective only because it artificially kept the currency exchange rate below the inflation rate. That led to a remarkable development when retail prices and salaries in the US dollar equivalent were rapidly growing while in real terms wages were actually falling (Graph 4.3).

One of the major aims of this policy was the restoration of the credibility of the national currency among business people and the population. However, not only did this measure fail to stop the internal flight of capital and savings into foreign currencies, but it also had significantly stimulated the process of "dollarisation" of the Russian economy. Artificially low exchange rates also meant that imports to Russia became cheaper while exports became dearer. This put Russian producers into a difficult situation, forcing them to sell internally or to export their produce at significantly lower prices. While Russian exports in 1995–96 continued to grow, that mainly happened as a result of dumping prices that were used by many Russian producers. However, since 1995 Russia started to rapidly increase its dependence on imports.

The 1995 financial stabilisation was also based on large spending cuts to the state budget. In 1995, for the second time since the reform began, the real per capita income recorded a sharp fall of 13%. At the same time the gross volume of wage arrears had risen to 0.8% of GDP. Tax evasion became massive with non-payments of taxes by the end of the year amounting to almost 11% of the gross federal budgetary expenditure (Table 5.4).

However, the decisiveness of the government in pursuing its policy of financial stabilisation did bring some important and positive results by the end of 1995. The rate of inflation in Russia had fallen from 117.8% in January to 103.2% in December 1995.[21] The deficit of the

Table 5.4   Gradual Reform – Year Two: Social and Economic Results, 1995 (indices; constant prices)

	1995 as % of 1994
GDP	96%
Budget deficit in 1995, % of GDP	2.9%
Non-payments of taxes,	
% of gross federal budgetary expenditure in 1995	10.9%
Industrial production	97%
Agricultural production	92%
Inter-enterprise debts at the end of year, % of GDP	14.4%
Capital investment	87%
Foreign investment, billion US dollars	2.73
including financial only	0.54
Real average income of the population	87%
Inflation (CPI)	315%
Life expectancy, male	100.7%
Life expectancy, female	101.1%
Unemployment as % of economically	
active population (ILO methodology)	8.8%
Unpaid wages at the end of year, % of GDP	0.81%
Annual external borrowing, billion US dollars	9.0
Annual internal borrowing, billion US dollars	23.3
Estimated capital flight, billion US dollars	18.5

state budget was reduced to a manageable 2.9%. In 1995 printing of money covered only 7.2% of budget deficit which was a very sharp fall from 76.1% just one year earlier.

These spectacular achievements became possible only through significant increase in government's external and internal borrowing. The budget deficit in 1995 was mainly covered by external credits (52%) and through internal borrowing (41%). In 1995 the volume of principal and interest payments on foreign credits that Russia had to pay had grown almost five times. Repayment of credits became the largest item in the federal budgetary expenditure after military spending. That was despite the fact, that Russia managed to negotiate with its Western creditors a rescheduling of 38.5% of the due credit payments.[22]

During 1995 the government also sharply increased its reliance on internal sources of credit. Issues of state securities – GKOs and "federal bond notes" (OFZ) – became regular while their total sales in US dollar equivalent increased in 1995 by more than 7 times and reached US$23.3 billion or 6.4% of GDP. At the end of the year the state debt on GKO-OFZ issues was equal to 3% of GDP while debt servicing amounted to 2% of GDP.[23]

The growing confrontation over the second stage of privatisation left the budget without significant revenues that the government planned to receive through cash sales of non-privatised enterprises and state-owned shares in partially privatised companies. In the first half of 1995 the government received only US$22.3 million from privatisation which amounted to just 2.5% of the planned figure.[24] This situation forced the government to seek alternative ways of promoting its privatisation effort. In March–April the government started negotiations with a number of Russian private banks which offered cash in return for trusteeship over state shares in privatised companies. In May this proposal received government approval and in August the Russian president issued a decree which outlined the procedure of what became known as "loans-for-shares" auctions.[25]

The auctions took place in November–December 1995. The companies that were tendered at the auctions included some of Russia's most profitable companies in oil-production, metallurgy, wood processing and transportation. On average, offering prices for controlling block of shares in these companies was more than 30% below their current market value[26] despite the fact that, in turn, Russian market value was also significantly undervalued if compared to international standards. In addition, some of most important of these auctions, for instance the auction of shares in the major oil company Yukos on 8 December, were organised by one of the bidders that, unsurprisingly, won the tender.[27]

The total revenues that the government managed to receive from "loans-for-shares" auctions totalled US$872.8 million or 1.4 times more than the gross revenue from cash privatisation during that year.[28] Combined revenues from these privatisations equalled 6.8 trillion roubles, which was still below the target level of 8.7 trillion[29] that the government planned to receive through cash privatisation at the start of the year.

"Loans-for-shares" auctions had a strong impact on the future development of the new Russian capitalism. First, these auctions had demonstrated the weakness of the government's strategy of reform even in such easy-to-implement parts as sales of state property. Incapability of the government to raise significant amounts of money through the sales of most lucrative enterprises in the minerals sector was surprising, given the importance of this sector for Russian and world economies. Second, the way these auctions were organised and managed, as well as their results, gave grounds for speculations about the fairness and openness of government's reform policies. The existing "special relationship" between the government and the Russian big business fully came into open after these auctions were held, leaving no doubts about the oligarchic nature of the ruling Russian regime. And, third, the results of these auctions sparked off an ongoing rivalry within Russia's business elite over the issue of state privileges. The Russian banking community which earlier in most cases was united in promotion of its corporate interests, since late 1995 has become increasingly divided.

In December 1995 new parliamentary elections were held in Russia. These elections demonstrated a significant rise in the electorate support for opposition parties. That was a clear signal to the Yeltsin regime that, if no immediate measures are taken, the coming presidential elections will mark the end of its power in Russia. Therefore, since early 1996 major efforts of the president and the government were redirected towards presidential elections. Issues of the future economic development and the promotion of reform were pushed aside for most of 1996.

5.4   Presidential elections (1996)

The political platform on which Yeltsin and his team entered the 1996 pre-election campaign had two major economic points. The first was the promise to pay off all wage arrears to the population. This issue has become a cause for the growing dissatisfaction of the population with the government's policies. Thus, large part of the government effort was aimed at reaching visible and quick improvement in the situation with delayed wage payments.

The other important point in the government's pre-election economic strategy was promotion of reform achievements. This policy was mainly targeted towards new Russian businessmen, managers of privatised enterprises, state bureaucrats and regional leaders. In order to strengthen its case the government was using a combination of political methods ranging from demonisation of opposition's plans and offers of cheap state credits and subsidies to entering into pre-election alliances with business elites and influential social groups.

Election concerns pushed the government to postpone and even to reverse its earlier attempts aimed at reaching financial stabilisation in Russia. Any significant direct or indirect cuts to social spending, industry or agriculture made on the eve of elections would inevitably undermine Yeltsin's chances of winning the crucial July 1996 elections. Although no aggregate and reliable data on government spending before the elections is yet available, there is little doubt that the government expenditure during that period had grown immensely. Yeltsin was making rounds of national trips and in most of the regions he was giving away huge sums of money and was promising even larger amounts if he was to be elected.

From March 1996 the government, through putting an extra pressure on national reserves and Russian borrowing channels, started to pay off wage arrears. Although there were no funds available to cover all of the debt to state employees, a significant portion of the debt for current months was paid off while the rest of the debt the government promised to clear after the election (Graph 5.1).

These economic measures, as well as the intense pre-election political manoeuvring which will be discussed in the next chapter, helped to bring Yeltsin back to power. However, immediately after the elections the government was faced with an even more difficult economic situation than before, which partly evolved as a result of the pre-election overspending. While Russia's budget was becoming dangerously imbalanced, the state reserves were running extremely low and sources of new credit were hardly available.

In order to improve this situation the government turned back to the implementation of contractionary fiscal policies of 1995. As could be seen from Graph 5.1, after the election state spending on wages was

Graph 5.1   Growth of Wage Arrears in 1996

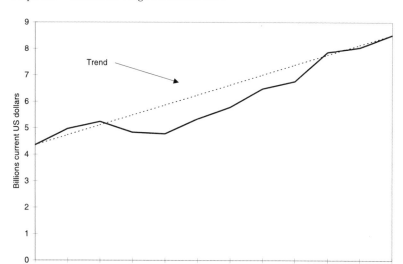

significantly reduced and by the end of 1996 the growth of wage arrears was back to the same trend as at the start of the year. By the end of the election year the gross amount of unpaid wages had grown to an all-time record of 2.1% of GDP.

These measures, however, could only partially cover the huge budget deficit. All other budgetary spending, including issues of credits to industry and agriculture, was also reduced leading to a further accumulation of inter-enterprise debts which in 1996 totalled almost 23% of GDP. In turn, cash-stripped enterprises could not pay their taxes. By the end of the year the state budget did not receive tax payments equal to 17.4% of the gross federal budgetary expenditure (Table 5.5).

However, austerity measures of the Russian government helped Russia to evade a major fiscal crisis. Despite the increased spending in the pre-election period, the budget deficit for 1996 was only slightly larger than in 1995: 3.3% of GDP as against 2.9% in 1995. This was achieved mainly through a significant increase in internal and external borrowing. During 1996 Russia's external debt increased by US$21 billion and reached US$128 billion. Debt servicing in 1996 excluding the rescheduled part of the due debt payments[30] had grown to 12.5% of all budgetary expenditure. That prompted the

Table 5.5   The Year of Elections: Social and Economic Results, 1996
(indices; constant prices)

	1996 as % of 1995
GDP	94%
Budget deficit in 1996, % of GDP	3.3%
Non-payments of taxes,	
% of gross federal budgetary expenditure in 1996	17.4%
Industrial production	95%
Agricultural production	93%
Inter-enterprise debts at the end of year, % of GDP	22.8%
Capital investment	82%
Foreign investment, billion US dollars	13.2
including financial only	10.0
Real average income of the population	106%
Inflation (CPI)	122%
Life expectancy, male	103.4%
Life expectancy, female	100.1%
Unemployment as % of economically	
active population (ILO methodology)	9.4%
Unpaid wages at the end of year, % of GDP	2.5%
Annual external borrowing, billion US dollars	21
Annual internal borrowing, billion US dollars	57.9
Estimated capital flight, billion US dollars	21.0

Russian Deputy Finance Minister to make a warning statement that if Russia continued to borrow money at the same rate, by 1998 it would be in no position to meet its debt servicing requirements.[31]

The most dramatic increase in state borrowing during 1996 was in the level of internal state debt. Issues of GKO-OFZ increased from US$23.3 billion in 1995 to US$57.9 billion in 1996 reaching 13.2% of GDP. The growth of internal borrowing led to a boom in stock market operations with Russian government bond notes and other securities. That made Russia the most lucrative securities market in 1996 for foreign investors.[32]

While Chernomyrdin managed to retain his post of prime minister after the presidential elections, in August 1996 Yeltsin introduced a significant government reshuffle, including the appointment of a prominent banker, Vladimir Potanin, to the post of the first deputy prime minister in charge of economic policy. Following that President Yelstin approved a package of 60 emergency revenue-raising measures.[33]

Introduction of new austerity measures helped to raise slightly the level of state revenues; however it did not stop the development of an acute financial crisis in Russia. Tax collection levels remained extremely low, prompting the government in October 1996 to establish an Emergency Commission with the sole responsibility of improving the situation with tax payments.

Despite the introduction of funding cuts and an increase in borrowing, the state budget remained heavily unbalanced. That forced the government again, like in 1995, to seek support from Russia's new capitalists – bankers and businessmen who continued to show strong interest in the proposed privatisation of state assets in mining, oil and energy sectors of the national economy. Appointment of Potanin to a top government post was the first sign of the recognition by the state of the need to co-operate with the local business community. Potanin's appointment had significantly intensified the rivalry within that community.

As a result of political and economic pressures during the election year, the Russian state budget was seriously undermined. Russia's internal and external public debt had grown substantially, while social problems associated with the reform were as acute as ever before. Temporary improvement of the situation immediately before the elections was and could not have been a long-lasting process. Rather, that was a pre-election trick used by Yeltsin in order to secure voters' support. However, that did not solve any of the problems that from the start were associated with or directly derived from the strategy of reform chosen by Russia in 1992.

5.5   The Chubais' reform (1997–98)

Russian government's successes in overcoming of inflationary effects of the 1996 pre-election promises could be largely attributed to one of the closest associates of President Yeltsin, Anatoly Chubais. Gaidar brought Chubais into the Russian government. From the start of "voucher privatisation" and until he was sacked by Yeltsin from the government in January 1996, Chubais headed the Russian privatisation campaign. In 1994–95 he also was the driving force behind Russia's attempts of financial stabilisation. After he left the government, he was put in charge of Yeltsin's election campaign headquarters. After Yeltsin's re-election he again assumed a central role in the state strategic planning. In December 1996 Chubais was appointed the head of the Administration of the Russian President. In March 1997 after another government reshuffle he and another close ally of Yeltsin, governor of Nizhnii Novgorod Boris Nemtsov, become first deputy premiers.

The Chubais-Nemtsov team was in control of the economic policy in Russia for most of 1997 and early 1998. Achieving and maintaining of financial stabilisation again became the cornerstone of the government's policy. The return to contractionary policies, which were abandoned in the late 1995, on the eve of presidential elections, demanded similar governmental actions. Reduction of the deficit of the state budget became the major goal. The same way as earlier, this was done solely through fiscal means, i.e. through cutting state expenditure and increasing the flow of budgetary revenues. The continuing economic crisis and the spread of "shadow economy" in Russia, which earlier already resulted in chronic and acute problems with tax collection, left the government with only two realistic options for realisation of its fiscal plans. These were a further reduction of state spending and increased flow of non-tax revenues into the budget through sales of state property and borrowing.

It needs noting that, as a result of the significantly reduced budgetary spending in the previous years, during 1997 the space for the government's fiscal manoeuvring has become increasingly limited. Any further large cuts to state support to the national economy and the military, as well as on social development, were certain to provoke a massive social and even political resistance. In addition to that the Chubais-Nemtsov team was under political pressure to fulfil, at least partially, the Yeltsin's pre-election promise to pay off all wage arrears to the population. This latter task meant that during 1997 the government had also to abandon an important tool of balancing the budget that it was successfully applying during all years of reform, i.e. delays of salary payments to state employees. Moreover, despite its limited resources, the Russian cabinet also had to find significant sums of cash that could be redirected towards reducing of the state debt on wages.

In the course of 1997 this task became one of the most important in the government's policy. By the end of the year, despite the mobilisation of all available financial resources, the government managed to reduce wage arrears from the state budget only by a small margin. At the same time the gross volume of delayed salaries in real terms remained almost unchanged. In early 1997 unpaid wages from the state budget amounted to 9.5 trillion current roubles; a year later this figure was 7.0 trillion. During the same period, between January 1997 and January 1998, the total volume of wage arrears increased from 48.6 trillion current roubles to 52.6 trillion.[34]

While almost immediately after the 1997 budget law came into force, top Russian officials publicly expressed concerns about the ability of the government to fulfil it.[35] In fact, in its actions the government was often ignoring the budget and acting in accordance with presidential decrees, many of which contradicted budgetary provisions. This allowed the government to implement some radical cuts to state spending which never had a chance to be approved by the parliament. In April–May 1997 the Chubais-Nemtsov team made public its plans to end the practice of state subsidising of communal services. Some major reductions on military spending were also introduced during that time.

However, these attempts did not yield any significant results. Rather, they provoked a strong public resistance to government policies. Thus, in June and September 1997 the lower house of Russian parliament, the Duma, had effectively blocked the government proposal aimed at reforming of the system of social benefits.[36] If approved, these measures would have resulted in a significant reduction of state subsidies for community services and rent. At the same time government cuts to military spending led in June–July to a series of public protests and demonstrations which involved army personnel, and even prompted a top pro-government politician to state that the armed forces were on the edge of mutiny.[37]

The failure of these attempts to reduce the expenditure side of the budget prompted the government in mid-1997 to direct most of its efforts towards increasing the flow of revenues to the budget. However, any progress in that direction was dependent on a significant improvement in tax collection. This issue was in the centre of government policies since the start of the reform, but despite all efforts levels of tax collection continued to fall. Most of debts came from corporate taxpayers. In turn, the latter were divided into two major groups. The first group included large companies, which did not pay their taxes in full because they failed to receive due payments for their services or products from consumers. These companies included major gas, oil and electricity corporations. The other group was made of mainly medium-sized companies which were in deep financial crisis, had experienced large falls in output and often simply did not have funds in their accounts to pay taxes. A growing number of these companies were successfully using their insolvent situation for bargaining with local and federal authorities for additional subsidies or cheap loans. Many of these companies were also involved in various tax evasion schemes.

Numerous attempts by the Chernomyrdin government to resolve the tax collection crisis brought only temporary results. The acute budgetary crisis in Russia forced the Chubais-Nemtsov team in May–June 1997 to take some decisive steps in order to improve tax collection. The main target of these measures was the first group of corporate tax debtors. The government ordered that either 15 large companies pay their tax debt to the state in full or face bankruptcies. By late June 1997 all of these companies had repaid their debts; however, many of them were forced to take large commercial credits in order to do that.[38]

Significantly increased revenues to the state budget[39] enabled the Russian government to bring the budget into balance, at least for a short period of time. That led to an improvement of Russia's international credit standing, prompting the World Bank to approve a special loan to cushion the social effect of the reform and the IMF to resume regular payments of its three-year loan to Russia.

These government's efforts helped to postpone the impending fiscal and political crisis in Russia. However, the need to pay off the state debt on wages and the rapidly accumulating public debt on other budgetary spending meant that the relief was very temporary.[40] In addition, by mid-1997 the effectiveness of another major source of state revenues – internal borrowing – was becoming negative (see Graph 2.4). That meant that new issues of state bonds could no longer cover gross repayments of principal and interest on the previously released bonds. Since August 1997 the net budgetary gain from issuing of internal bonds was zero to negative. In order to keep this bond market afloat the government was borrowing more and more money. This policy put an enormous pressure on the Russian budget and, finally, resulted in the collapse of the Russian bond market and in general meltdown of the Russian financial and banking system in August 1998.

The falling attractiveness of internal borrowing had prompted the Russian government to start issues of state bonds on external markets. In November 1997 Russia issued its first Eurobond with a repayment period of 5 years and managed to raise about US\$1 billion. In March 1997 the second 7-year Eurobond raised US\$1.2 billion, although at significantly higher premium. That did not stop the Russian government from floating a 10-year, US\$2 billion Eurobond in June. The money received from these issues was mainly directed towards repayment of the public debt on salaries.[41]

The shrinking base for budgetary revenues, both from internal and external sources, forced the Russian government in July 1997 to boost its privatisation programme. Between 1 July 1994 when cash privatisation was started and early 1997 the total revenues from sales of state property amounted to slightly more than 1.5 billion US dollars

Table 5.6 Russia: Privatisation in Major Branches of Economy

a) Dynamics of privatisation

	1992	1993	1994	1995	1996	1997	1998
Total number of privatised companies, thousands	46.0	42.9	21.9	10.2	5.0	2.7	2.1
Number of companies in trade and catering as % of all privatised	49.8	41.5	34.2	37.9	29.0	27.3	27.3
Gross revenues received from privatisation.[a]							
in billion current roubles	...	450	1 067	3 815	3 234	26 230	17.5
in billion 1990 roubles[b]	...	1.25	0.73	0.94	0.55	3.75	2.30
in million US dollars[c]	...	467.9	468.8	832.0	630.6	4 550.7	1806.5

b) Share of private sector in gross output (%)

	1992	1993	1994	1995	1996	1997	1998
Industry	14.0	55.1	80.1	90.3	90.8	91.1	...
Agriculture[d]	32.9	43.0	45.5	48.5	49.2	50.1	...
Retail trade	59.0	77.0	85.0	87.0	91.0	92.0	...

NOTES:
[a] Excludes revenues in vouchers (privatisation cheques): 46.8 mln cheques in 1993 and 55.5 mln in 1994.
[b] Calculated using GDP deflators.
[c] Calculations based on annual average official exchange rate of rouble to USD.
[d] Private farms and ancillary households only.

Sourced and calculated from:
Rossiiskaya Federatsiya v 1992 godu, Moscow: Goskomstat, 1993, pp.66–75; *Rossiiskii statisticheskii ezhegodnik. 1994*, Moscow: Goskomstat, 1994, pp.187, 227–31, 300; *Rossiiskii statisticheskii ezhegodnik. 1995*, Moscow: Goskomstat, 1995, pp.232–6, 317; *Rossiya v tsifrakh. 1996*, Moscow: Goskomstat, 1996, pp.131, 264, 270–2, 286–9, 316; *Sotsial'no-ekonomicheskoe polozhenie Rossii, janvar'-iul' 1996 g.*, Moscow: Goskomstat, 1996, p.195; *Sotsial'no-ekonomicheskoe polozhenie Rossii, janvar'-oktyabr' 1996 g.*, Moscow: Goskomstat, 1996, pp.207–14; *Sotsial'no-ekonomicheskoe polozhenie Rossii, 1997 g.*, Moscow: Goskomstat, 1998, p.230; *Rossiiskii statisticheskii ezhegodnik. 1997*, Moscow: Goskomstat, 1997, pp.334, 378, 469; *Sotsial'no-ekonomicheskoe polozhenie Rossii, yanvar' 1998 g.*, Moscow: Goskomstat, 1998, pp.116–8; *Rossiiskii statisticheskii ezhegodnik. 1998*, Moscow: Goskomstat, 1998, pp.388, 443, 588; *Sotsial'no-ekonomicheskoe polozhenie Rossii, yanvar' 1999 g.*, Moscow: Goskomstat, 1999, pp.143–5.

(Table 5.6). This was significantly less than the government initially planned. However, between late 1995 and mid-1996 the privatisation campaign in Russia was largely halted due to uncertain outcome of the presidential elections. Following Yeltsin's victory, privatisation issues were again on top of the government's priority list. The Russian banking sector that funded Yeltsin's election campaign and, consequently, had greatly increased its influence over making of the state policy, emerged as the main contender for the privatised state property. While, due to political pressures and uncertainties, bankers were forced to take a unified position before the election, after elections were over they immediately found themselves in competing camps.

However, the competition between Russian banks during the post-election privatisation auctions that were held in late 1996 was still far from the peak levels that it has reached a year later. One of the most important of these auctions, the sale of 33% of the shares in Russia's second-largest oil company AO Yukos, was organised by Menatep bank and, not surprisingly, won by that bank's subsidiary company.[42] Another Russian large private bank, Inkombank, came as a winner of the other important auction when, also through a subsidiary company, it acquired 8.5% of stake in the Unified Energy System (EES), the operator of the national grid.[43] In both cases banks did not operate alone: special bank and corporate consortiums were formed to bid in these auctions. Consortiums largely mirrored existing factions within the Russian banking and business community, which since 1993–94 was *de facto*, divided between a small number of competing financial-industrial groups.

The struggle between rivalry business groups became very intense in 1997 after the government announced that it was putting on sale shares of some of Russia's most lucrative companies.[44] In addition to the sale of stakes in the national telecommunications company and some major oil corporations that was planned a year ago, but was postponed until after the elections, the Chubais-Nemtsov team also attempted to sell the 40% of shares that were held by the state in the national gas monopoly, Gazprom. However, the strong resistance from Gazprom management against such privatisation forced Russia's young reformists to abandon their plans. Instead, Gazprom underwent minor restructuring and was obliged by the government to pay off its tax debt.[45]

On 25 July, at the first major privatisation auction of 1997, the government sold 25% plus one share of the national telecommunications company Svyazinvest. This auction was won by a consortium headed by Oneksimbank, a commercial bank ran by the former Russian deputy prime minister Vladimir Potanin.[46] Two weeks later Potanin's bank again came as a winner at another auction and received 38% of stake in the metals giant Norilsk Nickel.[47] While the first auction was generally considered to be fair because the winning bid was far larger than the rival bid,[48] the second auction was widely considered rigged by Oneksimbank. In 1995 this bank won a "loans-for-shares" tender when it lent the government US$170 million in exchange for control of the state share in Norilsk Nickel. Two years later, Oneksimbank bought out that stake for just US$250 million. Thus, after repayment of the loan the net revenue of the government from the sale of its control in the world's largest nickel producer was a mere US$80 million.[49]

Results of these two auctions led to a resumption of the struggle between major Russian business groupings. The shaky peace deal that was reached between Russia's leading businessmen before 1996 presidential elections was broken. The conflict immediately spilled over to the national mass media which, by mid-1997, was already fully controlled by rival business groups. Russian newspapers, TV and radio were giving diametrically opposite assessments of these privatisations. In addition to that, a series of reports on shady deals involving major businessmen and their allies in the government started to leak into the press. Five days after the second auction was held, the Russian deputy prime minister in charge of privatisation, Alfred Kokh, was forced to resign.[50]

By September the intensity of the bank war started to threaten the stability of the Russian political establishment. President Yelstin himself had to intervene by arranging a meeting with Russia's top bankers and asking them to stop rivalries.[51] This presidential appeal, however, had almost no effect. A new scandal broke out in mid-November involved a number of top Russian politicians who allegedly received large royalties from a publishing company linked to Oneksimbank. The royalties were paid for contributions to a book on privatisation that even has not been published.[52] This scandal led to the sacking of the new privatisation minister along with two other top officials. Chubais, who was also involved in the "book scandal", survived. However, on 20 November Yeltsin stripped both Chubais and Nemtsov from their important ministerial posts, respectively as finance, and fuel and energy ministers.[53]

The struggle between financial-industrial groups based around major Moscow banks continued to intensify until late November 1997 when the fallout from the Asian financial crisis had led to a significant rise in the cost of borrowing on international financial markets. In this situation

Russian banks, which had only limited resources of their own and in order to be able to compete in privatisation auctions had to seek foreign credits, became increasingly distracted from new privatisation offers that the Russian government was preparing.[55] Eventually, many of these planned privatisation auctions had to be cancelled, while the government again had to fulfil its spending promises through increased borrowing on domestic and foreign markets (Table 5.7).

Changes that took place at the end of 1997 were not the only factor that forced the government to postpone implementation of its plans for further privatisation. Under the new privatisation law, which came into effect on 2 August 1997, the Russian government could no longer stage closed or insider-dominated auctions of state property. According to this law, all sales had to be open and competitive. Moreover, the law required the government to submit its annual privatisation plan for approval by the parliament, which significantly limited the scale of future government manoeuvres in this area.[56]

Table 5.7   Chubais Reform: Social and Economic Results, 1997[54]
(indices; constant prices)

	1997 as % of 1996
GDP	100.4%
Budget deficit in 1997, % of GDP	4.4%
Non-payments of taxes, % of gross federal budgetary expenditure in 1997	30.6%
Industrial production	101.9%
Agricultural production	100.1%
Inter-enterprise debts at the end of year, % of GDP	29.2%
Capital investment	95%
Foreign investment, billion US dollars	32.5
including financial only	22.0
Real average income of the population	103.5%
Inflation (CPI)	111%
Life expectancy, male	102%
Life expectancy, female	100.8%
Unemployment as % of economically active population (ILO methodology)	9.0%
Unpaid wages at the end of year, % of GDP	1.8%
Annual external borrowing, billion US dollars	14.2
Annual internal borrowing, billion US dollars	77.4
Estimated capital flight, billion US dollars	20.0

The deadlock character of the economic policy, which was advocated by reformists in the period that followed the 1996 presidential elections, became evident in the course of 1998. The turbulence on international financial markets that accompanied the Asian financial crisis made it more and more difficult for the Russian reformist government to borrow large volumes of money abroad, whether through direct loans or through issues of state securities. Consequently, the external cash flow into Russia has become weaker. This happened exactly at a time when the government had to start making increasing volumes of repayments on some of its earlier debts, including internal debt on bond issues.

Right from the start of 1998 much of Russia's reform efforts were overshadowed by an impending collapse of its state financial system. Drastic efforts made by Chernomyrdin, Chubais and then by Kirienko aimed at averting this collapse by increasing volumes of external borrowing and introducing stricter taxation laws, had very little effect, probably with an exception of delaying the financial collapse by about five months. When in March 1998 Chernomyrdin was sacked (or organised his own sacking) by Yeltsin, Russian financial indicators were clearly pointing to a dangerously large imbalance between income and expenditure in the state budget. Thus, the August crisis of 1998 was easily predictable. It came as a logical completion of the earlier policy of the so-called reforms, which as its cornerstone had reliance on external funding rather than on the national sources of growth. The consecutive governments of Gaidar, Chernomyrdin, Chubais and Kirienko all proved unable to introduce far-reaching structural reforms into the command economy that Russia has inherited. In the course of reform years the already weak late-Soviet national growth base was devastated further, the precious mass support for reforms was wasted while Russian leaders preferred to move along an easy path of spending large amounts of money their nation did not earn.

By the end of 1998 the evolution of the Russian new capitalism was still far from being over. The August crisis had significantly undermined the positions and influence of Russia's emerging capitalist class. Particularly, in the last months of 1998 attempts made by the Primakov government and aimed at reinstating of state controls over Russia's financial flows have triggered new political struggles within the national elite. In this new post-crisis situation many tycoons of Russian business have found themselves under crossfire.

However, despite these recent developments the growth of influence of Russian capitalists in both the economy and in politics was rather impressive. Within a decade a quite disperse group of acting and former bureaucrats, petty businessmen, state industrial managers, and semi-legal and illegal dealers have organised itself into a number of nationally-based financial-industrial groups. These groups established direct links with state structures, both on local and national level.

The formal start of the second stage of Russian privatisation in 1994, and especially its activation after Yeltsin's victory in the 1996 presidential elections, almost immediately led to an intense struggle between major business groups for the control over the most lucrative shares of state property. The peculiarity of the Russian situation was that the competition between these groups took place in political rather than economic spheres. The level of political influence of that or other group and its connections to top officials have played far greater role in assuring a successful outcome of this struggle than financial and economic positions of any of these groups. That turned the federal government and Russian local state structures into an arena of rivalry of business groups. However, this development was largely provoked by the government itself, which was becoming increasingly dependent on large donations that were coming from the Russian business community. Such support came when the government found itself in an extremely critical situation having exhausted all other available sources of funding. Therefore, the government was forced to make concessions or to agree to special conditions under which this support could be possible. "Loans-for-shares" scheme was the first public manifestation of special relations between the government and Russia's new capitalists. In 1996, in return for the support to Yeltsin's election campaign, two leading businessmen received top government positions and, along with few others, "special treatment" at privatisation auctions.

The evolution of Russian new capitalism was largely directed by the strategy of reform that was chosen and pursued by President Yeltsin and his governments since 1992. It was the government policy that – through Gaidar's first reform steps – opened a niche for almost totally unlimited flow of resources from the state to private sector. Therefore, Russian new capitalists were in a way a creation of the Russian reformist government itself, like their predecessors were also a creation of the late Soviet system.

Mistakes made in the strategy and in the implementation of the Russian reform have also opened a way for the rapid growth of various forms of illegal economic activities in the country. Increasing pressures on part of the government, that in the last few years was desperately trying to raise the flow of revenues to the budget in a situation when the national economic output continued to slide, have greatly accelerated this process.

By the mid-1990s a significant part of economic activities in the Russian Federation were taking place outside the formal economy. "Shadow economy" experienced its most dramatic growth in the first two years of the reform. A number of factors stimulated this growth. Possibly the most important among these factors was a significant capital accumulation in the Russian informal economy. These money came from a variety of illegal and semi-legal operations, like misuse of state credits and credit fraud schemes, non-payment of contracts (particularly in the foreign trade sphere), the concealment of income and widespread tax evasion. Part of this capital was used to bribe officials, particularly those responsible for taking important economic decisions in the areas like issuing of export licenses and customs regulations.[57]

Illegal economic activities in the Russian economy mostly take place in the areas where traditionally significant amounts of cash are in circulation. These areas mainly include export industries, banking, trade and privatisation. A large share of unreported operations is taking place in Russia's major export-oriented industries: oil and gas production, ferrous and non-ferrous metallurgy, timber and fish production. In banking and finance informal sector has the strongest presence in currency exchange, inter-bank crediting and money transfers. However, the largest share compared to any other sector the "shadow economy" in the 1990s had in the retail and foreign trade where over half of all activities went unreported.[58]

According to the latest figures available from the Russian anti-crime authorities, in the first years of reform, during 1992–93, no less than 20% of oil and 33% of metals produced in Russia were later shipped out of the country illegally.[59] In 1996–97 official estimates of the share of "shadow economy" in Russia's GDP ranged between 22% and 50%. The lowest estimate came from the State Statistical Committee (*Goskomstat*) while the highest from Russian Prime Minister Chernomyrdin himself.[60] Goskomstat figure, widely believed to be understated, was calculated as a total of estimated shares of the informal sector in various branches of the economy. In 1996, according to Goskomstat, 63% of Russian foreign trade activity was not reported to the authorities (which was equal to 10% of GDP), 46% of agricultural production (4% of GDP), 11% of industrial output (4% of GDP), 9% of business activities in the sphere of transport and communications (1% of GDP), and 8% of construction (1% of GDP).[61]

At the end of 1996 Russian major state organisation which is responsible for fight against the economic crime, the Main Administration for Economic Crime of the Ministry of Internal Affairs, reported that the capital amassed and controlled by criminal groups amounted, in gross terms, to the equivalent of 60–70 trillion roubles which was about 40% of all the money in the circulation. Organised crime groups were controlling about 40 000 economic entities, which included approximately 500 commercial banks, 4 000 joint-stock companies and over 1 000 joint ventures. In addition to that, Russian criminal groups also established 1 500 commercial structures that acted as forefront legal bodies for their illegal economic activities.[62]

In 1997 Russian authorities managed to uncover 219 000 economic crimes or 20 000 less than in 1996. Out of the total number of these crimes committed in 1997, about 50% were in the sphere of foreign trade and another 33% were associated with privatisation, trade, banking and finance.[63]

An analysis of the modern Russian capitalism would be incomplete without a brief description of the development of small business. Many small businesses in Russia have their roots in the co-operative movement that boomed in the Soviet Union in the late 1980s. In their turn, the majority of these co-operatives, particularly those created in the production sphere, were offspring of the state-owned enterprises and, moreover, were often created by managers of these enterprises who were searching for ways of freeing themselves from the total control of the state.

About half of all functioning small businesses in post-Soviet Russia were small retail trade ventures and export–import firms (Table 5.8). Other areas of the economy where small business activities were significant included housing construction and renovation, industry and R&D. According to published statistics, during 1995 there was a significant growth in numbers of employed in small business; it was also reported that over 1 million jobs were created in that sector during that year alone.[64] In the following year, however, this was followed by even a more dramatic slump in employment numbers when, according to Goskomstat data, the total employment in small businesses has declined by 30%. The share of small businesses in the gross economic output in the second half of the 1990s was also decreasing: it fell from 18% in early 1995 to less than 12% in January 1998.

In regional terms, small business development in Russia varied greatly with most of these ventures established in large cities. In October 1996 22% of all Russian small businesses were operating in

Table 5.8 Small Business Development in Russia, 1993–98

	1 Jan 93	1 Jan 94	1 Jan 95	1 Jan 96	1 Jan 97	1 Jan 98
Total number, thousands	560.0	865.0	896.9	877.3	841.7	861.1
In percent						
Total number, including:	100.0	100.0	100.0	100.0	100.0	100.0
Industry	10.7	10.9	14.2	14.6	15.7	15.6
Agriculture	1.2	1.3	1.1	1.1	1.3	1.4
Construction	13.0	10.7	13.8	16.6	16.4	16.5
Transport and communications	2.5	2.2	2.0	2.3	2.4	2.5
Trade and Catering	49.2	46.0	46.8	42.7	42.7	43.3
Marketing	3.7	7.4	5.8	4.8	4.3	4.2
R&D	6.4	7.5	5.8	5.6	5.5	5.1
Other	13.2	14.1	10.7	12.2	11.7	11.4
Employment, thousands	…	8 600	8 480	8 945	6 269	6 515
Total output as % of GDP	…	…	17.9	12.0	10.0	11.7

Sources:
Rossiiskii statisticheskii ezhegodnik. 1994, Moscow: Goskomstat, 1994, pp.75–6; *Rossiiskii statisticheskii ezhegodnik. 1995*, Moscow: Goskomstat, 1995, pp.237–8; *Rossiiskii statisticheskii ezhegodnik. 1996*, Moscow: Goskomstat, 1996, pp.688–91; *Izvestia*, 22 January 1997; *Rossiiskii statisticheskii ezhegodnik. 1998*, Moscow: Goskomstat, 1998, pp.348–50.

Moscow and 10% St Petersburg, while shares of other areas did not exceed 4%.[65] In 1996 Moscow government collected 50% of its taxes from small businesses, while about 31% of the employed in Russia's capital city worked in small businesses. Shares of small businesses in employment in other regions were significantly lower, while in the Volga republic of Mordovia the share in 1996 was just 2%.[66] In 1997 24.2% of small businesses registered in Russia were based in Moscow and Moscow oblast' and a further 13.4% – in St Petersburg and Leningrad oblast'. In the same year small businesses operating in Moscow and St Petersburg accounted for 20% of the gross output of all small businesses in Russia.[67]

One of the most spectacular achievements of the 1992–97 Russian reform was mass privatisation of state property, which, as one recent study argued, was "unprecedented in world history".[68] By the end of 1996, 90% of the gross output of industry and the same share of the total retail trade turnover were coming from the private sector. Despite that, between 1992 and 1996 the total state revenue from privatisation amounted to 102.3 million privatisation vouchers and only to US$2.4 billion in cash (Table 5.6). However, during the same period an estimated US$80 billion left Russia in capital flight. Such a massive outflow of capital became possible largely as a result of the rush towards privatisation and mistakes that were made in its implementation, including an almost total withdrawal of the state from the regulation of the national economy.[69] The sale of some of Russia's most lucrative state-run businesses in energy and telecommunications in 1997, which brought an additional US$4.6 billion to the state budget, did not change the overall picture. In 1998 acute problems in the Russian economy forced the Russian authorities to cancel a number of initially planned or already postponed privatisation auctions. As a result, during 1998 the gross volume of revenues from privatisation in US dollar equivalent has dropped by over 60%. But even if we disregard direct and indirect financial losses associated with privatisation, one important argument that cancels most of gains made by privatisation still remains. The mass sale of state property failed to achieve its primary objective as was set by the reformists themselves: it did not result in any significant change in Russia's negative production dynamics.

As planned initially, privatisation of state property should have led to growth of efficiency in the economy, followed by an increase in gross output and accumulation of a significant investment capital within the country. The reality was quite the opposite: while efficiency in most sectors of the economy remained low and national production dynamics continued to go down, large amounts of capital were exported from Russia instead of being invested in its economy.

The major technical fault of the Russian privatisation model was in the fact that it made possible mass transfer of state-owned property to insiders. This later enabled managers of privatised firms to take full control over the new ventures. In the absence of an established capital market in Russia, such "directors' privatisation" was carried out with almost no competition. In the end, privatisation did not lead to any significant changes in the management of former state-owned enterprises, with most of these becoming even more ineffective than earlier.

Another extremely important negative outcome of Russian privatisation was that revenue from sales of state property, no matter how small, was mostly spent on subsidies to inefficient enterprises rather than being invested into the much-needed restructuring of the Russian economy. The chronic crisis of non-payments and wage arrears that quickly became the major concern of Russian governments soon after the start of the reform, forced the state to divert all of its available resources, including foreign credits and internal borrowing, towards payment of delayed wages and/or social subsidies. In essence, the Russian government was selling off state assets but continuing to keep the major part of the working age population on a direct or indirect unemployment benefit. At the same time very few new jobs were created, while investment into real sector of the economy reached its lowest levels ever during the 20th century.

As a result, a significant part of newly privatised companies never took off and became financially insolvent. However, bureaucratic or other connections of managers of these companies enabled them to receive various concessions or even direct state subsidies. The economic demands of these managers were strengthened by their publicly expressed warnings of grave social and political consequences which massive closures of enterprises were certain to cause. Thus, in the post-Soviet period the Russian state continued to provide subsidies to *de facto* bankrupt private companies almost in the same way it had done under the Soviet system, when all of these companies were state-owned.

The practice of state support to the national economy is not new, but the paradox of the Russian situation was that it happened on a mass scale and at a time when state resources were becoming increasingly and even dangerously limited. But even despite these state support actions, the crisis in the Russian economy continued to spread rapidly. But despite state actions, the crisis in the Russian economy continued to spread rapidly. According to Goskomstat, "in January–November 1997 the share of loss-making enterprises in the state sector [of industry] was 42.6% while in the non-state sector it was 49.0%".[70] In other words, the Russian private sector was less efficient than the state sector. In 1997, 60.4% of all Russian enterprises – private and state-owned – were loss making while the gross volume of losses reached 103.7 trillion roubles or US$17.4 billion. The share of loss-making enterprises in industry was 47.3%, in transport – 58.7% and in agriculture – 79.8%.[71] In 1998 with the spread of the financial crisis these dynamics became even more dramatic. The share of insolvent companies in industry increased to 49.2% and in agriculture to 83.1%. Out of the total number of enterprises that operated in the Russian economy (excluding small businesses, 55.2% in 1998 were making losses). The net balance of all financial activities of Russian enterprises in 1998 was a negative figure to the amount of 34.6 billion roubles or US$3.6 billion. The total volume of losses in the Russian economy was equal to astronomical 274.3 billion roubles (US$28.3 billion).[72] In US dollar terms, the latter figure was 1.6 times higher than in 1997, which was a stunning increase for one year even for Russia.

The figures above are quite amazing. They openly contradict the conventional economic theory, which says that the private sector of the economy in most cases is more efficient than the state-owned sector. Because privatisation in Russia, the way it was carried out, had very little effect on the management of enterprises, by 1997–98 almost half of private companies in Russia were loss making. However, the government retained its control over many profitable enterprises, which explains why the share of insolvent companies in the state sector was lower than in the private sector of the Russian economy.

Graph 5.2 gives yet another demonstration of the fact that Russian privatisation made almost no impact on the general economic development of the country. The graph shows that between 1990 and 1998 the share of private sector in the gross industrial output in Russia increased from 10% to over 90%. However, during the same period industrial production has fallen two times while the share of loss-making companies in the overall number of industrial enterprises has grown by 10 times. In other words, by 1999 it became clear that privatisation has failed to open a way for any significant growth in the national economy, thus failing to solve one of the most important problems of the Russian reform.

The way it was pursued in Russia, privatisation also significantly increased the growth of regional disparities in Russia. During the 1990s

Graph 5.2 Privatisation vs. Performance in Russian Industry (indices, %)

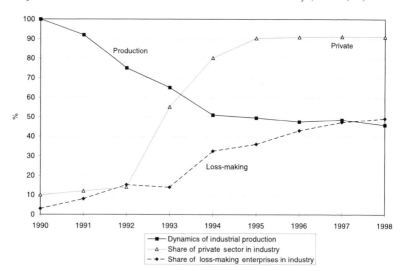

divisions between rich and poor regions became striking while the state had less and less resources at its disposal which could be used to balance differences in the regional development.

Map 5.1 below shows the breakup of net balances of industrial revenues and losses in various Russian regions at the end of 1997 or eight months before the peak of the financial crisis in Russia. The data are given in current US dollars and balances are recalculated on per capita basis. According to these data, only in five areas of Russia balances of the overall industrial performance were relatively high. These included major Western Siberian oil- and gas-producing regions of Tyumen', Khanty-Mansiisk and Yamalo-Nenetsk, mining and resource area of Krasnoyarsk in Eastern Siberia, as well as the Far Eastern mining province of Yakutia-Sakha. In these five regions overall industrial balance on a per capita basis was above US$300; in Yamalo-Nenetsk the balance was at Russia's top level of US$1,300.[73]

In the same year in the majority of Russian regions net balances of industrial output were between zero and US$299. Within the latter group regions that had per capita industrial balances of over US$100 included traditional manufacturing areas (Vologda, Vladimir, Moscow, Yaroslavl', Nizhnii Novgorod, Samara, Perm') and some metallurgy and

Map 5.1   Net Balances of Industrial Output in Russia by Region, 1997 (net balance of industrial revenues and losses on per capita basis, in current US dollars per year)

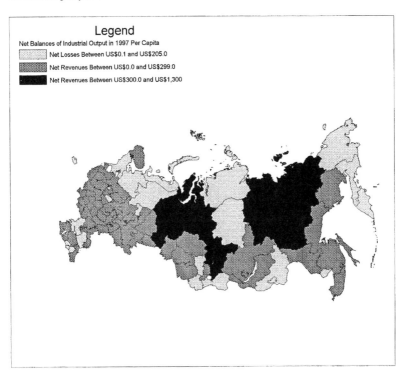

mining centres (Lipetsk, Tatarstan, Udmurtia, Magadan). In the rest of the regions within this group overall revenues received by the local industry approximately equalled gross losses.

The third group of regions consists of areas where net balance of the gross industrial output was negative. With exceptions of Ivanovo and Kemerovo, all of these areas are located in the distant parts of Russia: in the Caucasus, in the northern parts of European Russia, in the north and south of East Siberia, and in the Russian Far East. In the Soviet period these areas were traditionally major recipients of state subsidies. Dismantling of the Soviet system of economic management that took place in Russia after 1992, led to an acute economic crisis in these regions. By the end of 1997 the most hit by the crisis was the Koryak industry in the Russian Far East. The net per capita balance of its industrial output was a negative of US$203. Chukotka, also in the Far East, had a negative balance of US$180, Karelia in the North a negative balance of US$163, while in the major coal-producing region of Kemerovo net balance of industrial revenues and losses on a per capita basis was a negative balance of US$152.

To conclude, it is necessary to state that by 1998 the Russian reform strategy had produced a number of rather controversial results. While reformers managed to fulfil in part their primary objective by dismantling of the grossly ineffective Soviet system of state management of the economy, at the same time they failed to create in its place an effective and market-based economic system. Despite the fact that the majority of Russian companies have underwent privatisation and by the mid-1990s were mostly in the hands of private owners, they continued to be as ineffective as in the past. Privatisation, along with liberalisation of prices and demonopolisation of the foreign trade, also led to a considerable growth in economic crime and corruption in Russia. By the mid-1990s the Russian state has become a hostage to competing business interests, a situation that often made impossible any effective decision-making on economic issues. The first major auctions of state property, held under "cash privatisation" scheme in 1996–97, were a clear demonstration of this fact.

The sequence of reform steps that was chosen by Russia's first reformers, almost from the start has created a growing problem of balancing of the state budget. This problem became the major preoccupation of all consecutive post-Soviet governments in Russia and it left almost no time – and funds – for other no less important economic problems, like macroeconomic restructuring and growth of foreign investment. Russia in the post-Soviet period was borrowing significant amounts of money on external and internal markets, but almost all of this money was directed towards repayments of Soviet-style social benefits or towards supporting ineffective industrial and agricultural enterprises which should have been restructured – or closed – a long time ago. The proceeds from privatisation, no matter how small they were,[74] were also used for the same purposes. At the same time the Russian reform, albeit (fire) sale of state property, was largely halted.

The evolution of Russia's new capitalism was inseparable from and a product of the development of Russian political structures in the post-Soviet period. In the following chapter we will look into the contemporary Russian political development in a greater detail.

Notes

1. For example, see Scott Thomas and Heidi Kroll, "The political economy of privatisation in Russia", *Communist Economies & Economic Transformation*, Vol.5, No.4, December 1993, pp.445–459; L. D. Nelson and I. Y. Kuzes, *Property to the People. The struggle for radical economic reform in Russia*, Sharpe, Armont N. Y., 1994; L. D. Nelson and I. Y. Kuzes, *Radical Reform in Yeltsin's Russia*, Sharpe, Armont N. Y., 1995; Igor Birman, "Gloomy prospects for the Russian economy", *Europe-Asia Studies*, Vol.48, No.5, July 1996, pp.735–750; V. Mau, "Stabilization, elections, and perspectives of economic growth. The political economy of reform in Russia", *Problems of Economic Transition*, Vol.40, No.4, August 1997, pp.5–26; D. L. Weimer (ed.), *The Political Economy of Property Rights. Institutional change and credibility in the reform of centrally planned economies*, Cambridge UP, 1997.

2. The way privatisation and liberalisation of economy were carried out, they also significantly increased regional economic disparities in Russia, particularly between resource-rich areas and the rest of the country. See Igor V. Filatotchev, Roy P. Bradshaw, "The geographical impact of the Russian privatization program", *Post-Soviet Geography and Economics*, Vol.36, No.6, June 1995, pp.371–384.

3. Data in this and the following summary tables are taken from tables and sources contained in the previous chapters of this book.

4. Joseph R. Blasi, Maya Kroumova and Douglas Kruse, *Kremlin Capitalism: Privatising the Russian Economy*, Ithaca and London: Cornell University Press, 1997, p.xvii.

5. "Russia: debt rescheduling", *OAEEDB*, 4 October 1993.

6. A great number of recent publications had focused on the issues of privatisation in Russia. Some of the most important include Stephen Fortescue, "Privatisation of Russian industry", *Australian Journal of Political Science*, Vol.29, No.1, March 1994, pp.135–153; Susan J.Linz, "The privatisation of Russian industry", *RFE/RL Research Report*, Vol.3, No.10, March 1994, pp.27–35; Pekka Sutela, "Insider privatisation in Russia: speculations on systemic change", *Europe-Asia Studies*,Vol.46, No.3, 1994, pp.417–435; Simon Clarke (ed.), *Conflict and Change in the Russian Industrial Enterprise*, Cheltenham: Elgar, 1996; Alexander S. Bim, "Ownership and control of Russian enterprises and strategies of shareholders", *Communist Economies & Economic Transformation*, Vol.8, No.4, December 1996, pp.471–500; Stephen Fortescue, *Policy-Making for Russian Industry*, Houndmills, Hampshire: Macmillan Press; New York: St. Martin's Press, 1997; Susan J. Linz, "Russian firms in transition: champions, challengers and chaff", *Comparative Economic Studies*, Vol.39, No.2, Summer 1997; Stephen Fortescue, "Privatisation, corporate governance and enterprise performance in Russia", *Russian and Euro-Asian Bulletin*, Melbourne, Vol.7, No.5, May 1998, pp.1–9.

7. Joseph R. Blasi, Maya Kroumova and Douglas Kruse, Op.cit., p.xviii.

8. *Rossiiskii statisticheskii ezhegodnik. 1995*, Moscow: Goskomstat, 1995, p.276.

9. Between 1992 and 1994 direct state subsidies to enterprises were slashed from 32% to 5% (Joseph R. Blasi, Maya Kroumova and Douglas Kruse, Op.cit., p.190).

10. Another reason for the reduction of the gross inter-enterprise debt was the growth of barter trade operations that many enterprises started to use as means of payment. These non-monetary activities by the end of the year became widespread and led to a significant complication of the procedure of tax collection.

11. See *OAEEDB*, 5 April 1994 and 21 September 1995.

12. *Rossiiskii statisticheskii ezhegodnik. 1995*, Moscow: Goskomstat, 1995, p.231. For an overview of the dynamics and results of "voucher privatisation" in Russia see: Hilary Appel, "Voucher privatisation in Russia: structural consequences and mass response in the second period of reform", *Europe–Asia Studies*, Vol.49, No.8, December 1997, pp.1433–1450.

13. In April 1994 the government's privatisation strategy was summarised in the speech to the parliament by one of architects of the Russian reform, Anatoly Chubais. This speech was later published as an article in the leading Russian theoretical journal on economics. See Anatoly Chubais, "Itogi privatizatsii v Rossii i zadachi sleduyushego etapa", *Voprosy ekonomiki*, No.6, 1994, pp.4–9.

14. See *OAEEDB*, 22 January 1993 and 14 November 1996.

15. Joseph R. Blasi, Maya Kroumova and Douglas Kruse, Op.cit., p.41.

16. There were also other serious problems that arose from this model of privatisation. See: Igor Filatotchev and Adam Swain, "Problems of restructuring of former state-owned enterprises in Russia, Hungary and China: case studies of car-making firms", *Russian and Euro-Asian Bulletin*, Vol.6, No.6, June 1997, pp.1–11; Pekka Sutela: "Insider privatization in Russia: speculations on systemic change", Europe-Asia Studies, Vol.46, No.3, 1994, pp.417–435.

17. See "Russia: share distributions", *OAEEDB*, 2 April 1997.

18. *Izvestia*, 30 December 1994.

19. *Interfax Business Report*, No.72, 13 April 1995.

20. In April 1995 consumer prices were growing at an average rate of 0.28% a day, in May – at 0.25% a day, in June – at 0.21% and in July – at 0.17%. At the end of the year the daily increase of consumer prices was 0.10% which was significantly lower than 0.53% in January 1995 (*Sotsial'no-ekonomicheskoe polozhenie Rossii, 1995 g.*, Moscow: Goskomstat, 1996, p.156).

21. *Rossiiskii statisticheskii ezhegodnik. 1996*, Moscow: Goskomstat, 1996, p.377.

22. "Russia: external finances", *OAEEDB*, 21 September 1995.

23. Calculated from: *Sotsial'no-ekonomicheskoe polozhenie Rossii, 1995 g.*, Moscow: Goskomstat, 1996, pp.209–211.

24. *Interfax Business Report*, No.159, 17 August 1995.

25. On the background of "loans-for-shares" auctions see *Interfax Business Reports* Nos.79 (24 April 1995), 91 (12 May 1995) and 92 (15 May 1995).

26. See *Moskovskie novosti*, 21 November 1995.

27. *OMRI*, No.239, 11 December 1995.

28. By the end of 1995 the gross income from cash privatisation amounted to US$618 million (Calculated from *Sotsial'no-ekonomicheskoe polozhenie Rossii, 1995 g.*, Moscow: Goskomstat, 1996, p.126).

29. *Sotsial'no-ekonomicheskoe polozhenie Rossii, 1995 g.*, Moscow: Goskomstat, 1996, p.126; *Interfax Business Report*, No.159, 17 August 1995.

30. In September 1996 it was reported that these amounted to about US$20 billion (*The Financial Times*, 14 September 1994).
31. "Russia economist warns of crisis", *Associated Press (AP)*, 18 December 1996.
32. "Russia: the stock market boom", *Russian and Euro-Asian Bulletin*, Melbourne, Vol.6, No.1, January 1997, pp.10–14.
33. *Dow Jones News Service*, 18 September 1996.
34. *Sotsial'no-ekonomicheskoe polozhenie Rossii, yanvar' 1997*, Moscow: Goskomstat, 1997, pp.160–162; *Sotsial'no-ekonomicheskoe polozhenie Rossii, 1997 g.*, Moscow: Goskomstat, 1998, pp.247–249; *Sotsial'no-ekonomicheskoe polozhenie Rossii, yanvar' 1998*, Moscow: Goskomstat, 1998, p.186.
35. *Monitor*, Vol.III, No.42, 28 February 1997.
36. *RFE/RL*, No.60, 25 June 1997 and No.128, 30 September 1997.
37. Gareth Jones, "Yeltsin ruining army, Russia faces breakup – general", *Reuter*, 24 June 1997; *Monitor*, Vol.III, No.128, 1 July 1997.
38. See: "Gazprom repays giant debt", *AP*, 25 June 1997; Julie Tolkacheva, "Russia wage promises may be too good to be true", *Reuter*, 1 July 1997; John Thornhill, "Russia: Foreign reserves grow 55%", *The Financial Times*, 3 July 1997.
39. Tax repayments from only one company – Russia's gas monopoly Gazprom – during June 1997 were equal to 0.6% of the country's GDP (Peter Henderson, "Russian promises tough to keep, but markets happy", *Reuter*, 4 July 1997).
40. On 1 July 1997 the government announced that it repaid all of pension arrears to the population or about US$3 billion. This success was reached, however, through redirection of all government's recent borrowings (March 1997 Eurobond, credits from international organisations) as well as the tax return from Gazprom into pension payments.
41. *OAEEDB*, 20 December 1996; *The Financial Times*, 14 March 1997; *Monitor*, Vol.III, No.61, 27 March 1997 and Vol.III, No.122, 23 June 1997.
42. "Analysts say 'rigged' big gives Menatep control of Yukos", *Dow Jones News Service*, 23 December 1996.
43. "Russia: EES auction", *OAEEDB*, 28 January 1997.
44. See *OMRI*, No.42, 28 February 1997.
45. For details of the struggle that surrounded plans to restructure and privatise Gazprom see: *Interfax Daily Report*, 19 March 1997 and 4 April 1997; "Russia: demonopolisation decree being readied – Yasin", *Reuter*, 24 March 1997; *Monitor*, Vol.III, No.60, 26 March 1997; "Mission impossible?", *St Petersburg Times*, 31 March–6 April 1997; *RFE/RL*, Vol.1, No.5, 7 April 1997; "Nemtsov oulines planned measures to control monopolies", *ITAR-TASS*, 4 April 1997; *RIA-Novosti*, 9 April 1997; *The Financial Times*, 10 April 1997 and 16 April 1997; "Battle over natural monopolies heats up", *Prism*, Vol.3, No.5, 18 April 1997; *Moskovskie novosti*, 13 April 1997; "Bori Young Turks", *Business Week*, 28 April 1997.
46. *Izvestia*, 26 July 1997; "Russia: Telecoms privatisation", *OAEEDB*, 31 July 1997.
47. *Kommersant-Daily*, 12 August 1997.
48. US$1.875 billion against US$1.170 billion (*OAEEDB*, 31 July 1997).
49. Stephanie Baker, "Russia: privatization really a state disguised fire sale", *RFE/RL Report*, 8 August 1997 cited in: *Johnson's Russia List (JRL)*, 11 August 1997.

50. *Nezavisimaya gazeta*, 14 August 1997.
51. "Yeltsin reads bankers the riot act", *Monitor*, Vol.III, No.171, 16 September 1997.
52. For more information see Russian newspapers between 13–16 November 1997.
53. *RFE/RL*, Vol.1, No.164, 20 November 1997.
54. Sources: *Sotsial'no-ekonomicheskoe polozhenie Rossii, 1997 g.*, Moscow: Goskomstat, 1998; *Sotsial'no-ekonomicheskoe polozhenie Rossii, yanvar' 1998 g.*, Moscow: Goskomstat, 1998; *Russia Notes*, 28 May 1998; *RIA-Novosti*, 3 June 1998.
55. In late August the government announced its privatisation plans for 1998. 66 separate sales were to be organised including the sale of another 25% of Svyazinvest and state holdings in large oil companies and Aeroflot (*RIA-Novosti*, 26 August 1997). In mid-November, just before the Asian crisis struck Russian financial markets, the State Property Minister revealed that during the last six weeks of 1997 the government planned to receive from privatisation a further 10 trillion roubles which was almost equal to all proceeds from sales of state property that the state received since the beginning of the year (12 trillion roubles) (*RFE/RL*, Vol.1, No.158, 12 November 1997).
56. *Kommersant-Daily*, 27 August 1997.
57. The development of "shadow economy" and organised crime in Russia were in the centre of two recent studies: V. Papava and N. Khaduri, "On the shadow political economy of the post-communist transformation. An institutional analysis", *Problems of Economic Transition*, Vol.40, No.6, October 1997, pp.15–34; Tanya Frisby, "The rise of organised crime in Russia: its roots and social significance", *Europe–Asia Studies*, Vol.50, No.1, January 1998, pp.27–50.
58. *Delovoi Mir*, 21 November 1996 and *OMRI Digest*, No.38, 24 February 1997.
59. *Delovoi Mir*, 21 November 1996.
60. See: *Interfax-AiF*, No.22, 2–8 June 1997; *OMRI Digest*, No.231, 2 December 1996; Janet Guttsman, "Russian economy is not all that it seems", *Reuter*, 29 November 1996.
61. *Interfax-AiF*, No.22, 2–8 June 1997.
62. *Izvestia*, 15 October 1996; *Komsomolskaya pravda*, 12 November 1996; *Delovoi Mir*, 21 November 1996; *RIA-Novosti*, 3 December 1996.
63. *Sotsial'no-ekonomicheskoe polozhenie Rossii. 1996 g.*, Moscow: Goskomstat, 1997, p.206; *Sotsial'no-ekonomicheskoe polozhenie Rossii. 1997 g.*, Moscow: Goskomstat, 1998, p.301.
64. *Monitor*, Vol.III, No.15, 22 January 1997.
65. *Sotsial'no-ekonomicheskoe polozhenie Rossii, yanvar'-fevral' 1997 g.*, Moscow: Goskomstat, 1997, p.89.
66. *Izvestia*, 22 January 1997.
67. Calculated from: Regiony Rossii. 1998, Vol.2, Moscow: Goskomstat, 1998, p.300–4.
68. Joseph R. Blasi, Maya Kroumova and Douglas Kruse, *Kremlin Capitalism: Privatising the Russian Economy*, Ithaca and London: Cornell University Press, 1997, p.167.
69. For more discussion on capital flight see V. Tikhomirov, "Capital Flight from Post-Soviet Russia", *Europe–Asia Studies*, Vol.49, No.4, June 1997, p.591–615.

70. *Sotsial'no-ekonomicheskoe polozhenie Rossii, 1997 g.*, Moscow: Goskomstat, 1998, p.36.

71. *Sotsial'no-ekonomicheskoe polozhenie Rossii, yanvar' 1998 g.*, Moscow: Goskomstat, 1998, p.166.

72. *Sotsial'no-ekonomicheskoe polozhenie Rossii, yanvar' 1999 g.*, Moscow: Goskomstat, 1999, p.215–6.

73. The data used in Map 5.1 are recalculated from: *Sotsial'no-ekonomicheskoe polozhenie Rossii, yanvar' 1998 g.*, Moscow: Goskomstat, 1998, pp.285–286.

74. Another important problem associated with the Russian privatisation is the gross undervaluation of the country's capital stock. According to one observer, "when they were privatised, Russia's biggest 15,000 companies had a collective value of about $14bn – equivalent to the then market capitalisation of Kellogg, the US cereal company" (John Thornhill, "Russia: the risks and rewards of mass privatisation. Why are Russia's corporate assets so cheap", *The Financial Times*, 6 September 1997). While this problem existed right from the start of privatisation, when vouchers had a fixed value that quickly diminished with the growth of inflation, the undervaluation of assets became more striking at the second, cash stage of privatisation. However, during the last few years Russian businesses were putting a growing pressure on the government asking the latter not to increase prices at privatisation auctions. The major reason given was a "patrotic" one: if prices go up, Russian companies which do not have enough funds, will not be able to compete with foreigners who then will easily win all tenders. The undervaluation of privatised property left the state with large losses. The most radical assessment of these losses was presented by a State Duma committee and equalled 9.5 quadrillion roubles for the period of 1992–96 (*Delovoi Mir*, 2 April 1997). See also D. Willer, "Reasons for the low valuation of Russian shares", *The Economics of Transition*, Vol.4, No.2, October 1996, pp.449–457.

6
The Dynamics of Political Change

In this chapter we will briefly analyse main trends in the post-Soviet political development of Russia. However, we do not intend to repeat many recent studies that specifically focused on this issue. Rather, our objective is to investigate what was the interrelation between social and economic processes that developed in Russia in the 1990s, and the nature and direction of its political change. In this respect, of particular interest to us are issues related to the current state of relations between the federal and regional authorities, dynamics of economic perform- ance and changes in political preferences of the population in Russian provinces.

Our main argument is that a transition to a *stable* and *long-lasting* democracy should come as a combination of two major factors: politi- cal change and economic transformation of the society. In different historical, ethnic and geo-strategic situations these two tasks were met in a variety of ways. However, the essence of the problem of transition and its future success was mainly limited to the question of what should come first: political or economic change. Attempts to address these two tasks simultaneously were often unsuccessful because of the complexity and close interrelation of existing problems in a pre- transitional society. This frequently results in a failure on part of the ruling elite to control or to redirect the development of a society through the use of political structures, which are also undergoing fun- damental restructuring. That leaves these elites with limited and often inconsistent means of influencing complex and difficult processes of change in social and economic spheres.

Recent developments in Eastern Europe and the former Soviet Union saw the political change come first, ahead of profound economic and social transformations. That happened as a consequence of a number of important factors, but mainly because of the inability of the communist regimes to adapt to the rapid changes that took place in these societies. In the late 1980s and the early 1990s political reforms were viewed by many reformists as the most important step toward a more deep transformation of the society; these changes were much easier and faster to attain and their results, therefore, were more visible to people and the outside world. Despite the importance of these political transformations, they could not and did not provide an answer to a more complex and fundamental issue of how and when an economic change could happen.

6.1   Some general remarks on transition

A peaceful transition to another state and/or economic system in a society comes as an attempt by one or a group of elites to avoid a revolutionary (violent) change. In other words, transition takes place only when the conflict in a society is already present and, moreover, when this conflict carries a potential of evolving into a violent overthrow of the existing power structures. Therefore, the basic feature of a peaceful transition is that the ruling elite itself under growing pressures on the part of the inter- and/or extra-state opposition initiates it. This nature of transition frames its main objective as a way of securing future ruling elite's access to power and, at the same time, of decreasing the level of confrontation in the society. Traditionally this objective was implemented through the use of a number of means:

(1)   Introduction of a controlled process of political and economic reforms in a society.
(2)   Entering into negotiations[1] with the opposition (especially with the openly anti-establishment part of it).
(3)   Finally, giving away the power in small portions in exchange of guarantees of a limited access to power structures and/or social and economic privileges in the future.

In many recent cases of transition reaching of a significant stage in the process of transition was considered by a significant part of population, at least initially, as an indicator of the success of the transition process on the whole. For instance, many Russian and foreign observers saw the fall of the communist party rule and the following disintegration of the USSR as the proof of an irreversible democratic change in the former Soviet Union. However, no matter how significant and historical these events might have been, they only signalled the beginning of a new and more complex stage in the transition process, but not the end of that process.

In effect, the transition as a process of building a stable and long-lasting democracy in the post-Soviet Russia began with these historic changes. In the early 1990s the final outcome of this transition still remained very vague and unclear. It is of crucial importance, therefore, when analysing successes and failures of transition to be able to distinguish between series of important events, decisions or proclaimed moves that often form the transitional process, and the attainment of genuine irreversible changes in a society.

Profound changes normally are not accompanied by a visible or symbolic event and, for that reason, are much harder to determine. In the political sphere probably the most vital feature of this change is the achievement of reasonable levels of stability and control in a transitional society. It is essential that such stability comes from mass political (and ideological) support to the newly established regime and is also accompanied by the popular support of economic reform. While in the periods of big political upheavals a significant part of the population is prepared to suffer materially, provided that the political ideals they strive for are achieved, as the time passes these attitudes may change dramatically, especially if the early political victories are not followed by material gains from the reform for the majority of population. Therefore, to attain a lasting stability in a society it is essential that a profound economic restructuring that bring benefits to most of the people follow the political reform.

The evolutionary nature of the process of transition and its main feature as a negotiated process mean that in the political area a compromise between opposing political forces forms the basis of transition. Thus, from its start a transition, as a compromise solution, cannot meet all of the demands of conflicting forces in a society; it may and often leads to a significant decrease in the level of conflict in a society, but not to its total elimination.

The idea of compromise (or balance of forces) forms the most important feature of any democratic system. As such, in transitions to democracy it can be and is viewed not only as means, but also as a major objective of the whole political process. However, if confrontation is deeply-rooted in the society (that often happens when the issue of property redistribution is on the agenda) and the society has a history of undemocratic tradition (as was the case in the Soviet Union), reaching of a compromise may in the future greatly undermine the effectiveness of reform measures and even pose a serious threat to the stability in the country.

Conflicting parties enter into negotiation in a transition process solely because of their good will: there is no clear victory or defeat for either of them at the start of negotiations. Their ability to manoeuvre is limited only by their support base and the ambitions of their political leaders. Neither party is in a winning position at this stage; otherwise compromise settlement could hardly be on an agenda. Neither party is bound by limits of a certain political system, just because the very issue of negotiations is about the introduction of a new system. Thus, all parties participating in a transition process are likely and tend to view concessions they make as temporary, linked to a certain (transitional) environment and, for that reasons, as tactical. As soon as a compromise solution is found, the major issue that arises is to what extent those who reached it are prepared to follow its provisions in the future. There could be no long-lasting guarantees to that and, as modern history demonstrates, even constitutions, let alone transitional agreements, could be re-written fairly easily.

The issue of transforming of these temporary transitional agreements into a more lasting balance of powers within limits of new political system is the key to a successful political transition to democracy. However, compromises reached along the way of transition do not necessarily reflect the existing balance of political forces in a society. The ruling elite enters negotiations just because it feels that it is rapidly losing its support base. On the other hand, it tries to secure as much of its powers as possible. The result of negotiations, therefore, does not necessarily represent the real balance of power in the society. Through entering into negotiations the opposition, which at the start of transition enjoys far stronger popular support than the ruling elite, abandons one of its most significant earlier objectives, i.e. obtaining of a total political control. Later, in the course of negotiations, it is also forced to modify or even sacrifice a number of its other, most extreme, demands. This is often accompanied by a decline in the level of popularity of the opposition and by the growth of tensions (and even conflicts) inside its leadership.

Conflicting parties that enter into transitional negotiations are rarely represented by just two forces: the government and the opposition. Each of the two parties is frequently a coalition of various political movements and groups and that often makes the whole process of transition even more difficult to manage. On the one hand, in the eyes of the people transition becomes more valid and representative if the negotiation process incorporates as many political movements as possible. But, on the other hand, the broader is the spectrum of representation, the greater are chances of fragmentation in the post-transition politics (both along party and across party lines). In this situation compromise settlements are harder to reach, particularly between the most extremist forces on the left or on the right. What often happens is that the latter are often excluded from the final arrangements, because their irreconcilable and inflexible positions are very difficult to accommodate into any compromise agreement. That exclusion, however, lays a foundation for the growth of new conflicts in the future.

The "anti-extremist" feature of a transition process means that it normally rests upon moderate political forces which leaders are prepared for a compromise. In the post-transition period these forces very often quickly move to the centre of political spectrum in a society. The speed of this change depends upon the rate of growth in popularity of the extremist forces that were left outside the initial transition agreements.

The evolutionary political change normally has one or a number of symbolic acts that could be viewed as crucial points in the process of (political) transition. In the case of Russia, these acts were: the election of a prominent opposition leader as the first president of Russia in June 1991; an attempt on part of the former ruling elite to restore its power in full (August 1991 putsch); and the Belovezhsk agreements on the disintegration of the Soviet Union signed on the initiative of the Russian president in December 1991. Symbolic events serve as significant factors in political mobilisation within a society. These events normally either symbolise a beginning of the process of transition to political democracy or, more often, an end to a very significant stage in that process.

In addition to their unifying effect, these events give a rise to hopes for a better future and to growth of mass expectations of quick and successful resolution of major problems that exist in a society. This is also accompanied by the rise in the preparedness of the people (at least majority of them) to wait for few years until their hopes will start to realise. Thus, at the start of transition a society gives an important "political credit" to political leaders when most of errors and faults in their policies do not necessarily undermine their credibility and support among the population.

However, the luxury of this "political credit" is not given forever: there are clear limits as to what extent the population is prepared to wait. Length of this period differs between countries and situations, but rarely exceeds one to two years. After that "credit" starts to gradually expire, while the level of support of political leadership becomes increasingly dependent on the successes (or faults) in their policies, the same way as it happens under a "normal" political process.

Although this "credit" time is often long enough for the introduction of political reforms in a society, it is still a very short period for getting results from almost any reform in the social or economic sphere. Transition, as opposed to revolution, does not give any of its leaders a total power and the benefit of implementing socio-economic measures that can quickly satisfy a significant part of the population such as redistribution of property, nationalisation, etc. The transitional nature of the whole process demands for any significant decision to be negotiated between the major parties before it can be implemented. In practice that means that each important or radical decision, particularly in the economic field, is destined for long and often fierce political debates and negotiations. In this situation final arrangements are certain to differ greatly from the initial reform proposals. Thus, in most cases of modern transition, the newly created power structures prove to be more inefficient and time-absorbing decision-makers than the former (autocratic) systems.

The failure to materialise, at least partially, pre-transitional expectations and hopes of the population puts transition leaders into a difficult situation. Expiration of their "political credit" leads to a significant fall in their support base, which is accompanied by a growth in the popularity of extremist forces. The society becomes fragmented and more difficult to manipulate as political conflicts within it re-emerge again. In contradiction to those who participated in the transition agreements, extremists have an important advantage of being opposed to these agreements from the start.

Under these circumstances the ruling elite finds itself trapped in a difficult situation greatly resembles the one that existed on the eve of transition. However, there is one important distinction: democratisation of the political life that came as the first (and often the only) major success of the transition, does not give political leaders the advantage of the use of autocratic means of government, at least not to the same extent as in the past. The growth of new opposition makes the dividing line between former opponents, those who entered the transition arrangements, thinner and less significant. Irreconcilable enemies of the pre-transition period later often find themselves in one political camp.

This emerging threat of new authoritarianism gives transition leaders a moral ground to seek undemocratic means to fight it. Machiavellian principle becomes the cornerstone of new policies, while the former fighters against tyranny gradually become new autocrats. Transitional leaders become less and less indulgent to the growing public critique of their undemocratic methods; caught in the trap of democratic balances and compromises, they also start to blame the very system they helped to create for blocking the future reform.

Thus, as proved by all recent cases of transition in Eastern Europe and the former Soviet Union, attempts to promote economic and social reform in transitional societies cause the emergence of new political crises. These crises happen in the situation of a declining support for the reformers, when earlier hopes for a rapid change for the better start to disappear in the population. The majority of people start to feel "deceived" by the politicians who failed to keep their earlier promises. The content and consistency of the policies of reform starts to raise more doubts among the population, the fact that is immediately exploited by the new opposition. While part of the electorate turns to extremists, the majority prefers to abstain from active participation in the political life. Mass political disillusionment, apathy and ideological vacuum spread in the society, making the positions of the radical opposition even stronger.

Growing confrontation in the society is also accompanied by a significant rise in the mass political activity associated with economic developments, like strikes and demonstrations. Economic demands of strikers soon become mixed with political demands, giving radicals a sudden and strong mass following. Political life becomes increasingly fragmented, both on the national and local levels. While on the national level that leads to a significant growth in popularity of anti-establishment forces (fascists, nationalists, and communists), on the local level the new political crisis boosts separatist tendencies (territorial and ethnic nationalism). However, despite the fact that these two tendencies have one cause – the inability of the ruling elite to deliver the promised change, their objectives are not the same. At the time when national radicals want to seize all the power to promote their political views on the national arena, local nationalists want to separate from this arena and to establish themselves as undisputed rulers in their own territory. Although temporary alliances between the two groups of radicals are possible and often do take place, in a strategic perspective the conflict of interests between them has a capacity to provoke a new political crisis in the country.

If not reversed, the development of such a situation soon leads the society into a new pre-revolutionary situation, which in its many features resembles the one that existed at the start of transition. Presence of new democratic political structures, formed at the first stage of transition, do very little to lower the level of this growing confrontation, particularly if the latter is caused by the strife for total power. Clever political manoeuvring and inclusion of some of the radicals into the established political structures helps to defuse this conflict and even may lead to its disappearance in the long run. However, the latter might happen only if the grounds for the growth of this extremism are eliminated in the society through promotion of social and economic reforms that accommodate the interests of the majority of the people.

The problem is that promotion of social and economic reforms, at least in the initial phase, sparks off a new wave of confrontation rather than defuses it. Any profound restructuring of a society, particularly if it includes changes in property rights, cannot be carried out to the satisfaction of all social groups. There will always be groups that will be set to lose, either materially or politically. It is natural that these groups will resist the change. This resistance comes at different levels: in the decision-making process with opposition hampering or even blocking reform attempts; in general politics through the growth of various forms of extremism; and within the society itself through a growing social stratification and confrontation between the "winners" and the "losers".

The growing political isolation of parties that entered into transitional agreements and their failure to promote a radical socio-economic reform leaves the ruling elite with two options. One is to step down (either through elections or through resignation), thus leaving the whole transition process largely uncompleted and in the hands of the radical opposition. Under this option there is a great deal of possibility that the transition to democracy and market economy will end here, at least in the form promoted by earlier reformists. Radicals are certain to reverse many gains already made, starting with changes to the process of democratic decision-making because it contradicts and blocks their strife for the total control of state power.

The other option left for the ruling elite to save the reform process is to initiate undemocratic change itself, rather than leaving it in the hands of the radical opposition. Although this option also leads to the growth of authoritarianism in a society, changes in or even dismantling of the democratic decision-making structures are explained by the reformists as a necessary measure which is taken as a last step in order to prevent the national disaster – the coming to power of radicals. In this situation the parties that entered into transitional agreements start to feel less and less bound by them. Continuing attempts on part of the ruling elite aimed at incorporation of the radical opposition into the establishment become more and more often mixed with openly anti-democratic policies. Under these circumstances the objective of saving democratic gains through implementation of some undemocratic measures gradually transforms into an objective of saving the ruling elite's access to power by openly anti-democratic means.

The above logic of development can be found in almost every modern transitional society. It shows that the political transformation of a society does not automatically mean the irreversibility of the whole process of transition. Unless the political change is accompanied by quick and far-reaching social and economic reforms, it is certain to lead to a new wave of confrontation in the society. No doubt, modern transitional societies greatly differ in the levels of their development, their international political status that determines the amounts of external assistance they receive, and the preparedness of their societies for a radical change. Historical, ethnic and territorial differences also play an important, if not crucial, role in that process. However, what is even more important is the quality and decisiveness of their leadership, particularly of those who lead transitional societies in the first stage of reform. In our view, the most important issue in transition is whether these leaders are able or not to make full use of the "political credit" given to them by their people at the start of reform. Misuse of this credit creates major problems in the years to come that carry a capacity of undermining or reversing the process of change.

In its very nature, the transition as a compromise settlement has a number of internal contradictions that can later evolve into a full-fledged conflict. While initially it provides a (temporary?) escape from the possibility of a violent change in a society (revolution, civil war, military coup or alike), transition based on a compromise (democratic) idea at the same time fails to solve some of the fundamental problems that had earlier led to the conflict. First, a compromise, which means that certain (if not many) of the significant demands of contradicting political forces are put aside or even temporary abandoned, usually leaves a general feeling of dissatisfaction among the followers of these political forces. That feeling starts to grow rapidly as soon as post-transitional difficulties start to grow. And, second, political alliances which are formed in the process of the first stage of transition and which are based on the balance between contradicting ideas, have proved to be more loose and unstable than those alliances which are based on a common set of objectives and ideology.

If we will take into consideration the fact that transitions to democracy, by definition, take place from and within a previously undemocratic (authoritarian, totalitarian, repressive) environment, that gives the whole process a number of integral problems that are certain to influence developments in a society for a long time to come. These problems include the following:

(1) In the process of transition the abandonment of former tight controls on public activities (which constitute an important feature of all undemocratic regimes) releases huge political potential in a transitional society. This potential develops not only through political but also through anti-state and anti-public channels (violence, organised and unorganised crime, corruption, extreme forms of nationalism, etc.). If rapid measures are not taken at the start, the state itself becomes the subject of these anti-state activities (corruption, lobbying, etc.), making it increasingly difficult to eliminate or even control the growth of these destructive tendencies only through democratic means.

(2) The lack of experience in structuralised political struggles in a democratic environment on part of the majority of the population (due to the undemocratic nature of the former state) makes electorate an easy target for various manipulations and influences coming both from pro-reform parties and from political demagogues, populists, extremists and nationalists.

(3) Democratic changes in the political system inevitably lead to a rapid decrease of political importance, as well as to a fall in material gains, of some major social groups that traditionally formed the basis of power of the old regime (army, police, security forces, bureaucracy, state management of the economy). The response from these groups comes in increased attempts aimed at securing their former political and social positions. That happens in a variety of ways: open or hidden pressures on the government, political and/or economic destabilisation or even sabotage, attempts of *coup d'etat*, etc.

The combination of the above factors adds to the political difficulties causes by the transition and leads to an upsurge in violence, crime, ethnic strives and to a general instability of many post-totalitarian societies. That either may result in a gradual collapse of the newly-established democracy or may leave the leadership with no other option but to rely on the use of force in promoting their policies, thus giving credit to the opposition's argument that these democracies in reality have much in common with the tyrannies they have just replaced.

6.2   The importance of social and economic reform

Conflict in a society – the one that initially triggers the transition – comes as a combination of political and economic pressures. In the process of transition economic demands (and subsequent reforms) prove to be much more difficult to implement than political ones. The visible peak in the process of transition in many recent societies came in the form of a political change, either through an adoption of a new constitution, new democratic elections, demolition of the old repressive political structures, incorporation of anti-establishment forces into the new government, etc. However, in reality the solution of more complex problems of transition only starts when the economic demands are put on the agenda. The memories of the long-awaited political change (that give new leaders a certain amount of initial "political credit") tend to fade away among their followers much faster than many politicians envisage. Their past political merits become less and less important in the light of the current economic difficulties experienced by the population, while opposition forces quickly pick up the latter as the main argument in their struggle for yet again new political change.

No matter how big a role political events, pressures and struggles might have played in the process of transition to democracy, in a strategic perspective political change is always preceded by an increase in social tensions and economic pressures in a country that force the former elite to seek a negotiated settlement. In the Soviet case, it was the need for modification, updating of technologies, increased industrial and agricultural output, and, subsequently, higher state revenues that triggered Gorbachev's perestroika in the mid-1980s. In 1985, when perestroika began, the Soviet leadership was in a full control of the society. The anti-state opposition hardly presented any threat to the regime and its victory was still a very distant possibility. Modest social and economic transformations, initiated by Gorbachev in the Soviet society, were in fact the first step in the direction of transition. At that time neither Gorbachev himself nor the majority of his followers ever publicly mentioned the issue of the political change.

Implementation of deep economic changes in the USSR soon proved to be impossible beyond the limits imposed by the existing political system. Even timid half-measures, that Gorbachev tried to implement, provoked a growing resistance within the ruling elite that viewed his policies as posing a real threat to its future existence. That forced the Soviet reformer to seek ways of limiting the influence of that elite, mainly through opening up of the political system. Thus, by the end of the 1980s the accent in reformist policies was shifted from the economic reform to political reform.

The logic of these developments is very important for our argument. It shows that while, at the early stage of transition, leaders view the necessity of introducing an economic change as the most vital task, realisation of which, if they succeed, can help them to consolidate their crumbling power and bring a certain level of stability into a society, their reform attempts often result in a split within the ruling elite. The only way to resolve this impasse is through pursuing a political reform, which further undermines the positions of the ruling elite. Political changes also give rise to an organised anti-government opposition and to the growth of popular pressures for an even broader and deeper political reform. At this stage economic issues, that initially triggered the whole process of reform, are pushed aside while political issues come into the forefront of transition struggles.

If transition states had stable, highly developed and independent economies, all this could be considered to be a less serious problem. But the whole problem immediately becomes more dramatic, if the economy is in a stalemate and/or in the need of fundamental restructuring. However, this latter feature makes a very important characteristic of all modern transitions to democracy. Thus, through following the above logic of transitional struggles, the old as well as the reformist leadership concentrates on reinforcing its political power, because until that goal is reached it is impossible to promote fast and radical changes to the economic and social systems. The delay in the implementation of a radical economic reform leads to a further intensification of the already existing present crisis, which, in their turn, increases even further levels of general instability in the society.

Any deep socio-economic change is much more complex and difficult to implement than most of political reforms. Very rarely economic reform can bring immediate results, and these often become visible already after the public patience and the "political credit" associated with it had to a large extent expired. In addition, a successful implementation of economic transformations is usually subject to meeting certain preconditions that are largely independent of political leaders. Such preconditions are the need of urgent and large investment into the economy, both domestic and foreign; the necessity to introduce a new system of redistribution of wealth in a society; an acute lack of properly educated management and skilled workforce that are capable to work in the new conditions. These tasks involve a significant increase in state spending (at a time when state budgets are shrinking as a result of the crisis), maintaining of high levels of consolidation of democratic forces in order to counter the growing resistance to the reform, and simultaneous restructuring of national management and educational systems.

Successful implementation of a reformist economic strategy also becomes problematic because of the limits imposed by the compromise nature of the transition process itself. In practice that means that through participation in this process conflicting political forces seek guarantees of implementation of the most important of their economic demands. Accommodation of all these demands, even in modified form, is difficult and often proves to be simply impossible.

Inability to bring quick and visible changes to the deteriorating socio-economic situation forces transition governments to appeal for aid to the international community. Although foreign assistance played an important and, in some cases, crucial role in recent transitions, for large countries like Russia, the ability of the West to provide financial or technical assistance are significantly lower than the existing need. In the end, only domestic sources can provide enough of support for the implementation of any credible and lasting change.

The gap between the ability of the new leadership to promote successful economic reform and the expectations of the majority of the population, which becomes larger in the process of transition, forces transitional governments to seek for ways to escape their growing isolation from the society. Traditional political means of doing so include appeals to the nation, public reveals of anti-government plots (real or faked ones), crackdowns on activities of extremist opposition and other "destabilising" forces, growing attempts to control mass media, and increased search of support of the army and the police. While these measures are clearly aimed at strengthening of the power of the governing elite, normally through limiting of the activities of both inter- and extra-state opposition, they are often officially interpreted as the (only) way to bring under the control the growing political and social unrest in a country, to restore stability and order, and to give boost to the socio-economic reform.

In addition to increased political manoeuvring, transitional elites also make attempts to revive the economic reform through a general revision of the earlier proclaimed economic objectives and strategies; introduction of a less liberal tax policy, new budget cuts and freezing of state wages; tightening of foreign trade controls and imposing more severe restrictions on foreign currency flows from a country; putting into effect new anti-strike laws and, in general, a more strict legislation on industrial relations. Variations in these or similar measures depend on situation in that or other country and on the acuteness of internal crisis. However, the general tendency towards the reduction of the scope of initial economic objectives and forecasts and, consequently, towards significant lowering of the level of public expectations about gains from the reform, was a dominating feature of recent developments in almost every transitional state.

Another important feature of some modern cases of transition is its cyclic development. As stated above, growing public pressures for a rapid economic reform often push transition governments to take a less democratic stand, both in political and economic areas. This provokes the growth of a new conflict in the society, on national and local levels leaving the ruling elite faced with two options: either to enter into a compromise agreement with the new opposition, or to attempt to reinstall its control in the country by generally undemocratic or even repressive means. However, in the long run, each option eventually leads to a significant decrease of power of the ruling elite. If the latter is not prepared to give up its position and to concede to defeat, the emergence of a revolutionary situation in a society becomes inevitable.

Development of transitional societies along the lines of a cycle of transition "conflict-negotiations-transition-new conflict" can, in theory, be infinite or, at least, could continue for decades. The latter was already demonstrated by modern histories of many Third World nations. Such a situation of a permanent conflict has a very destructive effect on the society, both in terms of human losses and the level of economic deterioration. What is more important, however, is that if a country cannot rely upon a stable economic base (and many of transitional countries cannot), then there seems to be no clear way out of this cyclic development.

The world history gives many examples when development of a nation along this cycle was eventually changed to a directional development. However, there seem to be only two ways of how that happened. Firstly, this cyclic stagnation can be broken by a mass revolutionary revolt, civil war or coup that brings to power a political force (or an alliance of political forces) that are not bound by any former compromises. As a result of their clear victory, these forces also do not tend to enter into any sort of new compromise agreements with the opposition, not at least in the first years or even decades of the post-revolution period. Secondly, the cyclic development can be changed through a total curtailment of democracy by the ruling elite or by one of its factions. This usually is accompanied by introduction of a regime of "strong power", seen by the new autocrats as the only way of securing their dominant positions and stabilising the political and economic situation in the country. Any of these two options could hardly be regarded as a democratic development. In socio-political terms they actually signify a turn to the authoritarian past, a step back from liberal democratic values that prompted the initial transition.

The core of the problem of a simultaneous transition to a democratic political system and a modern economic structure lies in the question of whether it is possible or not to introduce the required economic change in a society through a democratic political system. We argue that, judging from the experience coming from many recent cases of transition, that was proven to be largely impossible. Economic reform in a broad sense – the one that demands a deep social reconstruction and the change of the national system of wealth distribution – cannot be effective without a significant reduction of social and economic privileges of those social groups that were the main beneficiaries under the old regime. The latter are certain to resist these changes, thus giving rise to a new conflict in a society. The fact that many of these beneficiaries continue to occupy important bureaucratic positions gives them power to halt the implementation of the reform. This resistance might take a great variety of forms, while attempts by the reformist part of a transition government to reach an agreement with these groups can hardly be successful.

In other words, in the process of transition it is clearly impossible to reduce or eliminate social and material privileges of certain social groups through attainment of their voluntary agreement to that. While direct negotiations lead to nowhere, democratic decisions passed by, say, a parliamentary majority do not automatically mean the readiness of the groups that are set to lose to agree to these changes. At the same time the ruling elite cannot reside to the use of force or other ways of direct pressures. These cannot be regarded as an acceptable and democratic practice, because such measures openly confront the basis of a transitional democracy: a national political compromise or a political accord.

Thus, attempts to promote a broad economic reform often trigger social (and, then, political) resistance in a transitional state. Ultimately, such attempts can only be successful if they are accompanied by measures to fight this resistance. However, a democracy based on an idea of the national compromise (transitional democracy) by its very definition cannot have access to such measures; in that feature it significantly differs from an often limited democracy which is established by a victorious political force in the post-revolution period (revolutionary democracy).

There is no doubt that a reverse to an undemocratic form of government through limiting the power of democratically-elected institutions does not automatically provide a solution to many social and economic problems of a transitional country. In fact, an authoritarian rule can be and is often even more destructive than a weak and unstable democracy. The regime of "strong power" could be capable of promoting an economic change if at least it has a clear vision of what it wants to achieve, a realistic strategy and capabilities to do that, and the support from a significant part of the population. However, often undemocratic regimes do not have these features. Autocrats may come to power through utilising the social need for a genuine economic reform, but reform does not necessarily form the basis of their future policies. Authoritarian powers open ways for quick enrichment to the new elite and the latter's fight against privileges of the past frequently leads to creation of new social privileges. This reveals a more general problem that is associated with an authoritarian rule, let it be initially "progressively-orientated" or a regressive one. As soon as it establishes a total control of the power, the only limitations to that power that may exist are purely subjective, i.e. dependent on a good will of the ruling elite. Thus, the evolution of an undemocratic regime can easily be reverted from progressive to regressive, which might happen without any dramatic surface changes, like revolutions or armed rebellions.

The above logic of transition to democracy explains why often transitional changes result in growing instability and, in the long run, may open way to dictatorships or lead to civil wars. As a very weak form of statehood, a transitional democracy is doomed to be changed sooner or later for a more stable social order. If we can use military terminology, then transitional arrangements, from the point of view of national political struggles, represent a form of a "cease-fire" agreement, rather than that of a final "peace treaty". In a transitional agreement neither side perceives that it has been totally defeated and, thus, it still reserves the right to gain (or regain) the state power sometime in the future. This brings only a temporary solution to the conflict in a society, but often did not stop the conflict from re-emerging at a later stage and in different forms.

The idea of creating a stable democracy solely through a peaceful transformation of political structures proves to be a rather impracticable concept in many modern cases where complex socio-economic realities exist. While successful in promoting (limited) political changes, transitional developments fail to reach the objective of economic transformation mainly because of the strong resistance on part of the old ruling elite. Thus, political transition often brings a delay to the solution of the existing social conflict, but not the solution itself.

Transition as an evolutionary way of transforming society demands time, control and stability. Successive generations of "democratically-orientated" leaders do not necessarily pave the way for implementation of a long-lasting democratic change. The continuing decline in economic and social conditions often leads to the growth of instability and to the emergence of a revolutionary situation. Impatience of the population grows, leaving transitional governments with less time for promotion of an effective reform, while their control of the situation is greatly undermined by a strong resistance from the old elite. As a result, these governments often fail to stop the emergence of anarchical (pre-revolution) situation, which significantly increases the possibilities for a sufficiently populist and ruthless leader (movement) to seize the power.

As it has been demonstrated by many modern transitional experiences, an introduction of reform program is a prerequisite but not a solution to avoiding of a revolutionary scenario. What is necessary is to have reform implemented, and that can only be achieved by a strong government. However, without implementation of a fundamental economic reform, anarchy may gradually well take over, paving a way to a new form of dictatorship.

External forces can and do play an important role in ensuring that transitional developments will not lead to the emergence of a new authoritarianism. However, the direction and volumes of external assistance are directly associated with strategic interests of foreign powers and that creates an extremely uneven distribution of this assistance between transitional states. For historic, geographic, strategic or economic reasons, some of transitional states receive far larger amounts of aid and are treated by aid donors differently, than the others. Consequently, the role that these external factors play in internal developments also differs greatly. As demonstrated by some modern transitional cases in Eastern Europe, large and carefully planned foreign assistance can help to break the vicious cycle of transitional development through strengthening the initial political change by profound social and economic reforms. However, in many other transitional democracies, particularly in those in the former Soviet Union, economic reform is still in its initial phases while the future of transition developments remains unclear.

6.3 "Nomenklatura" revolution in Russia

Like all other former communist states, Russia's transition from communism has been beset by problems of transforming of economic, social and political structures along Western-type democratic lines. Though ways these problems were addressed in different post-communist states varied greatly, their major outcomes were rather similar. These outcomes could be summarised in the following: (a) transition turned out to be a much more complicated and prolonged process than envisaged initially; (b) reforms were accompanied by dramatic, and in some cases devastating, falls in economic output, by the growth of social tensions and impoverishment of large masses of population; and (c) political life in the transition period became polarised, fragmented and highly unstable. In the Russian case, reforms also led to one more significant result: to the loss of internal (USSR) and external (Eastern Bloc) empires and, consequently, to a decline of its status of a great power.

These problems produced a set of dilemmas that Russia is still struggling to solve. Many of these dilemmas come as a product of a collision between the Russia's past and the ideal future that market reformists would have like Russia to reach. Other dilemmas have their roots in the century-long debates between communist and capitalist ideologies. Some of the most important of these dilemmas could be presented in the following questions:

1. Can economic transformation accompany economic growth?
2. How to reconcile (market economy) liberties with the strife for social justice?
3. Is it possible to implement deep economic transformations exclusively through the use of democratic means when that is accompanied by a prolonged period of hardships, uncertainties and, most probably, poverty for the majority of the people?
4. What in the long run becomes more important to the larger part of the population: social comfort or political and economic freedom?
5. And, in more general terms, is there a way to escape the growing contradiction between disorder (chaos), which becomes the main feature of the first transitional stages, and the yearning of the people towards stability (order)?

The list above is by no means full. Many of these dilemmas may be attributed to post-Soviet struggles between the forces of change, generally represented by democratic reformers, and the forces of "order", generally bound up with the forces of the past (conservatives/communists, etc.). Although historically these dilemmas were solved through dramatic social upheavals and were often followed by civil wars, the contemporary transformation was different. In Russia, like many other post-communist societies, the solution of these dilemmas was attempted through a peaceful, evolutionary change. And although ultimately the Soviet regime proved to be too weak to halt this change, that, however, did not mean that at a later stage the old elite would continue to act as a passive observer of these dramatic changes.

Irrespective of whether the events in the Soviet Union that took place during August–December 1991 could be called a revolution or not, there is little doubt as to their great historic significance. While a large variety of factors contributed to this change, in our view the most important of them is the fact that the Soviet rule was ended mainly as a result of actions undertaken by one faction of state and party bureaucracy (nomenklatura).[2] In short, the 1991 Russian revolution could be called a coup within the establishment. While the state power did change hands, it was carried out only within and between various parts of the Soviet elite. This change manifested a defeat of unionists/ internationalists (i.e. supporters of an imperial union-state, USSR) by separatists/nationalists (advocates of independent states).[3] The Gorbachev's populist rhetoric about democracy soon was followed by timid attempts of a political reform, greatly weakening the positions of unionists. By the early 1990s the rise of Yeltsin, who in his policies had successfully used a blend of nationalism and anti-communism, signalled that the resentful part of the Soviet bureaucracy was quickly gaining a substantial popular support. It was not long before separatists, first in Russia and then in all other Soviet republics, took the state power into their hands.

This important feature of the 1991 Russian revolution as a predominantly nomenklatura event explained the remarkable easiness and swiftness with which it was carried out. Amazingly, the change of power was not accompanied by any significant resistance, albeit the abortive August putsch, even despite the fact that the participation of masses in these events was comparatively very low. In the end, it was the Soviet nomenklatura in the republics, which initially preferred to abstain from supporting the Russian revolution, that gained most from it: after the Soviet Union had collapsed, republican leaders received the total power over their territorial entities.

If we analyse the consequences of the disintegration of the Soviet empire by a criterion of who were those who gained most from it, politically and materially, the post-Soviet realities clearly demonstrate that in all of the republics, as well as in most localities within Russia, a significant part of the old elite easily managed to retain their access to the state power. Moreover, following the 1991 change, their control of the state social and economic structures was greatly strengthened. While part of the old nomenklatura continued to occupy leading political positions, others became involved in a variety of legal and semi-legal business operations. In the past many civil servants and party functionaries could not easily do that because of the limitations imposed by the code of civil practice or by party discipline.

This nomenklatura character of the 1991 "revolution" to a large extent helps to explain the response of the new Russian leadership to developments that followed. It also sets the limits of how far this leadership was prepared to go in its reform attempts and transformations. Even now, six years after the events of August–December 1991, many Soviet-era bureaucrats continue to be in top positions within the establishment, they frame Russia's politics and manage its economy. For instance, in 1995 former secretaries of the local party committee headed 83 out of 89 Russian local and regional administrations. About one fifth of the largest enterprises that changed hands during the voucher stage of privatisation, became private property of their previous "red directors"; another 60% were controlled by them.[4]

Another important feature of the Russian transition is its strongly regionalist and separatist nature. In this regard it is important to note that, by definition, nomenklatura (or bureaucracy) is not a social stratum, a political party or a class. It can be identified as a group of people who are united in that group by their social affiliation (civil service) and by an above-average level of loyalty to the current regime, but at the same time often have different and even contradictory professional, egoistic and social interests. In many cases nomenklatura represents the most career-obsessed and politically fragmented part of a society. Specific conditions of the last years of the Soviet power made many state and party bureaucrats dependent on top-placed patrons and informal connections, more than ever before.[5] This process, in turn, led to a creation of numerous factions within the state and party bureaucracy based on personal, geographic and professional links.

The 1991 revolution gave Russian local and regional leaders an opportunity to claim unlimited power over their territories, in the same way as the Belovezhsk agreement on the disintegration of the

USSR had given to Soviet republican bureaucrats. That was the price that Yeltsin and his supporters had to pay for their reliance on separatism in the fight against the Soviet central power.[6] Yeltsin, who was later joined by other Soviet republican leaders, uncompromisingly rejected the political platform of the August 1991 coup leaders, including their ideology (communism), their objective (re-unification) and suggested means (the strengthening of central controls). Instead, he adopted a policy which was based on a "democratic anti-communism", separatism and on a gradual move towards loosening of the central power.

Thus, one of the main results that followed the Russian nomenklatura revolution was a serious weakening of the central state structures. The disintegration of the USSR and granting of total independence to republics meant that all mechanisms of control over republican bureaucracies were removed. The process did not stop there, however, and was soon followed by the growth of separatist demands within Russia itself.

The rapid rise of separatism created a whole set of new political and economic problems in Russia and in many other ex-Soviet states. Many of these problems, for instance the problem of halting a further disintegration of the state, could be overcome through reinstating of a strong central control. However, that meant that President Yeltsin and his supporters had to abandon their earlier ideology and to reside to policies that they have publicly scorned just only a few years ago, during the 1991 putsch. If they attempted to increase the power of central authorities in any significant way, this would immediately be interpreted by their separatist followers as a step back from their earlier "democratic" values and the pro-independence drive. The complexity of this dilemma lies in the fact that the continuation of policies based on separatism will in the future inevitably lead to the breakup of the Russian Federation, in the same way as it had already led to the collapse of the USSR.[7]

While during the first years of the post-Soviet development Russian leadership managed to keep separatist pressures under control, by the mid-1990s this was becoming a more and more difficult task. All traditionally multi-ethnic societies, as distinct from predominantly immigrant polyethnic societies, that exist today within boundaries of one nation-state have one common feature: a high level of concentration of power in the federal/central authority. Although this high centralisation of state power often is the major source of ethnic conflicts in that societies (e.g., in Russia, the other former Soviet republics, the former Yugoslavia, South Africa, India, etc.), the strength of the centre allows to keep separatist ethnic pressures under control, not allowing these nation-states to fall apart. However, any signs of weakness of the central power are often immediately followed by the growth of separatist pressures.

The weakness of the Russian central authority in the aftermath of the collapse of the USSR (1991–92) gave rise to regional demands of a greater independence on such a mass scale that some observers even compared that with the early stages of feudalism.[8] Initially, majority of these demands came from Russia's ethnic minorities: Tatars, Chechens, Ingushs, Bashkars, Buryats, Yakuts, etc. The level of confrontation between local separatists and the federal authorities varied greatly; however, the most exceptional case was that of Chechnya where in 1994 that confrontation led to a bloody and destructive war. By the mid-1990s ethic groups were joined by a growing number of territories that had predominantly Russian populations (Urals, Siberia, the Far East, St Petersburg, Moscow, Tyumen', etc.).[9] The Russian federal government responded to these pressures by entering into separate agreements with each region that demanded greater independence. By the end of 1997 already 35 out of the total of 89 regions, or 39% of all Russian administrative entities, had signed separate treaties with central authorities.[10]

It is important to note that the strength of separatist tendencies varied greatly across Russia. While in the majority of regions the role of central authority was rarely questioned, in other regions demands for greater independence were very strong. These divisions between regions stem from a variety of historical, political and economic factors. In each case combination of these factors is different; however, causes for separatism remain the same all over Russia. Firstly, Russian regions differ by the ethnic composition of their population and the history of their relations with Moscow. Separatism does not enjoy the same level of support in all of ethnic entities. It is stronger where there is a history of conflict in relations with Moscow and where local elites had managed to mobilise nationalist feelings into mass political movements.

Secondly, the strife for cultural – and political – independence from the centre is often accompanied by economic demands that in most cases play a far more important role than the ethnic factor. Economic causes for separatism also explain why it gains popularity in some predominantly Russian areas. From the socio-economic point of view, separatist regions are divided into two major categories. In the first category are Russia's wealthiest regions. These are pure donors to the Russian federal budget and their pressures for a greater independence from the centre are mainly framed by clear material gains.[11] The other category, on the contrary, is made up from Russia's poorest regions. The latter in the 1990s have experienced large and painful cuts to the level of subsidies they used to receive from the centre. As a result there was a dramatic increase in mass poverty in all of these regions creating favourable conditions for the growth of various forms of political extremism in these territories. Often this extremism is combined with other historical or ethnic factors, or used in political ambitions of local leaders, providing a fertile ground for a rapid increase in the local separatism.[12]

6.4   Political fragmentation in post-Soviet Russia

Given that the post-1991 changes in Russia were a nomenklatura revolution, the next important question that arises is: what role did the population, mass movements and anti-nomenklatura political parties play in Russia's transformations? The answer to this question is the key to understanding the politics of transition in Russia.

In general it can be stated that in Russian post-Soviet developments the electorate often played a passive role. This political passivity arose from the Soviet political culture, when mass politics, elections, etc., in the form they existed, where nothing more than a façade to the undemocratic political system. However, during the first few months after the failed August coup mass expectations of the coming "real change" were high in society. These expectations could have been easily transformed into the mass pro-democratic political activity, if free democratic elections were held at the time. But that did not happen, mainly because of the lack of interest in such mass political activity on part of the new Russian establishment. The separatist factions of nomenklatura which acquired access to the total power after August 1991 events, were not interested in making any steps that could have jeopardised their ruling positions immediately after they have gained control of the state power.

Only a year after the historic August 1991 events in Moscow, the dominant political attitude among the population was again passive and very similar to the response of the Soviet electorate under the communist system. That response came as a result of realisation by the larger part of the population that the only real gain from the 1991 "revolution" was only a change to the old ideological façade. The new Russian establishment started to quickly lose its popular support; even populist promises and anticommunist rhetoric coming from the president and the government did very little to revert this trend.

This was accompanied by appearance of new conflicts within the establishment: between the centre and the regions, and between the legislature and the executive. Like the Soviet nomenklatura earlier, the post-Soviet Russian ruling elite was becoming increasingly isolated. This isolation was even deeper than before, because, in contrast to communists, post-Soviet Russian leaders had no longer at their disposal party structures that could help them in consolidating their political and ideological control over the society.

The political vacuum, in which the new Russian leadership found itself soon after 1991, was also a logical consequence of the nomenklatura revolution. As a predominantly bureaucratic event, this revolution was a negation of the old regime by its own servants, where each of the bureaucrats had their own personal or career interests in mind. In the course of this change a selfish part of the former Soviet bureaucracy draped itself in the cloaks of a greater self-rule for provinces, demanding the dismantling of a centralised control. Immediately after the "revolution" occurred, however, the victorious "democratic" movement that brought this part of bureaucracy to power had become rapidly fragmented. With the collapse of the Soviet party and state structures, the major factor that kept this rebellious bureaucracy unified had quickly disappeared. Russian regional leaders, like feudal landlords, started to demand more and more independence from the Russian centre, prompting whole set of new conflicts between regional and national leaders as well as between different regional elites within Russia.

In a situation where masses were becoming increasingly politically indifferent, those who came to the ballot boxes could easily identify politicians/parties that they didn't trust, but would often find it difficult to tell whom they would like to support. That was a direct continuation of the traditional Soviet political behaviour, when taking a positive stand through supporting a party or an ideology, was equal to an active opposition to the regime. At the same time, a "silent opposition" to the existing order, expressed through a mass political inactivity, was rarely punishable. This negative political attitude divided the Soviet society into "them" (the elite or nomenklatura) and "us" (the ordinary people). The widening of the gap between the two groups – the establishment and the people – was symptomatic of the growing political and social crisis of the Soviet system in its last decades of existence. However, the appearance of a similar gap in the post-Soviet period was unexpected and initially viewed by the elite as an atavism of the past.

The growing political indifference of the population and the low levels of the mass political activity have created in Russia a political vacuum or, as James Alexander puts it, a "stateless" environment.[13] This also resulted in an increasing estrangement of the state power from the people. In such a situation the interrelation between the state and the masses became thin and easy to break. Rudiment political organisations, absolute majority of which were too small and low-influential, were not able to fulfil the role of political parties as stabilising elements in a multi-party democratic system. The inability of Russian post-Soviet political structures to channel or to accommodate the aspirations of the electorate gradually resulted in the growing fragmentation of politics. The more actively Russian politicians tried to reconcile growing mass negation of the post-Soviet political and economic order with their own political agendas, the more fragmented and confrontational the Russian political life became.

Political fragmentation is not always a negative sign. In the history of many modern democratic societies the process of fragmentation of political life often preceded the formation of major parties. However, in some countries, particularly in the Third World, the heritage of authoritarianism, coupled with the absence of established mass political organisations, pushed societies into political decay, chaos and disintegration, which, consequently, led to the establishment of an authoritarian rule. This was accompanied by large-scale social and economic crises and often created a pre-war situation.

In the last years of the Soviet Union the political life was characterised by a clear-cut divide between "pro-reformists" and "anti-reformists". This split went through all sectors of social life, including even the party and state structures. When in the late 1991 the former ruling elite was defeated following the disintegration of the USSR, the grounds for this divide, in its earlier form, had disappeared. Leaders of opposition were now in the ruling positions. This change of places was accompanied by an increase in the complexity of political choices that voters had to make. The result was a growing fragmentation in Russian politics, both on the national and regional levels.

The first studies of Russia's modern regional political preferences started to appear in the late 1980s, when the first contested elections were held in the Soviet Union.[14] These studies revealed a phenomenon that in the later years became the dominant feature of Russian regional politics: a deep political divide between Russia's southern and northern regions. While the majority of electorate in Russian southern provinces tends to support left/nationalist parties and movements, Russia's North mainly votes for democrats and pro-reform parties. Sergei Chugrov has called that "the phenomenon of the 55th parallel"[15] because the dividing line almost exactly coincides with this longitude. In his view, the existence of this phenomenon is based on income and economic disparities between the rich North and the poor South, and on different levels of urbanisation. In the North more urbanised Northern population tends to be more democratically inclined that more conservative rural voters in the South.

A clear dividing line in the 1989 parliamentary elections, the presidential elections of June 1991 and at the April 1993 referendum represented the political split between Russian regions.[16] However, the continuing fragmentation of the Russian political arena made the political choices of the electorate in the first post-Soviet elections in December 1993 more complex and mixed.[17] In Map 6.1 we have grouped all major political parties that contested the 1993 parliamentary elections into two major categories: left/nationalist and democratic/state. The Russian communist

Map 6.1   Regional Distribution of Votes Between Major Political Trends in December 1993 Parliamentary Elections

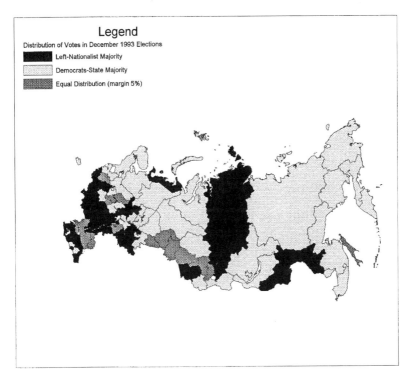

party, the nationalist Liberal democratic party and the Agrarian party formed the first group, while the second group consisted of Russian political movements with a predominantly democratic orientation: Russia's Choice, Yabloko, Women of Russia, Party of Russian Unity and Accord and Democratic Party.[18] The map shows regions where any of these two groups received the majority of votes, as well as regions where distribution of votes was equal or close to equal (margin between polar votes of less than 5%).

According to the map, the electorate in all of southern and Western regions of the European Russia, with few exceptions, had given its total support to left/nationalist parties. Other important strongholds of these parties included Eastern Siberia and southern part of the Russian Far East (Amur oblast' and Jewish autonomous region). A significant part of Russian southern regions in December 1993 also gave equal numbers of votes to left/nationalist and pro-reform parties. On the other hand, in the northern parts of European Russia and in the major part of the Russian Far East democratic parties enjoyed a largely unrivalled support.

Voting patterns in the Russian Far East present a very interesting case. Due to the fact that economic crisis in this part of Russia is generally much deeper than in the European regions and, consequently, population's sufferings are much greater, one would assume that this should automatically translate into a significantly lower support for democratic (pro-state) parties than anywhere else in Russia. The reality is quite opposite. With the only exception of traditional agricultural oblasts, the majority of voters in the Far East had cast their votes for democrats. Such "non-conformist" electoral behaviour can be explained by the fact that voters in the Far East tend to support political leaders that were never publicly associated with the present or past ruling elites, the nomenklatura. These leaders could represent left, right or centre of the political spectrum. That fact explains why both nationalist Zhirinovsky and pro-market reformer Yavlinsky gained far larger shares of votes than any other candidate directly associated with the former or current regime.[19]

The next important elections in Russia were held in December 1995.[20] At that stage the political fragmentation in the Russian society was at its peak. More than 40 political parties contested parliamentary seats, the number of alliances they formed in the course of the election campaign was even greater. For instance, when the parliamentary election campaign was already in the full swing, the media, according to our calculations, reported on 37 separate cases of splits, new coalitions and factional fights within Russian political movements that took place within just one week.[21]

Despite the high level of political fragmentation, the results of these elections had demonstrated that the process of consolidation of Russian political forces was gaining momentum. The new Duma was dominated by parties that were in an open opposition to both the president and his course of reforms. The communist party faction became the largest in the parliament, controlling more than a third of votes in the Duma. That forced other factions, notably the democrats, to take joint voting positions more often than ever in the past.

The December 1995 elections marked the beginning of a new stage in the consolidation of political forces in Russia. The political fragmentation that during the first years of reform made Russian politics extremely unstable and generally unpredictable has started to gradually disappear. The previous two Russian parliaments – the one elected in Soviet times and the other in December 1993 – in their daily proceedings were in fact even more fragmented than the Duma elected in 1995. Thus, while the former were was much easier for President Yeltsin to manipulate and to deal with, in the case of the 1995 parliament Yeltsin was frequently forced to rely on means of direct pressure like the use of his wide presidential powers rather than on a clever political manoeuvring.

6.5   The role of the presidency

The 1995 parliamentary elections were also a clear demonstration of the fact that in the mid-1990s the process of polarisation of Russian politics had led to a significant decline in the influence of the "middle" groups, both in the parliament and in the society. The political arena was becoming more clearly divided between the extreme trends, whether on the left or on the right. The "middle" group, true liberal democrats, was rapidly getting squeezed out of Russian politics by the anti-communist ruling elite and its increasingly pro-communist/ nationalist opposition.

The Yeltsin's regime had its main ideological base in anti-communism. It can also be added that, at least in the first years of the reform, the political function of this regime was a further decentralisation of the Russian state. At the same time, the political platform of conservatives/communists could be described as an anti-anti-communist (which is predominantly but not necessarily pro-communist), re-unificationist (supportive of the restoration of the USSR) and pro-centralist (promotion of the idea of a strong central power as opposite to region-alism/separatism). Modern Russian communists, as demonstrated by the 1995–96 election campaigns, publicly recognised the necessity of a mixed economy and agreed that there were limitations to the use of planned methods in the state management. At the same time, they made no secret of their plans to reverse privatisation and to re-nation-alise some key industries. However, in contradiction to traditional communist ideologues, in the area of ethnic/national relations the new Russian communist leaders are outspoken advocates of (Russian) nationalism rather than the late Marxists' internationalism.

The most uncompromising opponents of communists are regional-ists, many of whom, like communists, come from the ranks of the former communist party and Soviet state nomenklatura. Regionalists (separatists) are, in the eyes of modern Russian communists and nationalists, the ones to blame for the collapse of the USSR. If a com-munist/nationalist coalition ever comes to power, there is little doubt that it will attempt to prosecute the separatist "renegades". This explains why regionalists often make the most ardent anti-communists in contemporary Russia.

Despite their political differences, regionalists, like communists, gen-erally use the same political tactics. In the promotion of their objec-tives they also tend to rely heavily on the use of bureaucratic institutions and open (direct) means of political pressure. Russia's most outspoken regionalist, President Yeltsin, used a very "communist-like" policy in dealing with his opponents in the parliament in October 1993, as well as during the war in Chechnya in 1994–96. On many recent occasions regionalists acted as "soul brothers" of communists, demonstrating that they have roots in the same former Soviet elite (nomenklatura), but in its different faction, the local bureaucracy.

Regionalists do not have a united political base. They draw their political support from local elites and these often have different politi-cal views and even seek contradictory objectives. Therefore, in general, regionalists tend to have an extremely vague political platform and often pursue controversial policies. When we discuss the role that regionalists played in post-Soviet Russian political developments, it becomes clear that on many occasions the personality of the Russian President, Boris Yeltsin, had played a crucial role in framing and direct-ing of their political orientation. Initially it was Yeltsin and his close associates that choose anti-communism and decentralisation of the state power as the two major cornerstones of their policy. By the early 1990s their fight against the domination of the centre allowed them to mobilise diverse political aspirations of regionalists into a single political platform.

While in the early 1990s separatism was a very effective tool in combating the weak Soviet central power, in the post-Soviet period the growth of regionalism and separatism had increasingly started to block Russia's national development. In post-Soviet Russian politics the earlier conflict between separatism and unionism within the USSR was transformed into increasing tensions between (local) regionalism and federalism. However, because of his earlier political commitments, Yeltsin found it impossible to denounce this separatist ideology, even when it started to threaten the future of the Russian federal state. This made Yeltsin's domestic policies extremely contradictory. As the national leader, Yeltsin was forced to defeat the unity of the Russian state, while his major political support came from the separatist (anti-union) forces. That explains many controversies in Yeltsin's policies and the fact that, when internal conflicts in Russia reached critical levels like in the case of Chechnya, Yeltsin preferred to abstain from taking radical decisions that could have easily undermined his major power base.

Another implication of Yeltsin's contradictory policy was that it allowed him to rely upon and to manipulate this rather vague power base of his. The diverse nature of regionalists made it impossible for Yeltsin, even if he wished to do so, to maintain any viable and structuralised political organisation. If created, such political structure was doomed to be subject to internal contradictions, as were all of the political parties and movements set up by Yeltsin's close associates. However, it is our view that Yeltsin was actually never interested in establishing his "own" movement or party. A direct association with any party would immediately limit his scope for manoeuvre and in the long run would make him grossly dependent on party politics. Instead, Yeltsin systematically rejected all appeals and pressures to join or even to give his strong public backing to any one political movement. In the end it was Yeltsin who played the crucial role in guaranteeing that the post-Soviet Russian political life remained unstructuralised, extremely fluid and, consequently, very unstable. It was in this situation of a constant instability that Yeltsin found it easy to secure his own dominating position in the political system and to cleverly manipulate the opposing political forces. He understood that any formalisation of Russian politics would eventually destroy his main political strength, which was based on the vagueness and the populist nature of his political platform that allowed him to easily shift the blame for any political or economic failures of his government on someone else.

Thus, instead of creating in Russia a formalised political system based on democratic principles, Yeltsin was continuously playing a major destabilising role in Russian politics. He surrounded himself with weak and relatively unknown politicians, who either had no power base of their own or enjoyed a very modest political support on the national arena. In such a case their major political strength was solely in their alliance with Yeltsin. The latter is proved by the fact that in every single case political movements formed by Yeltsin's close associates had rapidly disintegrated as soon as these associates were out of president's favour. This equally applies to Gaidar's Russia's Choice, Shakhrai's Party of Russian Unity and Order, and Chernomyrdin's Russia is Our Home movement.

Beyond the Potemkin village of nominally democratic and elected institutions,[22] the Russian post-Soviet political system was as far from a Western-type democracy, as was the late Soviet system. As Richard Sakwa puts it:

> While in the West politics is formalized, ritualized and conventional, in Russia, by contrast, politics is raw, unaggregated and barely mediated by parties, movements or convention. The country is a hyper-politicized society in the sense that most forms of social life remain subject to bureaucratic regulation; at the same time it is effectively de- or apoliticized in that mediating structures of political life remain embryonic. Individuals have constantly to make political and social choices marking sudden transitions from infantilism to political adulthood – without an intervening period in which to mature.[23]

By the mid-1990s, with the escalation of economic and political crises in Russia, the objective of his own political survival had become the top priority of Yeltsin's policy. In order to achieve that he was prepared to sacrifice his principles, closest associates and to enter into new and unexpected alliances. The high level of fragmentation of Russian politics, itself a product of Yeltsin's earlier policies, was starting to endanger his own position in power. In an attempt to keep its hold of power in a situation of an increasing "political vacuum" in the Russian society the Yeltsin's administration had only two major options: either to give up to popular pressures and to step down (thus opening a way towards formalisation of the Russian politics) or to continue its political manoeuvres while keeping the society under control by increasingly undemocratic means. The events of October 1993 had clearly demonstrated that Yeltsin's choice was the latter option. In the aftermath of these events Yeltsin had a free hand in ruling the country which he used to consolidate his power within the establishment. As a result, in December 1993 Russia received a constitution that cemented a strong presidential power and provided the president with a variety of "constitutional" counter-measures to resist in the future any possible opposition from the parliament to his rule.[24]

In the post-1993 Russian constitutional system it is the president, and not the parliament, who has most of the power. This explains why both the political elite and the electorate had given significantly less importance to the December 1995 parliamentary elections than to the presidential elections that were held half a year later.

In the first half of 1996 all Russian major political parties were fully absorbed by preparations for the elections which were generally viewed as the most decisive political battle in Russia since the collapse of the Soviet Union. The opposition led by the communist party entered into electoral pacts with other pro-communist/nationalist parties and movements creating a united "front of national-patriotic forces". This pro-communist bloc carefully abstained from nominating of its candidates to the Russian government, which was formed after the newly elected parliament had started its sitting in January 1996. Communists and their allies also refused to enter into any talks with the president who in their rhetoric, in contrast to their earlier tactic of evading open criticisms of the president, was now made personally responsible for all the faults and mistakes in Russia's reform policy. However, the greatest setback of the opposition was a lack of bright personalities and election organisational skills. The communist candidate for presidency, Gennady Zyuganov, could hardly attract any support from the younger part of the Russian electorate, while opposition's pre-election appeals and programmes were mainly directed towards the older part of the population, leaving younger and more educated voters indifferent. These age and educational characteristics of communist supporters were further strengthened by the urban–rural divisions, when opposition forces were generally significantly more successful in attracting the voters' support in rural areas rather than in Russian towns and cities.

For Yeltsin contesting the elections was a very risky political exercise. According to all opinion polls held in the early 1996, Yeltsin's chances of winning these elections were almost non-existent. Despite that, he decided to stand for the re-election, ignoring the advice from some of his closest security and military advisers to postpone the elections.[25]

Yeltsin appointed Anatoly Chubais, one of his closest allies who until early 1996 was in charge of Russian privatisation campaign, to head his election headquarters.

Yeltsin entered the election campaign with a political platform, which was based around the same main issues that already brought him popularity in the past: anti-communism and decentralisation. However, in 1996 his anti-communist campaign was more aggressive and was aimed at provoking a mass fear of communist dictatorship and of the threat of inevitable civil war in Russia. The issue of decentralisation (or of increased powers of local authorities) was clearly given a low priority status. That did not stop Yeltsin from making a number of important reshuffles in regional structures and from cleverly using financial levers to influence the regions.

But the closer the election date was, the clearer was the need for Yeltsin to modify his election strategy because it was not bringing him the necessary support. Yeltsin's hope was in undertaking a number of popular (populist) measures that could quickly change the balance of forces in his favour. In March 1996, the first time since the wage arrears started to grow in 1992, the Russian government announced its decision to pay off delayed pensions and wages to state employees. Indeed, salary payments did start to come, which could happen only at the expense of greatly increased state borrowing. In April Yeltsin's supporters opened wide and active pro-Yeltsin campaign in the mass media while president himself went on a two-month tour of the Russian regions.

As a presidential candidate Yeltsin was a completely changed person. There were no more visible health problems that were inseparable from his image during 1994–95. He was articulate, and looked healthy and determined. He did his best to promote a "strong man" image of himself. At the end of May in an unexpected move he even reached a cease-fire agreement with Chechen separatists, which was never fully implemented but did help to soften criticism of his Chechen policy on the eve of elections.

By the time the first round of presidential elections took place on 16 June 1996, Yeltsin's chances of victory were already comparable to those of the opposition. That was a remarkable achievement, given the fact that six months earlier the opposition had a sweeping victory at the parliamentary elections and that Yeltsin's own standing in the opinion polls was one of the lowest among Russian politicians. However, without understating the important role that Yeltsin's personal features had played in reversing the election results, it should be noted that it was profound changes he introduced in his political platform that made many Russian voters give their votes for Yeltsin. The strong showing of opposition had forced Yeltsin to re-think and re-define his policy so substantially, that on the eve of elections communist leader Zyuganov had complained that Yeltsin was "already implementing" communist policy.[26] With the sole exception of denouncing the ideology of communism, Yeltsin's pre-election programme had no major differences with the political platform of his main opponents, the communists. Both platforms were based on two main principles: the promotion of Russian nationalism and a "socially-orientated" reform. This was a noticeable change from the "liberal", pro-Western and free-market rhetoric of Yeltsin's earlier political statements.

Presidential elections were held in two rounds in June–July 1996. In the second round Yeltsin had joined forces with one of his nationalist opponents, General Alexander Lebed. That move made it possible for Yeltsin to get a majority of votes and to defeat his main rival, communist leader Zyuganov. Yeltsin's victory came at the expense of not only his ideological concessions, but also his health. Between the two rounds of elections Yeltsin suffered a heart attack and he spent most his time during the first year of office in hospitals. In exchange for political and electoral support, Yeltsin also had to make important political concessions to the most important players that provided him with this crucial support. These included General Lebed who immediately after the elections started to broker his own way into Kremlin through openly undermining Yeltsin's authority; Russian bankers that funded Yeltsin's re-election campaign and after the elections had received most favourable treatment in privatisation auctions and other government financial activities; and regionalists that have significantly increased their autonomy from the centre following Yeltsin's victory.

The results of the first round of the 1996 presidential elections can serve as a very good indicator of changes that took place in political preferences of the Russian electorate.[27] While voting patterns in the December 1995 parliamentary elections had shown extremely high levels of political fragmentation, voting in the June elections was in regional terms much more consolidated. Map 6.2 shows the regional distribution of votes in the June 1996 elections between the two major political trends: left/nationalist parties (communists, "liberal-democrats", Lebed) and democratic/state parties (Yabloko and Yeltsin). In 1996 the North-South political divide in Russia became even clearer than in the 1993 elections (see Map 6.1). With the exception of the city of Moscow and northern regions, majority of votes in the European

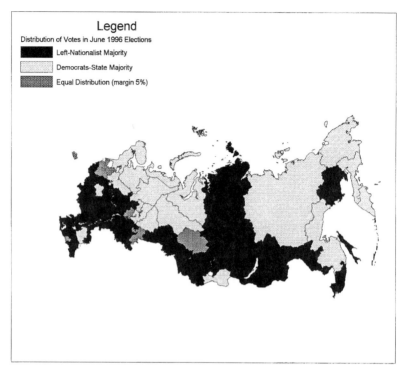

Map 6.2   Regional Distribution of Votes between Major Political Trends in the First Round of Presidential Elections, June 1996

part of Russia in the first round of the 1996 presidential elections was cast for left/nationalist parties. Elsewhere in Russia in all of the areas where in 1993 democrats and nationalists got equal votes, by 1996 nationalists were in a clear majority. In 1996 the number of regions in a "middle" voting group (equal distribution of votes) was also much smaller than in 1993.

In Tables 6.1 and 6.2 we have listed areas where the majority of votes were cast for either of the two main political trends. Major Russian industrial cities (Moscow, St Petersburg, Sverdlovsk and Khabarovsk) in 1993–96 were the strongholds of democratic/state parties along with the major mining areas in the North and some of Russia's ethnic republics. Between 1993 and 1996 the support for pro-state parties had increased in Moscow and the area, in St Petersburg and the area, in Sverdlovsk, Perm' and Sakha, while in all other areas it has fallen. Ethnic republics in the

South of Russia form one of the most important regional groups that traditionally support left/nationalist parties. Other areas where these parties in 1993 and 1996 elections had a clear majority include agricultural and industrial regions in European Russia. In 1993–96 only in the North Caucasus regions of Dagestan and Karachaevo-Cherkesia the support for left/nationalist parties had fallen slightly, while in all other areas it had increased, sometimes dramatically.

In general, Tables 6.1 and 6.2 reveal a clear and direct link between voting preferences and income levels of the electorate in Russian regions. We have selected 30 Russian regions with the most striking differences in per capita income distribution patterns and grouped them into three major categories: nine Russian regions[28] are in a "high-income" category, eight in a "medium-income" category[29] and the remaining 13 regions[30] fall into a "low-income" category. Socio-economic differences between these regions are represented in Table 6.3 below. While in 1996 in high-income areas the share of income in Russia's total was twice higher than the share of population, the situation in low-income areas was opposite with the gross income share 1.7 lower than the share of population. At the time when the first

Table 6.1   Areas with the Largest Portion of Votes Cast for Democratic-State Parties, 1993–96
(% of all votes in the area)

	December 1993	June 1996
Moscow	63.2	69.7
Tyva Republic	68.6	66.9
Sverdlovsk Oblast	57.1	65.5
St Petersburg	61.0	65.0
Perm Oblast	62.5	63.4
Ingushia Republic	82.5	62.4
Sakha Republic	50.1	57.7
Karelia Republic	60.2	57.6
Chukotskii Autonomous Okrug	56.3	55.4
Arkhangelsk Oblast	55.3	52.7
Moscow Oblast	49.4	52.7
Kamchatka Oblast	56.2	52.3
Khabarovskii Krai	52.9	51.9
Komi Republic	53.6	50.8
Murmansk Oblast	59.0	50.8
Leningrad Oblast	48.6	49.6
Kabardino-Balkaria Republic	52.2	48.2

Table 6.2   Areas with the Largest Portion of Votes Cast for Left-Nationalist Parties, 1993–96
(% of all votes in the area)

	December 1993	June 1996
North Osetia Republic	57.5	76.2
Oryol Oblast	64.5	71.4
Adygeya Republic	52.5	71.4
Tambov Oblast	62.0	71.1
Stavropolskii Krai	62.4	70.4
Dagestan Republic	75.7	69.8
Smolensk Oblast	61.8	69.6
Altaiskii Krai	61.0	69.6
Voronezh Oblast	57.2	69.6
Mordovia Republic	66.5	69.5
Karachaevo-Cherkesia Republic	69.6	69.1
Penza Oblast	62.5	69.0
Belgorod Oblast	63.2	68.5
Chuvashia Republic	55.0	68.4
Kursk Oblast	65.0	67.4
Bryansk Oblast	58.2	67.3
Ulyanovsk Oblast	56.1	66.5
Ryazan' Oblast	55.4	66.0
Lipetsk Oblast	58.2	65.9
Chita Oblast	50.4	64.9
Pskov Oblast	61.5	64.8
Orenburg Oblast	53.5	64.2
Marii El Republic	51.2	63.0
Amur Oblast	50.9	62.4
Volgograd Oblast	53.0	60.9

round of presidential elections was held, the average per capita income in high-income areas in real terms was less than 5% lower than in 1990; in low-income areas it was more than 38% lower.

It is no surprise, that, given the existing income differences between Russian regions, voting patterns in the three income categories also varied significantly. As demonstrated by the results of all major elections held in the post-Soviet period, there is a direct interrelation between income levels of the electorate and the support it gives to one of the two major political trends (see Table 6.4a). While in high-income areas left-nationalist parties received a lower share of votes than pro-government parties, the situation was completely reverse in the low-income areas. Between 1993 and 1996 in all categories the support for both trends had increased significantly which

Table 6.3   Shares in the Population and the Gross Income in 30 Russian Regions
(Russia's national totals = 100)

a) Shares in the Russia's population, 1996

High income areas	18.7
Medium income areas	13.1
Low income areas	12.9

b) Shares in the gross income of the Russian population

	December 1993	December 1995	June 1996
High income areas	27.98	40.87	38.20
Medium income areas	12.71	10.51	10.22
Low income areas	9.19	6.81	7.76

c) Dynamics of the average real per capita income as % of 1990 level, 1990 = 100

	December 1993	December 1995	June 1996
High income areas	80.69	115.38	95.34
Medium income areas	73.22	59.26	50.92
Low income areas	58.02	42.08	42.36

Calculated from:
Rossiiskii statisticheskii ezhegodnik. 1994, Moscow: Goskomstat, 1994, pp.510–512;
Pokazateli sotsialnogo razvitiya Rossiiskoi Federatsii i ee regionov. Moscow: Goskomstat, 1993, pp.105–107; *Uroven' zhizni naseleniya Rossii. 1996*, Moscow: Goskomstat, 1996, pp.65–67;
Sotsial'no-ekonomicheskoe polozhenie Rossii, yanvar'-iuyl' 1996 g., Moscow: Goskomstat 1996, pp.261–262.

was symptomatic of the general polarisation in political attitudes of the Russian society and the decline of centrist, "middle" political groups and forces. In high-income areas the number of votes cast for mainstream parties in 1993–96 increased from 64% to 96% and with state parties receiving 1.6 times more votes than nationalists in the first round of the 1996 presidential elections. During the same period in middle-income areas the voters' support for the mainstream parties had grown from 53% to 96% while shares of the two groups in 1996 were almost equal (difference of less than 5%). In the low-income category of regions political polarisation of voters was even more dramatic: mainstream parties there had increased their gross share from 51% in 1993 to almost 100% in 1996. In June 1996 the number of votes cast for nationalists in these regions was 2 times higher than the number cast for pro-government parties.

Table 6.4   Income Disparities and Political Polarisation in Russian Regions, 1993–96

a) Voting patterns in 30 regions (as % of all votes cast)

	December 1993	December 1995[a]	June 1996
High income areas:			
Left-nationalist	27.6	26.0	37.4
Democratic-state	35.9	22.8	58.4
Medium income areas:			
Left-nationalist	37.2	31.2	50.8
Democratic-state	26.0	17.2	45.1
Low income areas:			
Left-nationalist	44.5	41.8	63.3
Democratic-state	16.7	14.3	33.6

b) Voting patterns in groups of regions[b] (as % of all votes cast)

	December 1993	December 1995[a]	June 1996
Mining areas			
Left-nationalist	33.9	40.5	58.2
Democratic-state	20.1	11.3	32.2
Manufacturing areas			
Left-nationalist	30.2	26.0	40.4
Democratic-state	36.9	21.8	55.8
Agricultural areas			
Left-nationalist	42.5	41.5	66.7
Democratic-state	18.1	11.6	30.4

NOTES:
[a] Due to an extremely high level of political fragmentation at the December 1995 elections, numbers of votes cast for Russian mainstream parties were significantly lower than in 1993 or in 1996.
[b] *Mining areas:* Kemerovo, Tyumen' and Sakha only.
   Manufacturing areas: St Petersburg, Samara and Khabarovsk only.
   Agricultural areas: Belgorod, Krasnodar and Stavropol only.

Calculated from:
Vybory Prezidenta Rossiiskoi Federatsii, 1996. Elektoral'naya statistika, Moscow: TsIK, 1996; *Russian Regional Explorer: Geography, Economy, Ecology, Government.* Washington-Moscow: Russian Info&Business Center and MagicInfo, 1996.

Although income levels had a significant effect on the election results in most Russian regions, another factor that in some cases had played even a more important role in framing of political preferences of voters was the level of education of the population. In Table 6.4b we presented

voting results in the three groups of regions with different economic profiles. In real terms, in June 1996 the average per capita income in mining areas was 86% of the 1990 level compared to 64% in manufacturing areas and 49% in agricultural areas (see Table 4.16b). However, pro-state parties enjoyed the largest level of support in manufacturing areas (56% versus 40% for left-nationalist parties), where an average level of education of electorate is significantly higher than in mining or agricultural areas. In mining areas pro-state candidates received 1.8 times less votes than the opposition. Even in the area with the Russia's highest per capita income, Tyumen', the support for nationalists in the first round of the 1996 presidential elections was more than 50% of the total vote.

To summarise, one can say that three major factors determined Russian voters' behaviour in the post-Soviet elections. These factors were (a) the traditional divide between the industrial North and the agricultural South with a border around 55th parallel, (b) large and increasing income disparities between the regions, and (c) the level of education of the electorate. Despite the high level of fragmentation in the formal Russian politics, between 1993 and 1996 there was a significant consolidation in political attitudes the electorate, mainly around the two major political trends. In general, left-nationalist parties had dramatically increased their support and were set to win the 1996 presidential race. The victory of Yeltsin came only as a result of his clever political manoeuvring, incorporation of major nationalist demands into his own pre-election programme and, finally, the election alliance with a nationalist leader. However, it is highly unlikely that either Yeltsin or any other leader from the "state/democratic" group will be able to use the same tactic again in the future elections. By the mid-1990s the Russian political arena was already set for the left/nationalist victory and all political indicators pointed towards a conclusion that such a victory was only just a matter of time.

6.6   Russian nationalism and the search for a national idea

The changes in political attitudes of the Russian electorate in the post-Soviet period were mainly ideologically motivated. As Michael Urban noted, in Russia

> a discourse of identity forfeits from the outset the possibility of constructing some other nation onto which might be loaded the negative moment in the recreation of a national community. As a consequence, this negative moment has circulated through Russian politics

generally, informing the code of communication with the vexed categories of identity (and culpability), and transposing onto domestic conflicts the manichaean logic of unqualified nationalism.[31]

Shifts in political preferences of Russian voters were also indicative of the continuing process of search for an ideology (or a set of national symbols) that could bring unity and a clear sense of national identity to this deeply divided nation. Consolidation trends that appeared in the mid-1990s on the Russian political arena demonstrated that, on the one hand, this process was strengthening the division of the Russian society around the two major political groups (democratic-state and left-nationalist), each having a completely different social and economic agenda. On the other hand, however, the growing similarity of political programmes of these two groups, which became apparent during the 1996 presidential elections, also manifested that Russian political elites were essentially starting to share a common ideological ground.

During the last years of existence of the Soviet Union its' official ideology, Marxism–Leninism, was politically dead. In fact, it was the opposition to this ideology that brought unity into the ranks of the opposition. Anticommunist platform was shared by liberals and nationalists, extremists and fighters for religious freedoms. It was a powerful unifying ideological tool, but its' major drawback was that it could have been effective only until the time when the enemy – the Soviet state and the communist party rule – continued to exist. When in the late 1991 the Soviet Union collapsed and the communist party disintegrated, anti-communism had immediately started to lose its magnetism. Despite attempts of the Yeltsin regime to keep anticommunist rhetoric alive, the former unity in the opposition ranks was rapidly giving way to political fragmentation.

Within months after the collapse of the communist rule Russian liberals had formed numerous competing parties and organisations; the same happened to the left/nationalist opposition and the remnants of the Soviet communist party. In this situation the Yeltsin administration could no longer rely on a continued support from the united democratic bloc because it ceased to exist. However, Yeltsin realised that an association with any single party or movement would greatly limit the scope for future political manoeuvring and would eventually undermine his chances of staying in power. The only way to save his position at the top of the establishment was for Yeltsin to distance himself – politically but not necessarily ideologically – from his earlier support base which was now rapidly crumbling. The result was an appearance of the "above politics" attitude that by the mid-1990s became the dominant feature of the political platform of the Yeltsin regime.

The process of political fragmentation in post-Soviet Russia was also accompanied by a growing political indifference on part of the society. High levels of political enthusiasm of the masses that were characteristic of Russian developments in the late 1980s and the early 1990s, have started to give way to a growing confusion of the electorate when the Russian political arena became fragmented. That created a certain "political vacuum" when a large share of the population preferred to abstain from an active involvement in the political life. Although that seems to be a natural response of voters in a fragmented political environment, political indifference very soon started to transform into a growing political isolation of the ruling regime threatening its chances for political survival. To overcome that, the Yeltsin administration had to come up with new populist slogans that could unite a significant part of the electorate and help this regime to stay in power. Thus, just a few months after the collapse of the USSR the Russian leadership had started to actively search for a new national idea.

The official policy of the Yeltsin administration was always based on nationalism although that, until recently, was not recognised officially. However, in its development the Russian contemporary nationalism had passed several stages. In the early days of Russia's independent development, which followed the abortive August 1991 coup, policies of the Russian leadership were mainly framed around what can be called *"regionalist nationalism"*. This version of nationalism had its roots in political demands of regional elites that wished to acquire more independence from the central authority.[32] Because the latter was mainly associated with the Soviet Communist Party, "regionalist nationalism" was strongly anti-communist and anti-integrationist. Negation of the internationalist communist ideology led to the growth of the Russian nationalistic sentiment among Russia's ruling elite. New Russian leaders were at that time both rigid anti-communists and exponents of the ideas of "great Russia". Despite an apparent controversy, this "regionalist nationalism" was both pro-Russian and pro-Western. The West was viewed as a "natural ally" of Russian liberal nationalists in their struggle against communists whose attitudes were considered to be generally anti-nationalistic and anti-Western.

However, by the early 1993 it became clear that this version of nationalism could not fulfil one of its main objectives: it could not unify the Russian nation. Political and social differences between various factions of the Russian leadership, most notably expressed in emerging rifts between the President and the parliament, and between the centre and the periphery, were much stronger than the officially proclaimed policy of achieving unity of all Russians in the sake of re-building a "great Russia". During this second stage of development of the new Russian nationalism (1992–94) anti-communist and pro-Russian sentiments were gradually replaced by appeals to Russian traditions and cultural heritage. The change was to a large extent provoked by re-emergence of the Russian communist movement, which also attempted to combine communist ideology with nationalism.[33]

This *"heritage nationalism"* was aimed at finding grounds for national unity in the "great Russian history and culture". The earlier harsh criticism of the Soviet heritage started to give way to a policy which was based on drawing a dividing line between the Soviet "state" and the "people's" heritage. Everything Soviet was no longer automatically declared to be evil. At the same time attempts were made to link liberal ideology to Russian traditional values, thus presenting it as a part of the Russian popular heritage.

The split between communists (centrists) and anti-communists (regionalists) which was exposed in the growth of "regionalist nationalism" by 1993 in the official ideology was transformed into a distinction between "false" nationalists (like communists who were propagating internationalist ideas, alien to this understanding of the Russian heritage) and "true" Russian nationalists (anti-communists and liberals at the same time). Since that time the policy of "restoration" of traditional Russian values received a clear blessing from the state. "Traditionalist" actors, writers and publicists received a warm official welcome while the cash-strapped Russian state found large amounts of money to construct and rebuild heritage monuments.[34] In the centre of this traditionalist revival was the Russian Orthodox religion, its church, morals and traditions. It became fashionable for Russian political and business leaders to show their adherence to religion in public, despite the fact that many of them just a few years where communist party bureaucrats and, therefore, professional atheists.

By the mid-1994 Russia's search for a new national identity had received yet another twist when attempts on part of the Russian leadership to find unity in the Russian heritage failed to stop the growing split in the society. It became clear that "heritage nationalism" was incapable to halt the continued growth of "regionalist nationalism". Russian regional elites were demanding greater independence from

Kremlin, while separatist tendencies in some Russian regions (particularly in the North Caucasus) were stronger than ever before. This nationalist feeling was in the early 1990s successfully utilised by Yeltsin and other Soviet republican leaders as the major tool in dismantling of the Soviet (communist) centre. But by 1994 it was boomeranging back and threatening the existence of the united Russian state itself. In addition to that, official attempts to appeal to Russian heritage as a unifying factor had greatly stimulated the growth of imperialist sentiments inside Russia which, in their turn, provoked separatist and anti-Russian responses from non-Russian ethnic communities inside and outside Russia.

"Heritage nationalism", the same way as "regionalist nationalism" earlier, failed to strengthen the national unity in Russia mainly because it was based on dividing rather than unifying principles. Both versions of nationalism could only be effective when they targeted political enemies inside Russia, increasing, and not eliminating, existing divisions between regionalists and centrists, and between traditionalists and modernisers. The breakup of the Chechen War had clearly demonstrated that continuation of an official policy based on these divisions would lead to an extremely destructive result. In such a situation the only practical way to consolidate the nation and to reverse the process of Russia's further disintegration was to search for (or to invent) an external threat. It is important to stress that by the mid-1990s many opposition parties, including communists, industrialists and neo-fascists, already actively used this tactic. Steady growth of their popularity, on the one side, and the escalation of the conflict between central power and regional elites, on the other, have forced the Russian leadership to accept a new version of nationalism as its official ideological platform.

The new version of modern Russian nationalism was in many ways a logical continuation of "heritage nationalism". However, the focus of the latter was transformed from internal (Russia's history, traditions and culture) to external developments and was based on a clear-cut distinction between Russia (and its "unique" and "special" destiny) and the rest of the world. Russia's national interests were no longer seen by Russian leaders as necessarily coinciding with or even non-confrontational to the interests of other major powers, while strong nationalistic overtones in official statements that came from Kremlin had distanced the Russian leadership from its former Western allies. Although much of Yeltsin's nationalist rhetoric nothing more than a pre-election manoeuvre and was still far from becoming a real policy, it was a striking deviation from Yeltsin's earlier pro-democratic and generally pro-Western statements, signifying that by the time of the 1996 presidential elections the emerging *"anti-Western nationalism"*[35] was gradually becoming the third version of the post-Soviet Russian nationalism.

Anti-Western sentiments were gaining strength within the Russian leadership during the larger part of 1995; these sentiments received a significant boost in the official ideology after the success of left/nationalist opposition in the December 1995 parliamentary elections. However it were the 1996 presidential elections that cemented this process. The secret of Yeltsin's re-election could largely be attributed to his outstanding adaptation skills. By the time the final results of these elections were announced, Yeltsin had completely changed his earlier liberal/pro-Western image. He successfully imported nationalist rhetoric of his major opponents, presenting himself as a "true" Russian nationalist and anti-Westerner who was prepared for a resolute fight to establish the "law and order" and to keep the unity of the Russian state.[36] The only significant difference between Yeltsin and his main challenger, communist leader Zyuganov, was in their formal ideological platforms. While proclaiming basically the same (nationalist) policies, the two men held opposite views on the ideological colour of this nationalism. From that point of view the 1996 elections could be interpreted as a struggle between two variations of the same "anti-Western nationalism": one, based on the link between Marxism and the Russian "heritage nationalism", and the other derived from regionalists' anti-communism and the same "heritage nationalism".

After the presidential elections were over, the transformation of this new "anti-Western nationalism" into an official political platform of the Russian ruling elite was halted, although it was not dropped off completely. The need to maintain good relations with the West, the main financial donor of the Russian reform programme, forced Yeltsin to take a much more cautious approach on this matter. In addition to that, attempts by Yeltsin and his associates to consolidate the crumbling Russian nation through centralisation of state power along "great nation" lines were met by a growing resistance on part of regional elites which were the main winners of post-Soviet decentralisation.

By the time when in the late 1996 Yeltsin finally reappeared on the Russian political arena after a long period of illness, nationalistic and anti-Western overtones in his policy statements were no longer present. However, the ideological base of his regime remained extremely weak, while the process of disintegration of the Russian nation was still gaining pace. At the same time the erosion of moral and value systems in Russia was reaching dangerous levels.[37] Realising that the need to find a firm ground for national unity became acute as never before and that continuation of the political and ideological vacuum in Russia carried a potential of destroying his own regime, Yeltsin publicly called on authorities and the people "to generate a new ideology for the new Russia". Presidential aide Georgy Satarov was even given the responsibility to overlook the process of search "for the national idea", and the semi-official "Rossiiskaya gazeta" announced a contest for the best "Idea for Russia".[38]

In September 1997 Yeltsin's close associate, Russian vice-premier Boris Nemtsov, in a series of public interviews disclosed what the new "national idea" was about. Called *"people's capitalism"*, it was an ideology, which combined Western liberal values with the strife for a strong state and social protection. "People's capitalism" was seen as the next, democratic phase of Russia's capitalist development, which should follow the initial phase of "nomenklatura capitalism" and the current phase of "oligarchic capitalism".[39] The most important feature of this new ideology was its attempt to merge Western liberalism and a belief in market freedom with demands to re-install strong (central) state. The latter were a central point of "anti-Western nationalism"; however, in the ideology of "people's capitalism" the crucial anti-Western part of this version of Russian nationalism was taken out.

"People's capitalism" was a rather clumsy, controversial and generally unworkable solution to the Russian ideological crisis. The call for recreation of strong state, as proposed by authors of "people's capitalism", was in an open contradiction to their objective of a further liberalisation and decentralisation of the economy, while at the time when the weak and penniless Russian state could not fulfil its current social obligations, it was unrealistic to expect that it can afford to offer any additional social guarantees to its people.

"People's capitalism" was another utopia, very similar to the Bolshevik utopia of communism and also open to broad interpretations. Despite the fact that Yeltsin publicly endorsed the idea of "people's capitalism",[40] the public reaction to it was rather sceptical. For many Russians who politically and financially lost more in the reform years than they have gained, capitalism became firmly associated with its post-Soviet Russian version and all of its injustice, crime and evils. Therefore, any attempt to place capitalist ideals into the basis of a new national ideology in Russia was doomed to failure. This was soon realised by the Yeltsin administration. By the end of 1997 "people's capitalism" was no longer mentioned in any official statements that came from Kremlin. In December 1997 Yeltsin's former chief of staff, Sergei Filatov, convened a congress of Russian intellectuals, intelligentsia, and appealed for their support in defining the "national idea".[41]

Intensification of crisis tendencies in the Russian economy during 1998 moved the debate on the new "national idea" to the bottom of the list of political priorities. Political survival has become the major objective of Yeltsin and his close associates. The collapse of the Russian financial market in August 1998 had significantly undermined the credibility of the Russian political elite. Any ideology that was artificially created and promoted from the top of the political hierarchy even in the pre-August 1998 period was met with a great deal of scepticism both by the population and regional elites. But in the aftermath of the 1998 collapse it became clear that attempts to reconstruct or re-design a new national ideology were doomed to failure. Thus, by the end of 1998 this issue has completely disappeared from the Russian political agenda.[42]

Ideological weakness of the Yeltsin regime, as demonstrated by the lack of success in its attempts to find a "national idea", was indicative of a fundamental problem faced by Russian democrats in the post-Soviet era. This problem related to the rapid narrowing of their political base in the electorate at a time when the popularity of left/nationalist forces was on the rise. Incorporation of "anti-Western nationalism" into his election programme helped Yeltsin to ensure victory in the 1996 presidential elections. However, this political move could not be a lasting one, because any practical steps aimed at pursuing of an anti-Western policy and at recreation of a strong state would immediately alienate Yeltsin's major supporters: Western leaders and Russian regional elites. Forced to abandon its support for the growing Russian nationalism, the Yeltsin regime in the post-1996 period continued to slip into a deeper political isolation. At the same time nationalist sentiments among the Russian electorate were growing stronger while proponents of the new Russian nationalism, like Moscow mayor Yuri Luzhkov and General Alexandr Lebed, were receiving a massive support.

Despite the crucial role that it can play in Russian nation-building, national unity alone will not be enough for ensuring a lasting stability that Russia desperately needs. The lack of a sound programme of social and economic reconstruction that forms the basis of official policy is a much more serious problem which is harder to tackle than many ideological issues. The absence of such a programme in the future can lead to a situation when some of Russia's "heritage values", including adherence to an authoritarian rule,[43] might gain dominant position over "imported" liberal values that Russian nationalists already claim to be in conflict with the Russian culture and traditions. And these "imported" values might well include economic liberalism, political rights and freedoms, and a multiparty democracy.

Notes

1. I use the notion of "negotiations" in a broad sense, i.e. as a synonym of a negotiated settlement. In practice, a political transition may not necessarily include a *single* and *prolonged* process of constitutional talks/negotiations (like, for instance, in the South African case in 1992–94). Instead, it can be realised through a *series* of *relatively short* talks as it were in the post-Soviet case in Russia, where constitutional talks, that continued no more than 4 months at each given year, were held in 1990, 1991, 1992 and 1993.

2. The role of nomenklatura in the modern Russian transition has been in the centre of a number of recent studies, particularly those by Olga Kryshtanovskaya. See: O. V. Kryshtanovskaya, "Transformatsiya staroi nomenklatury v novuyu rossiiskuyu elitu", *Obshestvennye nauki i sovremennost'*, No.1, 1995, (p.64); O. Kryshtanovskaya, "Finansovaya oligarkhiya v Rossii", *Izvestia*, 10 January 1996; Olga Kryshtanovskaya, Stephen White, "From Soviet *nomenklatura* to Russian élite", *Europe–Asia Studies*, Vol.48, No.5, July 1996, pp.711–734; N. V. Petrov, "Politicheskie elity v tsentre i na mestakh", *Rossiiskii monitor*, No.5, 1995; James Hughes, "Sub-national élites and post-communist transformation in Russia: a reply to Kryshtanovskaya & White", *Europe–Asia Studies*, Vol.49, No.6, September 1997, pp.1017–1036; Nikolai Rabotyazhev, "K voprosy o genezise i sushnosti nomenklaturnogo kapitalizma v Rossii", *Mirovaya ekonomika i mezhdunarodnye otnosheniya*, No.1, 1998, pp.38–51.

3. "Internationalism" as an ideology formed the core of the national policy pursued by Soviet communists since the formation of the USSR. In theory, "internationalism" was viewed by Soviet ideologues as a force, which was in irreconcilable opposition to "nationalism", considered to be a destructive force and a major obstacle to the "social progress". But in practice, the policy of Soviet leaders was to a large extent continuation of the imperial policy of the Tsarist Russia. The political, cultural and ethnic dominance of the Russian (Slav) nation formed the basis of this policy. While providing significantly more cultural and language freedoms to non-Slavic nations, Soviet leaders insured that all major levers of political and economic management in the Soviet Union were controlled by Russians (and other Slavs). This control was part and parcel of the dominating "unionist" policy, which was aimed at strengthening of a highly centralised union-state rather than a loosely unified federal state. The unionist, pro-integration policies were so effective that it was not until 1990 that a Russian faction was finally formed in what was the major power structure in the country: the Communist Party itself. By that time all other Soviet republics had long

established their own parties. These were formally headed by representatives from local ethnic groups, but in practice were managed by their deputies, all of which were ethnic Slavs. See also article by Dominic Lieven on "The Russian empire and the Soviet Union as imperial polities", *Journal of Contemporary History*, Vol.30, No.4, October 1995, pp.607–636.

4. Reports in *Vlast' i ekonomika* (Post-Factum), 18 September 1995, and *Monitor*, 18 August 1995. See also Susan J. Linz, "Red executives in Russia's transition economy", *Post-Soviet Geography and Economics*, Vol.37, No.10, December 1996, pp.633–651.

5. Since 1985, through his continued support for the policy of *perestroika* Gorbachev put many of state and party bureaucrats into a situation of growing uncertainty on the nature, content and final goals of reforms that he initiated. That provoked the start of a rapid decline of the power of the union political structures. The state and the party power became increasingly disseminated among a variety of local, regional, republican, ethnic and other groups and organisations. This weakness of the central power precluded the formal disintegration of the Soviet Union. See Robert J. Kaiser. *The Geography of Nationalism in Russia and the USSR*, Princeton, NJ: Princeton University Press, 1994.

6. Theodore Friedgut, Jeffrey Hahn (eds.), *Local Power and Post-Soviet Politics*, Armonk: M. E. Sharpe, 1994.

7. See Robert J.Kaiser, "Prospects for the disintegration of the Russian Federation", *Post-Soviet Geography and Economics*, Vol.36, No.7, September 1995, pp.426–435; Jean Radvanyi, "And what if Russia breaks up? Towards new regional divisions", *Post-Soviet Geography and Economics*, Vol.33, No.2, February 1992, pp.69–77.

8. Vladimir Shlapentokh, "Early feudalism – the best parallel for contemporary Russia", *Europe–Asia Studies*, Vol.48, No.3, May 1996, pp.393–412.

9. For some recent reports and analysis of the growth of separatist tendencies in Russian regions see: Charles M. Becker and David D. Hemley, "Interregional inequality in Russia during the transition period", *Comparative Economic Studies*, Vol.38, No.1, Spring 1996; Gerald M. Easter, "Redefining centre-regional relations in the Russian Federation: Sverdlovsk Oblast'", *Europe–Asia Studies*, Vol.49, No.4, June 1997, pp.617–636; Kamil Ivanov, "Razlichiya mezdu regionami ugrozhayut bezopasnosti Rossii", *Ekonomika i zhizn'*, 1997, No.8; Aleksandr Kasimov, "A diamond set in gold: the Republic of Sakha. Big money as a factor in big-time politics", *Prism*, Special Issue, Part 3, December 1996; Daniel R. Kempton, "The Republic of Sakha (Yakutia): the evolution of centre-periphery relations in the Russian Federation", *Europe-Asia Studies*, Vol.48, No.4, June 1996, pp.587–614; Peter Kirkow, "Distributional coalitions, budgetary problems and fiscal federalism in Russia", *Communist Economies & Economic Transformation*, Vol.8, No.3, September 1996, pp.277–298; Peter Kirkow, "Local self-government in Russia: awakening from slumber?", *Europe–Asia Studies*, Vol.49, No.1, January 1997, pp.43–58; Peter Kirkow, "Russia's regional puzzle: institutional change and economic adaptation", *Communist Economies & Economic Transformation*, Vol.9, No.3, September 1997, pp.261–288; Vladimir Mau and Vadim Stupin, "The political economy of Russian regionalism", *Communist Economies & Economic Transformation*, Vol.9, No.1, March 1997,

pp.5–26; Anna Paretskaya, "Russian central authorities seek new formula for relations with the regions", *OMRI Analytical Brief*, No.460, 13 November 1996; Judith Perera, Andrei Ivanov, "Resource-rich Tyumen region faces breakup... and poverty", *InterPress Service (IPS)*, 3 December 1996; "Russia: regional results", *OAEEDB*, 11 April 1997; Denis J. B. Shaw, "Bids for autonomy by Northern regions of the Russian Federation", *Post-Soviet Geography and Economics*, Vol.34, No.5, May 1993, pp.319–321; "Urals governors denounce federal government", *OMRI*, No.27, 7 February 1997.

10. Alexander Krylovich, "Thirty-five Russian regions are building their relations with the federal centre on a treaty basis", *RIA-Novosti*, 30 October 1997.

11. In 1997 there were only eight donor-regions in Russia: Moscow, Lipetsk, Samara, and Sverdlovsk oblasts, Krasnoyarsk krai, Bashkortostan, and the Khanty Mansi and Yamal Nenets autonomous areas in Western Siberia (*Rossiiskie vesti*, 6 August 1997).

12. The rise of separatism is not the only manifestation of the growth of popular support of various extremist tendencies in post-Soviet Russia. In other poor regions, where there are no special historical, political or ethnic grounds for demanding independence, it is anti-separatist (or pro-"strong government") views that were rapidly gaining popularity during the 1990s. See Andrei Ryabov, "Rost politicheskogo ekstremizma v Rossii", *Vek*, No.35, September 1997.

13. James Alexander, "Uncertain conditions in the Russian transition: the popular drive towards stability in a 'stateless' environment", *Europe–Asia Studies*, Vol.50, No.3, May 1998, pp.415–444.

14. See V. A. Kolosov, N. V. Petrov, L. V. Smirniagin (eds.), *Vesna-89: Geografia i anatomiya parlamentskikh vyborov*, Moscow: Progress, 1990. For an excellent recent overview of Russian regional politics see Jerry F. Hough, "The political geography of European Russia: republics and oblasts", *Post-Soviet Geography and Economics*, Vol.38, No.2, February 1998, pp.63–95.

15. See: Sergei Chugrov, "O regionalnoi fragmentatsii rossiiskogo politicheskogo soznaniya", *Mirovaya ekonomika i mezhdunarodnye otnosheniya*, No.1, 1998, p.31; Darrell Slider, Vladimir Gimpel'son, Sergei Chugrov, p.720.

16. Ibid.; Ralph S. Clem, Peter R. Craumer, "The geography of the April 25 (1993) Russian referendum", *Post-Soviet Geography and Economics*, Vol.34, No.8, October 1993, pp.481–496.

17. For a detailed overview of regional voting patterns in the December 1993 elections see: Darrell Slider, Vladimir Gimpel'son, Sergei Chugrov, "Political tendencies in Russia's regions: evidence from the 1993 parliamentary elections", *Slavic Review*, Vo.53, No.3, Fall 1994, pp.711–732; Ralph S. Clem, Peter R. Craumer, "The politics of Russia's regions: a geographical analysis of the Russian election and constitutional plebiscite of December 1993", *Post-Soviet Geography and Economics*, Vol.36, No.2, February 1995, pp.67–86; Lisa A. Baglione and Carol C. Clark, "Participation and the success of economic and political reforms: a lesson from the 1993 Russian parliamentary elections", *The Journal of Communist Studies and Transition Politics*, Vol.11, No.3, September 1995.

18. Although the division of Russian political parties into these two categories makes our main argument clearer, we fully recognise that there were

significant differences in programs and in policies of parties within each category. See also Darrell Slider, Vladimir Gimpel'son, Sergei Chugrov, pp.715–717.

19. Sergei Chugrov, "O regionalnoi fragmentatsii rossiiskogo politicheskogo soznaniya", *Mirovaya ekonomika i mezhdunarodnye otnosheniya*, No.1, 1998, p.34.

20. These elections were in the focus of a number of recent studies. See: Sergei Chugrov, "Elektoralnoe povedenie rossiiskikh regionov: statisticheskii analiz itogov vyborov dekabrya 1995 g.", *Mirovaya ekonomika i mezhdunarodnye otnosheniya*, No.6, 1996; Ralph S. Clem, Peter R. Craumer, "The geography of the Russian 1995 parliamentary election: continuity, change, and correlates", *Post-Soviet Geography and Economics*, Vol.36, No.10, December 1995, pp.587–616; M. Steven Fish, "The predicament of Russian liberalism: evidence from the December 1995 parliamentary elections", *Europe–Asia Studies*, Vol.2, March 1997, pp.191–220; John O'Loughlin, Michael Shin, Paul Talbot, "Political geographies and cleavages in the Russian parliamentary elections", *Post-Soviet Geography and Economics*, Vol.37, No.6, June 1996, pp.355–385; Ian McAllister, Stephen White and Olga Kryshanovskaya, "Voting and party support in the December 1995 Duma elections", *The Journal of Communist Studies and Transition Politics*, Vol.13, No.1, March 1997; Vladimir Tikhomirov, "New political balance in Russia: an analysis of the December 1995 Russian parliamentary elections", *Russian and Euro-Asian Economics Bulletin*, Vol.5, No.1, January 1996, pp.1–4; Steven White, "The 1995 elections to the Russian State Duma", *The Journal of Communist Studies and Transition Politics*, Vol.13, No.1, March 1997; Stephen White, Matthew Wyman & Sarah Oates, "Parties and voters in the 1995 Russian Duma election", *Europe–Asia Studies*, Vol.49, No.5, July 1997, pp.767–798; Matthew Wyman, "Development in Russian voting behaviour: 1993 and 1995 compared", *The Journal of Communist Studies and Transition Politics*, Vol.12, No.2, June 1996.

21. Various newspaper and cable wire reports between 10th and 17th of September, 1995.

22. For some recent commentries on the type of political system in post-Soviet Russia see: Vitaly Tretyakov, "Kommunizm, fashizm ili diktatura 'Partii vlasti'?", *Nezavisimaya gazeta*, 21 May 1998; "State of Russian democracy leaves something to be desired", *Monitor*, Vol. IV, No.100, 26 May 1998.

23. Richard Sakwa, "Subjectivity, politics and order in Russian political evolution", *Slavic Review*, Vol.54, No.4, Winter 1995, p.962.

24. Under the 1993 constitution it becomes very difficult, if not at all impossible, for the parliament to impeach the president, provided that the upper house of the parliament, the Federation Council, consists mainly of president's supporters and nominees. On the other hand, the president can fairly easily dissolve the parliament and announce new elections. He also can also override parliamentary decisions and has the right to issue decrees to substitute laws until the parliament passes the latter. The president also nominates (and dismisses) all members of the Russian government. The prime minister is nominated by the president and then has to be supported by the lower house of the parliament, the *Duma*. For a recent detailed study of the 1993 Russian constitution see: Lee Kendall Metcalf, "Presidential

Power in the Russian Constitution", *Journal of Transnational Law & Policy,* Vol.6, No.1, Spring 1996.

25. See, for instance, reports in *Kommersant-Daily,* 23 April 1996, *Nezavisimaya gazeta,* 11 April 1996, *Izvestia,* 21 June 1996.

26. See *Interfax Daily News Report,* 9 May 1996.

27. For a more detailed overview of these elections see: Sergei Chugrov, "O regionalnoi fragmentatsii rossiiskogo politicheskogo soznaniya", *Mirovaya ekonomika i mezhdunarodnye otnosheniya,* No.1, 1998, pp.29–41; Sarah Oates, "Regional support in the 1996 Russian presidential elections", *The Journal of Communist Studies and Transition Politics,* Vol.13, No.1, March 1997; A. V. Oblonsky, "Paradoxes of Russian political development", *The Journal of Communist Studies and Transition Politics,* Vol.13, No.1, March 1997; John Lowenhardt, "The 1996 presidential elections in Tartarstan", *The Journal of Communist Studies and Transition Politics,* Vol.13, No.1, March 1997; Marie Mendras, "Interpreting the Russian elections: Yeltsin and the Great Divide in Russian society", *East European Constitutional Review,* Vol.5, Nos.2–3, Spring–Summer 1996, pp.51–63; Stephen White, Richard Rose, Ian McAllister, *How Russia Votes,* London: Chatham House Publishers, 1997.

28. Moscow, Karelia, Sakha, St Petersburg, Perm', Kemerovo, Tyumen', Irkutsk and Kamchatka.

29. Arkhangelsk, Kaluga, Moscow Oblast', Krasnodarskii Krai, Udmurtia, Omsk, Tomsk and Magadan.

30. Pskov, Vladimir, Ivanovo, Ryazan', Marii El, Mordovia, Tambov, Kalmykia, Penza, Ulyanovsk, Dagestan. Rostov and Kurgan.

31. Michael Urban, "The politics of identity in Russia's postcommunist transition: the nation against itself", *Slavic Review,* Vo.53, No.3, Fall 1994, pp.733–734.

32. For one of the first discussions of that phenomenon see Rastam Narzikulov, "New privileges: post-perestroika variant", *Moscow Times,* No.42, 18–25 October 1992, pp.10–11.

33. Amending itself to the growing nationalist wave in the Russian society, the Russian Communist Party even dropped atheism as one of its core policy principles while its leader Zyuganov was publicly baptised.

34. For more on the nationalist revival in Russia see Stephen G.Wheatcroft, "History in Russia since the unleashing of the energy of history (January 1987) and the fall of the USSR (December 1991): ten years on the archive and historical front, 1987–1996", pp.92–129, and Henrietta Mondry, "'Political philology': nationalism in the Russian literary press (1993–1996)", pp.133–141. Both articles in Vladimir Tikhomirov (ed.), *In Search of Identity: Five Years Since the Fall of the Soviet Union,* Melbourne: CRE-AS, 1996. See also Vera Tolz, "The national debate over nation-building in post-communist Russia", *Prism,* Vol.4, No.10, 15 May 1998, Part 2.

35. Some Russian observers prefer to call it "state nationalism" (*gosudarstvennyi natsionalizm*). This term stresses the priority given by proponents of this version of nationalism to interests of the state as distinct from interests of various factions within the Russian leadership or society. Although this interpretation does not imply that Russian state interests should necessarily collide with the interests of any particular foreign power, recent developments in Russia demonstrate that it is the spread of Western influence

(often understood in the most general terms) that supporters of this new Russian nationalism want to halt more than anything else.

36. Although much of this nationalist talk came not from Yeltsin, but from his new Security Advisor General Lebed, by placing Lebed into a prominent position and by giving him a free hand in interpreting his policies, Yeltsin had thus informally approved of this change.

37. See Mikhail Gorshkov, "Economic and psychological crisis erodes Russian mentality", *Nezavisimaya Gazeta-Scenarios (RIA-Novosti)*, No.6, June 1997.

38. Anna Ostapchuk and Yevgeniy Krasnikov, "'Kreml' posetila ideya", *Moskovskie novosti*, No.38, 21–28 September 1997.

39. See *Moskovskie novosti*, No.38, 21–28 September 1997; "Committed to democratic capitalism: IC interview with Boris Nemtsov", 25 September 1997, *www.intellectualcapital.com*; "Popular capitalism in Russia?", *Monitor*, Vol.3, No.182, 1 October 1997; "Russian deputy premier favors revival of Russian nation", *Interfax*, 3 October 1997.

40. *Moscow Times*, 26 September 1997.

41. Kathy Lally, "Russia, short on ideas, looks to intelligentsia", *Baltimore Sun*, 8 December 1997.

42. The 1998 economic crisis was also accompanied by a considerable growth of political and social instability in the country. As a result, in the last months of 1998 the level of confrontation among opposing factions of the Russian elite was increasing rapidly, prompting the government to appeal for a "political peace". In early 1999 Russian government announced that it has developed a programme to fight political extremism. A few weeks later that was followed by a statement made by Prime Minister Primakov in which he proposed to sign a treaty on "political stability" between the president, the parliament and the government. However, these appeals had very little effect (see *Monitor*, Vol.5, No.3, 6 January 1999; *RFE-RL Newsline*, Vol.3, No.18, 27 January 1999, Part I).

43. For a recent discussion of this subject see Grigorii Vainshtein, "The authoritarian idea in the public consciousness and political life of contemporary Russia", *The Journal of Communist Studies and Transition Politics*, Vol.11, No.3, September 1995, pp.272–285; Frederic J. Fleron, Jr., "Post-Soviet political culture in Russia: an assessment of recent empirical investigations", *Europe–Asia Studies*, Vol.48, No.2, March 1996, pp.225–260.

7
Conclusion

Throughout its modern history Russia has always been a deeply divided and unequal society. Even during the period of communist rule, despite the proclaimed principles of equality and social justice in "the state of workers and peasants", the Russian society remained highly stratified in political (access to power), social and ethnic terms. In the last decades of the Soviet rule this stratification was extended to include the growing income inequality.

With the collapse of the Soviet Union and the start of Russia's attempts to reform, the removal of a system of state-imposed controls over many areas of social and economic activity has led to the rapid growth of internal divisions in Russia. By the mid-1990s these divisions had evolved into serious contradictions between Russia's rich and poor, between the elite and the people, and between better-off and worse-off regions. All of these contradictions make the current political situation in Russia highly unstable and unpredictable. There remains a constant possibility of the emergence of a new conflict that might come in various forms from a political revolt to a social upheaval or a nationalist (separatist) upsurge.

The increase in social and political tensions within the Russian society has been taking place against the background of a major economic crisis. This created a situation when interrelation between negative political and economic trends has led Russia into a vicious circle of crisis development. Each political crises had a devastating effect on the economy, while a crisis of the economy, in its turn, destabilised the future political situation even further. Crime levels were on the increase, social inequality was spreading throughout Russia and society was becoming more and more violent. As Perotti recently noted a highly unequal, polarized distribution of resources creates strong incentives for organized individuals to pursue their interests outside the normal market activities or the usual channels of political representation. Thus, in more unequal societies individuals are more prone to engage in rent-seeking activities or other manifestations of sociopolitical instability, such as violent protests, assassinations, and coups.[1]

The growth of influence of various extremist forces in the Russian political life in recent years has also come as a response to the growing crisis of the national economy. One-sided, unfinished and often politically biased measures, through which Russian reformists attempted to transform the Soviet system of economic management, have greatly accelerated the development of this crisis and led to a formation of what Peter Rutland called a "schizophrenic economy".[2]

Until 1997 the Russian economy was not showing any signs of growth. In the first two years of the post-Soviet reform (1992–93) government actions were largely paralysed by the strong anti-reform opposition in the parliament. The conflict between the executive and legislature reached its peak in the autumn of 1993. The adoption of the new Russian constitution in December 1993, which put most of the state power into the hands of the president, resolved the earlier political conflict and, at least theoretically, has opened the way for the continuation of the stalled reform.

That, however, did not happen. In Table 7.1, I have put together some major indicators of Russian economic, financial and social developments during the five years (1993–97). According to data from *Goskomstat*, presented in this table, in 1997 the earlier negative trend in Russia's economic growth was finally reversed when GDP has registered a small growth for the first tome since the collapse of the USSR. This growth, however, clearly contradicts some other data in the same table. For instance, since 1993 there were no real signs of recovery or significant growth in the two basic sectors of the Russian economy, industry and agriculture. This continuing fall in output has led to a serious contraction in the taxation base of the government, with the gross volume of unpaid taxes increasing by 1.6 times between 1993 and 1997. As it was revealed recently, GDP growth figures were derived by Russian statisticians through increasing their estimates of the share of the shadow economy in the gross domestic product. In 1997 this share was estimated as 23%, a significant rise from 20% in previous years. Because no recalculations were made for the earlier period, this

Table 7.1   Some General Indicators of Russia's Performance in 1993–97

	1993	1994	1995	1996	1997
Gross Domestic Product					
Dynamics of GDP, 1993 = 100[a]	100.0	87.4	83.9	78.9	79.2
Annual change, %	–12.0	–13.0	–4.0	–6.0	0.4
Federal Budget					
Revenues, 1993 = 100[ab]	100.0	113.0	108.3	93.0	90.2
as % of planned	...	69.0	106.3	81.2	74.3
Expenditure, 1993 = 100[a]	100.0	98.9	65.6	58.6	57.0
as % of planned	...	57.0	96.8	81.5	77.3
Budget deficit, 1993 = 100[a]	100.0	85.0	23.1	24.4	24.0
as % of expenditure	50.1	43.1	17.7	20.9	21.1
as % of GDP	10.7	10.4	2.9	3.3	3.2
Deficit covered by (% to total):					
Internal bonds (incl. GKO-OFZ)	0.9	9.0	40.7	55.2	38.2
Foreign borrowing	12.4	14.9	52.2	44.8	61.8
Credits of the RCB	86.7	76.1	7.2	0.0	0.0
State Borrowing					
Foreign debt in US$, 1993 = 100[c]	100.0	118.8	129.7	123.9	136.6
Gross sales of internal bond notes (GKO-OFZ) in US$, 1993 = 100	100.0	1 328.0	10 053.2	25 052.7	23 840.2
Principal & interest repayments on foreign credits in US$, 1993 = 100	100.0	142.9	485.9	685.3	...
Rescheduled debt payments as % of all repayments due	...	25.4	38.5	...	...
Overdue Social Payments					
Gross wage arrears, 1993 = 100[ac]	100.0	123.4	143.4	349.2	330.1
Unpaid wages as % of gross monthly wage fund in all national economy	7.7	17.3	27.1	85.7	66.7

Table 7.1 *continued*

	1993	1994	1995	1996	1997
Performance of the Economy					
Industrial output, 1993 = 100	100.0	78.5	76.1	71.9	73.3
Agricultural output, 1993 = 100	100.0	88.0	80.9	75.3	75.3
Gross volume of unpaid taxes, 1993 = 100[ac]	100.0	80.5	94.7	135.5	162.7
Inter-enterprise debt, 1993 = 100[ac]	100.0	37.1	33.6	50.1	61.7
Dynamics of capital flight, 1993 = 100	100.0	150.4	141.2	157.3	152.7
Social Dynamics					
Average income:[c]					
in US dollars, 1993 = 100	100.0	85.0	202.0	262.9	289.7
in constant prices, 1993 = 100[a]	100.0	112.0	97.9	97.9	101.3
Unemployment, 1993 = 100[cd]	100.0	131.7	154.6	163.5	153.8
CPI, % of annual change[a]	940.0	315.0	231.0	121.6	111.0

NOTES:

[a] In constant prices. Calculated using GDP deflators.
[b] Russian statistics on revenues of the federal budget include internal and foreign loans.
[c] As at the end of the year.
[d] ILO methodology.

change resulted in a sudden growth in Russia's GDP indicators in 1997.[3]

Despite these statistical inaccuracies, it should be noted that in 1993–97 the Russian government had managed to reach significant progress in some areas, particularly in the spheres of finance and monetary policy. The rate of inflation during that period has fallen dramatically from 9.4 times in 1993 to just 1.1 times in 1997. Deficit of the federal budget has been reduced by more than four times. Dynamics of average income in constant prices and in US dollar equivalent indicated that the real exchange rate of rouble to US dollar has grown by almost three times in 1993–97.

However, these achievements came at the expense of many other important areas. While budgetary revenues in 1997 remained at approximately the same level as in 1993, the expenditure has fallen almost twice. The latter meant that many state employees were regularly not being paid their salaries in time. The gross volume of unpaid wages in the national economy in 1997 was 3.3 times higher than in 1993. The earlier practice of covering budgetary deficit through printing of the money (or issuing of credits by the Russian Central Bank) was completely halted by 1996, while the additional budgetary funding was now coming solely from state borrowing. Between 1993 and 1997 Russia's foreign debt increased by more than one-third. At the same time internal debt has grown many-fold, reaching in early 1998 US$65 billion[4] or about a half of the gross external debt. In 1997 issues of internal bond notes were almost 240 times higher than in 1993 (Table 7.1). By 1997 the gross volume of state borrowing had reached dangerous levels. In May 1998 Deputy Finance Minister Vladimir Petrov was quoted as saying that Russia was in no position to take any additional loans, because by the year 2000 repayments of the current state debt will constitute about 70% of the Russian budgetary expenditure.[5]

The crisis that erupted in the Russian economy in August 1998 signified the collapse of one of the major achievements of the Russian reform – the stability of its financial and monetary systems. During just one month of August 1998 the fall in the exchange rate of the national currency, the rouble, to US dollar was comparable to the change during the preceding two-and-a-half years. Between the end of July and the end of December 1998 rouble/US dollar rate increased by 3.3 times, while between the end of 1995 and July 1998 the increase in the rate was only 1.3 times.[6] The spread of financial crisis has left Russian reformists, who still continued to blame the pro-communist opposition for failures in the domestic policy, with almost no arguments that could support a thesis of even partial success of the Russian reform. The collapse of the national monetary and banking system, highly controversial and, from an economic point of view, overtly inefficient privatisation, total disarray in what was left of the Soviet state sector and management structures, crisis in the agriculture which resulted in critical dependence of Russia on foreign food and aid supplies, political apathy of voters and their total disillusionment in the strategy of reforms against the background of rapidly increasing extremism and nationalism – these were just a few results of the Russian reformist experiments in the 1990s.

It can be stated, however, that economic problems of contemporary Russia to a large extent were caused by political factors. With the exception of hard-line communists, most of whom operate outside the Russian communist party, very few in Russia have questioned the need of transformation and restructuring of the Soviet state-run economy. However, the lack of progress in achieving of this major goal points out to the fact that it was as important to identify the aim of transformation, as to outline a clear strategy of reaching it and to ensure that implementation of this strategy will be supported by a certain level of political consensus in the society. However, the latter were the two most important areas where the Yeltsin administration had failed to reach any success. Instead of political consensus, the Russian establishment throughout all years of reform was torn apart by an ongoing confrontation. This included a whole set of conflicts between the executive and the legislature, between the centre and the periphery, between major political trends and even inside them, between rich and poor, both in social and geographic terms, and within the business community as well as within other important social strata.

Many of these conflicts appeared as a result of weakening of the central state power, particularly in the first years of the reform. That had seriously destabilised Russian political structures and eventually led to the rise of new authoritarianism in the 1993 constitution. Since 1993 the Russian political system had largely lost its internal mechanism of development and became increasingly inflexible. Any significant political move in Russia became dependent, and in many cases could only come from one man, president Yeltsin. The future of the Russian reform also became a hostage to Yeltsin's mood and choices of advisers, while economic fluctuations in the recent years tended to copy cardiograms of Yeltsin's heart.

The profound mistake first made by Soviet and then Russian reformists was in believing that the establishment of political (multiparty) democracy could and will significantly foster the implementation of the economic reform. According to recent studies in the theory of economic growth, there cannot be found "any difference in the growth performance of democracies compared to nondemocracies". However, empirical evidence suggests that

> [p]olitical instability reduces growth. This result is particularly strong for the case of unconstitutional executive changes such as coups, as well for changes that significantly changes the ideological composition of the executive. The effect of instability on growth is less strong for the regular and frequent turnovers typical of industrial democracies. ... Finally the occurrence of a government change increases the likelihood of subsequent changes, suggesting that political instability tends to be persistent.[7]

Attempts in Russia to implement a broad political reform along with a deep transformation of the national economy had greatly incapacitated the ability of reformists to pursue any radical reforms, whether political or economic. The adoption of the 1993 constitution indicated that the Yeltsin government was ready to sacrifice some earlier democratic gains and to turn to increasingly non-democratic ways of rule as the means of promoting a radical economic reform. However, the growing political isolation of reformists, which was demonstrated by the results of parliamentary elections held on the same day when the new constitution was adopted, forced them to seek ways of retaining their power base, at least within the establishment. The support of Yeltsin's policies by regional leaders became the most crucial factor in the survival of his regime.

The rise of regionalism in the post-Soviet Russia has undermined the authority of federal structures even further. Moreover, through its reliance on the support of regional leaders the central government has become a hostage to their demands for more and more independence. The spread of the economic crisis made the existing differences in socio-economic performance between regions even deeper and in recent years have led to widening of the gap in political preferences between the regions (Table 7.2). Voting patterns in the first round of the 1996 presidential elections indicated towards an emerging split in regional political attitudes of the Russian electorate, when the support of democratic and pro-state parties was becoming increasingly limited to main metropolitan areas of Russia ("manufacturing group") while the rest of the electorate was giving preferences to left and nationalist

Table 7.2   **Economic and Political Development of Groups of Regions**

a) Dynamics of economic and social development in 1997 (as % of 1990)

	Industrial output	Agricultural output	Investment	Per capita income
Mining regions	61.6	69.4	30.7	102.7
Manufacturing regions	40.0	70.7	25.8	69.5
Agricultural regions	51.6	53.0	20.8	58.4

b) Political preferences, June 1996 (as % of all votes cast)

	Democratic/state parties	Left/nationalist parties
Mining regions	32.2	58.2
Manufacturing regions	55.8	40.4
Agricultural regions	30.4	66.7

movements and organisations. However, even within their major support areas the total vote for pro-state parties in 1996 was significantly lower than in 1993.

The growing political isolation of the Yeltsin regime has prompted it to modify its political strategy in the course of and after the 1996 presidential elections. However, that again placed the issue of implementation of a radical economic reform on the bottom of the government's priority list. Although economic issues have been in the centre of state policy ever since the early 1992, an analysis of government's reform efforts suggests that until late 1998 there was no clearly defined and realistic strategy of reform. In effect, all of the post-Soviet reform attempts in Russia were never completed. The only significant reform results that the Russian government can put to its credit include liberalisation of prices and trade in 1992, an extremely dividing and controversial privatisation of 1992–97, and the fiscal stabilisation of 1995–97. Any positive effects that the latter two reforms might have had were, however, washed away by the August 1998 crisis. Even in their initial phases these reforms had serious side effects, like significant falls in the population living standards, growth of the shadow economy and the general criminalisation of the Russian economy, increase in illegal export of capital from Russia, accumulation of wage arrears, rise of the levels of indebtedness of the Russian state, etc. And, most importantly for the future, these reform measures significantly accelerated the growth of social and political divisions within the Russian society.

An analysis of Russian strategies adopted since the start of the reform in 1992 suggests that their major goals were the breakup of the Soviet system of economic management (privatisation, decentralisation and demonopolisation) and stabilisation of the financial situation in Russia. These measures coincided with a type of advice that the Russian government was constantly receiving from some of its major donors, foremost the International Monetary Fund. By the mid-1990s most of these goals were reached. Inflation rates have significantly fallen, while the value of the Russian national currency was rising rapidly. Privatisation of state property was entering its final stages, while decentralisation of economic activities has reached levels beyond which it was starting to threaten the political and economic unity of the Russian state. Demonopolisation of major corporations was also progressing, albeit slowly, due to a fierce opposition to such measures both within their management and within the Russian political system.

However, even before the August 1998 crisis it became clear that these achievements had a very limited effect on the general development of the Russian economy, which continued its uninterrupted fall. It is my strong belief that many current problems in Russia and much of sufferings of its people come from the fact that Russian reformists had adopted a fundamentally wrong strategy of reform. Instead of concentrating their efforts on the transformation of the basics – the economic structure that Russia inherited from the Soviet Union and on stimulating the local production, reforms were aimed at mostly cosmetic changes to the ownership of Russian companies. Any serious structural change of the economy demands significant volumes of investment, but instead financial resources were decentralised, privatised and diverted from the production sphere, while foreign credits were mostly wasted. Prospects for modernisation of the Russian economy and the development of new technologies were also seriously undermined with the *de facto* collapse of the Russian scientific and R&D potential.

Contrary to some recent observations,[8] this study suggests that there is a strong and direct interrelation between economic and political developments in post-Soviet Russia. The spread of economic crisis has played a crucial role in polarisation and radicalisation of the Russian political life. In turn, the weaker the Russian economy was, the more dependent it became on the outcome of political developments. Political favouritism was gradually replacing a sound economic strategy, the same way as since 1993 the future of a multiparty democracy in Russia fell more and more into the shadow of the Russian imperial authoritarianism. Given recent changes in political attitudes of the Russian population, it can be stated that by the end of 1998 Russia was even farther away from achieving its initial reform objectives, than it was at the very start of reform in 1992.

Notes

1. Perotti, Roberto, "Growth, income distribution, and democracy: what the data say", *Journal of Economic Growth*, Vol.1, No.1, June 1996, p.151.
2. Rutland, Peter, "Russia's unsteady entry into the global economy", *Current History*, Vol.95, No.603, October 1996.
3. *The Financial Times*, 25 March 1997.
4. *Russia Notes*, 28 May 1998.
5. Georgy Osipov, "Pravitel'stvo raskololos' v ozhidanii katastrofy", *Segodnya*, 8 May 1998, p.1.
6. Calculated from various issues of *Sotsial'no-ekonomicheskoe polozhenie Rossii*, 1996–99.
7. Alesina, A., Ozler, S., Roubini, N., and Swagel, Ph., "Political instability and economic growth", *Journal of Economic Growth*, Vol.1, No.1, June 1996, p.205.
8. See Michael McFaul, "Russia: the sky has not fallen", *Washington Post*, 19 May 1998.

Bibliography

Statistical sources

Ekonomicheskoe polozhenie regionov Rossiiskoi Federatsii, Moscow: Goskomstat, 1994.

Ekonomika Rossii (Goskomstat monthly statistical reports), Moscow: Goskomstat, 1996.

Kapital'noye stroitel'stvo v Rossiiskoi Federatsii, Moscow: Goskomstat, 1994.

Narodnoye khozyaistvo Rossiiskoi Federatsii. 1992, Moscow: Goskomstat, 1992.

Narodnoye khozyaistvo RSFSR v 1987 g., Moscow: Goskomstat, 1988.

Narodnoye khozyaistvo RSFSR v 1988 g., Moscow: Goskomstat, 1989.

Narodnoye khozyaistvo RSFSR v 1990 g., Moscow: Goskomstat, 1991.

Narodnoye khozyaistvo RSFSR. Statisticheskii sbornik, Moscow: StatUpravlenie RSFSR, 1957.

Narodnoye khozyaistvo SSSR v 1960 godu, Moscow: TsSU, 1961.

Narodnoye khozyaistvo SSSR v 1988 g. Statisticheskii ezhegodnik, Moscow: Goskomstat, 1989.

Narodnoye khozyaistvo SSSR za 60 let, Moscow: TsSU, 1977.

Narodnoye khozyaistvo SSSR, 1922–1982, Moscow: TsSU SSSR, 1982.

Nauchno-tekhnicheskii progress v SSSR. Statisticheskii sbornik, Moscow: Goskomstat, 1990.

Nauka v Rossii. 1996, Moscow: Goskomstat, 1996.

Nauka v Rossiiskoi Federatsii. Moscow: Goskomstat, 1995.

O razvitii ekonomicheskikh reform v Ross.Federatsii (Goskomstat monthly statistical reports), Moscow: Goskomstat, 1992–1993.

Pokazateli sotsial'nogo razvitiya Rossiiskoi Federatsii i ee regionov. Moscow: Goskomstat, 1993.

Promyshlennost' Rossii. 1996, Moscow: Goskomstat, 1996.

Promyshlennost' Rossii. 1998, Moscow: Goskomstat, 1998.

Regiony Rossii, 1997, Volumes 1 & 2, Moscow: Goskomstat, 1997.

Regiony Rossii, 1998, Volumes 1 & 2, Moscow: Goskomstat, 1998.

Rossiiskaya Federatsiya v 1992 godu. Statisticheskii ezhegodnik, Moscow: Goskomstat, 1993.

Rossiiskaya Federatsiya v tsifrakh v 1993 godu, Moscow: Goskomstat, 1994.

Rossiiskii statisticheskii ezhegodnik, 1994, Moscow: Goskomstat 1994.

Rossiiskii statisticheskii ezhegodnik, 1995, Moscow: Goskomstat 1995.

Rossiiskii statisticheskii ezhegodnik, 1996, Moscow: Goskomstat 1996.

Rossiiskii statisticheskii ezhegodnik, 1997, Moscow: Goskomstat, 1997.

Rossiiskii statisticheskii ezhegodnik, 1998, Moscow: Goskomstat, 1998.

Rossiya v tsifrakh. 1996, Moscow: Goskomstat, 1996.

Rossiya-1993. Ekonomicheskaya konyuktura. Nos.1–4, Moscow: Tsentr ekonomicheskoi konyuktury, 1993.

Rossiya-1994. Ekonomicheskaya konyuktura. Nos.1–4, Moscow: Tsentr ekonomicheskoi konyuktury, 1994.

Rossiya-1995. Ekonomicheskaya konyuktura. Nos.1–4, Moscow: Tsentr ekonomicheskoi konyuktury, 1995.

Rossiya-1996. Ekonomicheskaya konyuktura. Nos.1–4, Moscow: Tsentr ekonomicheskoi konyuktury, 1996.

Rossiya-1997: Ekonomicheskaya konyuktura. Nos.1–4, Moscow: Tsentr ekonomicheskoi konyuktury, 1997.

Sel'skoe khozyaistvo Rossii. 1995, Moscow: Goskomstat, 1995.

Sel'skoe khozyastvo SSSR. Statisticheskii sbornik, Moscow: Goskomstat, 1988.

Short-term economic statistics. Commonwealth of Independent States, 1980–93, Moscow: Statkom, 1993.

SNG: Statisticheskii byulleten', (monthly statistical reports from the CIS' Statistical Committee), 1993–97.

Sodruzhestvo Nezavisimykh Gosudarstv v 1994 godu. Statisticheskii ezhegodnik, Moscow: Statkom, 1995.

Sodruzhestvo Nezavisimykh Gosudarstv v 1995 godu. Kratkii spravochnik, Moscow: Statkom, 1996.

Sodruzhestvo Nezavisimykh Gosudarstv v 1995 godu. Statisticheskii ezhegodnik, Moscow: Statkom, 1996.

Sodruzhestvo Nezavisimykh Gosudarstv v 1996 godu. Statisticheskii ezhegodnik. Moscow: Statkom, 1997.

Sodruzhestvo Nezavisimykh Gosudarstv v 1996 godu. Statisticheskii spravochnik, Moscow: Statkom, 1997.

Sodruzhestvo Nezavisimykh Gosudarstv v 1997 godu. Statisticheskii spravochnik. Moscow: Statkom, 1998.

Sotsial'no-ekonomicheskoe polozhenie Rossii (Goskomstat monthly statistical reports), Moscow: Goskomstat, 1993–1998.

Sotsial'noe razvitie Rossiiskoi Federatsii v 1992 godu, Moscow: Goskomstat, 1993.

Sotsial'naya sfera Rossii, Moscow: Goskomstat, 1995.

Sravnitelnye pokazateli ekonomicheskogo polozheniya regionov Rossiiskoi Federatsii, Moscow: Goskomstat, 1995.

Statistical Handbook 1993: States of the Former USSR. Washington DC: The World Bank, 1993.

Statistical Handbook 1994: States of the Former USSR. Washington DC: The World Bank, 1994.

Statistical Handbook 1995: States of the Former USSR. Washington DC: The World Bank, 1995.

Statistical Handbook 1996: States of the Former USSR. Washington DC: The World Bank, 1996.

Statistical Handbook 1997: States of the Former USSR. Washington DC: The World Bank, 1997.

Statistical Handbook: States of the Former USSR. Washington DC: The World Bank, 1992.

Uroven' zhizni naseleniya Rossii. 1996, Moscow: Goskomstat, 1996.

Vneshnie ekonomicheskie svyazi SSSR i Sodruzhestva Nezavisimykh Gosudarstv v 1991 g., Moscow: EVIK, 1992.

Books and articles

Aage, Hans, "Russian occupational wages in transition", *Comparative Economic Studies,* Vol.38, No.4, Winter 1996.

Ajello, Robin, "Why Moscow is selling advanced weapons to Asian friends ...and foes", *Asiaweek*, 7 February 1997.

Alesina, A., S. Ozler, N. Roubini and P. Swagel, "Political instability and economic growth", *Journal of Economic Growth*, Vol.1, No.1, June 1996, pp.189–211.

Alexander, James, "Uncertain conditions in the Russian transition: the popular drive towards stability in a 'stateless' environment", *Europe-Asia Studies*, Vol.50, No.3, May 1998, pp.415–44.

Appel, Hilary, "Voucher privatisation in Russia: structural consequences and mass response in the second period of reform", *Europe–Asia Studies*, Vol.49, No.8, December 1997, pp.1433–50.

Artisien-Maksimenko, P., and Yu. Adjubei (eds.), *Foreign Investment in Russia and Other Soviet Successor States*, New York: St.Martin's Press, 1996.

Aslund, Anders, *How Russia Became a Market Economy*, Washington DC: Brookings Institution, [1995].

— "Russian banking: crisis or rent-seeking?", *Post-Soviet Geography and Economics*, Vol.37, No.8, October 1996, pp.495–502.

Aslund, A., and R. Layard (eds.), *Changing the Economic System in Russia*, London: Pinter Publishers, 1993.

Atta, van, D. (ed.), *The "Farmer Threat": the Political Economy of Agrarian Reform in Post-Soviet Russia*, Boulder, Colorado: Westview Press, 1993.

Babaeva, L. B., M. P.Kozlov et al, *Malyi biznes v Rossii: sotsial'nye tipy i sfery deyatel'nosti*, Moscow: Rossiiskii nauchnyi fond, 1995.

Baglione, Lisa A., and Carol C. Clark, "Participation and the success of economic and political reforms: a lesson from the 1993 Russian parliamentary elections", *The Journal of Communist Studies and Transition Politics*, Vol.11, No.3, September 1995.

Bald, Joachim, and Jim Nielsen, "Developing efficient financial institutions in Russia", *Communist Economies & Economic Transformation*, Vol.10, No.1, March 1998, pp.81–94.

Bass, Ilya, and Leslie Dienes, "Defense industry legacies and conversion in the post-Soviet realm", *Post-Soviet Geography and Economics*, Vol.34, No.5, May 1993, p.302–17.

Becker, Charles M., and David D. Hemley, "Interregional inequality in Russia during the transition period", *Comparative Economic Studies*, Vol.38, No.1, Spring 1996.

Begg, David, and Richard Portes, "Enterprise debt and financial restructuring in Central and Eastern Europe", *European Economic Review*, Vol.37, No.2/3, April 1993, pp.396–407.

Berger, Mikhail, "Place on secret bank list still proof of legitimacy", *St Petersburg Times*, 26 January–2 February 1997.

Bernstein, Jonas, "Enter the corporate state", *The Moscow Times*, 19 September 1997.

Bim, Alexander S., "Ownership and control of Russian enterprises and strategies of shareholders", *Communist Economies & Economic Transformation*, Vol.8, No.4, December 1996, pp.471–500.

Birman, I., "Gloomy prospects for the Russian economy", *Europe–Asia Studies*, Vol.48, No.5, July 1996, pp.735–50.

Blasi, J. R., M. Kroumova and D. Kruse, *Kremlin Capitalism: Privatising the Russian Economy*, Ithaca and London: Cornell University Press, 1997.

Blum, D. W. (ed.), *Russia's Future: Consolidation or Disintegration?*, Boulder, Colorado: Westview Press, 1994.

Boeri, Tito, "Transitional unemployment", *The Economics of Transition*, Vol.2, No.1, March 1994, pp.1–25.

Borisenko, E. N., *Prodovol'stvennaya bezopasnost' Rossii: problemy i perspektivy*, Moscow: Ekonomika, 1997.

Boyco, M., *Privatising Russia*, Cambridge, Mass.: MIT Press, 1995.

Brada, Josef C., "The political economy of communist foreign trade institutions and policies", *Journal of Comparative Economics*, Vol.15, No.2, June 1991, pp.211–38.

Brooks, K., and Lerman, Z., *Land Reform and Farm Restructuring in Russia*. Washington, DC: The World Bank, 1994.

Brui, B., I. Zbarskaya and A. Volkov, "O sovremennom sostoyanii i prognoze smertnosti naseleniya Rossiiskoi Federatsii", *Voprosy statistiki*, Moscow, No.3, 1997, pp.54, 56.

Chernichovsky, D., H. Barnum and E. Potapchik, "Health system reform in Russia: the finance and organization perspectives", *The Economics of Transition*, Vol.4, No.1, May 1996, pp.113–34.

Chubais, Anatoly, "Itogi privatizatsii v Rossii i zadachi sleduyushego etapa", *Voprosy ekonomiki*, No.6, 1994, pp.4–9.

Chugrov, Sergei, "Elektoralnoe povedenie rossiiskikh regionov: statisticheskii analiz itogov vyborov dekabrya 1995 g.", *Mirovaya ekonomika i mezhdunarodnye otnosheniya*, No.6, 1996.

— "O regionalnoi fragmentatsii rossiiskogo politicheskogo soznaniya", *Mirovaya ekonomika i mezhdunarodnye otnosheniya*, No.1, 1998, pp.29–41.

Clark, Bruce, and Chrystia Freeland, "Russia: $50bn awaits tax reform", *The Financial Times*, 7 February 1997.

Clarke, Simon (ed.), *Conflict and Change in the Russian Industrial Enterprise*, Cheltenham: E. Elgar, 1996.

— (ed.), *Management and Industry in Russia: Formal and Informal Relations in the Period of Transition*, Aldershot: E. Elgar, 1995.

Clem, Ralph S., and Peter R. Craumer, "The geography of the April 25 (1993) Russian referendum", *Post-Soviet Geography and Economics*, Vol.34, No.8, October 1993, pp.481–96.

— "The geography of the Russian 1995 parliamentary election: continuity, change, and correlates", *Post-Soviet Geography and Economics*, Vol.36, No.10, December 1995, pp.587–616.

— "The politics of Russia's regions: a geographical analysis of the Russian election and constitutional plebiscite of December 1993", *Post-Soviet Geography and Economics*, Vol.36, No.2, February 1995, pp.67–86.

"Committed to democratic capitalism: IC interview with Boris Nemtsov", 25 September 1997, *www.intellectualcapital.com*.

Connor, W. D., *Tattered Banners: Labor, Conflict, and Corporatism in Postcommunist Russia*, Boulder, Colorado: Westview Press, 1996.

Cooper, Julian, *The Soviet Defense Industry: Conversion and Economic Reform*, London: Royal Institute of Economic Affairs, 1991.

Cramer, Peter R., "Regional patterns of agricultural reform in Russia", *Post-Soviet Geography and Economics*, Vol.35, No.6, June 1994, pp.329–51.

Dembinski, Pavel H., *The Logic of the Planned Economy. The Seeds of the Collapse*, Oxford: Clarendon Press, 1991.

Duflo, E., and C. Senik-Leygonie, "Industrial restructuring in Russia: early reactions of firms to the shock of liberalization", *The Economics of Transition*, Vol.5, No.1, May 1997, pp.45–62.

Easter, Gerald M., "Redefining centre-regional relations in the Russian Federation: Sverdlovsk *Oblast*", *Europe-Asia Studies*, Vol.49, No.4, June 1997, pp.617–36.

Ekonomicheskaya i sotsial'naya geografiya Rossii, Moscow: RON-PRESS, 1997.

Ellman, Michael, "The increase in death and disease under 'katastroika'", *Cambridge Journal of Economics*, 1994, Vol.18, pp.329–55.

Ernst, M., *Transforming the Core: Restructuring Industrial Enterprises in Russia and Central Europe*, Boulder, Colorado: Westview Press, 1996.

Evans, Jr., Alfred B., "The decline of rural living standards in Russia in the 1990s", *The Journal of Communist Studies and Transition Politics*, Vol.12, No.2, June 1996.

Feshbach, Murray, "Comments on current and future demographic and health issues", *Johnson's Russia List*, 10 June 1997.

Filatotchev, Igor V, and Roy P. Bradshaw, "The geographical impact of the Russian privatization program", *Post-Soviet Geography and Economics*, Vol.36, No.6, June 1995, pp.371–84.

Filatotchev, Igor, and Adam Swain, "Problems of restructuring of former state-owned enterprises in Russia, Hungary and China: case studies of car-making firms", *Russian and Euro-Asian Bulletin*, Vol.6, No.6, June 1997, pp.1–11.

Filipov, David, "Evasion schemes tax Russia's economy", *Boston Globe*, 28 October 1996.

Fish, M. Steven, "The predicament of Russian liberalism: evidence from the December 1995 parliamentary elections", *Europe–Asia Studies*, Vol.2, March 1997, pp.191–220.

Fleron, Jr., Frederic J., "Post-Soviet political culture in Russia: an assessment of recent empirical investigations", *Europe-Asia Studies*, Vol.48, No.2, March 1996, pp.225–60.

Friedgut, T. H., and J. W. Hahn (eds.), *Local Power and Post-Soviet Politics*, Armonk, N.Y.: M. E. Sharpe, 1994.

Flynn, J., P. Kranz and C. Matlack, "Grabbing a corner on Russian aluminium", *Business Week*, 6 September 1996.

Fortescue, Stephen, "Privatisation of Russian industry", *Australian Journal of Political Science*, Vol.29, No.1, March 1994, pp.135–53.

— "Privatisation, corporate governance and enterprise performance in Russia", *Russian and Euro–Asian Bulletin*, Melbourne, Vol.7, No.5, May 1998, pp.1–9.

— *Policy-Making for Russian Industry*, Hampshire: Macmillan Press; New York: St. Martin's Press, 1997.

Frenkel', A. A., *Ekonomika Rossii v 1992–1996 gg.: tendetsii, analiz., prognoz*, Moscow: Finstatinform, 1996.

Friedgut, Theodore, and Jeffrey Hahn (eds.), *Local Power and Post-Soviet Politics*, Armonk: M. E. Sharpe, 1994.

Frisby, Tanya, "The rise of organised crime in Russia: its roots and social significance", *Europe–Asia Studies*, Vol.50, No.1, January 1998, pp.27–50.

Gaddy, C. G., *The Price of the Past: Russia's Struggle with the Legacy of a Militarized Economy*, Washington, DC: Brookings Institution, 1996.

Gaidar, E. T., *Russian Reform/International Money*, Cambridge, Mass.: MIT Press, 1995.

Gay, W., *Capitalism with a Human Face: the Quest for a Middle Road in Russian Politics*, Lanham, MD.: Rowman & Littlefield, 1996.

Gill, G. J., *20th Century Russia: the Search for Power and Authority*, South Melbourne: Nelson, 1994.

Goble, Paul, "Buying out Russia", *RFE/RL*, 4 March 1997.

Goldman, M. I., *Lost Opportunity: Why Economic Reforms in Russia Have Not Worked*, New York: W. W. Norton & Co., 1994.

Gorshkov, Mikhail, "Economic and psychological crisis erodes Russian mentality", *Nezavisimaya Gazeta-Scenarios (RIA-Novosti)*, No.6, June 1997.

Gregory, Paul, and Robert Stuart, *Soviet Economic Structure and Performance*, 4th Edition. N.Y.: Harper & Row, 1990.

Guttsman, Janet, "Russian economy is not all that it seems", *Reuter*, 29 November 1996.

Halligan, Liam, and Pavel Teplukhin, "Investment disincentives in Russia", *Communist Economies & Economic Transformation*, Vol.8, No.1, March 1996, pp.29–52.

Hanson, Philip, "Russia's 89 Federal Subjects", *Post Soviet Prospects*, Vol.IV, No.8, August 1996.

Heleniak, Timothy, "Economic transition and demographic change in Russia, 1989–1995", *Post-Soviet Geography and Economics*, Vol.36, No.7, September 1995, pp.446–56.

Hewett, Edward A., *Reforming the Soviet Economy: Equality versus Efficiency*, Washington, DC: Brookings Institution, 1988.

Holzman, Franklyn D., *Foreign Trade Under Central Planning*, Cambridge, Mass.: Harvard University Press, 1974.

Hough, Jerry F., "The political geography of European Russia: republics and oblasts", *Post-Soviet Geography and Economics*, Vol.38, No.2, February 1998, pp.63–95.

Hughes, James, "Sub-national élites and post-communist transformation in Russia: a reply to Kryshtanovskaya & White", *Europe–Asia Studies*, Vol.49, No.6, September 1997, pp.1017–36.

Iarygina, Tat'iana, "Poverty in rich Russia", *Problems of Economic Transition*, Vol.37, No.8, December 1994.

Iovchuk, S., and I. Kvashnina, "Foreign capital investment in Russia: status and outlook", *Problems of Economic Transition*, Vol.39, No.12, April 1997, pp.43–54.

Ivanov, Kamil, "Razlichiya mezdu regionami ugrozhayut bezopasnosti Rossii", *Ekonomika i zhizn'*, 1997, No.8.

Johnson, Juliet, "High noon for Russia's banks", Loyola University, Chicago, 6 November 1997. Paper published in *Johnson's Russia List (JRL)*, 17 December 1997.

Kaiser, Robert J., "Prospects for the disintegration of the Russian Federation", *Post-Soviet Geography and Economics*, Vol.36, No.7, September 1995, pp.426–35.

— *The Geography of Nationalism in Russia and the USSR*, Princeton, NJ: Princeton University Press, 1994.

Kampfer, J., *Inside Yeltsin's Russia: Corruption, Conflict, Capitalism*, London: Cassell, 1994.

Kasimov, Aleksandr, "A diamond set in gold: the Republic of Sakha. Big money as a factor in big-time politics", *Prism*, Special Issue, Part 3, December 1996.

Kempton, Daniel R., "The Republic of Sakha (Yakutia): the evolution of centre-periphery relations in the Russian Federation", *Europe-Asia Studies*, Vol.48, No.4, June 1996, pp.587–614.

Khanin, G., "Kak rabotayut rossiiskie banki", *Eko*, No.6 (238), 1994, pp.49–53.

Kirkow, Peter, "Distributional coalitions, budgetary problems and fiscal federalism in Russia", *Communist Economies & Economic Transformation*, Vol.8, No.3, September 1996, pp.277–98.

— "Local self-government in Russia: awakening from slumber?", *Europe-Asia Studies*, Vol.49, No.1, January 1997, pp.43–58.

— "Russia's regional puzzle: institutional change and economic adaptation", *Communist Economies & Economic Transformation*, Vol.9, No.3, September 1997, pp.261–88.

Klugman, Jeni (ed.), *Poverty in Russia: Public Policy and Private Responses*. EDI Development Studies, Washington DC: The World Bank, 1997.

Koen, Vincent, and Steven Phillips, *Price Liberalisation in Russia: Behavior of Prices, Household Incomes and Consumption During the First Year*, Washington, DC: International Monetary Fund, Occasional Paper No.104, July 1993.

Kolosov, V. A., N. V. Petrov and L. V. Smirniagin (eds.), *Vesna-89: Geografia i anatomiya parlamentskikh vyborov*, Moscow: Progress, 1990.

Kornai, Janos, "Transformational recession: the main causes", *Journal of Comparative Economics*, Vol.19, No.1, August 1994, pp.39–63.

Krylovich, Alexander, "Thirty-five Russian regions are building their relations with the federal centre on a treaty basis", *RIA-Novosti*, 30 October 1997.

Kryshtanovskaya, Olga V., "Finansovaya oligarkhiya v Rossii", *Izvestia*, 10 January 1996.

— "Kto segodnya pravit bal v Rossii", *Argumenty i fakty*, No.21, May 1997, p.4.

— "Rich and poor in post-communist Russia", *The Journal of Communist Studies and Transition Politics*, Vol.10, No.1, March 1994, pp.3–24.

— "Transformatsiya staroi nomenklatury v novuyu rossiiskuyu elitu", *Obshestvennye nauki i sovremennost'*, No.1, 1995.

Kryshtanovskaya, Olga, and Stephen White, "From Soviet *Nomenklatura* to Russian Élite", *Europe-Asia Studies*, Vol.48, No.5, July 1996, pp.711–34.

Kunin, V, "Tax evasion on the rise in Russia", *RIA-Novosti*, 5 December 1996.

Kuznetsov, A. P., *Foreign Investment in Contemporary Russia: Managing Capital Entry*, New York: St. Martin's Press, 1994.

Lally, Kathy, "Russia, short on ideas, looks to intelligentsia", *Baltimore Sun*, 8 December 1997.

Lamdany, R., *Russia: the Banking System During Transition*, Washington, DC: The World Bank, 1993.

Lamghammer, R. J., M. J. Sagers and M. Lucke, "Regional distribution of the Russian Federation's export earnings outside the former Soviet Union and its implications for regional economic autonomy", *Post-Soviet Geography and Economics*, Vol.33, No.10, December 1992, pp.617–34.

Lapidus, Mikhail K., et al, *Understanding Russian Banking: Russian Banking System, Securities Market, and Money Settlements*, Kansas: Mir House, 1997.

Lavigne, Marie, *The Economics of Transition: From Socialist Economy to Market Economy*, London: Macmillan Press, 1995.

Lerman, Z., Y. Tankhilevich, K. Mozhin and N. Sapova, "Self-sustainability of subsidiary household plots: lessons for privatization of agriculture in former socialist countries", *Post-Soviet Geography and Economics*, Vol.35, No.9, November 1994, pp.526–42.

Lieven, Dominic, "The Russian empire and the Soviet Union as imperial polities", *Journal of Contemporary History*, Vol.30, No.4, October 1995, pp.607–36.

Linz, Susan J., "Red executives in Russia's transition economy", *Post-Soviet Geography and Economics*, Vol.37, No.10, December 1996, pp.633–51.

— "Russian firms in transition: champions, challengers and chaff", *Comparative Economic Studies*, Vol.39, No.2, Summer 1997.

— "The privatisation of Russian industry", *RFE/RL Research Report*, Vol.3, No.10, March 1994, pp.27–35.

Logue, J., S. Plekhanov and J. Simmons (eds.), *Transforming Russian Enterprises: From State Control to Employee Ownership*, Westport, Conn.: Greenwood Press, 1995.

Lokosov, V. V., and I. B. Orlova, *Pyatiletka No.13: vzlety i padeniya*, Moscow: Akademia, 1996.

Lowenhardt, John, "The 1996 presidential elections in Tartarstan", *The Journal of Communist Studies and Transition Politics*, Vol.13, No.1, March 1997.

Lukyanova, Lidia, "If they get rid of the 'shuttle traders', then who will feed and clothe Russia?", *Prism*, February 1997, Vol. III, Part 2.

— "Will Russia get a 'smarter' tax policy?", *Prism*, Vol.II, November 1996, Part 3.

Lushin, S., "The fiscal and payments crisis", *Problems of Economic Transition*, Vol.40, No.5, September 1997, pp.36–48.

Lyle, Robert, "Russia: huge foreign investment hinges on reforms", *Radio Free Europe/Radio Liberty News Service*, 13 January 1997.

Lyubskii, Mikhail, "Valyutnoe regulirovanie: Novaya skhema kontrolya", *Ekonomika: Analiz, otsenki, prognozy*, Moscow: Agentstvo ekonomicheskikh novostei, No.11, 1–15 June 1994.

Malle, Silvana, *The Economic Organisation of War Communism*, Cambridge: Cambridge University Press, 1985.

Marshak, V.D., "Mezhregional'nye finansovye potoki", *Region: ekonomika i sotsiologia* (Novosibirsk), No.1, 1998.

Matlack, Carol, "Helping the Russian mafia help itself. Tax exemptions have become a gold mine... for gangsters", *Business Week*, 9 December 1996.

Matvievskaya, E. D., *Inostrannyi kapital v Rossii 1995–1996 gg.*, Moscow: Institut ekonomiki, 1996.

Mau, Vladimir, "Stabilization, elections, and perspectives of economic growth. The political economy of reform in Russia", *Problems of Economic Transition*, Vol.40, No.4, August 1997, pp.5–26.

Mau, Vladimir, and Vadim Stupin, "The political economy of Russian regionalism", *Communist Economies & Economic Transformation*, Vol.9, No.1, March 1997, pp.5–26.

McAllister, I., S.White and O.Kryshanovskaya, "Voting and party support in the December 1995 Duma elections", *The Journal of Communist Studies and Transition Politics*, Vol.13, No.1, March 1997.

McAuley, Alastair, "The determinants of Russian federal-regional fiscal relations: equity or political influence?", *Europe-Asia Studies*, Vol.49, No.3, May 1997, pp.431–43.

Mendras, Marie, "Interpreting the Russian elections: Yeltsin and the Great Divide in Russian society", *East European Constitutional Review*, Vol.5, Nos.2–3, Spring–Summer 1996, pp.51–63.

Menshikov, Stanislav, "State enterprises in transition", *Transitions*, Vol.35, No.1, pp.125–48.

Menshikova, Olga, "Novye bednye na rynke truda", *Moya Gazeta*, 30 October 1996.

Metcalf, Lee Kendall, "Presidential power in the Russian constitution", *Journal of Transnational Law & Policy*, Vol.6, No.1, Spring 1996.

Migratsionnye protsessy i rossiiskii nauchno-tekhnicheskii potentsial: sotsial'no-ekonomicheskie posledtstviya migratsii nauchnykh kadrov, Moscow: IMEPI RAN, 1996.

Mikheev, D., *Russia Transformed*, Indianapolis, Ind.: Hudson Institute, 1996.

Mondry, Henrietta, "'Political philology': nationalism in the Russian literary press (1993–1996)", in: V. Tikhomirov (ed.), *In Search of Identity: Five Years Since the Fall of the Soviet Union*, Melbourne: CRE-AS, 1996, pp.133–41.

Moore, John H., "Science, technology and Russia's future: two legacies", *Communist Economies & Economic Transformation*, Vol.9, No.1, March 1997, pp.43–60.

Narzikulov, Rastam, "New privileges: post-perestroika variant", *Moscow Times*, No.42, 18–25 October 1992, pp.10–11.

Nelson, L. D., and I. Y. Kuzes, *Property to the People. The struggle for radical economic reform in Russia*, Sharpe, Armont NY, 1994.

— *Radical Reform in Yeltsin's Russia*, Sharpe, Armont NY, 1995.

Neumann, I. B., *Russia and the Idea of Europe: A Study in Identity and International Relations*, London, New York: Routledge, 1995.

Nikolayev, Alexander, "'Alligators' conquer arms market", *Panorama*, 1997, No.4.

Noren, James H., "The Russian military-industrial sector and conversion", *Post-Soviet Geography and Economics*, Vol.35, No.9, November 1994, pp.495–521.

— "Statistical reporting in the states of the former USSR", *Post-Soviet Geography*, Vol.35, No.1, January 1994, pp.13–37.

Nove, Alec, *An Economic History of the USSR 1917–91*, Harmondsworth: Penguin Books, 1992.

Nuti, D. Mario, "Russia: the unfinished revolution", *International Economic Outlook*, June 1994, pp.3–8.

O'Loughlin, J., M. Shin and P. Talbot, "Political geographies and cleavages in the Russian parliamentary elections", *Post-Soviet Geography and Economics*, Vol.37, No.6, June 1996, pp.355–85.

O'Prey, K. P., *A Farewell to Arms? Russia's Struggle with Defense Conversion*, N.Y.: Twentieth Century Fund Press, 1995.

Oates, Sarah, "Regional support in the 1996 Russian presidential elections", *The Journal of Communist Studies and Transition Politics*, Vol.13, No.1, March 1997.

Oblonsky, A. V., "Paradoxes of Russian political development", *The Journal of Communist Studies and Transition Politics*, Vol.13, No.1, March 1997.

Ostapchuk, Anna, and Yevgeniy Krasnikov, "Kreml" posetila ideya', *Moskovskie novosti*, No.38, 21–28 September 1997.

Owen, T. C., *Russian Corporate Capitalism from Peter the Great to Perestroika*, N.Y.: Oxford University Press, 1995.

Papava, V., and N. Khaduri, "On the shadow political economy of the post-communist transformation. An institutional analysis", *Problems of Economic Transition,* Vol.40, No.6, October 1997, pp.15–34.

Paretskaya, Anna, "Russian central authorities seek new formula for relations with the regions", *OMRI Analytical Brief,* No.460, 13 November 1996.

Perera, Judith, and Andrei Ivanov, "Resource-rich Tyumen region faces breakup... and poverty", *InterPress Service (IPS),* 3 December 1996.

Perotti, Roberto, "Growth, income distribution, and democracy: what the data say", *Journal of Economic Growth,* Vol.1, No.1, June 1996, pp.149–87.

Petrov, N. V., "Politicheskie elity v tsentre i na mestakh", *Rossiiskii monitor,* No.5, 1995.

Petrov, N. V., S. S. Mikheyev and L. V. Smirnyagin, "Regional differences in the Russian Federation: social tensions and quality of life", *Post-Soviet Geography and Economics,* Vol.34, No.1, January 1993, pp.52–8.

Philips, Alan, "Russia bled dry as $1bn a month is smuggled out", *The Electronic Telegraph,* 6 June 1997.

Puffer, S. M. (ed.), *Business and Management in Russia,* Aldershot, UK: E. Elgar, 1996.

Rabotyazhev, Nikolai, "K voprosy o genezise i sushnosti nomenklaturnogo kapitalizma v Rossii", *Mirovaya ekonomika i mezhdunarodnye otnosheniya,* No.1, 1998, pp.38–51.

Radvanyi, Jean, "And what if Russia breaks up? Towards new regional divisions", *Post-Soviet Geography and Economics,* Vol.33, No.2, February 1992, pp.69–77.

Razzakov, F. I., *Bandity vremen kapitalizma: khronika rossiiskoi prestupnosti 1992–1995 gg.,* Moscow: EKSMO, 1996.

Reddaway, Peter, "Russia heads for trouble", *The New York Times,* 2 July 1996.

Rose, Richard, and Yevgeniy Tikhomirov, "Who grows food in Russia and Eastern Europe?", *Post-Soviet Geography and Economics,* Vol.34, No.2, February 1993, pp.111–26.

Russian Economic Reform: Crossing the Threshold of Structural Change. A World Bank Country Study Report. Washington: The World Bank, 1992.

Russian Regional Explorer: Geography, Economy, Ecology, Government. Washington-Moscow: Russian Info&Business Center and MagicInfo, 1996.

Rutland, Peter, "Russia's unsteady entry into the global economy", *Current History,* Vol.95, No.603, October 1996.

Sachs, Jeffrey D., "Russia's struggle with stabilisation", *Transition,* Vol.5, No.5, pp.7–10.

Saint Paul, Gilles, and Thierry Verdier, "Power, distributive conflicts, and multiple growth paths", *Journal of Economic Growth,* Vol.2, No.2, June 1997, pp.155–68.

Sakwa, Richard, "Subjectivity, politics and order in Russian political evolution", *Slavic Review,* Vol.54, No.4, Winter 1995, p.962.

Sánchez-Andrés, Antonio, "Privatisation, decentralisation and production adjustment in the Russian defence industry", *Europe–Asia Studies,* Vol.50, No.2, March 1998, pp.241–55.

Sarafonov, M., and N. Lirov, "Begstvo kapitala iz Rossii", *Ekonomika i zhizn',* 1992, No.38, p.9.

Sedik, D., C. Foster and W. Liefert, "Economic reforms and agriculture in the Russian Federation, 1992–95", *Communist Economies & Economic Transformation,* Vol.8, No.2, June 1996, pp.133–48.

Senik-Leygonie, Claudia, and Gordon Hughes, "Industrial profitability and trade among the former Soviet republics", *Economic Policy*, Vol.15, October 1992, pp.353–86.

Seregin, V. P., V. P. Stepanov and E. D. Khalievskaya, *Inostrannyi kapital v Rossii*, Moscow: Mezhdunarodnaya akademiya informatizatsii, 1994.

Severin, Barbara, "Observations on regional aspects of food availability in Russia", *Post-Soviet Geography and Economics*, Vol.36, No.1, January 1995, pp.41–57.

Shamkhalov, F. I., and V. V. Kotilko, *Predprinimatel'stvo v Rossii: regional'no-otraslevoi aspekt*, Moscow: Ekonomika, 1997.

Shaw, Denis J. B., "Bids for autonomy by Northern regions of the Russian Federation", *Post-Soviet Geography and Economics*, Vol.34, No.5, May 1993, pp.319–21.

— "Russia's division into 'rich' and 'poor' regions", *Post-Soviet Geography and Economics*, Vol.34, No.5, May 1993, pp.323–25.

Shelley, Louise I., "The price tag of Russia's organized crime", *Transition: The Newsletter About Reforming Economies*, Washington: The World Bank, February 1997.

Shkolnikov, V., "Zdorovie naselenia Rossii", *Voprosy statistiki*, Moscow, No.3, 1997, p.74.

Shlapentokh, Vladimir, "Early feudalism – the best parallel for contemporary Russia", *Europe-Asia Studies*, Vol.48, No.3, May 1996, pp.393–412.

Sinel'nikov, S., *Byudzhetnyi krizis v Rossii: 1985–1995 gody*. Moscow: Evraziya, 1995.

Sizov, A., *The Russian Economy: From Rags to Riches*, Commack, N.Y.: Nova Science Publishers, 1995.

Slider, D., V. Gimpel'son and S. Chugrov, "Political tendencies in Russia's regions: evidence from the 1993 parliamentary elections", *Slavic Review*, Vo.53, No.3, Fall 1994, pp.711–32.

Smith, Alan, *Russia and the World Economy: Problems of Integration*, London and New York: Routledge, 1993.

Specter, Michael, "Deep in the Russian soul, a lethal darkness", *The New York Times*, 8 June 1997.

Standing, G., *Russian Unemployment and Enterprise Restructuring: Reviving Dead Souls*, N.Y.: St. Martin's Press, 1996.

Stanovlenie rynochnoi ekonomiki v Rossii, Moscow: Moskovskii obshestvennyi nauchnyi fond, 1997.

Steele, J., *Eternal Russia: Yeltsin, Gorbachev and the Mirage of Democracy*, London: Faber and Faber, 1994.

Stoner-Weiss, Kathryn, *Local Heroes: The Political Economy of Russian Regional Governance*, Princeton University Press, 1997.

Strategiya razvitiya Rossiiskoi ekonomiki i programma pervoocherednykh shagov, Moscow: Institut ekonomiki, 1996.

Sutela, Pekka, "Insider privatization in Russia: speculations on systemic change", *Europe-Asia Studies*, Vol.46, No.3, 1994, pp.417–35.

— "The role of banks in financing Russian economic growth", *Post-Soviet Geography and Economics*, Vol.38, No.2, February 1998, pp.96–105.

The Changing Social Benefits in Russian Enterprises, Paris: OECD, 1996.

The Guidelines of the Programme for the Medium Term Social and Economic Development of Russia. The Report of the Russian Academy of Sciences prepared for

Duma Hearings. Part One: The Concept of Overcoming of Recession, Moscow, May 1997.

— Part Two: The Development Prospects of National Economy Sectors, Moscow, May 1997.

Thomas, Scott, and Heidi Kroll, "The political economy of privatisation in Russia", *Communist Economies & Economic Transformation*, Vol.5, No.4, December 1993, pp.445–59.

Thornhill, John, "Russia: a quiet revolution", *The Financial Times*, 19 August 1997.

— "Russia: the risks and rewards of mass privatisation. Why are Russia's corporate assets so cheap", *The Financial Times*, 6 September 1997.

Tikhomirov, Vladimir (ed.), *Anatomy of the 1998 Russian Crisis*, Melbourne: CERC, 1999.

Tikhomirov, Vladimir, "Capital flight from Post-Soviet Russia", *Europe-Asia Studies*, Vol.49, No.4, 1997, pp.591–615.

— "Food balance in the Russian Far East", *Polar Geography*, Vol.21, No.3, July–September 1997, pp.155–202.

— "Investment crisis in Post-Soviet Russia", in: H. Shibata and T. Ihori (eds.), *Welfare State, Public Investment and Growth*, Tokyo: Springer-Verlag, 1998, p.221–55.

— "New political balance in Russia: an analysis of the December 1995 Russian parliamentary elections", *Russian and Euro-Asian Economics Bulletin*, Vol.5, No.1, January 1996, pp.1–4.

Tolkacheva, Julie, "Russian banks face deadly competition from the West", *Reuter*, 5 September 1997.

Tolz, Vera, "The national debate over nation-building in post-communist Russia", *Prism*, Vol.4, No.10, 15 May 1998, Part 2.

Tompson, William, "Old habits die hard: fiscal imperatives, state regulation and the role of Russia's banks", *Europe-Asia Studies*, Vol.49, No.7, November 1997, pp.1159–86.

Tretyakov, Vitaly, "Kommunizm, fashizm ili diktatura 'Partii vlasti'?", *Nezavisimaya gazeta*, 21 May 1998.

Ulyukaev, A. V., *Ekonomika i politika epokhi reform i potryasenii*, Moscow: Evraziya, 1997.

Urban, Michael, "The politics of identity in Russia's postcommunist transition: the nation against itself", *Slavic Review*, Vo.53, No.3, Fall 1994, pp.733–4.

Vainshtein, Grigorii, "The authoritarian idea in the public consciousness and political life of contemporary Russia", *The Journal of Communist Studies and Transition Politics*, Vol.11, No.3, September 1995, pp.272–85.

Vybory Prezidenta Rossiiskoi Federatsii, 1996. Elektoral'naya statistika, Moscow: TsIK, 1996.

Wallich, C., *Fiscal Decentralisation: Intergovernmental Relations in Russia*, Washington DC: The World Bank, 1992.

Watson, Robin A., "Interrepublic trade in the former Soviet Union: structure and implications", *Post-Soviet Geography and Economics*, Vol.35, No.7, September 1994, pp.371–408.

Webster, L. M., *Newly Privatised Russian Enterprises*, Washington DC: The World Bank, 1994.

Wegren, Stephen K., "From farm to table: the food system in post-communist Russia", *Communist Economies & Economic Transformation*, Vol.8, No.2, June 1996, pp.149–84.

Wegren, Stephen K., and Frank A. Durgin, "The political economy of private farming in Russia", *Comparative Economic Studies,*Vol.39, Nos.3–4, Fall–Winter 1997.

Weimer, D. L. (ed.), *The Political Economy of Property Rights. Institutional change and credibility in the reform of centrally planned economies*, Cambridge, Cambridge University Press, 1997.

Wheatcroft, Stephen G., "History in Russia since the unleashing of the energy of history (January 1987) and the fall of the USSR (December 1991): ten years on the archive and historical front, 1987–1996", in: V. Tikhomirov (ed.), *In Search of Identity: Five Years Since the Fall of the Soviet Union*, Melbourne: CREAS, 1996, pp.92–129.

White, S., R. Rose and I. McAllister, *How Russia Votes*, London: Chatham House Publishers, 1997.

White, S., M. Wyman and S. Oates, S., "Parties and voters in the 1995 Russian Duma election", *Europe–Asia Studies*, Vol.49, No.5, July 1997, pp.767–98.

White, Steven, "The 1995 elections to the Russian State Duma", *The Journal of Communist Studies and Transition Politics*, Vol.13, No.1, March 1997.

Willer, D., "Reasons for the low valuation of Russian shares", *The Economics of Transition*, Vol.4, No.2, October 1996, pp.449–57.

Williams, Carol J., "Russia reels out more red tape to protect ruble currency", *The Los Angeles Times*, 11 October 1997.

Wyman, Matthew, "Development in Russian voting behaviour: 1993 and 1995 compared", *The Journal of Communist Studies and Transition Politics*, Vol. 12, No.2, June 1996.

Yavlinsky, Grigory, *Laissez-Faire Versus Policy-Led Transformation: Lessons of the Economic Reforms in Russia*, Moscow: Center for Economic and Political Research, 1994.

Yavlinsky, Grigory, and Sergey Braguinsky, "The inefficiency of *Laissez-Faire* in Russia: hysteresis effects and the need for policy-led transformation", *Journal of Comparative Economics*, Vol.19, No.1, August 1994, pp.88–116.

Zecchini, Salvatore (ed.), *Lessons from the Economic Transition: Central and Eastern Europe in the 1990s*, Dordrecht-Boston-London: Kluwer, 1997.

Zel'dner, A. G., *Agrarnyi sektor ekonomiki Rossii na poroge XXI veka*, Moscow: Institut ekonomiki, 1995.

Newspapers, cable reports and periodicals

Asiaweek, Hong Kong.

Associated Press (AP), Washington.

BISNIS Briefs, Washington DC.

Biznes-fakt, Agentstvo ekonomicheskikh novostei, Moscow.

Biznes-TASS, Moscow.

Boston Globe, Boston.

Business Week, Hightstown, NJ.

Delovoi mir/Business World, Moscow.

Dokumenty (a monthly supplement to "Ekonomicheskie novosti"), Moscow.

Dow Jones News Service, New York.

EAST:Economies and Societies in Transition, Newsletter of the EAST Center, the University of Pennsylvania, Philadelphia.

Economica Weekly Press Summary, Moscow.

Ekonomika i zhizn', Moscow.

Ekonomika sel'skogo khozyaistva Rossii, Moscow.

Ekonomika: Analiz, otsenki, prognozy, Agentstvo ekonomicheskikh novostei, Moscow.

Ezhenedelnyi informatsionnyi byulleten', Rabochii tsentr ekonomicheskikh reform pri Pravitel'stve RF, Moscow.

Finansovye izvestia, Moscow.

IEWS Russian Regional Report, the Institute for EastWest Studies, New York.

Interfax Business Report, Moscow.

Interfax Daily News Report (Interfax), Moscow.

Interfax Report on Food & Agriculture, Moscow.

Interfax-AiF, Moscow.

InterPress Service (IPS), Moscow.

ITAR-TASS Daily Report, Moscow.

Izvestia, Moscow.

Johnson's Russia List (JRL), Washington DC.

Kommersant-Daily, Moscow.

Komsomolskaya pravda, Moscow.

Krestyanskie vedomosti, Moscow.

Megapolis-Express, Moscow.

Monitor: A Daily Briefing on the Post-Soviet States, The Jamestown Foundation, Washington DC.

Monitoring obshestvennogo mneniya/The Russian Public Opinion Monitor, Moscow.

Moskovskie novosti, Moscow.

Moya gazeta, Moscow.

Nezavisimaya gazeta, Moscow.

Nezavisimaya Gazeta-Scenarios (RIA-Novosti), Moscow.

Open Media Research Institute (OMRI) Daily Digest, Prague.

Open Media Research Institute (OMRI) Economic Digest, Prague.

Oxford Analytica Eastern European Daily Brief (OAEEDB), London.

Panorama, Moscow.

Post-Factum Weekly News Digest, Moscow.

Prism: a Bi-Weekly on the Post-Soviet States, The Jamestown Foundation, Washington DC.

Radio Free Europe/Radio Liberty News Line (RFE/RL), Prague.

Reuter, London.

Rossiiskaya gazeta, Moscow.

Rossiiskie vesti, Moscow.

Russia Notes, Moscow.

Russian and East European Finance and Trade, New York.

Russian and Euro-Asian Bulletin, Melbourne.

Russian Economic Trends, London.

Russian Information Agency – Novosti Daily Report (RIA – Novosti), Moscow.

Russian Information Agency – Novosti Economic Daily News, Moscow.

Segodnya, Moscow.

St Petersburg Times, St Petersburg.

The Economist, London.

The Electronic Telegraph, London.

The Financial Times, London.

The Los Angeles Times, Los Angeles.

The Moscow Times, Moscow.

The Moscow Tribune, Moscow.

The New York Times, New York.

The Wall Street Journal, New York.

Transition: The Newsletter About Reforming Economies, The World Bank, Washington.

Transitions, Brussels.

Trud, Moscow.

Vek, Moscow.

Vestnik ekonomicheskikh reform, Rabochii tsentr ekonomicheskikh reform pri Pravitel'stve RF, Moscow.

Vlast' i ekonomika, Post-Factum, Moscow.

Voice of America (VOA), Washington DC.

Voprosy ekonomiki, Moscow.

Voprosy statistiki, Moscow.

World Development Report. The World Bank. New York: Oxford University Press, 1994–1997.

World Economic Outlook, Washington DC: International Monetary Fund, 1995–1997.

Index